LIVING THE Hiplife

LIVING THE
Hiplife

Celebrity and
Entrepreneurship
in Ghanaian
Popular Music

JESSE WEAVER SHIPLEY

Duke University Press

Durham and London   2013

Designed by Heather Hensley

Typeset in Chaparral Pro by Westchester Publishing Services

Library of Congress Cataloging-in-Publication Data
Shipley, Jesse Weaver.
Living the hiplife : celebrity and entrepreneurship in
Ghanaian popular music / Jesse Weaver Shipley.
p. cm.
Includes bibliographical references and index.
ISBN 978-0-8223-5352-2 (cloth : alk. paper)
ISBN 978-0-8223-5366-9 (pbk. : alk. paper)
1. Rap (Music)—Ghana.   2. Rap musicians—Ghana.
3. Popular music—Ghana.   4. Hip-hop—Ghana.   5. Ghana—
Songs and music.   I. Title.
ML3503.G4S55 2013
781.6309667—dc23   2012034575

Duke University Press gratefully acknowledges the support of
The Office of the Provost at Haverford College, which provided
funds toward the publication of this book.

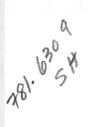
DEDICATION

Thorne Shipley

CONTENTS

LIST OF ILLUSTRATIONS

Plates   PLATES FALL BETWEEN PAGES 138 AND 139

Figures

ACKNOWLEDGMENTS

This book goes out to all the people who listened and talked, shook their heads and smirked. I am grateful for the input and ideas of so many different people in multiple locales. Research for this book has been generously funded and supported by Fulbright-IIE; Wenner Gren Foundation; University of Chicago; Bard College; Haverford College; Museum for African Art in New York; Third World Newsreel; British Council of Ghana; Carter G. Woodson Institute for African American and African Studies at University of Virginia; School of Performing Arts at University of Ghana, Legon; National Theatre of Ghana; International Centre for African Music and Dance (ICAMD); Bokoor African Popular Music Archives Foundation (BAPMAF).

I must thank many people for countless contributions large and small. I thank, in Chicago: Jean Comaroff, John Comaroff, Beth Povinelli, Andrew Apter, Nancy Munn, Michael Silverstein, Susan Gal, Ralph Austen, Liz Garland, Jen Higgins, Laurie Frederick, Barney Bate, Jane Guyer, Paul Liffman, Anne Balay, Anne Chien. In Virginia: George Mentore, Hanan Sabea, Wende Marshall, Jemima Pierre, Scott Saul, Joseph Miller, Reginald Butler, and Michelle Kisliuk. In Annandale: Chinua Achebe, Diana Brown, Mario Bick, Laura Kunreuther, Yuka Suzuki, Tom Keenan, John Ryle, Peter Hutton, Helon Habila, Patricia Pforte, and Ali Feser. In Johannesburg: Jyoti Mistry, Dzino, Thuli Skosana, Maria McCloy, Shizeeda Osman, Eric Worby, and Achille Mbembe. In New Brunswick: Michael Warner, Brent Hayes Edwards, and Sareeta Amrute. In Philadelphia: Laurie Hart, Maris Gillette, Zolani Ngwane, John Jackson, Linda Gerstein, Kim Benston, Israel Burshatin, Koffi Anyinefa, Susanna Wing, Andrew Friedman, Linda Bell, and Kathy McGee. In circulation: Michael Hanchard, Tina Campt, Marina Peterson, Alex Dent, Anne Maria Makhulu, Ruti Talmor, Hylton White, Binyavanga Wainaina, Tom Burke, Candice Lowe, Bayo Holsey, Rosalind Morris, Jim Smith, Harvey Neptune, Kamari Clarke,

Ben Talton, Lisa Binder, Stephanie Newell, Ato Quayson, Tyrone Simpson, Roy Grinker, Charlie Piot, Brian Larkin, Paul Kockelman, Saskia Koebschall, Jason Lee, and M One of Dead Prez. With Duke University: Ken Wissoker, Leigh Barnwell, Susan Albury, Bonnie Perkel, and Debbie Masi (Westchester Publishing Services). In and out of Accra: Reggie Rockstone Ossei, Panji Anoff, Rab Bakari, John Collins, Willie Anku (late), Esi Sutherland-Addy, Mohammed Ben Abdallah, J. H. K. Nketia, Farouk Abdallah, Aminata Abdallah, Kofi Anyidoho, Africanus Aveh, Yaw Asare (late), Esi Ansah, Nana Aqua Anyidoho, David Donkor, Kwesi Brown, Judith Nketia, Cynthia Delali Noviewoo, Akramah Cofie, Habib Iddrisu, Kelvin Asare Williams, Dhoruba Bin Wahad, Gavin Webb, John Akomfrah, Gyedu Blay Ambolley, Sidney, DJ Black, Grey, Nkonyaa, Kochoko, M3nsa Ansah, Wanlov, Lazzy, Prodigal, Promzy, Eli Jacobs-Fantauzzi, Hashim Haruna, Obour, Ronny, Bright, DJ Ronny Boateng, D-Black, Okyeame Kwame, Zela Limann Ossei, Phoebe Ossei, Ricci Ossei, Felicity Antwi, Diana Afi Kofitiah, Samuel Otoo (Ghana Boy), Birte Hege Owusu-Addo, Paa Kwesi Holdbrook-Smith, Nate Plageman, Eric Don Arthur, Korkor Amarteifio, Gibril, Blitz the Ambassador, M.anifest, Mzbel, Abrewa Nana, Eddie Blay, Kweku T, Ben Angmor Abadji, Jeff Cobbah, George Mensah Britton, and Akoto. I must thank William Loren Katz, Giles Weaver, Burke Shipley, and Virginia Shipley. And, finally, my deepest gratitude to Tabetha Ewing.

An earlier version of the opening section of chapter 5 appeared in "Creativity and the Limits of Political Agency," in *Creativity in Crisis: After Afro-Pessimism*, edited by Anne Maria Makhulu, Stephen Jackson, and Beth Buggenhagen (University of California Press, 2010). An earlier version of the second part of chapter 5 and reworked introductory material appeared in "Aesthetic of the Entrepreneur: Afro-Cosmopolitan Rap and Moral Circulation in Accra, Ghana," *Anthropological Quarterly* (2009). An earlier version of historical sections from chapters 2 and 3 appeared in "The Birth of Ghanaian Hiplife: From Black Styles to Proverbial Speech in African Hip Hop," in *Hip Hop Africa: New African Music in a Globalizing World*, edited by Eric Charry (Indiana University Press, 2012).

Throughout the book I follow my informants' informal descriptions in using "Akan" and "Twi" somewhat interchangeably to refer to related, mutually intelligible languages, of which Asante Twi, Akuapem Twi, and Fante are the most prevalent. If speakers or musicians specify, this is indicated. Likewise in transcribing and translating lyrics I follow the notion that in this musical oral form the notion of definitive translation is less important than the ways in which participants are themselves a part of translations. I, therefore, have sought out translations that reflect this and used English language orthography as this is the way that most participants write and text Akan languages despite its inability to capture certain elements. At times I use pseudonyms in reference to interviewees to protect them from embarrassment or conflict.

Aesthetics and Aspiration

We are listening to bling music,
which thumps and talks about hip
and hop, gold and going places.

There is no past, everything is sampled.

—BINYAVANGA WAINAINA, *One Day*
  I Will Write about This Place

Don't Go There

For several years, Nescafé, an affiliate of Nestlé Corporation in Ghana, sponsored a series of regional competitions for amateur hiplife musicians. Aspiring musicians performed while music industry judges assessed their star potential.[1] In mid-2004 each of the nation's ten regions held preliminary competitions; the winners went to the national finals in Ghana's capital, Accra. Reggie Rockstone, considered by many to be the originator of hiplife music, was mentoring a young group of rap artists called the Mobile Boys and entered them in the competition.

The Mobile Boys—Grey, Kochoko, Nkonyaa, and Bedsheet—all in their twenties, have stories that are common to a generation of disenfranchised youths in Ghana and across the continent. They reflect patterns of rural-to-urban migration of youths seeking work and inspiration, success, and pleasure in the city just as those before them have. They take small jobs and hustle, and rely on friends for support and lodging. Grey (Thomas Antwi) explains, "I couldn't finish school because my mother didn't have money for school fees. . . . I don't know my father, but he never supported me so I don't worry about him. I used to play football but when I hurt my knee, I put all my energy into making it as a musician. That is my hope."[2] The first time he heard them rap, Reggie was struck by their lyrical talent. "These kids would hang around the neighborhood . . . some of them sleeping in a nearby abandoned building. . . . When I heard them, I was blown away. I mean they could flow. I decided to invest in developing them as a group."[3] For several years Reggie supported the boys, giving them a place to stay and providing recording time at his studio. He hoped his investment would lead to their success, which in turn would reflect well upon him.

Reggie recalls they were known in Accra's hip-hop "underground scene . . . But to put out an album that is going to sell is not easy, even for me or other well-known stars." He laments that while private radio was central to promoting early hiplife artists, stations increasingly demanded "payola," illicit cash payments from artists and producers to play songs. Unknown artists struggle to reach mainstream audiences. Making connections with leading musicians, producers, and corporate sponsors is a way in. Finding such a famous patron as Reggie appeared to be a path to success for the aspiring rappers.

To give the rappers exposure, Rockstone featured them on his 2003 "Mobile Phone Song." Each rapper's verse tells humorous tales of romance, lying, and hustling, all made possible by using a mobile phone. It reflected a funny saying circulating in Accra: "Everyone with a cell phone is a liar," which links mobile technology to the power of creative speaking. After the song was released and people saw the group with Reggie or backing him up at shows, they would shout, "Hey, that's the Mobile Phone Boys," and the name stuck.

The Nescafé competition was a way for the company to rebrand itself for youth markets. As one radio executive explains, promoting undiscovered artists gives them a good public image and does "something useful for the community." The winners would be thrust into the public eye, receiving a recording contract, music videos, a house for a year, and ten million cedis cash. The Mobile Boys, with their polished lyrical skills, easily won the Accra regional competition and looked forward to the national finals, held the night of September 17, 2004, on an outdoor stage at Kwame Nkrumah Circle. A popular venue known to local audiences, this stage often hosted events such as massive all-night charismatic church services and healing sessions, as well as popular concert party variety theatre shows sponsored by Unilever, and football skills competitions sponsored by Guinness. The Nescafé event was well publicized and free, attracting a slightly rowdy crowd of several thousand people, dominated by teenagers and young adults, with boys outnumbering girls. Workers carrying small tankards on their backs served Nescafé drinks to the crowd.

The Mobile Boys' performance proved a crowd favorite, garnering huge cheers. "We thought we had won," recalls Grey. After the various groups performed, the show's MC, K.O.D. of Radio Gold, announced that the group Praye from Kumasi had won. Crowd members shouted their disappointment and screamed for the Mobile Boys. Grey explains, "Praye's music is more local dance beats. They don't really rap. . . . But they are nice guys. Their name . . . refers to an Asante proverb, 'If you take one broom straw out of the broom it will break, but together it is strong.' It refers to strength in unity." Reggie was angry and mounted the stage with the Mobile Boys in tow. Taking the mike from K.O.D., he shouted to the crowd, "if you no think Mobile Boys win make some fucking noise!" He tossed the mike to the ground and left. Reggie later explained to me that he did not think the competition was fair. "I had a call from a friend of mine. It turns out they already knew who they wanted to win and I wasn't informed. . . . They could have . . . pulled me aside and said, hey Reg, don't go there because we got this planned."

Although the Mobile Boys lost amid accusations of competition fixing, several months later Nescafé contacted them. Kochoko explains, "It's shocking to us after that bogus competition. Nescafé asked us to do an advertisement. It's unbelievable. . . . We did it for them and it's on the air." They adapted the lyrics of their song "Don't Go There" to promote Nescafé. According to Grey, "The song is about . . . showing respect. . . . If something is important to me, then you should not destroy it. 'Don't go there.' We just rewrote a verse." The Mobile Boys sang the track mostly in the Akan language with only the hook in English.

When the Mobile Boys get their Nescafé. Don't go there. Nescafé.
Kochoko, Grey, Nkonyaa love the taste. Don't go there. Nescafé.
All the security guards drink it to stay awake. Don't go there.
There are three and one in a sachet. Don't go there.
The taste! It's already got milk and sugar in it. One sachet per cup.
N to the E to the S to the C to the A to the F to the E. Nescafé, hey![4]

For the Mobile Boys, getting paid to adapt one song was small compensation for the frustration at watching another group garnering the fame and support they felt they had earned. The hopes and frustrations of this competition demonstrate this book's concern with various processes of mediation and circulation that are central to this musical genre's social significance. In a more abstract sense, this competition shows how performers struggle to convert musical value into sustained celebrity-status and economic value. I trace how an aesthetic of hiplife emerges as artists make pleasurable music amid the tensions of contemporary urban Ghana's political and economic transformation. Hiplife is a symbolic realm through which youths on the margins reimagine themselves as socially authoritative, free-thinking public speakers. At the same time, corporate, state, and media institutions attempt to harness youth styles—and their images of self-expression—for other purposes, demonstrating the potentials and hazards of the free market.

Making Music, Making Value

This book examines the sociohistorical emergence of Ghana's hiplife music as a new genre and its centrality to changing ideas of Ghanaian identity. It follows how hiplife makes and transforms various kinds of value—aesthetic, moral, linguistic, and economic. Hiplife is a popular music genre that fuses hip-hop sampling, beatmaking, and rap lyrical flow with older forms of highlife music, Akan storytelling, and proverbial oratory. Like highlife before it, hiplife is musically eclectic. It is defined less by a specific rhythm or orchestration than by techniques that blend black diasporic music and style into established local performance genres. Throughout the twentieth century, black diasporic popular culture has had a particularly potent influence on Ghanaian aesthetics. Hip-hop, in particular, appeals to young Ghanaians through its emphasis on the liberatory potential of black male speaking. Young Ghanaian rappers infuse the direct bravado of hip-hop with traditional respectful oratory and familiar highlife rhythms, legitimizing it in the eyes of a broader Ghanaian public. In this sense, artists have made themselves into mediators of foreignness, transforming new fashions for local consumption.

I argue that this musical genre produces an aesthetic and moral configuration that celebrates entrepreneurship. Hiplife's entrepreneurial spirit aligns music-making with self-making, as unknown hiplife artists strive to transform themselves into influential stars. The specific aesthetic practices that make linguistic and bodily transformations in the musical realm are the same values that make a good entrepreneur. This book follows the story of how celebrity becomes a form of value production central to both music and entrepreneurship. Tensions and controversies around hiplife reveal the cultural implications of free-market transformations that have dominated Ghanaian society over the past two decades. New electronic and digital circulations are central to this development, as is the role of artists and producers as social mediators.

Young male hiplife musicians who rise to fame represent a new kind of Ghanaian celebrity for the neoliberal era, and complicate simplistic dichotomies between state and market. Celebrity artists mediate value for an evolving Ghanaian society. Hiplife stars are public emblems of entrepreneurial success, converting musical pleasure and images of leisure and success into celebrity. Fame, in turn, becomes a form of currency, transforming ephemeral signs of social status into material value. Artists initially seek success through informal music circulations. Subsequently, corporate and media interests appropriate artistic celebrity to brand products for an emerging Ghanaian market. The state also tries to use new market-oriented tastes to gain public support. As aspiring artists recognize that their success hinges upon fashioning an image of celebrity—and that financial support for music comes primarily from corporate sponsorship and market recognition—they increasingly create personal brands, striving to be made into corporate icons for mobile service providers, drinks, and household goods. In the context of the free market, the freedom of personal expression itself becomes a disciplinary practice that organizes power and value.

Drawing on sociolinguistic approaches, I emphasize how musical meaning is actively made and contested in lived social contexts of production, circulation, and reception. Taking an actor-centered approach, this book is particularly concerned with how performers claim authoritative public stances by linking disparate performance registers, and how audiences, who tend toward conservative interpretations, try to make sense of innovative signs within established performance structures. In the process, culturally specific notions of circulation and mediation call into being new Ghanaian moral publics. Performers and audiences rely on the referential aspects of songs, styles, and performances to connect musical aesthetics to moral qualities and to the potentials of economic value production. Thus, I use aesthetics to refer to a set of changing principles and contexts through which participants structure affect and taste. In practical ways actors draw on these values to interpret familiar signs, adopt stances, and introduce new signs, in the process amending the principles of interpretation. By making young musicians into national icons emboldened with the power to make economic and moral value, hiplife provides youths with transformative possibilities, but also reveals the limits of social mobility. Though my focus is on the sociohistorical specificity of hiplife, this African urban genre has broader implications for global music amid technological and corporate changes that have provided new opportunities for musicians to reach audiences but also new forms of constraint. Hiplife musicians cultivate bodily and linguistic aesthetics to make and circulate music through changing electronic production and digital distribution networks representing broader changes in music industries across the globe.

Circulation in the City

In 1980s Accra, hip-hop became popular among a handful of elite, internationally oriented youths. At clubs and school concerts, enthusiasts imitated American styles of rapping, DJing, and break dancing. Youth interest in hip-hop styles reflected changing generational tastes as their parents' highlife, soul, and R&B seemed outdated. In contrast black American rap stars represented a new Afro-cosmopolitan swagger that they could emulate.

After several years of protosocialist military governance, Ghana was transitioning toward privatized, liberal rule. Ghana's 1992 democratic constitution mandated state privatization, initiating the rapid proliferation of private radio, television, advertising, and production media. With rising business opportunities, numerous Ghanaians—many with experience in media industries—returned from self-imposed economic exile in Europe and America. Young adults from villages across the country also increasingly came to Accra as the capital city promised new opportunities for work and pleasure.

Reggie Rockstone was one of those who returned from abroad to Accra and began rapping in Twi over heavy hip-hop beats and samples of Ghanaian highlife and Nigerian Afrobeat. Born Reginald Asante Ossei in London to Ghanaian parents, he attended Accra's prestigious Achimota College for secondary school, though he spent most of his time break dancing. Moving to London in the mid-1980s after finishing school, he recalls being "bitten by the hip-hop bug" and honing his English-language rap skills in the nascent London hip-hop scene. When he returned to Accra in 1994, he was surprised at how local rap was focused on imitating American styles. "Some kids didn't even understand English that well. They were just copying the flow. . . . To make hip-hop local [we had to rap] in local languages and address issues that were important to my people here." Reggie is credited as the originator of hiplife, coining the term to describe his blend of the nostalgic sounds of old Accra with hip-hop's new bravado. He explains, "I took the 'hip' from hip-hop and the 'life' from highlife. . . . At first people thought [rap] was foreign. . . . Including the highlife sound [made] the older crowd listen. . . . I had to blend languages and styles, mix it up so local people would respect the music."[5]

Reggie's music both made it cool to rap in Ghanaian languages and made hip-hop acceptable to a broad Ghanaian public. His successful, innovative blend relied upon his unique fluency in local and foreign musical forms developed through a life of frequent movement between Ghana, London, and the United States. His music established a pattern for musical transformation that subsequent artists used to further develop hiplife as a local, blended genre. It inspired a generation of younger artists, without direct access to transnational travel, to reinterpret hip-hop for local audience tastes.

I first met Reggie in 1997 when he performed at the Pan African Historical Theatre Festival (PANAFEST) in Cape Coast, Ghana. His presence as a headlining performer confounded how visitors and locals alike understood what constituted African music. The state-run festival was established in 1992 to show cultural "connections among black peoples" and to use African performance and art to unite Africans from the continent and the diaspora.[6] For state organizers and private sponsors, this semiannual festival was a chance to encourage African diasporic peoples to visit and establish long-term connections with Ghana. The weeklong program in 1997 featured traditional dance troupes from across Africa, contemporary African theatre, diasporic musical groups, an academic conference, and an arts and crafts fair. Reggie, wearing military fatigues, performed to a large crowd of youths at the Cape Coast Centre for National Culture, next to stalls selling traditional carvings, cloth, and leather goods. Contrasting with other artists at the event, Reggie was a new kind of Ghanaian celebrity. He confounded institutional ideas of Pan-Africanism in favor of the tastes of young irreverent, commercial-oriented audiences. "Reggie is hot. . . . They need us more than we need them," his manager, Paa K, quipped to me outside the PANAFEST offices while negotiating Reggie's appearance fee. Many African diasporic attendees were uncertain how to interpret his music. "This isn't African," one commented. "Is he from Ghana or what?" Another stated, "I didn't come all the way here to listen to American music."

The following year my sense of the growing and unique significance of hip-hop in Ghana was solidified. One Saturday I was backstage at the National Theatre of Ghana chatting with actors. We were struck by the fact that, while only a small audience was watching their play by an important Ghanaian playwright in the main auditorium, hundreds of energized teenagers were behind the theater rehearsing for an upcoming rap competition. The National Theatre was hosting Kiddafest, a youth variety show meant to celebrate Ghanaian culture. Due to popular demand, organizers had recently agreed to include a rap segment, as long as performers rapped in what they referred to as "local" African languages and used nonprofane lyrics that told morally positive stories. At the time, I was studying modern stage theatre and I was struck by how youth interest in hip-hop was changing official state notions of what constituted African culture. Interest in hip-hop had spread from elite urban students to mass urban and rural youths as evidenced by the diverse rap performers coming to compete at the theater. While critics saw the music as un-African, morally corrupt, and foreign, as rap gained local recognition, audiences increasingly identified it as an African genre.

Hip-hop's particular aesthetics of cutting, mixing, and sampling provided a vast array of techniques for synthesizing various melodies, lyrics, languages, and rhythms. Over time, excitement about new generic blends unexpectedly inspired youth interest in older performance genres as beatmakers manipulated electronic production technology to replicate highlife rhythms and rappers sought out traditional proverbs to enrich their lyrics. Rappers experimented with adapting lyrical flows to suit "local" languages. They used various languages, Akuapim Twi, Asante Twi, Fante, Ga, Ewe, Hausa, Dagbane, and Pidgin English, instead of copying American English styles. While English is Ghana's official national language, dominating institutional and civil contexts, and Ga is the language indigenous to Accra, the capital city is defined by its multilingualism. While some rappers used other languages, most blended Akon languages, the country's lingua franca, with some Pidgin and English.[7]

While Accra's vibrant live music scene of the 1970s had been devastated by a decade of economic and political instability, hiplife's use of new technology led to a new age of public music. Cheap beatmaking software and computer-based production technology allowed young artists to experiment and record music in home studios when musical instruments and professional recording facilities were difficult to find. The rise of numerous private radio stations was also crucial to hiplife's rise, as radio DJs needed new music to fill the airwaves and reach the youth market.

By 1999 a critical mass of local hiplife hits flooded Accra's airwaves and clubs. Hiplife provided a sound track for urban youths. Hiplife lyrics and fashions celebrated youth possibilities with an African urban élan and reflected Accra's renewed vibrancy. Layers of overlapping local music played from taxis, markets, drinking spots, Internet cafés, and compound houses. DJs at parties, clubs, and funerals played a blend of hiplife, highlife, and gospel along with American R&B and pop tunes. New local music created a feeling of national belonging. As one market trader commented to me in 1998, "We want to hear our own Ghanaian music. Songs that we understand and speak to us, not some foreign stories."[8]

Accra's jumbled soundscape has been dominated by three main genres: gospel, highlife, and hiplife. Each genre represents a competing social imaginary through its associated fashions, sounds, and social spaces. The popularity of gospel signifies the increasing power of neo-Pentecostalism across the country, while highlife represents an older, specifically Ghanaian way of narrating daily struggle and urban-rural relations. Hiplife stands out through its celebration of newness and emphasis on individual bravado. For some youths, gospel and highlife are, as Grey explained, "too local" and "too slow."[9] Hiplife provides symbolic access to Afro-cosmopolitan worlds and its forms of performative power. As Scooby Selah of hiplife group TH4 Kwages explained, it also is a "real" reflection of daily life. "Hiplife is the way that we do things . . . in Accra. It shows how we live. It is our life."[10]

As the music's popularity grew and stylistic variations arose, reflexive debates about what constituted the genre and its social significance also spread. Hiplife provides youths with a way to narrate life in Accra. As a historical center of trade between Africa and the West, Accra is a city that faces two directions: toward rural West African life and the urban metropoles of Europe and America. Hiplife, and reflexive discussions about it, reflect the cultural and economic movements of mobile youths within Ghana. It also reflects the increasingly transnational nature of Ghanaian nationhood, connecting Ghanaians in London, New York, and around the world through Internet file sharing and social networking. Hiplife songs address current moral and social dilemmas: the pleasures and perils of nightlife; hopes of international travel; ambivalence toward young women's skimpy dress; consequences of young men's desires for wealth and sexual conquest; frustrations of political corruption; and dreams of becoming a star musician. The music's digital circulation amplifies and speeds up public debates around current issues. In producing, circulating, and consuming music, young artists and listeners forge a dispersed, national public and become narrators of moral nationhood at home and abroad.

When I began researching hiplife, I focused on analyzing live concerts. Over time I realized, that for fans and artists, the public relevance of this musical performance genre lay primarily in its electronic circulations. Presence at live shows seemed to be confirmation of a mobile electronic network, rather than an end in itself. I began to increasingly follow circuits of musical production and reception through recording studios, radio stations, urban markets, and cyberspaces, tracing how electronic tracks took on meaning and shaped social interactions. I got to know producers, rappers, DJs, media people, and beatmakers as they traveled and performed in and outside of Ghana. I traced the political and commercial appropriations of music and networks of mobile file sharing. I gathered life histories of performers—both famous and unknown—to understand the music's relevance across social classes and cultural-linguistic groups.

In 2003 Reggie Rockstone and I began collaborating on filming the story of hiplife. Over the following decade I shot video of interviews, recording sessions with celebrity and struggling artists, live shows, radio sessions, street events, and scenes of music in daily life, eventually making two feature documentaries and numerous shorts and music videos.[11] The process of filming hundreds of hours of footage and editing it in conjunction with feedback from hiplifers has informed my understandings of the music as a form of self-representation. At times my camera gave me anonymity in the midst of a highly mediatized landscape. At other times my camera's presence reoriented the nature of a performance or conversation. These moments were instructive in revealing the structures of events and how artists wanted to present themselves for public consumption. Participating in hiplife networks as a filmmaker has allowed me to understand the intertwined relationships between music making and marketing, and the importance of narration and public image to artistic success.

Hiplife musical production and consumption align youth interests with market-based forms of value and the promises and anxieties of entrepreneurship. The free market's valorization of entrepreneurial skills is reflected in artistic styles that focus on individual virtuosity. In Ghana, as ideologies of private ownership and individual business aspiration overtook notions of state and collective progress, as they have in much of the liberalizing world, youths invested their hopes for prosperity in market-based practices (Comaroff and Comaroff 2000). Hiphop's ethos celebrating the black male hustler suited the state's new free market–oriented focus on the entrepreneur as ideal citizen. Neoliberalism entails "myths of the citizen as consumer and markets as sovereign entities" (Giroux 2008, 140). Hiplife posits the musician as agentive self-fashioning subject striving for individual success and mobility. Private media technologies emphasize personal freedoms: specifically the right to free expression and to shape oneself and market tastes through consumer choice—though this idea of freedom also constrains subjects as they are increasingly beholden to market logic.

Mediation, Circulation, and Control

Theories of mediation and circulation give insight into how hiplife participants use various semiotic registers and technological forms in their performative self-fashioning (Samuels et al. 2010; Stokes 2004; Meintjes 2003). Hiplife is rooted in skills of mediation in various ways: Music mediates stylistic transformations, which in turn mediate moral and social debates. Electronic technologies mediate new publics and speech communities. DJs and producers mediate artistic fame. Beatmakers and rappers mediate among competing musical and linguistic registers. Artists mediate the interplay between aesthetic and economic value (figure 1).

Recent theories of circulation revive older anthropological interests in how exchange practices produce social relations and subjectivities by structuring relational obligations (Mauss 2000). Following Malinowski, anthropologists have focused on circulation, arguing that meaning and place are produced in the processes and mediations of movement. That is to say, the idea of stasis is made through motion; and circulation is "a cultural process with its own forms of abstraction, evaluation, and

FIGURE 1 Fan takes mobile phone picture with Reggie Rockstone. Photograph by the author.

constraint" (Lee and LiPuma 2002, 192). Electronic technologies provide new channels for exchange and obligation, restructuring relations through new forms of potential and constraint (Brennan 2010; Peterson 2010; Larkin 2008; Engelke 2007; Eisenlohr 2006; Hirschkind 2006). In particular, the reflexive aspects of technologies of mediation and movement shape the ways that new community affiliations coalesce (Mazzarella 2004; Tsing 2004; Gaonkar 2002; Geschiere and Nyamnjoh 2000).

Across performance genres, debates about meaning drive social circulation through the power and pleasure of interpretation. Ghanaian dance, music, and oratory display a high degree of reflexivity. Ghanaian popular aesthetics tend to value precise control of language and bodily movement; audiences are sensitive to subtle actions of performers and scrutinize them. In many traditions of oral mediation, the performers' job is explicitly to arbitrate between different worlds and different registers (Anyidoho 1983). For example, in Akan courts, the chief's political and legal relationships with his subjects are mediated through an Okyeame, a wise spokesperson who uses proverbs to translate and embellish the public speech acts of the chief (Yankah 1995). The Okyeame also mediates potentially dangerous speech from visitors directed to the chief to protect him from harmful intent. In Akan languages, words are efficacious and potentially dangerous (Obeng 1997; Anyidoho 1983). Language is understood to be performative; that is, participants recognize that language is not only referential but shapes the world it is describing. Language use takes on morally good or bad positions. Respect and authority are given to those who skillfully contain and poetically direct the social power of speech (Yankah 1995, 16, 125). In this sense, elegance and indirection are highly valued. Speaking authority is associated with proverbial speech (*bu me be*), metaphoric speech (*kasakwan*), indirection and innuendo (*akutia*), and rumor (*konkonsa*) (Yankah 1995).

Yet in many traditional contexts youths are not supposed to speak publicly, let alone use proverbial, formal oratory.[12] Young rap lyricists, and by association their audiences, appropriate the public authority of traditional court orators in contexts previously inaccessible to them. Songs take on the formal features of proverbial speech as morality tales for a Ghanaian citizenry. Lyrical hooks become detachable, highly mobile catchphrases that move across publics orally, electronically, and digitally. New communities of belonging are mediated through audience interpretations and embellishments of music as it circulates. Hiplife songs become socially relevant through their transportability as proverb-like speech fragments. They connect dispersed publics through circulatory practices honed in traditional forms of oratory and refashioned for electronic modalities.

Hiplife's aesthetic value, then, is judged through an artist's ability to blend elegant, respectful language with innovative referential practices. Following Reggie's example, rappers established a formula that combined personal deictics—first-person forms of address and signs that focus audience attention on an individual artist's attitude, dress, and verbal skill—and the use of traditional music and proverb-like statements that gave words and rhythms authority by deferring authorship to a traditional cultural collective. Audiences celebrated young rappers who referenced established oral and musical registers as new mediators of traditional wisdom. This, in turn, gave them the authority to introduce stylistic innovations. In this sense, successful performers structure an interaction, by assuming "an authoritative voice . . . which is grounded at least in part in the knowledge, ability, and right to control the re-centering of valued texts," reconnecting them in new ways (Bauman and Briggs 1990, 77). In valorizing the skills of blending and mediating disparate styles, this genre marks its practitioners as mediators situated between the modern West and the rural traditional village.

In hiplife's poly-linguistic lyricism, audiences enjoy the uncertainties of translation rather than seek definitive interpretations of songs.

Song makers become famous for their use of obscure proverbs or morally controversial lyrics as they drive controversy and deliberation. Translation, according to Walter Benjamin (1969), is always incomplete, an active process of fragmentation and transformation. Especially in a society that values proverbial speech, debates, and disagreements about lyrical meaning are crucial to a song's elegance, authority, and mobility.

Diaspora and the Productivity of Disjuncture

Why does hip-hop provoke strong, polarizing reactions? In scholarship and popular media, African hip-hop is often either romanticized or demonized. Proponents see the global spread of hip-hop as part of an international movement in which musical connections represent historical unity and facilitate political and social transformations (Osumare 2007). But critics argue that hip-hop promotes American and commercial "contamination" of Africa's "pure" music traditions. In the first guise, hip-hop is posited as something intrinsically African. In the second, it is foreign and threatens to disrupt the radical difference that Africa represents as a site of cultural origin. Debates about origins and connections are themselves productive aspects of the development of hiplife in Ghana. Examinations of African popular culture argue that popular pastiche aesthetics reflect Africans' alternative experience of modernity as embodied critical agency (Cole 2001; Barber 1997; Waterman 1990). Indeed, Hanchard (1999) posits that Afro-modernity emerges through shared black experiences of violence and exclusion that lead to horizontal, non-state-based affiliations. Hiplife is an example of how black youths in the "global shadows" transform value, turning marginality and disconnection into a form of moral public recognition. Notions of diasporic disjuncture and return shape how young urban Africans self-consciously use diasporic culture to forge something new.

Reflexive debates about the stylistic elements that constitute the music and the moral, cultural, and racial requirements of authentic hip-hop have been central to the genre since its inception. Hip-hop-related musical genres in various locales promote reflection on community belonging. The music's irreverent techniques for remixing older styles lead to discussions of musical influence and connections, and in the process discussions of social and moral issues (cf. Saada-Ophir 2006; Stavrias 2005). The music's malleability and reflexive tendencies also lead to its easy transportability to new contexts as youths can use local sounds to make something new while claiming membership in a global community of successful, outspoken artists. They can sound unique but be part of something bigger, be radical, and be controversial while striving for official recognition.

Since hip-hop's emergence in the 1970s as an eclectic musical and social style pioneered by mostly black and Caribbean New York youths, it has evolved into a global force of youth-oriented morality and commerce. Its four main elements—rapping/MCing, DJing, graffiti writing, break dancing/B-boying—evolved through a self-conscious aesthetics of improvisation, rebellion, creativity, and humor. The hip-hop sound provided an atmosphere that encouraged eclectic influences. DJs extended break beats, cutting back and forth between two turntables with copies of the same record. Developing this new kind of sonic environment allowed MCs to rap, improvise and toast, and layer other sounds over a looped beat. It was both endlessly repeatable and changeable to suit audience tastes. As its popularity spread from DJ and MC performances at parties and clubs in predominantly black urban communities, its aesthetic was reified as a representation of black community for internal and external contemplation and consumption. Early hip-hop celebrated oral dexterity in freestyle rap battles and ciphers. The music became established through radio play and record label attention, shifting from underground party music to musical expressions of post-civil rights black consciousness. At the same time, as packaged representations of African American life, hip-hop was appropriated by mainstream commodity culture.

Two main strands of hip-hop emerged that reflected the tension between the music's racial politics and commodification: socially conscious music and gangster rap (cf. Forman and Neal 2011). As with many diasporic forms, politically conscious hip-hop relied on an idealized image of Africa as a place of symbolic origin, for example, the imagery of Afrika Bambaataa and the Universal Zulu Nation. Even as controversies about violent lyrics emerged in the 1980s, hip-hop began to be accepted as a mainstream musical form, popular with middle-class white suburban listeners. Its growing record sales relied on repackaging old tropes of romanticized black creativity, violence, and hypersexuality (Rose 2008; Dyson 1993). The rapper, as an icon of masculine agency able to re-create himself through an elegant control of language, embodied the contradictory legacy of public representations of black culture: the threat of a violent black male gangster and the potential of a creative antihero struggling against racial oppression

(DeGenova 1995b; Dent 1992). As hip-hop became central to American popular culture in the era of privatization, the image of the black gangster transformed into that of the black business entrepreneur, with the ubiquitous idea of hustling blurring the line between official and illicit forms of value production.

Hip-hop's remixing techniques and its ability to blend radical politics, thuglife, and commercial marketability gave it an unusual portability (cf. Fernandes 2011; Alim et al. 2008; Watkins 2005). By the early 1990s youths across Africa and around the world began adapting hip-hop practices and symbols in decidedly local, expressive terms (Charry 2012; Perullo 2011; 2005; Ntarangwi 2009; Weiss 2009; Haupt 2008; Fernandes 2006; Mitchell 2001). Youths recontextualized signs of black diasporic, masculine self-fashioning to mark racial, ethnic, linguistic, and class differences under a variety of conditions—from impoverished North Africans in Paris's banlieues to alienated Japanese bourgeois youths to disenfranchised Brazilian favela dwellers (Caldeira 2006; Condry 2006; Durand 2003; Cornyetz 1994). Hip-hop in many locales valorizes the disenfranchised, usually male, microphone-wielding speaker. Through rap, an MC enunciates the possibilities of a public stance from which he has been previously excluded in race and class terms (Jackson 2005).

Hip-hop-related subgenres across Africa strive for national and linguistic specificity while claiming membership in a global hip-hop community, with New York—and Paris for some Francophone artists—as its symbolic center. For the most part, African hip-hop artists focus on national audiences while presupposing intimate links to a broader Pan-African hip-hop imaginary. As artists struggle to make hip-hop locally relevant by deploying national cultural and linguistic signs, connections among artists across Africa have been harder to forge. In Senegal, youths used hip-hop bravado as a code of moral responsibility linking African American rebellion and French protest, with traditions of griot performance, Islamic moral discourse, and Wolof language use. During the 2000 presidential elections, hip-hop artists helped sway young voters bringing Abdoulaye Wade to power with a referendum tied to generational change (Herson 2007). In 2011–2012, when President Wade tried to stay in power despite growing public dissatisfaction, rappers used their public platform to give local protests international exposure. In Tunisia in 2011, rapper El General helped inspire public outcry at state oppression and corruption that led to the populist ousting of the government. Across Africa critics protested that hip-hop was foreign and morally corrupting, but many youths saw it as a way to reinvigorate traditional forms of respect, morality, and language use that were neglected by society at large. Hip-hop in Kenya and bongo flava in Tanzania, Naija pop in Nigeria and kwaito and hip-hop in South Africa have all re-created large internal markets and have helped develop music industries in the context of state privatization, celebrating local expressive traditions in self-consciously creative, modern forms.

Hiplife incites moral outrage among its critics, who see it as disrespectful. But unlike Senegalese hip-hop artists, who are directly engaged in politics, Ghanaian hiplife practitioners are often more interested in earning respectability than in making political interventions. Musical variations across Africa demonstrate different ways that African youths re-deploy hip-hop's dominant image of young black male voicing geared toward capitalist accumulation and consumption. Hip-hop in the United States—as both counterculture and mainstream corporate product—provides "not only an 'explicit focus on consumption'" but "an alternative means of attaining status for urban African American and Latino youths who face unemployment, racism, and marginalization in a post-industrial economy" (Tricia Rose in Maira 2000, 333). For African youths, hip-hop promotes desires for the bodily and material markers of capitalist consumption and accumulation, though it does so through black images of protest and authority. Where Africa is marginalized within global political economy, hip-hop marks a path to cosmopolitanism, as well as a counternarrative critique of racial-economic inequality that underlies it.

Hip-hop is increasingly a way in for visitors to Africa. While some come to Africa seeking difference, others seek connections. Hip-hop serves both purposes. A growing number of American students on study-abroad programs and "alternative" travelers across the continent are captivated by the familiar difference of "local" hip-hop. A number of alternative Web sites and independent record labels promote Afropop and hip-hop as forms of global modern connection.[13] Multinational corporations also have recognized the potential of African hip-hop for branding and connecting youth markets around the world. For example, Coca-Cola adapted "Wavin' Flag," a song by Canadian-based Somalian rapper K'naan, as its anthem for the 2010 FIFA World Cup. Its lyrics called for freedom through sport as the first football World Cup held in Africa was promoted in the language of Pan-African unity. In addition, the U.S. government has promoted hip-hop in Africa to counteract the "potential of Islamic fundamentalists to make inroads on the continent" by showing a "positive image of America."[14] These examples of appropriation show the potential of hip-hop to simultaneously articulate with various local and global circulating discourses.

Recent studies show how African American, Caribbean, and black British music deploy techniques of mixing, copying, and amplifying as embodied expressions of histories of oppression and violence against black peoples from the slave trade to colonialism to corporate extraction (Veal 2007). Diasporic urban black youths create electronic sonic aesthetics that reflect their ongoing experiences of displacement and raise political and moral issues in the language of Pan-African obligation. Sonic metaphors of disjuncture and mobility provide both a form of belonging and an embodied history of diasporic dispersion (Gilroy 1993).[15]

While scholars and popular audiences recognize that diasporic music is built upon African musical forms, when African artists incorporate diasporic styles, they are criticized for copying something foreign or being culturally inauthentic. Indeed, some scholars from both Africa and the United States continue to critique serious intellectual inquiry on African hip-hop as an inappropriate way to understand African locales. Hip-hop in Africa, which claims both African and diasporic origins, unsettles the predisposition to define Africa through radical difference, especially in relation to performance and public culture (Holsey 2008; Kapchan 2007; Silverstein 2004; Ebron 2002). It raises questions about the historical relationships between Africa and global blackness and the directions of influence (cf. Shepperson 1960).

Value, Semiotics, and the Body

Value—moral, linguistic, aesthetic, economic—is actively made in all sorts of social action (Graeber 2001). I use a social theory of value to explain how hiplife, as a form of cultural production, transforms value among these realms. Qualities associated with hiplife include celebrity, success, hipness, linguistic dexterity, confidence, mobility, and control. Hiplife artists struggle to convert their labor into value in a number of ways: fusing disparate musical registers into a new genre; making traditional styles cool and foreign ones local; turning musical talent into public recognition, recognition into fame, and fame into money. In these transformations, actors align themselves with established social virtues as a way to gain acceptance for new forms of value (Guyer 2004, 18–20). For example, Reggie Rockstone shaped local music because he was adept at aligning himself with both hip-hop swagger—he was cool—and with established local styles, which made people pay attention to his eclectic music and fashion.

Social actors fashion themselves in relation to established aesthetic principles that emerge through sociohistorically specific types of production and labor. According to Terence Turner (1984), Marx's theory of value shows that production is not solely a material process but mediates between social practice and cultural meaning. Marx's notion of production is not limited to commodity manufacturing and abstracting labor, but defines a symbolic process in which social actors fashion themselves and, in the process, produce and transform the material conditions of society. For Marx value is the "transformation of the dynamic content of productive activity into the category of meaning" (Turner 1984, 7). For example, Turner's (2007) research on Kayapo "social skin" shows that dress and adornment are cultural practices that reinforce and challenge social hierarchies and produce value through displays of the body. In this sense, "labor must be understood in terms of cultural forms of consciousness, not economics" (Turner 1984, 7). Electronic music production and digital media change the relationship between labor, economic value, and aesthetics. Unknown artists refashion themselves as public figures by taking advantage of the circuits of value conversion that electronic musical labor allows.

The value transformations Munn (1986) describes among Gawan traders provide an interesting comparison to the ways in which Ghanaian musicians try to make names for themselves through digital music circulation, travel, and publicity. In both locales, actors associate themselves with positive qualities and virtues that bring fame, which in turn produce new forms of value. Munn's use of Peirce's notion of qualisign—which refers to a quality that works as a sign—shows how moral virtues are assessed in aesthetic terms, which then determine how labor is converted into economic value. For musicians in Ghana and traders in Gawa, value is made in symbolic processes focused on the body.

For Gawans, Munn argues, value transformations rely on an actor's ability to symbolically extend his or her relevance across social spacetime.[16] Through social action a core set of virtues or qualities is assessed in relation to positive and negative moral polarities. Social practices that reflect qualities of expansiveness, outwardness, and collective simultaneity extend spacetime, whereas activities that focus on interiority, heaviness, and personal consumption reflect negative values and compress spacetime. For example, individuals who exchange shells or are successful in gardening and travel make a name for themselves, gain personal fame, and in the process accrue value for their group. In contrast, excess personal consumption reflects selfishness and brings negative valuations associated with witchcraft. In successfully exchanging Kula shells across other islands, Gawans transform themselves at home. Here fame is produced in an "externalizing process involving the separation of internal elements of Gawa . . . and their transaction into the inter-island world" (Munn 1986, 6). In this process, the self is transformed through its outward projection in objects and values and the return of these values as fame. These exchanges are shaped by communal assessments that positively value the successful exteriorization and spreading of one's name "overseas" and negatively value the inverse failure to circulate.

Munn and Turner are concerned with socially normative processes through which actors aspire to fame and recognition within established cultural systems and circuits of exchange. Conversely, black expressive genres in a variety of contexts show how marginalized groups invert dominant value polarities, remaking community affiliations under conditions of political-economic change. As Hebdige's ([1979] 1996) examination of British punk and ska shows, disenfranchised youths try to invert normative aesthetic values by remaking their bodies through dissonant and initially unappealing pastiches. Here fashioning the body is a way of projecting identity into the world and remaking value for those excluded from society's main circuits of exchange and social reproduction.

As these new systems of moral-aesthetic valuation gain public recognition, the terms of personal and bodily freedom are drawn into consumer-oriented marketplaces of taste. As some economists, in fact recognize, free-market economies are not simply places of exchange but are themselves productive of value (LiPuma and Lee 2004). In making music, hiplife artists associate themselves with virtues of travel, translation, and celebrity to remake themselves as entrepreneurs who can transform aesthetic value into economic value. In this transformation aspiring musicians try to make themselves into celebrities. In understanding how fame is made, Peirce's notion of an indexical icon is useful as it demonstrates how signs work in multiple ways to simultaneously link various symbolic registers. Achieving celebrity status entails garnering attention to the body of the artist. An indexical icon is a sign that works by both pointing toward other signs (indexical) and by resembling signs (iconic). The indexical and iconic aspects of signification, then, link bodily aesthetics to broader moral, linguistic, and social virtues.[17]

Working for Fame

To return to my opening story: Young musicians like the Mobile Boys become astute social analysts in their struggles to find success and make a name for themselves. In assessing the social landscape, they searched for avenues to transform themselves from unknown artists into celebrities. The Mobile Boys recognized that private radio was crucial to hiplife's initial popularity but that rapid technological changes provided new opportunities for making and circulating music.

After Praye won the Nescafé competition, they became one of the most popular hiplife groups through the financial support, professional music videos, studio production, and publicity that they received. They produced party tracks with danceable highlife-oriented electronic beats and catchy, easily repeated Akan-language hooks; quite a different brand of hiplife from the Mobile Boys' undanceable hard-core hip-hop beats and elaborate rap lyrics. Praye's look was fresh and flashy, in contrast to the Mobile Boys' tough street image. In a cover photo for Ghana Music .com in 2009, Praye posed with gold lamé jackets and designer sunglasses conveying an image of success. Their track, "Angelina," was a major hit in 2008 and 2009; digital copies of the song and its video— which intercuts scantily clad women dancing with the group at a club— circulated widely on the Internet and played in African nightclubs from the Bronx to London to Accra.

Music people explain fame, each with their own formula. DJ Ronny Boateng, who spins for Ghanaians in New York, feels artists need to cater to audience tastes. "I like Praye because they have a beat, the old time feel. . . . Ghanaian audiences want to dance. . . . The Mobile Boys are great rappers but . . . as a DJ it does not please the crowd. . . . It needs to be marketable."[18]

Praye's music and look were tailored and marketed for mass appeal. The Mobile Boys were frustrated watching artists like Praye become popular while they struggled to gain recognition even with their underground following and Rockstone's patronage (figure 2). Nkonyaa (Johnny

FIGURE 2 Mobile Boys on a music video shoot. Photograph by the author.

Torsah) of the Mobile Boys explains the changes in the music business: "At first producers invested in releasing albums. . . . But there were too many bribes and not enough sales. . . . Investors . . . were losing money. So we are looking for other ways to reach the audience. Now you have to put out a video or hit single first, then you get called to do live shows, then you do the album. Now we perform for a little money or free . . . to get our name out there. . . . People love our music, but we are not making money."[19] Instead of trying to make money from sales, artists recognize that they need to release singles and mixtapes to gain renown before they will get paid to perform. Nkonyaa continues, "The money now is in [headlining] live shows at the beach, for corporate sponsors. But you have to have your album out to be legit . . . and money to make videos and advertisements. You have to look successful and people will like your music." Nkonyaa laments that the Mobile Boys had a chance to be sponsored by Guiness but turned it down. "They wanted us to change our names to the Extra Smooth Boys if we signed with them for 100 million. That's a lot of money. But Reggie said we should not do it because they would own everything we did. But now we have nothing anyway so . . ."[20] In observing the music industry Nkonyaa recognizes that garnering an image of existing success is itself important to public interest even if it entails compromise. Without the sheen of market value audiences remain suspicious of aesthetic worth.

Music increasingly circulates solely in digital form, as artists burn CDs or use flashdrives to give songs to DJs. Fans share files through music Web sites, online social networking, and Bluetooth from their phones. Some songs find quick success circulating as MP3 files to club DJs and radio stations. But many artists with one or two hits quickly fade from public attention, unable to translate sudden success into a lasting musical presence. DJ Black of Joy FM laments, "Some kid will have one hit and think he is famous. Meanwhile he has no money. To be a long-term success and really make money in Ghana music is not easy."[21]

Aspiring managers hustle to bring undiscovered artists to public attention by signing them to small labels but most lack the capital to invest in studio time, advertising, music videos, and radio and television play. Musicians, beatmakers, and managers struggle to figure out the vagaries of the market and how money is made when no one is buying music and technologies of circulation change so quickly.

Grey sees hiplife through a lens of hard work and professionalism (figure 3). "I know that if I keep rapping and keep up my hustle . . . look for every opportunity, I will succeed. It is not an easy business. . . . When any manager or promoter calls me to do a show or feature on someone else's track in the studio, I am ready with my lyrics. Ask anyone in the industry; they all respect me for being always on point. Now I am just waiting for my time." Hopeful artists without personal connections pay established producers for beats and studio time.[22] Grey cannot afford to pay so hustles to connect with DJs, producers, and promoters. "I do little things, like I will buy them credit [prepaid units for mobile phones] and text them the code number if they need it. Then if they are having an event they will think of me. I have good relationships with people at TV stations so that when my music video is ready I can take it to them and they play it for a cheaper rate. So if I have money I save it for that."

Neoliberal popular culture tends to emphasize rags-to-riches fantasies of unknown individuals becoming successful through chance and talent. The Mobile Boys' frustration and continued struggle illustrate the strength of musicians' aspirations. Hiplife becomes a form of production, reliant on the manufacture of leisure, celebrity, and aspiration as productive of value. In popular music financial compensation does not come through wage labor exchanges but in converting images and sounds into fame and the idea of success, which entails uncertainties and risks

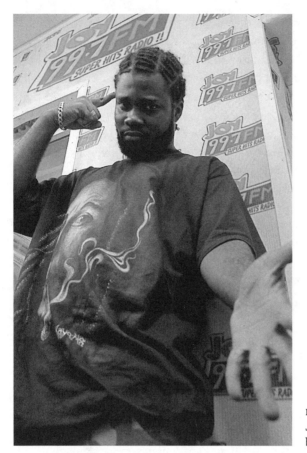

FIGURE 3 Grey at
Joy FM. Photograph
by the author.

as well as the potential for material wealth. The entrepreneurial potential to earn wealth from musical products relies on practitioners' abili-
ties not only to make music but also to make their own authority as
purveyors of popular taste.

Chapter Outlines: The Making of an Entrepreneurial Aesthetic

The ethnographic narratives in this book follow numerous artists, songs,
and fashions as they circulate across urban and transnational spaces in
order to understand the exchanges between musical aesthetics and
publicity that make hiplife into a socially significant genre. The chapters progress chronologically, showing the historical development of
the music from highlife through the early years of hiplife to second-
and third-generation artists. They also move geographically, looking at
the transnational circulations that defined the music's early years, ex-

amining hiplife as the soundtrack of millennial Accra, and following its subsequent travels with Ghanaians abroad.

The first two chapters show that hiplife, while appearing new, builds on an established pattern of semiotic layering. They describe how Ghanaian popular culture relies on a logic of value transformation in which black diasporic forms are fused with established performance genres. Chapter 1 traces how highlife, an eclectic popular dance music that emerged in the 1920s and developed further through jazz and soul music influences, is defined not through a particular rhythm or lyrical form but rather through a style of mediation and pastiche that incorporates new black and foreign musical forms into sounds that come to define locality. Foreign aesthetics are first understood as modern, both threatening and exciting, but once incorporated by Ghanaian musicians, they become aspects of national tradition. Chapter 2 then describes the social and political conditions and musical forms through which hip-hop came to Ghana by showing how it destabilized Ghanaian state ideas of national culture in the context of privatization in the 1990s.

The third and fourth chapters show that the birth of hiplife relied on the same patterns of appropriation that have long been central to highlife. Chapter 3 focuses on Reggie Rockstone's return to Ghana from London and his centrality in making hip-hop local and making highlife cool. Reggie's story illuminates the role of celebrity in making value and reshaping authoritative speaking practices. This chapter also chronicles the rise of private media and the processes through which hip-hop gained local legitimacy. Chapter 4 then examines how young rappers and beatmakers elaborated on Reggie's Akan-language rap, regrounding hip-hop—often understood as a foreign form—in locally recognizable language registers and performance traditions.

The fifth and sixth chapters examine the principles of urban and electronic musical circulation. Successful hiplife songs provide morally controversial proverb-like lyrics that become easily detachable phrases able to move across various publics. In these circulations, aesthetically pleasing songs are transformed into morally potent commentaries. Provoking moral controversy in pleasurable form is a powerful way for artists to find musical renown. Chapter 5 explores the importance of humor and parody in driving musical circulation. It examines the technological changes that lead artists and audiences to focus increasingly on digitally circulated hit singles. To illustrate these changes, I follow two hits that became parodies of political sincerity during the 2000 and 2004 national presidential campaigns. Chapter 6 focuses on the work of a female hiplife artist to consider the gendering of the genre and how notions of entrepreneurship and public voicing rely on ideas about hypermasculine agency.

The seventh and eighth chapters demonstrate how hiplife artists engage in various transnational circuits of Ghanaians abroad to make music and convert travel and musical labor into aesthetic value. Hiplife, as mediated through Internet and digital technologies, turns displacements and disjunctures around race and nation into new economic possibilities. Chapter 7 examines digital circulation and informal labor exchanges between New York, London, and Accra in the making of an album. The final chapter examines the transnational connections and disconnections provoked by hiplife concerts for Ghanaians living in the Bronx, New York. Hiplife provides Ghanaians abroad, living in the midst of a diverse black community, a unique sonic nationhood by signifying Twi rap as cultural tradition. Whereas hip-hop was initially seen by many as foreign, within a few years, hiplife as a hybrid genre became the embodiment of Ghanaianness.

Each chapter elaborates a different aspect of how hiplife artists and audiences make and circulate the music, how it is emotionally experienced as pleasurable or offensive, and how debates about moral and linguistic value shape aesthetic values. In all of these processes, practitioners are concerned with how to make themselves into musical celebrities. In the prevalent figure of the entrepreneur, artists find a performative model for presenting success and claiming authoritative speaking. An economy of moral critique drives the music's circulation, reshaping national, racial, generational, and cultural affiliations in the language of entrepreneurship. In the making of a new public culture of circulation, artists find creative possibilities as well as structuring constraints.

As Ghanaian urban youths help craft a new public culture for the privatizing state, they, in some measure, dictate how electronic technologies and transnational mobility become integrated into Ghanaian daily life. In order to examine these changes, I ask how a popular music becomes a language of moral nationhood; how a small group of young men become arbiters of style for a national public that values generational hierarchy and traditional modes of speaking; what the gendered implications of value making in popular realms are; and how established language ideologies get reinscribed through hip-hop. In qualities of musical control and balance, and moral debates sparked by making, circulating, and listening to music, young hiplifers challenge how Gha-naians experience tradition and modernity. Artists and audiences ne-gotiate the disjunctures between ideas of national culture and the chang-ing location of national collectivities in the language of beats and rhymes. As aspiring artists struggle to fashion musical tastes, they remake themselves in the process.

This book is not a history of hiplife nor does it attempt to compre-hensively catalog artists, songs, and stylistic differences. Any scholarly attempt to pin down a popular movement is bound to fail for the sim-ple reason that popular tastes and fashions change so quickly that—to paraphrase Hegel—writings on popular culture only appear when the object of study is hopelessly out of fashion. Instead, I examine how youths make and listen to hiplife, fashioning it into a socially sig-nificant genre, to explain broader principles of how value is made and transformed through circulation.

CHAPTER 1

Soul to Soul

VALUE TRANSFORMATIONS AND DISJUNCTURES
OF DIASPORA IN URBAN GHANA

In 1973 musician Gyedu Blay Ambolley released his song "Simigwa Do," an irreverent mix of funk guitar and R&B organ over a highlife beat. Soul music and fashion, which blended urbane sex appeal and black empowerment, were all the rage in Ghana and across Africa. Ambolley's soul-highlife captivated young audiences, though his provocative lyrics scandalized older listeners for being too sexual. What's more, he sounded like James Brown chanting in Fante and English (see figure 4). Unlike the subtle storytelling that characterized older highlife lyrics, Ambolley's were striking in how they directly addressed and provoked his audience: "If you don't know how to do it. Just listen to me. I'm going to show you how to do it." Thirty years later, Ambolley's specific blend of highlife and soul and his confident, directive lyrics, as one young artist explained to me, made him "a rap pioneer . . . even before there was rap music." This song demonstrates how African diasporic fashions and sounds have been central to Ghanaian popular culture throughout the twentieth century. Indeed, across different epochs musical innovation has been defined by a mastery of the art of incorporation rather than by a specific sound or look.

From the 1920s through the 1960s, highlife reflected populist fantasies about elite modern life, revealing mass audience concerns with urbanization, economic inequality, and nationalism. Each generation used popular music to create a soundscape for social transformation.

FIGURE 4 Gyedu Blay Ambolley performing in Accra, 1970s. Photograph used with permission of John Collins and BAPMAF.

Audiences thrilled at the latest highlife innovations that presented an image of African modern life, both full of potential and potentially hazardous. Highlife and its associated concert party theatrical style synthesized jazz, church cantatas, vaudeville, ragtime, soul, Afro-Latin dance, and rock with established forms of storytelling and neo-traditional music and dance. Highlife became integral to generational change as it incorporated various foreign black styles into new, but recognizably Ghanaian, idioms. Over time, each musical variant came to represent tradition and nationhood, against which next-generation innovations were, in turn, assessed. Musical experimentation reflected young artists' struggles to reach new audiences and to gain wealth and success in the process.

The appropriation and reinterpretation of Afro-cosmopolitan styles is at the center of highlife. Its stylistic power is based on an indexical and iconic parallelism in which this blended genre simultaneously points to ideas of progress and tradition. In this logic, Afro-cosmopolitan signs connote a set of virtues—freedom, aspiration, and movement—while markers of traditional music ground these values in familiar sounds.

Hybrid genres require artists who can control foreign, particularly black, forms of expression, transforming them into locally legible styles (Erlmann 1999; 1991). These artists are purveyors of taste who facilitate symbolic exchanges between Ghana and Afro-cosmopolitan worlds. They distill multiple, disparate sonic influences into a sound that defines Ghanaian nationhood through an aesthetic of newness.

Though diasporic forms have influenced many popular African styles, the confluence is not one of simple formal affinity or historical reconnection. The "return" of diasporic forms to Africa raises questions about mistranslation and disjuncture among black peoples as much as it does cultural affiliations (Edwards 2003). Beyond the dichotomy of white colonizer and black colonized, there is a third influential figure in African cultural discourse: the black foreigner. Because they challenge simplistic racial dualisms, black foreigners are not easily drawn into the racial-cultural oppositions that shape dominant understanding of colonial and postcolonial power. They are not the opposite, but not the same; African, but not; not colonial, except sometimes; not white, but somehow foreign. Disjunctures between Africans and diasporans are, in fact, productive of new cultural configurations. As artists struggle to interpret diasporic fashions for Ghanaian audiences, they actively remake African urban life as an Afro-cosmopolitan world. In this chapter I ask what semiotic work African diasporic signs do for Ghana. My purpose is to describe a logic of aesthetic appropriation and valuation that emerges through the history of highlife and later shapes hiplife music.

Highlife and Black Culture in the Gold Coast

Ghanaian urban culture has a long history of irreverently picking apart and reconstituting aspects of foreign black popular culture.[1] Various diasporic forms have been crucial to highlife's development. The music's history shows a pattern of indigenization of foreign styles and a movement from the use of English to local languages to reach mass audiences (Avorgbedor 2008). The term "highlife" became popular in the 1920s among urban poor congregating outside elite nightclubs where African musicians played ballroom and orchestral music mixed with some African tunes; through these dances listeners on the streets aspired to "live the highlife" (Collins 1996).

At the time, the Gold Coast's main coastal trading cities, Takoradi, Cape Coast, and Accra, were experiencing an economic boom. They developed infrastructure and civil service to support the export of cocoa, timber, and gold. Booming trade led to the development of an African middle class with growing tastes for foreign commodities. At the same time, multinational corporations began to recognize the potential of opening African markets. Sir Frederick Gordon Guggisburg, Gold Coast's governor from 1919 to 1928, was a liberal reformer interested in developing the colony's modern institutions. During this time, major educational, urban, and transportation infrastructures were built, including Takoradi's deepwater harbor, railway lines, Accra's main Korle Bu hospital, and Achimota School. With a growing class of workers and civil servants who had leisure time and money, European record companies recognized a potential market for popular music and, beginning in the 1920s, sought out African musicians, shipping records and record players to Africa (cf. Cole 2001). By the 1950s West African musicians were recording singles and LP albums in large numbers and record-pressing plants across Africa became big business, peaking in the 1970s (Agovi 1989).[2]

Highlife's varying instrumentations, rhythmic patterns, and melodies emerged from a pastiche of African, black diasporic, and European styles reflecting the movements of workers, sailors, preachers, and entertainers across the Atlantic, beginning in the late nineteenth century. Freed slaves and West Indian soldiers deployed by the British to fight the Asante, Yoruba, and others in West Africa brought Afro-Caribbean music. White and black American vaudeville and minstrel shows and itinerant Pentecostal preachers toured West Africa in the early twentieth century. Missionary schools spread Christian hymns and cantatas. European piano music, American sea chanteys, goombay from the Caribbean via Sierra Leone, Liberian Kru two-finger guitar, and accordion mixed with Ga and Fante musical traditions from Gold Coast towns (Collins 2002; 1996, xii–xvii).

By the 1920s highlife had synthesized numerous influences into three distinct styles: dance orchestra, brass band, and palm wine guitar band (Collins 1996, xiii).[3] Swing and jazz, spread by West African troops abroad and Allied troops stationed in Gold Coast during World War II, reoriented elite dance orchestra music of the 1930s toward smaller dance bands playing at urban clubs and halls. These included Jerry Hansen's Ramblers, King Bruce's Black Beats, and Stan Plange's Uhurus. E. T. Mensah's Tempos were especially successful with a "fusion of swing, calypso, and Afro-Cuban music with highlife" (Collins 1996, xv). With brass, strings, and drum sections, these jazz-oriented bands dominated urban nightlife across West Africa.[4]

In contrast, guitar bands played for rural and nonelite urban audiences. "Yaa Amponsah"—the name of an early highlife song—refers to the melody and chord progression that structures this style of guitar band highlife. These bands evolved in conjunction with concert party variety theatre troupes creating traveling multimedia music, theatre, and comedy events (Cole 2001). Early groups performed mostly English- and Pidgin-language songs suitable to an elite Gold Coast ethos. In the early 1950s, guitarist E. K. Nyame's Akan Trio pioneered the staging of proverb-like morality plays in Akan languages that revolved around original highlife tunes.[5] The Jaguar Jokers, African Brothers, CK Mann, Ghana Trio, and T. O. Jazz, among others, had eclectic guitar bands attached to theatre troupes that toured the country with the latest highlife music, original plays, and comedy. The relationship of highlife to concert party is significant in that it linked contemporary popular music to a tradition of Ananse trickster moral storytelling, in which lyrics gave indirect moral messages (Cole 2001; Sutherland 1975).

Soon after helping organize the 1948 Fifth Pan-African Congress in Manchester, England, Kwame Nkrumah returned to the Gold Coast to advocate for "self-government now." His political agitation against colonial rule sparked nationalist sentiment with a Pan-African orientation. As the struggle for independence intensified, highlife music and concert party theatre reflected this nationalist movement.[6] Nkrumah's Convention People's Party (¢PP) government supported a number of touring highlife and concert party groups, including the Workers' Brigade Concert Party, to build national and party sentiment through cultural expression, before and after independence on March 6, 1957 (Agovi 1989).[7] In his independence speech, Nkrumah stated that the "Independence of Ghana is meaningless unless linked up with the total liberation of the African continent." This reverberated through other political movements, affirming the importance of the new state's connections to Pan-African imaginaries and diasporic communities. Nkrumah supported African independence struggles around the continent and American civil rights movements, and he also linked cultural expression to nationalism and Pan-Africanist allegiance. His invitations to diasporic artists, choreographers, writers, and intellectuals to settle in Ghana demonstrated the ethos of Pan-African political and artistic collectivity he fostered.

The National Theatre Movement, under playwright Efua Sutherland's leadership, defined highlife, Ananse storytelling, and concert party as traditional cultural performances from which to develop Ghanaian modern theatre and national culture (Shipley 2004). Nkrumah's state supported highlife and concert party as symbols of indigenous expression. Amid the fervor of independence, with state encouragement for codifying national expressive forms, highlife and concert party were seen as traditional Ghanaian culture. At times, state recognition hindered the entrepreneurial tendencies of bandleaders, who were often less interested in politics and authenticity than audience excitement and financial success.[8] Bandleaders, reliant on gate fees, attracted local audiences by catering to their desires to hear the latest foreign and local hits and to incorporate new songs, styles, and instruments into their repertoire. As actor-musician Goldfinger recalls, the spirit of competition drove musical innovation. Artists learned theatre and music with an established band and then set out to become well known on their own. "[We used our] skills to become financially independent. . . . Most good musicians wanted to be artists in our own right, not controlled by some other bandleader. If you had the skills, that is what you wanted to do."[9] Musicians, inspired by audiences' eclectic tastes, continued to incorporate new styles. For young audiences, concert party and highlife groups touring the country provided spectacles of modern style and new technology for an emerging national audience (Shipley 2004; Cole 2001). In this way, highlife took on a crucial and contradictory symbolic role in mid-twentieth-century Ghana as simultaneously a marker of national cultural identity and traditional African performance, as well as a sign of modern, black cosmopolitanism.

Group names reflected growing links between black aesthetics and nationalist sentiment. For example, the Burma Jokers, made up of local World War II ex-servicemen stationed in Burma, renamed themselves Ghana Trio after the pivotal 1948 Accra riots, which followed a peaceful march in which colonial police killed four ex-servicemen. In 1963 the African Brothers took their name following President Nkrumah's initiation of the Organization of African Unity (Collins 1996, 33).

Following Nkrumah's overthrow in 1966, Ghana's Second Republic (1969–1972) aimed to liberalize the country, encouraging a spirit of entrepreneurship and free trade. Despite high inflation, currency devaluation, and unstable cocoa prices, independent music and theatre groups flourished in the early 1970s, as more urban nightclubs emerged and better roads and mobile electronic musical technologies facilitated rural tours.[10] Dance bands faded as guitar bands used jazz and rock instrumentation and electronic sound systems mixed with eclectic brass instruments and hand drums to more easily blend the latest soul, disco, reggae, R&B, rock, and Congolese music with established highlife rhythms. In particular, African American soul styles became a way for younger generations to distance themselves, through styles of speaking, dress, and the language of Black Power, from what they perceived as the British colonial orientations of their parents. Jaguar Jokers members, for example, began to dress in sequined jump suits and cover songs like James Brown's "I'm Black and I'm Proud" for rural and urban audiences. But these foreign tunes were reinterpreted for local appeal. Group leader Y. B. Bampoe recalled that to differentiate themselves from other groups, they introduced new songs, blending their hooks and melodies with older, familiar styles and rhythmic patterns to make them accessible. "Villagers want to hear the latest songs but you have to give them a highlife, give them a rhythm they can dance to, that is familiar. Then you slip in the new stuff . . . if you just played foreign music for villagers they would not like it; they would not dance to it like they do with highlife . . . which makes sense to them."[11]

Fela Kuti's Afrobeat and Osibisa's Afrorock are the two most successful examples of soul-oriented West African music that not only transformed the local musical scene but gained international recognition. Nigerian highlife musician Fela Kuti, by several accounts, formulated his Afrobeat style while staying in Accra in 1967, when he saw how excited audiences got when Ghanaian artists blended highlife with soul (Veal 2000). His subsequent sojourn in the United States exposed him to the Black Panther Party's radical politics and the latest African American music. This further developed his music's blend of African and diasporic music and fashion, invoking Pan-African culture to counter the perceived continuation of neocolonial oppression. One of the most influential African groups of its era, Osibisa was formed in England in 1969 by Ghanaian and Caribbean musicians. Teddy Osei and Mac Tontoh played in highlife dance bands in Accra. After moving to London, they developed their distinct Afrorock style that incorporated soul, funk, highlife, and folk rhythmic traditions that aimed, successfully, to make West African music more accessible to Western audiences and to bring rock and funk to African audiences.[12]

Soul to Soul

Over the course of the twentieth century, highlife established a pattern of eclectic appropriation in which artists and audiences used music and fashions to simultaneously mark a specific Ghanaian nationalism and cosmopolitan black belonging. Soul as mediated by highlife, in particular, had a profound influence on Ghanaian public life.

The Soul to Soul concert, held as part of Ghana's 1971 Independence Day celebrations, shows the fervor that soul music and fashion caused among Ghana's youth generation.[13] The state-sponsored event was coordinated by the Ghana Arts Council to celebrate national independence with African American music and popular expressions of black unity.[14] Youths from across Ghana traveled to the all-night show in Accra. One woman remembered sneaking out of secondary boarding school in Koforidua, in the Eastern Region, with several friends and traveling hours by bus to attend the show. She recalled the importance of soul styles to student life: "Students saw this concert as a major event. We admired and copied the way African Americans dressed. We formed copyright groups that imitated soul music in our talent shows. Soul to Soul was the culmination of this fascination with black styles."[15] In schools across Ghana, youths listened to African American records and imitated hairstyles, clothing, dances, and verbal expressions. "Copyright" musical groups imitated as closely as possible the sounds of the groups they admired. Another attendee recalled the excitement: "Kids who went to the show, even if they had no money would try to wear their best fashions . . . soul styles—bell-bottoms and wide shirt collars open down the front. If you did not have the right clothes you would take them from friends or relatives because you wanted to look hip."[16]

The Soul to Soul musicians arrived in Ghana with an entourage of 143 people amid massive publicity that proclaimed, "'SOUL ANGELS' IN TOWN."[17] The program began in the late afternoon at Black Star Square, a vast parade ground flanked by Independence Arch and the Atlantic Ocean.[18] Thousands began filling the square as darkness came. Ghanaian groups performed first, warming up the crowd for the American acts. Roberta Flack, the Staple Singers, Santana, and Wilson Pickett were much anticipated. Santana's blending of Afro-Latin dance rhythms with rock-and-roll instrumentation impressed the audience, later influencing a number of Ghanaian bands to experiment with fusing musical styles. Ike and Tina Turner, not well known to the audience, also awed the crowd. The national newspaper, the *Daily Graphic*, reiterated the excitement, using African American vernacular in its praise. "The dynamic dancing and singing display put up by Tina was admired by all. And as for the showmanship of Ike, man, it was no jive. He was on his job."[19] "Wicked" Wilson Pickett was the headlining musician. Referred to in the press as "Soul Brother no. 2" following James Brown, he performed in a black rhinestone-studded jumpsuit, open at the chest to reveal a gold medallion. He sang hits like "Midnight Hour," igniting the crowd by asking them, "How many of you think you got soul tonight!?" Later he sang to the audience, "Soul is in the heart, soul is everywhere. Soul is black and black is beautiful." As several observers recalled, when a singer from Voices of East Harlem raised her fist in a Black Power salute, many in the audience responded with cheers and followed suit. Tina Turner's concert anthem reflected an emotional return to Africa from a diasporic perspective. She sang, "Soul to soul. This is where it all came from; where the rhythm will turn you on. Back in our native homeland." For the black musicians, coming to Ghana was a symbolic return to an African point of origin. They thrilled at the welcome they received and the crowd's enthusiasm.[20]

The audience was also moved by the spirit of global racial unity. For Ghanaians, this diasporic return marked innovation and new possibilities for local transformation. Kwaa Mensah, a pioneer of palm wine highlife guitar, played at the concert though, according to several attendees, young audience members saw him as old-fashioned and uninteresting. Guitar band highlife represented modern innovation to the previous generation of Ghanaians who fought for independence. However, for urbanites and teens in the 1970s it marked rural backwardness and colonial life. Soul to Soul performers' dress, dance, music, and calls for racial unity created a buzz among audience members. Decades later, attendees still recalled in detail performers' outfits, including tight skirts and jeans, jumpsuits, bell-bottoms, sequined tops, bright wide-collared shirts, Afro hairstyles and wide sideburns, oversized sunglasses, and gold chains (figure 5). Youths used these fashions as a challenge to local social and political elites and their perceived continuities with European colonial influence. One attendee recounted that for young people, the concert provided a critique of their parents' generation, raised under colonial rule. "Those in power spoke like they wanted to be English, which seemed silly. Our elders, in the eyes of the youth, continued to value colonial ways of doing things . . . and we needed a way

FIGURE 5 The Black Beats performing. Photograph used with permission of John Collins and BAPMAF.

to comment upon that because as a youth in Ghana you could not directly stand up and criticize your elders. It was not proper."[21] African American music and style marked rebellion and innovation against what youths saw as their parents' old-fashioned, English ways of doing things.

Metaphors of Control, Proto-Rap, and the Making of a Musical Ancestor

Two musicians from the late 1960s and early 1970s demonstrate crucial features of how highlife incorporated soul and diasporic styles while maintaining the poetic indirection of storytelling traditions at the core of their aesthetic. This required the ability to control and deconstruct various genres and reassemble them in new authoritative configurations. This style of appropriation presaged hiplife.

Perhaps the most successful band of its generation, Nana Ampadu's African Brothers band structured songs around highlife's rhythmic bell patterns and melodies, integrating reggae beats and funk guitar riffs to make new dance styles. Ampadu wore a rhinestone-studded black jumpsuit, à la Wilson Pickett, and played innovative Afrofunk guitar. But twenty to thirty years later, he is remembered for playing "traditional" highlife. His hit song "Ebi Te Yie," one of the most influential highlife songs of his era, demonstrates his mastery of the indirect moral story-telling form (Anyidoho 1983). Released in 1967, one year after the military coup that overthrew Kwame Nkrumah, audiences and fellow artists interpreted its lyrics as a metaphor for political corruption. It follows the structure of *Anansesem* (Ananse trickster storytelling). The song is based on a folktale about a meeting of forest creatures. During the meeting, antelope continually tries to speak but is silenced by lion, who is sitting directly behind him, and who hits him every time he tries to make a point. Finally, antelope calls for the meeting to be canceled, reciting the song's title and its indirect moral point, "some of us are seated well, while others are not seated well at all." It was interpreted popularly, and by the authorities, as a critique of the purported silencing of public discourse by the coup-makers. Ampadu claims that he was young and did not intend the song as a political critique, but simply a story about animals from Akan folklore.[22] The government banned the song, which only made it more popular. The artist's denial of any political-moral intent fueled its popularity even more because of its uncertainty and openness to interpretation. The tale's circulation reflects the indirect style of Ananse storytelling, which was facilitated by its title's detachability as a proverbial phrase that became shorthand for the story's moral message. In the song, the antelope's predicament points to the possibilities and constraints of public speaking and the links between the right to speak and social authority. It reflects the established predisposition of audiences to read narratives as metaphoric and dual, simultaneously subversive and rooted in established reference. This issue also appears in hiplife when musicians draw upon storytelling to reposition the new music as a legitimate public genre.

Like Ampadu, Gyedu Blay Ambolley's music was notable for its detachable phrases that rapidly circulated across urban audiences. However, Ambolley's blend of highlife, funk, and Afrobeat emphasized the lyrical dexterity of the star performer and first-person narration over the content of the story. His style anticipated later musical transformations in Ghanaian hip-hop. In the early 2000s, after hiplife was established, listeners harkened back to Ambolley's 1970s music as a form of proto-rap.

As I describe above, his best-known song, "Simigwa Do," presented a pattern for integrating soul music into highlife's rhythm, reinventing the sound while referencing familiar musical patterns. After playing with a number of highlife bands, Ambolley released this hit single in

1973 under the group name the Steneboofs (Collins 1996, 88). Funk electric guitar chords and solo riffs are layered over horns, bongos, keyboard organ, and bass with a bell keeping the beat, creating a full Afrobeat sound.[23] Highlife is usually structured around one of several similar bell-pattern rhythms, including kpanlogo, sikyi, adowa, borborbor, konkoma, and gome.[24] "Simigwa Do" uses a kpanlogo highlife rhythm. Kpanlogo is a popular neotraditional Ga dance music emerging in 1960s Accra out of a combination of rock-and-roll dancing, Liberian Kru oge, Sierra Leonian goombay, and older highlife (Collins 1996, 110).[25] Initially, kpanlogo's sexually suggestive dance was seen as indecent. Otoo Lincoln, its originator, had to demonstrate it before Ghana's Arts Council to prove its musical legitimacy (ibid.).[26] While many traditional musics rely on polyrhythmic patterns including the ubiquitous 5 pulse bell pattern, much highlife, kpanlogo, and other popular styles compress these 5 pulses or beats into a 4/4 time pattern, fitting with jazz-, rock-, and blues-based signatures.[27] This provides a structure for infusing diasporic music with polyrhythmic traditions. As I will describe, despite its raucous popular origins, by the 1990s kpanlogo was identified as "traditional," a sonic nostalgia that made it central to the hiplife sound.

With the kpanlogo bell in the background, Ambolley's lyrics mix English and Fante, blending traditional-sounding chanting with R&B singing and vocalizations. The song opens with "The simigwa do! Brrrrr!" He chants over a funk-guitar progression,

Simigwa, you know is a kind of dance . . .
we've been doing in a place called Simi.
Tell them! That's a place you get together.
Groove together. And when everything gets . . .
we've got to do our own thing.
Now what we call the simigwa do.
Ready fellas? Yea! I said, ready fellas?

Using first-person narration, the singer calls on listeners to join in a collective celebration, describing and defining Simigwa in the process.

But Ambolley's song became controversial because listeners did not understand the song's chanting refrain, "Simigwa do." Some interpreted it as a loose vocalization of "Besin, menko di wo" (Let's go and have sex). Ambolley countered that he was chanting "Simigwa do." At times Ambolley was vague about the meaning. At other points, he defended the phrase. "In Fante it is a proverbial phrase which means the sort of composed dance done by a chief or well established person. He is sitting on a chair with so much pride as if he has achieved something and is in a happy mood, then an inner feeling makes him get up for a moment and dance. People thought it meant 'Let's go and have sex' but it wasn't like that" (Collins 1996, 88).[28] While I listened to the song with different people, some were confused. One fan noted, "It is Fante gibberish but maybe some of it is local slang that only a few people understand . . . No one knew what it meant, but it sounded so hip. . . . Others said it was a traditional saying, but I don't know."[29] Uncertainty of meaning heightened the catchphrase's power. The record was banned from radio play, though its popularity persisted and cemented Ambolley's reputation and nickname as the Simigwa Do Man. Another old-time fan felt Ambolley was an opportunist and "made up the phrase. No one knows what it means. People struggle to find meaning . . . When people said that's what he was saying he said, 'No no, that's not what I mean. . . .' That is why he is called the king of Simigwa, because only he understands what he is saying, ha ha! For the rest of the song, it is difficult to understand the words, unless you are pure Fante."[30] The ambiguity between profanity and "pure" traditional phrasing was driven by Ambolley's effective dodging of definitive interpretation and his blending of references to obscure tradition with the latest musical trends.

For my purposes here Ambolley's lyrics are important for their form rather than their content. They evoke listeners as members of a cool in-group, participants in an exclusive dance. As hiplife artist Reggie Rockstone said of Ambolley, "It didn't matter if you knew what he said. You knew right away he was hip."[31] His use of James Brown-esque vocalizations and first-person performative invocations of audience participation, like "Now I'm going to show you how to do it," distilled the essence of soul hipness for a local audience. As with Ampadu's "Ebi Te Yie," the ambiguity and the proverb-like detachability of the title "Simigwa Do" drove the song's circulation and popularity. Audiences were excited by indirect profanity, the possibility of hidden meaning, and the pleasures of controversy itself. Both artists balanced a familiar highlife sound with the innovative excitement of soul styles. The ability to create such an aesthetic balance would be significant later in the formulation of hiplife music, as following chapters will show.

The early 1970s were a crucial moment in musical transformation. Ghanaian musicians experimented with blending signs of blackness, Ghanaianness, and personal freedom in re-creating a national sonic landscape. Soul's emphasis on self-fashioning and bodily control encouraged local artists and audiences to see style as a realm of potential value transformation. Santana and Osibisa demonstrated how to incorporate African and Latin American rhythms and sounds into a rock structure that was accessible to African and international audiences. Highlifers like Gyedu Blay Ambolley, Nana Ampadu, and Ebo Taylor built upon highlife rhythms to incorporate soul, funk, jazz, and Latin elements.[32] Soul fashion, hairstyles, and forms of bodily expression, in the Ghanaian context, signified both racially specific black pride and the broader perception of Americans as having the ability to remake themselves through the force of personality. African American expression provided a language to reject British colonial social mores. Future Ghanaian leaders growing up in the 1960s defined political and social differences from their elders by embracing soul and R&B music and styles.

In the early 2000s when rap became popular, hiplifers recalled Ambolley with his chanting style as a musical ancestor. One fan remembers, "In his days Afrobeat was popular. So he was doing Afrobeat but behind it was chanting. So when people started rapping we remembered the same style with Gyedu Blay. Trying to look back to take something from our culture but in now looking back they were trying to do R&B and hip-hop in Akan. Many don't even know the influence of Ghanaian traditions on society and on hip-hop. What we see them doing from the present and what they thought they were doing is different."[33] While he had mostly been forgotten, suddenly he was recuperated by young musicians as the first person to rap in a Ghanaian language. Ambolley encouraged hiplifers' interest in his music by collaborating and performing with young artists. Whereas his contemporaries, like Ebo Taylor, continued to perform for audiences interested in highlife or Afrobeat, Ambolley attracted a new generation of rap fans.

Ghanaian Afro-Modern: Diasporic Disjunctures and Returns

Ghanaians with cosmopolitan aspirations use diasporic signs to refashion themselves as Afro-modern subjects, using signs of worldiness—particularly its black forms—to remake the local worlds they inhabit (Ferguson 1999, 211–213). Popular urban genres emerge from African artists' attempts to realign the differences among black peoples apprehended through style. A musician raised in Accra in the 1970s told me the following apocryphal story, which was recounted to him by a well-known writer. "In the 1960s a group of black Americans with Afros came to Accra. They spent time with a group of Ghanaians who had shaved heads who showed them around . . . providing proper Ghanaian hospitality. By the time they left, the Ghanaians had Afros and the African Americans had shaved heads." Several times, I have heard a similar story told as a joke: When you see a group of guys on the street, how can you tell who is African American and who is Ghanaian? Answer: The African Americans are wearing their Ghanaian hosts' traditional cloth and flowing *Agbadas* and the Ghanaians are wearing Western suits and urban fashions.[34]

The playful open-endedness of these stories, typical of indirect, proverbial speech (Obeng 1997), presents an inverted relationship between African diasporic and Ghanaian culture that allows for audiences to reflect on the history of these connections; they are intimately related to each other while simultaneously being opposites (Holsey 2008; Ebron 2002). They present an historical affinity in which both groups learn and gain value from the other. The humorous disjunctures among styles of dress represent the impossibility of existing in the same ontological space, a distance wrought by more serious historical disjunctures. Both hosts and visitors desire connection upon the diasporic "return" to Africa though they are slightly out of step with each other. The humorousness of copying hairstyles and clothing comes through the cultural-historical problem of substituting surface recognition for embodied knowledge. The image of mutual appropriation and inversion reflects a self-conscious recognition of both the intimacy and misunderstanding that urban Ghanaians draw upon in establishing a relationship to African diasporans.[35]

How Ghanaians narrate the relationship between diasporians and Ghanaians is telling of the ways foreign black aesthetics remake African localities. These stories acknowledge the local influence of black diasporic culture while introducing an element of reflexivity into judging the politics of aesthetic influence. In assessing black diasporic signs, a doubling occurs: if the copy were exact, then both would seamlessly blend and there would be no story to tell. The fact that each reuses the counterpart's style points to an affective affinity; both are seemingly transformed from the outside. In the process of appropriation there is both intimacy and distance, defined in the hopes and limits of style to convey a shared corporal experience. The cultural value placed on controlled mediation itself is demonstrated in numerous stories and jokes about Ghanaians who copy foreign styles too closely or those who affect

American or British English accents without ever having traveled abroad (jokingly referred to as LAFA or Locally Acquired Foreign Accents).

Diasporic returns to Ghana are often premised on idealizations of Africa as a site of (lost) symbolic origin rather than a place of active cultural production, whereas for Ghanaians, diasporic culture stands for the freedom of movement as well as the dissaffection of lost historical connection and distance from modern progress (Ferguson 2006). Black diasporic forms represent both foreign difference and racial-national recognition.

Other Globalizations: Why James Brown Is Not the Same in Accra as in Bamako

The centrality of diasporic styles to urban African life points to how Ghanaians strive for global connections through reconfiguring disjuncture. Disjunctures between diasporic and Ghanaian styles, and the local irreverent celebration of these differences, facilitate the stylistic transformation of foreign black styles into local Ghanaian ones. The logic of these value transformations provides a way to think about the subtleties of globalization from the margins.

In the late 1990s I sat in a friend's Accra house, looking through a family photo album with images from the 1970s. As a civil servant in his fifties, my friend dressed in tailored African print or dress shirts and slacks. But the black-and-white photos show him as a teen wearing tight polyester shirts, bell-bottoms, and platform shoes, along with a neat Afro and prominent sideburns. In the photos he poses confidently, with equally well-coiffed friends and girlfriends. "We had a band when we were in school. We were terrible! We tried to play James Brown and all those soul brothers . . . but it attracted the girls and we looked cool," he laughed. The pictures struck me because of how normal and prevalent soul styles were in 1960s and 1970s urban Africa; and how fashionable, playful images of urban Africa are often excluded from historical records of African life.

Comparing this to Manthia Diawara's account of soul styles in Mali reveals some of the differences within African interpretations of soul, showing that Ghana has a particularly intimate relationship to African diasporic styles.[36] Diawara describes how soul fashion inspired by diasporic icons like Mohammad Ali and "James Brown's music reconnected Bamako's [Mali's capital] youth to a pre-Atlantic slavery energy that enabled them to master the language of independence and modernity and to express the return of Africanism to Africa through Black aesthetics" (2002, 81). Diawara argues that James Brown provides a model of agency and possibility, a guide for how to be modern. He describes how the aesthetic of photographer Malick Sidibé not only captured portraits of Malian youths in soul styles but circulated and amplified the importance of these images in defining the hopes of Mali's postindependence generation. "Sidibé attained mastery of his craft by copying copies; that is, by following Bamako's youth, who were themselves following the black diaspora and the rock-and-roll movement" (ibid.). Diawara argues that photographs of stylistic duplication transform "the copy into an original" as images of Bamako youth copying soul styles become "masterpieces of the look of the 1960s" (ibid., 80).

As diasporic styles circulated through different forms of mediation—from music to gestures to clothing to photography—the power of teenagers in Bamako's imitations as symbols of agency and aspiration required a reflective distance from their diasporic referents. With the reclamation of photographs decades later, the participants look like originals only from a distance. While marking historical connections through aesthetic recognition, the symbolic logic of copying also distances the original by highlighting the unreality of this fantasy and the gap between the original James Brown and his Malian imitators. In a place like Bamako, the fantasy of closeness comes from a tacit acknowledgment that historical distance, exacerbated through long colonial experiences, is reinforced rather than undone through the symbolic return of a prodigal son like James Brown in the form of replicated clothing. The experience of Sidibé's photographs foregrounds not a singular sense of the transformation of imitators into originals but the simultaneity of the normality of soul styles in Bamako and their strangeness.

For Malian youths in the 1960s and 1970s, African American styles were viewed and represented from afar. As Weiss (2009) explains, in the 1990s African American styles shaped the fantasies and desires of Tanzanian youths who congregated around "hip-hop barber shops," striving to imagine new futures. Whether in postindependence Mali or neoliberal Tanzania, practices of copying fit within a logic of (post)colonial mimesis with a difference, where mirroring images of (foreign black) power provides a language for rethinking the future (Bhabha 1994). Signs of black difference, however, have different meaning in different locales. Whereas Bamako is away from the coast, a second city in Francophone Africa, and Arusha faces the Indian Ocean, youths in Accra and other

West African port cities have been part of intimate circuits of popular exchange with diasporic peoples throughout the twentieth century (Pierre 2012; Holsey 2008; Gaines 2006; Hasty 2005; Pierre and Shipley 2003; Drake 1982).

If the racial violence of the slave trade and colonialism were central to making the European nation-state, and this political entity continues to be structured around xenophobic and nationalist anxieties about racial policing (Goldberg 2002), then understandings of globalization and modernity need to take into account how racial disjunctures and discontinuities organize pathways of movement, influence, and transformation (Edwards 2003). For W. E. B. DuBois, African diasporic peoples made and maintained connections in the context of trauma and dispersal, embodied in the experience of exclusion rather than through an African cultural essence. In *Black Folk, Then and Now* DuBois ([1939] 1990) posits a theory of global history, arguing that the slave trade helped shape Europe culturally and economically, and that the historical connections among Africans on the continent and those scattered throughout the New World were forged through the violence and trauma of this extended moment. Drawing inspiration from German romanticism, DuBois posited that nationalism for African peoples across various locales emerged, not from shared language and territory, as with the German *volk* (folk), but rather in the shared historical experiences of dispersal and disjuncture.

Theories of globalization that emphasized technological velocity and deterritorialization (Appadurai 1996) emerged partially through enduring intellectual struggles to reconcile place-based ideas of culture and change-oriented histories in relation to African diasporic peoples. After DuBois, philosophers and analysts of black worlds oscillated between theories of historical continuity connections and cultural boundaries discontinuities. Herskovits ([1941] 1990) emphasized historical continuities between African and diasporic peoples as a way to validate diasporic culture. Ethnographic work on Caribbean societies further led to a recognition that contemporary cultural configurations needed to be understood through histories of political-economy and movement, as well as local narratives of and silences around these histories (Mintz 2012; Trouillot 1997). Even with the importance of black diasporic societies to the development of theories of globalization that dominated social analysis in the 1990s, scholars struggled to reconcile the centrality of African peoples to notions of modernity with their continued exclusion from it.

Michael Hanchard, building on Gilroy's (1993) work on the Afro-modern as counterculture, argues that Afro-modernity is "the selective incorporation of technologies, discourses, and institutions of the modern West within the cultural and political practices of African-derived peoples" (Hanchard 1999, 247). Hanchard's concern is not with the role of African diasporans in contributing to or participating in Western political configurations but rather lies in delineating the logic of black culture and politics in its own right. For Hanchard, black political communities are defined by a series of disjunctures that African peoples struggle within and against.

Hanchard's notion of Afro-modernity involves recognizing ontological differences as historical products. The spatial and "temporal dimensions of inequality" (Hanchard 1999, 263) get embedded in the fabric of modern collectivities—primarily the nation-state and its citizenry—that continue to structurally exclude black peoples from universal notions of modern belonging. Spatially, the global dispersal of black peoples creates disconnections. In this sense, black nationalism runs counter to the spatial project of the nation-state. But black publics have reimagined spatial dispersal through oppression as a potential form of shared history and collectivity. Temporally, black publics appear late in coming to modernity, blamed for the exclusions through which they have been marginalized. As Hanchard argues, the temporal disruption of community underlies the exploitation of black peoples and undermines their struggles for renewed organization. Notions of modern subjectivity and collectivity are built upon ideas of temporal and spatial continuity, stories of national-cultural origins, and shared language. Typically, epistemologies of nationalism theorize that citizen-subjects share a universal spatial-temporal framework (a nation-state) that defines modern being. For Hanchard, while black peoples have been blamed for their own spatial and temporal displacements, these are not failures to be corrected but rather built upon (Kelley 2003; Robinson [1985] 2000). Hanchard's notion of Afro-modernity focuses on theorizing the linkages between modern black political organization and black life-worlds. It provides grounding for ethnographic work on practice-based social forms like hiplife, in which local ideas of African diasporic connections and disconnections reshape collectivity in racialized terms. Though theories of black modernity must more clearly include African practices and locales as historically produced and globally engaged rather than as points of origin for diasporic disperals.

Gilroy's (1993) influential theorizing of the Black Atlantic has been criticized for excluding Africa in global circuits of black aesthetics and politics. Studies of jazz, reggae, blues, and hip-hop show how black diasporic music provides sonic metaphors of displacement from and unity with Africa (Veal 2007). Equally important, but less well documented, is the influence of diasporic cultural practices "back" on Africa. Cities like Accra are crucial to understanding black cosmopolitan networks. It is significant that most potent and popular forms of African music, worship, and theatre, throughout the twentieth century, have drawn on African diasporic modes of expression, making questions about connections and disjunctures and global racial inequality a subtext of so much African culture since the 1960s (Diawara 2002). In this light, if notions of Afro-modernity are to include African locales, more attention needs to be paid to the complex relationships between global black counter-publics and African cities and states.

The analysis of musical practices has provided a way to trace chains of influence from diaspora to African music and polities and to disrupt the ahistorical purity that surrounds popular and scholarly understandings of African music (Agawu 2003; Meintjes 2003; Veal 2000; Erlmann 1999; Collins 1996). Patterns of Caribbean and African American influence on Africa were greatest along mercantile trade routes and in urban centers along the coast. In South Africa, sailors brought jazz, blues, and Marcus Garvey's ideas of black nationalism, which shaped both the musical aesthetics and political ideologies of South African urban and migrant workers. Neighborhoods like Sophiatown in Johannesburg and District Six in Cape Town were centers of jazz and nightlife, with the music being seen as a marker of black identification and resistance and a threat to the apartheid state's racial order. In Kinshasa and Brazzaville, Cuban rumba and other influences helped shape "Congo" music, a Francophone "westernized African dance music" and later soukous. In Nigeria, juju music and later Afrobeat blended Latin American dance rhythms, soul guitar, and hymns with Yoruba praise singing (Veal 2000; Waterman 1990, 2).

A Logic of Appropriation: Symbolic Thirdness as Freedom and Inversion

In describing some of the changes in twentieth-century highlife in relation to a theory of Afro-modernity, my point is to show that Ghanaian popular culture is defined by an established logic of transformation in which artists craft diasporic signs into local artistic, economic, and moral value. Highlife is an eclectic genre, defined less by a particular rhythm or harmony than by a style of control and transformation. Diasporic signs in Africa provide a kind of promise; a debt is incurred that promises future connection. As the story of inversion in which African American visitors swap clothes and hairstyles with their Ghanaian hosts shows, from a Ghanaian perspective, exchanges with diasporic peoples are a form of cosmopolitan appropriation that embody debates about continuities and disjunctures among black peoples. Artists like Ambolley and Ampadu demonstrate an aesthetic of musical, lyrical, and bodily control. They incorporate soul music into familiar highlife rhythmic and storytelling structures that emphasize indirection and moral ambiguity. Ghanaian musicians' skills are judged by their ability to control black cosmopolitan signs and transform them into local registers. Integrating new music requires both bold artistic irreverence and the ability to make links to established, respected traditions.

Theories of copying imply replicating power to invert it; but copying black styles for Ghanaians involves a third term not defined by a simplistic dichotomy of colonizer and colonized, black and white, or foreign and local. This logic of musical appropriation is not a mimetic process that requires distance and duality. Mimesis is always both more and less than the original. Audiences assess not the exactness of a musical copy but how well musicians transform and synthesize foreign black styles into local legibility. This logic of transformation defines how Ghanaian artists turn a disparate set of musical styles and exchanges into a new synthetic and authoritative register. After decades of Ghanaian musicians synthesizing various influences into local popular dance music, highlife is defined more by a process of incorporating diasporic forms than by any particular rhythm, melody, or instrumentation. Musicians, audiences, and analysts alike have a hard time defining highlife—and, as we shall see, hiplife—but the debates about its origins and boundaries are themselves vibrant and pleasurable aspects of popular discourse; and, crucially, despite the myriad styles and subgenres, people know it when they hear it. While highlife was shaped by new appropriations and innovations from the 1920s through the 1970s, it also maintained familiar rhythms and melodies that defined a community of listeners. Musicians became good at understanding how to disarticulate various parts of songs—the instrumentations, rhythms, melodies, and lyrical structures—and reintegrate them with various other styles, similar to what electronic beat programmers did years later. They also became good at switching between styles and understanding how to transform foreign sounds for local audiences. Black foreign musical practices are emotionally charged ways of connecting to a global black collectivity while remaining specifically Ghanaian.

While Ghanaians at times associate African American culture with moral and sexual impropriety, its styles also provide each generation of Ghanaian youths with a language of possibility and the promise of freedom, placing a wedge between two sides of an old racial power dynamic. Diasporic styles stand in for newness that is also familiar. Evading the intractable, dialogic relationship between black and white, diasporic blackness allows youths to fashion new public voices.

Postcolonial theorists have argued that mimesis defined the productive ambivalence between colonial power and its opposition, and that the polarities of colonialism were enfolded into the postcolonial world (Bhabha 1994; Taussig 1992). Theories of mimesis in colonial contexts are built upon ideas of mimesis as signification, where a representation is understood to be produced in a dyadic relationship by copying the outside world. When participants reflect upon the sameness and difference embodied in a copy, self and other are produced and meaning is made. Copies show similarities, but in not being the same they heighten difference and open spaces for parody and inversion. Frantz Fanon's ([1952] 2008) psychoanalytic interpretations of DuBois's notions of blackness and doubling has been especially useful in breaking down post-Enlightenment assumptions that modernity was a universal historical endpoint rather than a symptom of an ongoing condition of power that relied upon continually symbolizing blackness, Africa, and colonized peoples as radical difference.

A theory of mimicry provides a way to link the history of the modern subject to the maintenance of colonial power. But mimicry is also a form of resistance for colonized peoples to embody, parody, and invert power effects. Colonial societies, and their postcolonial echoes, seem to encourage ambivalent copying, in which both colonizer and colonized copy each other, remaking themselves through a dialectic of power in which they see each other as both a reflection and an inversion; reiterating the Hegelian master-slave dialectic in which each relies upon the other for mutual existence. These entanglements imply a dyadic structural logic in which signs become meaningful in relation to their opposites. But the role of African diasporic signs in Africa destabilizes easy dyads of colonizee and colonizer, implying the importance of a third term in how participants actively engage the worlds in which they live (Erlmann 1999). Following Charles Peirce's notion of third-ness, which refers to how signification facilitates other "relations between relations" (Kockelman 2010, 407)—or the ways that sign-object relations mediate and produce other parallel relations among subjects and signs, signs and objects, and signs and contexts—the masterful incorporation of African diasporic signs into Ghanaian life facilitates new connections for those who can wield them, providing a certain semiotic freedom to claim new social stances. That is to say, diasporic signs in Africa are easily transmutable and open to interpretation; they do not stand in fully for self or other but shift between the two. They are more sensitive to context and require constant and masterful maintenance in aligning their meaning with local and foreign registers. The semiotic relationships of race and nation, local and foreign are built around black diasporic signs that signify agency and allow Ghanaians to actively align themselves with the freedom of transnational blackness while holding onto local aesthetic principles.

The influence of the African diaspora on Africa is profound. But part of this dynamic is the erasure of its own importance and continued revival of the idea of Africa as a place of origin.[37] In this dialectic of influence and erasure, the ability to mediate and appropriate foreign notions of blackness becomes a crucial performance value. This aesthetic is judged in terms of how musicians mediate and control new forms of speaking authority from the fragments of various older sonic forms and claim them as their own. Transformations in popular music give insight into how Ghanaian urban dwellers address problems of disjuncture and origins through embodied styles. The appropriation of global black styles that long defined Ghana's urban popular culture had important implications for the generation of Ghanaian youths growing up in the 1980s in the midst of new break-dance and rap crazes as well as state economic crises.

CHAPTER 2

Hip-Hop Comes to Ghana

STATE PRIVATIZATION AND AN AESTHETIC OF CONTROL

After leading two coups in 1979 and 1981, Flight Lieutenant Jerry John Rawlings became not only the nation's political leader but a populist icon. In its early years his youthful revolutionary government emphasized generational change, rejecting older military leaders raised under colonial rule. Rawlings orchestrated spectacular, charismatic speeches from the tops of tanks or after descending by rope from hovering helicopters (see figure 6). People recalled that he looked like a soul singer in his fighter pilot jumpsuit unbuttoned and open at the chest, short Afro hairstyle, and aviator sunglasses. His soul-inspired style reflected the state's collective Pan-Africanist aspirations. But by the mid-1980s the Ghanaian state was stuck between two contradictory positions. It was trying to maintain the image of a strong centralized state, while simultaneously privatizing its institutions and opening its markets to foreign investments and commodities. Culturally, youth interests were shifting toward the latest rap and breakdancing trends coming out of New York. For the new generation of teenagers, hip-hop replaced soul and R&B as the newest musical fashion craze. By the mid-1990s youths refashioned themselves and their relationship to ideas of progress and success through popular figures such as hiplife artists and church pastors rather than political leaders like Rawlings. This chapter traces the interrelationship between a growing interest in hip-hop and the privatizing state as it attempted to maintain control over public expressions of national culture. Central

FIGURE 6 Flight Lt. Jerry John Rawlings giving a speech from the top of a tank after 1979 coup.

to this dynamic was the question of whether hip-hop was understood as African or foreign.

Hip-hop was initially popularized as a marker of cosmopolitanism among elite youths and expatriate Ghanaians returning from living abroad. It subsequently attracted working-class youths who saw it as a sign of aspiration and a gateway to modern life. But the rising popularity of hip-hop also ignited debates about the moral implications of foreignness for youths and national development. As English-language hip-hop was commonly deemed foreign and morally corrupt, legitimizing the genre required integrating local language and performance idioms. Unexpectedly, one way this came about was through the National Theatre of Ghana's attempt to foster and promote Ghanaian culture by developing local-language rap competitions for youths.

The contested process of hip-hop's localization was an embodied debate about the tools necessary to craft individual success in a changing society. Particularly in emphasizing skills of aesthetic appropriation, local hip-hop pointed to new potentials for technologically driven, privatized popular music as a realm of wealth production. As the state seemed out of control, careening between centralized socialism and free-market liberalization, break dancing and rap focused on personal, bodily, and linguistic control. Dancers mastered improbable physical contortions and rappers flowed through linguistic acrobatics that valorized bodily precision in the face of social instabilities. Hip-hop also celebrated the figure of the entrepreneur in Ghana's nascent neoliberal society, tapping in to established business and entertainment models that the socialist state had quelled. The language of free-market economic transformation promoted private initiative and entrepreneurship as ways for Ghanaians to connect to the rest of the world. As the Ghanaian state became less prominent in shaping the populace's aspirations, the figure of the entrepreneur became the ideal citizen dominating political, economic, and cultural realms. State privatization gave rise to a new independent media beholden to the market, which fostered musical innovations that already infused youth culture. The music provided young Ghanaians with a soundtrack for marketization, with its celebration of the black hustler and the performative power of language and style.

Informal Economy: Balancing State Regulation and Privatization

Political-economic liberalization in the 1980s aligned an established entrepreneurial spirit with changing state interests. Struggles to control markets and trade—and the forms of cultural and economic value they shape—have been at the heart of Gold Coast and Ghanaian public life throughout the twentieth century. A culture of entrepreneurship has long been pervasive in Accra, a historical center for traders and middlemen. Indeed precolonial and colonial struggles among European powers and the Asante Empire centered around the control and regularization of trade routes to and from the West African interior through coastal ports (Allman and Tashjian 2000; Clark 1994). In Accra's markets formal and informal global and regional networks converge as all manner of goods and services are exchanged. Successful market traders are middlemen who master the art of networking, making value through the dynamics of exchange itself, though in moments of crisis they have often been demonized, blamed for broader social crises. Productive trade activity has alternatively garnered praise as a bedrock of good governance and incited moral panics that blame market activity for cultural-moral disintegration. At times, state interests have struggled to control competitive business practices; at other times, entrepreneurial interests have had free reign.

The notion of the informal economy, now common in social analysis, came out of Keith Hart's (1973) research in Accra's marginalized Nima neighborhood. The area, largely populated by Muslim immigrants from northern Ghana, was removed from established social and kinship networks, its residents excluded from official state contracts and the rights of citizenship. Hart argued that people who expect official support experience its loss as catastrophic. However, marginalized people, who have never had state support, create their own exchange networks. Rather than fight their political marginalization or withdraw from public life, the people of Nima made a new one. They sustained aspirations for future possibilities by creating their own networks of informal trade and a vibrant, unofficial economic life. They also diversified risk and increased chances for success by operating numerous diverse businesses at once. They were busy aspiring to succeed, not lamenting their marginalization; they were making trade networks through personal charisma and improvisation, rather than official structures. Social connections were converted into economic value.

From the perspective of the Ghanaian state, since independence in 1957 political difference has centered on the tension between free enterprise and state market regulation. After independence, Kwame Nkrumah's state aimed to centralize and regulate commerce. For example, in nationalizing the price of cocoa crops, Nkrumah argued that the state was obligated to support and protect farmers from global market fluctuations and that, conversely, profits from cocoa crops should benefit the nation, not just the farmers. After Nkrumah's overthrow in 1966, his opposition, led by Asante business elite and cocoa farmers, argued for decentralization and deregulation of business negotiations with international interests. Under Kofi Busia's Second Republic, the state moved away from centralized economics toward liberalizing policies to facilitate links between Ghana's economy and international markets. But currency instability, fluctuations in global cocoa prices, and inflation limited foreign investment and the stabilization of private business structures.

Colonel Acheampong's 1972 coup aimed to instill military discipline while continuing liberalization. But this government was known for *kalabule* or corruption, especially in relation to foreign luxury commodities. Food and commodity shortages led to rampant spread of informal trade networks. As one former civil servant recalls, in the 1970s if you went through legal channels or official government shops, things were scarce, but everything from petrol to basic foodstuffs to foreign luxury goods were abundant in unregulated markets run by market women rumored to be the girlfriends of military leaders. A common joke held that the state was ruled by "bottom power"—the large buttocks of market women incurred favors and controlled the decisions of men in power who were rumored to give Volkswagens to women they favored. During these economic fluctuations, touring bands and urban nightclubs flourished musically and financially. Highlife bandleaders' entrepreneurial spirit drove musical innovation as they competed with other groups for audiences. Making money from music embodied the spirit of an informal economy that still defines the life of so many people in Accra.

Perceptions of growing moral and economic indiscipline led to political upheaval in the early 1980s. On June 4, 1979, Flight Lieutenant Rawlings headed a coup d'état. His Armed Forces Revolutionary Council (AFRC) government oversaw the democratic election of Dr. Hilla Limann's People's National Party and the installation of Ghana's Third Republic. But, on December 31, 1981, Rawlings and his men returned in a second coup, citing lack of government control. This time he stayed in power as military ruler until 1992, and then as democratically elected president of the Fourth Republic until 2000.

Initially, Rawlings established a socialist-oriented government with the explicit aim of instilling discipline upon an economically out-of-control society. His regime encouraged the nation to turn inward to meet its economic needs rather than looking to foreign aid or international markets. They aimed to regulate Accra's culture of excessive, moral indiscipline and the conspicuous consumption of foreign goods. One woman, growing up in Accra during the 1970s and 1980s, remembers,

> People had been obsessed with foreign cars, clothes, everything. J. J. [Rawlings] wanted us to get back to our roots, to rely on our own resources. . . . Suddenly everyone in Accra had a garden and grew their own food; it was hard to get petrol to go to town. No one had money but no one was starving either; we all supported each other. . . . It's almost hard to remember that collective feeling because of how Accra became after that with all the foreign commodities again and kids acting like they were pop stars.[1]

The idealistic government encouraged the consumption of local Ghana-made goods and called for boycotts of foreign commodities. One Rawlings supporter-turned-journalist defended the need for the

1979 coup by recalling the intense economic indiscipline in Ghana. "The 'Kalabule' (corruption) . . . became so intense and unbearable that at a time EVERY GHANAIAN VIRTUALLY BECAME A CHEAT, SWINDLER, SMUGGLER, and a CHARLATAN."[2] One of the soldiers' most decisive and visible activities after the first coup was destroying Makola, Accra's main market, and publicly disciplining market women. From the perspective of the new state and its hopeful citizens, the informal market economy that flourished in the 1970s undermined good governance and civil progress. However, the activities traders were accused of—hoarding, cornering the market on commodities, and innovative marketing to consumers—were alternately understood as effective entrepreneurial activity by aspiring businesspeople who, unable to work through official channels, fashioned alternative networks of exchange.

While initially Rawlings's government called for national self-sufficiency and state centralization, by 1982 budget shortfalls necessitated Ghana's entry into an International Monetary Fund and World Bank-sponsored Structural Adjustment Program. While the government publicly advocated for state control, its agreements with the World Bank and the IMF mandated the privatization of state enterprises and opening local markets to foreign investments and commodities.

The music business, so vibrant in the early 1970s, struggled after the Rawlings coups. Government curfews banned movement from 6 PM to 6 AM for several years. Fuel shortages also curtailed Accra's nightlife, as well as the movements of concert party-highlife guitar bands that toured the countryside.[3] The forced return of over one million Ghanaians from Nigeria, food shortages, and drought exacerbated the national crisis. Government taxation on the importation of foreign musical instruments further crippled bands. Faced with poor resources for music education in schools and declining tour and gigging opportunities, many musicians left Ghana for the United States, Germany, Holland, England, and Nigeria. Since churches were not subject to instrument taxes, musicians who did not leave switched to gospel, performing for church services (Collins 2012). The lack of new, original music by Ghanaian bands caused the decline of the formerly vibrant recording industry, and only a few locally pressed albums and singles came out.

Playwright Mohammed Ben Abdallah became Secretary of Tourism and Culture and was particularly vocal in linking cultural identity to economic transformation.[4] He recalls trying to convince his more politically oriented colleagues of the importance of the arts. "Drought and fuel and food shortages affected us more because of Ghana's reliance on foreign markets for our raw materials and commodity imports. We wanted to reclaim control of our resources. . . . Cultural unity was crucial to that."[5] He was concerned with how cultural policy could support local economic control.

> [We] criticized previous regimes for perpetuating neocolonialism . . . and the dominance of foreign cultural influences on Ghanaians, in music, in dance, in drama, in the arts, in clothing that people wore and even the attempts by some of our women to lighten their skins with all kinds of creams. . . . Foreign music was played more than our music—[radio and television] programs generated from outside dominated our airwaves as compared to programs generated from within our country with inspiration from our culture. . . . [We] talked about the democratization of culture, culture institutions.[6]

The government supported regional and district cultural centers, reestablished moribund traditional festivals, and encouraged new ones. In Accra it built cultural institutions oriented toward Pan-Africanism, including the DuBois Centre, George Padmore Library, Kwame Nkrumah Mausoleum, and the National Theatre of Ghana. Education policies established cultural studies in schools to encourage the serious study of Ghanaian indigenous culture, dance, music, and languages (Coe 2005). For the first time the state established a ministry-level institution dedicated solely to culture: the National Commission on Culture. As its first chairman, Abdallah attempted to regulate all media, film, copyright, and arts programming and infrastructure related to culture.

Dance Revolution: From Disco to Break Dancing

As the military discipline and economic crises of the 1980s faded, nightlife in Accra began to make a modest comeback, but in new ways. When military curfews started at 6 PM, people went to early dance parties called "afternoon jumps." Curfews were pushed to 8 PM, then 10 PM. Amed, a teenage club goer whose father was a lecturer at the University of Ghana, remembers the excitement as nightlife returned. "Clubs would be open 3:30 to 9:30. People would go out and rush to get home on time."[7] International travel and access to foreign media eased. One early hip-hop enthusiast whose father was a minor government official joked to me, "If a new fashion or album comes out in New York, the next day it's in Accra." His brothers and sisters would wait for their uncle to return from Europe to bring the latest "fashions and music" from "up there."[8] Magazines, cassettes, videos, and later CDs and DVDs, were sent by relatives, sold by traders, or acquired by traveling elites.

Lack of instruments, dispersal of bands, and increasing availability of affordable, portable technologies meant that the musical landscape took on a decidedly electronic feel. "Spinners"—mobile DJs who provided music for funerals, outdoorings (celebrations of a child's birth), parties, and dances—were cheap to hire and could play a wide variety of the latest hits. Their use of electronic equipment—turntables, cassette decks, amplifiers, loud monitors, microphones, lights, and sound effects—excited people as spectacles of technology in rural and poor areas, and provided ways to have multiple musical styles without live musicians. Clubs and secondary school shows used DJs playing cassettes and LPs rather than bands and hosted disco and R&B dance competitions.

The new generation liked new kinds of black music. Reggae became more popular. The global disco craze inflected local tastes as well. And, of course, Michael Jackson captured people's imagination. Performers imitated him at numerous look-alike and dance competitions at clubs and secondary schools. Gospel highlife evolved through a rising interest in Pentecostalism and the migration of previously secular musicians into church bands. The subgenre of "burger highlife," influenced by Ghanaian musicians working in Germany, evolved as musicians traveled to Europe and brought back computer and synthesizer music. Kojo Antwi, Geroge Darko, and the Lumba Brothers, among others, transformed popular music after returning from Germany by infusing highlife with electronic sounds, rock and reggae, and new flashy looks.

Cheap video recording and screening technology facilitated access to foreign narrative films and music videos. Poor youths gathered at small video screening facilities that charged nominal fees. Elite kids passed around videotapes among their friends. One teenager recollects the importance of dance videos from abroad. "We would get so excited to watch again and again, just trying to see the styles and moves."[9] The explosion of big-budget American urban dance films—such as *Saturday Night Fever* (1977), *Grease* (1978), *Fame* (1980), *Flashdance* (1983), *Footloose* (1984), and *Dirty Dancing* (1987)—had a big impact. Early hip-hop films like *Wild Style* (1982), *Style Wars* (1983), *Breakin'* (1984), and *Beat Street* (1984) also inspired interest. Kids gathered to watch television shows like *Soul Train*. As Amed recalls, "People were moonwalking, spinning on their heads, doing the robot, directing traffic, locking, all those '80s moves. . . . It was *black* music. We *felt* it, but it was also so urban and American. It made us feel a part of what was happening outside when things in Ghana were rough. You got a few tapes—that was a big deal, so we paid attention to what we saw." He remembers the feeling of isolation: "We didn't have a lot of things. You felt isolated, even the wealthier kids; and hip-hop seemed like a way black kids in New York were taking control of the city, of being hip on their own terms. . . . Highlife was our parents' music, old-fashioned compared to spinners and their lights and heavy amps."[10] For urban youths, black American life provided an image of modern possibility and connection to a glamorous world out there.

Adjetey Sowah, who won a world freestyle dance competition in Holland in 1986, recalls going to dance competitions in 1981 and 1982 at Accra's Babylon Disco.[11] "Freestyle dance in Ghana started because Ghanaians played R&B, soul music, and stuff like that. . . . [You would] listen to the music and come out with your own moves. . . . People started watching American videos especially in 1983 after [Michael Jackson's] *Thriller* came out. Right? *Thriller* was it! . . . But I just don't watch those videos. . . . I try to change the style, to come up with my own moves. I say, 'Hey, these are the latest moves, let's change what is going on.'"[12] Young people were inspired to copy American dances from videos and creatively elaborate on them.

For select students at elite secondary schools, by the mid-1980s disco and R&B were superseded by a growing break-dancing craze. One student from Achimota School at the time remembers, "pop music like Bobby Brown, New Edition . . . James Brown, funk, reggae played in clubs. . . . [Some of us] thought Michael Jackson, who was all the rage, was really corny. We wanted to be more like the streets; and even more than hip-hop and soul music it was break-dancing competitions at first that started to spread."[13]

In school Reginald Ossei (later Reggie Rockstone) was well-known as a break-dancer. His father, Ricci Ossei, was from a small village near Kumasi. After earning a scholarship to school, Ricci eventually made his way to England in search of work. With a flair for fashion trends and innovative designs like "patch jeans," he became a successful fashion designer, starting one of the first fashion studios in Anglophone sub-Saharan Africa.[14] Reggie was born in London. His father led a rather cosmopolitan life, taking Reggie to America to stay with his new

African American wife. Reggie's mother thought he needed a different influence and took him to live in Kumasi. In the early 1980s his father sent him to Accra's elite Achimota College. As Reggie recalls, he was less interested in classes than in break dancing. As Ghana's political situation stabilized, Ricci became the fashion designer for political and cultural elites, later developing a new media business. Reggie inherited his father's charisma and flair for style. Amed, a schoolmate of Reggie's, recalls how his break dancing came out of the disco and Michael Jackson crazes. "I am sure he doesn't want to remember, but Reggie started with Michael Jackson–style dancing, then got into breaking. He was always leaving school, going off to dance competitions in Tamale, Kumasi, all over Ghana. Sometimes he would get stuck for a week someplace and we would have to make excuses for him. . . . In those days transportation was not easy. His father was not happy. But Reggie was so into it, he didn't care." From an early age, Reggie used his travel experience to claim legitimacy. "He had lived abroad so that gave him some urban cred. But he would also tell us that he spent time in Kumasi with local kids and that's where he got his Twi [language skills] and tough Kumasi [thing]."[15]

Learning and elaborating on disco, Michael Jackson, and then break-dancing styles gave youths in Accra an embodied way to imagine themselves as members of a broader black community during a period of social isolation. Within these allegiances, break dancing was the first of American hip-hop's four elements—break dancing/B-boying, MCing, DJing, and graffiti—to mark the generational shift away from 1970s soul styles.

Rap and Elite Language Use

Aside from the bodily aesthetic of break dancing, American-English rap lyricism provided youths with connections to African American urban life. While soul styles marked their parents' generation's break with colonial valorizations of Britishness, hip-hop gave youths a new public voice. Rap focused on the act of speaking itself as rebellious for young black men. With rap's popularity youth adopted inflections to sound African American, sparking debates about proper language use. Negotiating the relationship between English and Ghanaian languages became central to establishing rap's local legitimacy. As Susan Gal argues, "Language ideologies are never only about language. They posit close relations between linguistic practices and other social activities and have semiotic properties that provide insights into the workings of ideologies more generally" (2005, 24). Reflexive references to language use are themselves crucial to how language ideologies are contested or reinforced. Debates about appropriate forms of speaking were common to rap enthusiasts and critics. English remained Ghana's official language after independence, though debates continued about maintaining Ghanaian cultural identity when the state's language was not, in fact, anyone's mother tongue.[16] Language use in rap reflected these conundrums.

Rap's appropriation, as with earlier diasporic styles, reflected and reinforced Accra's class and language hierarchies. Rap first became popular with the children of elites in Accra, Kumasi, and in coastal boarding schools. Elite secondary schools in Ghana—as elsewhere in postindependence Africa—have been important centers for making cultural tastes and forging political connections (Wainaina 2011; Agawu 2003; Diawara 2002).[17] Hip-hop speaks to the dual dynamics of cultural exclusion for urban African elites. One student from Mfantsipim School explains that elite youths were caught between the expectations and entitlements of Western education and their ambivalence toward local culture. "Wealthy and politically connected kids . . . intellectuals, mixed-race kids; if you grew up in Accra, even though you were better off, you were kind of marginalized in a strange way from the West . . . and from traditional village life."[18] In addition, for children of Lebanese, Syrian, and Indian merchants and those of mixed parentage, hip-hop represented American coolness.[19] It provided an alternative vision of globalization from Eastern trade networks and the languages of their parents. For elite students who felt excluded from various forms of identity, hip-hop provided a Pan-African, global form of inclusion.

At first, teens lip-synched to recordings of American rappers, then began writing their own English raps, copying lyrical flows and themes.[20] They formed English-language rap groups for school variety shows. One student at Accra Academy in the 1980s recalls, "My favorite rappers were LL Cool J and Run-DMC. We didn't worry too much about the lyrics; it was more the overall message of these rich black guys who had such style and defiance. It made us feel tough . . . like we too could make money."[21] For elite—and later nonelite—youths, rap's appeal was not primarily the specific lyrical content but rather its linguistic form. Reggie remembers that kids less fluent in English "would not even understand anything they were listening to. They just heard the funky beats and felt a connection. . . . Especially early on it was the sing-song kind of hip-hop that became popular. People had to be able to hear the melody and dance to it."[22] American hip-hop appealed through its formal stylistic elements. While in the American context African American vernacular hip-hop connoted street toughness, in Ghana it pointed to a black cosmopolitanism associated with high social status.

BiBi Menson[23] was a pioneer of Accra's hip-hop scene in the 1980s. After attending Accra Academy, he got involed in music, eventually becoming program director for Radio Gold. He remembers how class hierarchies were re-created in small social circles of privileged children who congregated in open-air drinking spots in Adabraka and other neighborhoods. "We were into break dancing, rapping, and all the hip-hop culture. . . . Boys from [elite] schools . . . would always be at house parties or clubs. We would get together and talk big things, insulting each other. . . . Then there were the more local boys from down the ghetto— we used them as foot soldiers. . . . They would easily throw a punch for you. We were the loudmouths, trying to be heard." English was the primary language of elite school life, informally mixed with Pidgin, Twi, and other local languages. Privileged students, more fluent in English than their lower-class counterparts, acted as cultural translators and purveyors of taste, mediating the world for local consumption. African American vernacular style was the language of cosmopolitanism and the purview of elite youths. Mastery of these codes translated into status.

Menson noted how the symbolic power of African American inflected English youth styles. "We were into all this Yo Yoism and foreign life. . . . You dare not do it [rap] in the local language. You would be a laughingstock." English fluency was important. Through hip-hop, he said, laughing as he remembered, "Our accents changed. . . . We spent a lot of time trying to sound natural when we spoke with American accents."[24] New dance moves, musical styles, and informal speech patterns required practice to give the appearance of naturalness.

American rappers' Afrocentrism had the unintended consequence of garnering Ghanaian interest in African culture. In formal contexts, African styles and language use were looked down upon, as outdated or "colo" (colonial). Menson pointed out, "It's ironic. . . . In those days you couldn't wear kente cloth [traditional Asante fabric]. We had to wait for someone like Heavy D to wear kente caps before we saw it as acceptable to follow our own traditional forms of dress."[25] Nii Addokwei Moffat, of entertainment newspaper *Graphic Showbiz*, remembers that in the 1980s various Ghanaian musicians experimented with rap. In 1984 at a cultural performance held at the State House, dancer-musician Cecilia Adjei "asked why we can't rap in our local dialects. She tried something [in the Dagbane language] and so did I [in the Ga language] and several other artists and people found it . . . exciting." Atongo, an eclectic musician from the north of Ghana, also rapped in Hausa in the 1980s, though he never received the attention later rappers would.[26] As a rap competition promoter put it, rappers attempted "at first, to directly imitate their favorite American artists in style, music, and lyrics. . . . They were not ready to . . . make the music theirs."[27]

Initial receptions of hip-hop in Ghana revealed both young people's intimate affinity for African American life and their distanced admiration for the forms of modernity it proposed. For each generation, African American vernacular styles of speech, bodily comportment, and dress have been both signs of global racial affiliation and ways of claiming local distinction (Bourdieu 1984). Just as soul and R&B provided generational critiques of earlier jazz- and swing-influenced highlife, students in the 1980s marked rebellion against their parents' generation by using hip-hop to critique soul.

Ghanaian Diasporans Go to London, Play Black Music, and Come Home

The experience of Ghanaians who lived in London and returned to Ghana was central to developing hiplife's image and sound. Reggie Ossei left for London after school pursuing break dancing; seeking fame but unsure of where he would find it. As he recounts, he wanted "to pursue things on a bigger scale. . . . I wanted to make it in the big time." Many of his generation had left Ghana, fleeing corruption and decadence in the 1970s and austerity in the early 1980s. Staying with family in South London, he attended drama school for acting. He began traveling to New York, buying the latest hip-hop gear and urban fashion to sell in London, where they still were not easy to find. There he met up with Freddie, originally from Sierra Leone, who had attended Ghana International School. "Freddie and I were running partners from growing up in Accra." Reggie and Freddie, along with Jay and DJ Pogo, formed PLZ, an English-language hip-hop group.[28] Reggie recalls getting into rap, "I did not even know how to rap or play music; I was a break-dancer. So I just faked it until I figured it out."[29] Freddie recalls how they got their rap names. "One day we decided we were the stone family. He was Rock-stone and I was Funk-stone."[30]

At the time, black British life was dominated by Afro-Caribbeans, with African youths often subsumed within Caribbean communities. It was also defined by the close proximity to and racial tensions with white working-class youths (Hebdige [1979] 1996). Reggie remembers, "England at the time was a really racist place. They still thought about the whole colonial thing. Africans were looked down on. . . . Even some Jamaicans were confused about . . . West Africa . . . and looked down on us. It wasn't easy to be African."[31] As Ghanaian-British filmmaker John Akomfrah recalls, "Many Jamaicans and such didn't want to associate with Africans. We disturbed prevalent ideas of authenticity for Black culture as coming from the West Indies."[32]

Reggie and Freddie hung around with a mix of Caribbean and African youths as part of a nascent hip-hop scene including groups like London Posse, an influential early British hip-hop group. PLZ put out several records with a small label, Go for the Jugular, including the tracks "If It Aint PLZ" and "Build a Wall Around Your Dreams," and achieved minor local success.[33] London Posse portrayed the frustrations and violence of black life in London with reggae-inflected rap. PLZ, on the other hand, emphasized African American vernacular and style, even encouraging fans to think the group was from New York. Reggie remembers, "If people thought we were from New York, that helped our image on stage and on the street." A vibrant scene was emerging in South London but it lacked commercial appeal. "It was a small scene and it wasn't possible [for us] to break out in those days. . . . Anyway we were Africans doing African American music for Caribbean crowds . . . We couldn't exactly go to New York to make it there."[34]

Panji Anoff was also part of this music scene and would later help shape hiplife in Ghana. Of German and Ghanaian heritage, he was also born in Britain, moved to Ghana as a child, and then returned to England, where he studied mechanical engineering at Cambridge University. He worked as a journalist and for the BBC. A music producer and recording engineer, he helped manage PLZ. Panji recognized the fantastical ways Africa was seen and how hip-hop in England was stuck in the contradictions of exotic images. "Early hip-hop in London relied on African American images and ideas of Africa. . . . Africa itself, on the other hand, was seen as tribal or primitive."[35] He reflected on how these contradictions would lead to hiplife's development in Ghana:

> Hiplife really started with PLZ and their success as an American-oriented hip-hop group. Considering the [limited] interests of the [British] music industry in hip-hop at the time, PLZ had reached the limits of what they could do in Britain. . . . I mean, if they said they wanted to do African music, if they had started rapping in Twi [in Britain], that would have been the end of it. . . . They had traded on their American image in London for legitimacy. . . . So they could not go to New York or orient their music toward Africa.[36]

While Reggie was enamored of hip-hop's dual feelings of toughness and celebration, Panji was interested in broader explorations of global black music. In PLZ's struggles to gain recognition and their inability to bring African music to London audiences, Panji saw the opportunity to develop hip-hop into something that would draw on Ghanaian musical traditions instead.

For Paa K, another elite Ghanaian living in London, the differences between the experience of blackness in London and in Ghana revealed both the positive and negative aspects of ideas of black cultural unity. Paa Kwesi Holdbrook-Smith is from a well-known Fante family. His great-great-grandfather was one of the first barristers with a British law degree on the Gold Coast. Paa K attended an elite British boarding school, then worked in entertainment and events management in London before returning to Ghana, where he worked with early private radio and acted as Reggie's manager. For Paa K, as for Panji and Reggie, black culture provided a form of solidarity. "Black music gave us all—African, Caribbean, and South Asian—a soundtrack for living in a hostile country." But he also worried about the specificities lost in having to respond to British racism, "the Brits, the racism conflates a variety of nonwhite peoples with vastly different experiences and cultures." In this context black styles helped youths redefine forms of what Stuart Hall (1993, 225) calls "significant difference" within British society that negated black experience. "In public school [in Britain] I remember one white kid insulting me by saying, 'You Africans don't know anything about civilization.' I said to him, 'Look, I live in your country, speak your language, and understand your culture. I know your society better than you do. I also speak my language and a whole other culture. So who is the uncivilized one?'"

For Paa K the experience of youths in Ghana contrasted with that of black Britons. "Growing up in Ghana, black music and dress, and ways of talking from America and the Caribbean, gave us a modern sense of ourselves. We needed a language to connect to the rest of the world, especially our Africans in the diaspora. We wanted to be part of the world and [to] be free as individuals. We wanted to make money, to succeed, to have opportunities, instead of being controlled by . . . military regimes."[37] For Ghanaians in Ghana, black expressive practices acted as signifiers of foreign value, modernity, and personal success and freedom. For black youths in Britain, calypso, reggae, dub, and rap were forms of rebellious cohesion against racial and class-based exclusion.

The post–World War II influx of Afro-Caribbean, South Asian, and African immigrants to Britain sparked white working-class economic anxiety and racism. The "disruptions" to British life after the war centered on the traumas of the end of empire for both former colonizers and colonized and a sense of spatial and temporal displacement. Serious intellectual inquiry into popular culture also came out of this historical conjuncture of colonial race and urban class hierarchies in postwar Britain. British Cultural Studies emerged out of an analysis of the tensions and affinities between an increasingly alienated white working class and growing black British communities established through mass emigration to urban Britain (Carby 2007; Hall 1993).[38] Analytic interest in crises of social reproduction led to studies of youth style and expression as forms of agency and narration emergent through structural contradictions. For example, Hebdige's ([1979] 1996) small masterpiece *Subculture: The Meaning of Style* outlined the ways that black British styles were reappropriated in new configurations by white youths. It argued that popular culture provided a set of bodily practices through which marginalized youths inverted dominant aesthetic principles to rearticulate hierarchy and difference through personal expression. In resymbolizing music and dress, children of empire addressed their dual legacies of race and class discrimination. In these youth rituals of rebellion, new forms of racialized subjectivity emerged.

Black British urban communities came of age in the 1980s, as the state reoriented itself through Margaret Thatcher's free-market economics, cutting public funding for the arts, health, and education. Major riots broke out in Brixton and Birmingham in 1981, and again in Brixton in 1985, as African, Caribbean, and Asian communities responded to the endemic police brutality, racial violence, and mundane discrimination they faced in Britain.[39] This was the environment in which Reggie, Panji, Paa K, and other Ghanaians in diaspora became passionate about hip-hop.

Hip-Hop Spreads in Accra

Back in Ghana, while hip-hop had initially been the purview of elite youths, the authenticity and value ascribed to being from "the ghetto" in American rap music resonated for urban kids from poor neighborhoods. Hip-hop marked both a black cosmopolitanism and a masculinized resistance to marginalization. Boys living in crowded, poor neighborhoods with densely packed compound houses had secondary access to hip-hop as music and videos circulated across Accra. Teenage enthusiasts in the 1980s spawned interest among their younger siblings, born around 1980, setting the stage for the explosion of hiplife music twenty years later.

Hashim Haruna is part of this group. About ten years younger than hip-hop pioneers like Reggie, BiBi, and Panji, Hashim grew up in Nima, Accra's famously tough, crowded neighborhood of migrants from the Muslim north. Hashim moved to the United States while still in school, and in the mid-2000s he began promoting hiplife music in the Bronx, New York. Some of his childhood friends became rappers, including the well-known group VIP. He recalls that boys in Nima called their "bases"— yards, kiosks, and shade trees where they congregated—things like "the Bronx" and "Fly Away," representing "things they desired."[40] While wealthier youths frequented clubs and drinking spots, those in poor neighborhoods relied on informal meeting places, mapping new imaginaries onto spaces of daily living in the language of hip-hop. Youths in poor neighborhoods adopted hip-hop's valorization of ghetto life as a form of cultural capital. "Because I was from Nima, other kids thought I was tough and would admire my styles. I was really into hip-hop. And richer kids identified hip-hop with the ghetto. So when we got into hip-hop music and clothes, they would see us as tough and wanted to hang out with us." Hip-hop's ability to link African American street life and elite, foreign modernity validated the experiences of poor African youths.

Hashim remembers the wide influence of rap music videos. "In videos rappers always seemed so successful. Many kids wanted to be like that, to make money to help their families . . . so they tried to copy . . . their swagger." Hip-hop's images of strong black masculinity and rebellion resonated. What John Jackson has dubbed hip-hop's "nihilistic Don't-Give-a-Fuckness" (2005, 195), projected through visual and verbal images of excess, cars, cash, jewelry, and sexually available women, gave young men fantastical images of financial and sexual success.[41] Samuel Bazawule, who would make a career rapping as Blitz the Ambassador, recollects with a smile how they excitedly imitated fashions. "We would stand around burning barrels and wear Timberland boots and puffy jackets like we saw in the music videos. It wasn't until I moved to the U.S. years later that I realized they did that because it was cold in New York!"[42] The image of the hustler aligned leisure with aspiration. In young men's desire for wealth, the line between images of success and rebellion blurred. As music videos circulated in Accra, images of African American rappers appeared on T-shirts, paintings, and posters, and influenced fashion.

High unemployment in neighborhoods like Nima increased social pressure on young men to find work. Reminicient of Keith Hart's notion of informal economy, Hashim says, "In Nima everyone is a hustler. You have to constantly look for any opportunity to survive and support your family."[43] As in the case of rural South Africa (White 2010), lack of official employment, and separation of home from places where value could be accrued, created an ongoing crisis of masculinity in which young men struggled to build economic and social capital to support families and become respectable adults. In Accra, as hip-hop became a localized symbolic language, it communicated the aspirations of youths who did not have access to other networks for making value. Baggy pants, oversized chains, basketball sneakers or Timberland boots, sunglasses and goggles, baseball caps, name-brand and knockoff gear represented cosmopolitan success. Poor urban and rural youths used foreign, diasporic styles to connect them to modern life. A young barber who moves between Accra and his village near Keta in the Volta region explains, "If you are a young man, when you go back to your village after being in Accra for some time you are always sure to wear the latest hip-hop fashions. This shows that you are successful."[44] Poor young men identified with diasporic images of strong black masculinity; this marked both their marginalization and desire to find alternative routes to success.

Rapping and DJing suited kids who did not have access to musical instruments or a live music scene. Paa K recalls, "All of these kids who wanted to get into music began focusing on rapping because all they had was their voices." Several rappers recall that by the early 1990s, there were a handful of clubs where many young Ghanaians first listened to hip-hop. Some hosted rap performances and lip-synch competitions to the likes of Run-DMC, MC Hammer, and Heavy D.[45] BiBi remembers Joe Davis DJing at Miracle Mirage and hosting English freestyle rap events, though he began to encourage rappers to use local African languages. Early groups and performers consisted mostly of school-aged aspirants and included Talking Drums with Kweku T and Abeeku; Native Funk Lords, made up of Eddie Blay, CIL, Jake, and Tinney Quaye; Funkadelic; N'Effect; Nananom; Keteke; Cy Lover; Root I; Slim Buster; Nana King; Soul Black; General Marcos; Sammy B; CSI Posse; Roy Steel; Gosh MC; Kwame; and Swift. They chose names that reflected local interpretations of hip-hop bravado.

DJing crews and spinners sold mixtapes and beats at kiosks and markets around Accra to supplement their live DJ work for events, parties, and clubs. Kwame Amet Tsikata, the grandson of famed ethnomusicologist J. H. K. Nketia, grew up a hip-hop fan in Madina, a neighborhood north of Accra; later he took the stage name M.anifest. He recalls how little access they had to hip-hop when they were growing up, hungrily consuming the occasional track they heard on AM radio. In his neighborhood, kids would use prerecorded beats to practice rapping. "If you wanted beats to rap over, you would go buy them from [DJ] crews like Prime Cuts."[46] New music was easier and cheaper to get on cassette than vinyl and easier to copy, manipulate, and circulate. DJs sampled beats from foreign hip-hop, pop, R&B, and many other kinds of music for cassette mixtapes. Kwadwo Ampofo, better known as DJ Black, learned to make mixtapes as a young member of Prime Cuts. "We had this place in Osu where people came to buy tapes . . . No one taught me. I just would sit quietly watching. Then one day I started to do it and everyone was shocked at what I could do."[47] He recounts manipulating cassette decks to change the speed of playback and recording to match beats on various tracks. "We had to improvise. . . . We didn't have good technology." He DJed at clubs and then for one of the first radio hip-hop shows in 1998 on University of Ghana's Radio Univers, before taking a job at Joy FM.

DJ Azigiza Jr. was the first to make a national name for himself by rapping in Twi over electronic beats. He became a DJ and presenter for Joy FM, had his own television show highlighting local artists, and represented Ghana at international concerts in the West Africa subregion. While Azigiza's Twi-language rap was popular, as one young artist remembers, his "local style" conjured up images of an older highlife idiom and he "did not earn people's respect as a rapper." One fan remembers with a smile, "We loved him but, man, he was really corny. Just cheesy clothes. . . . Pants up really high, and a bad high-top fade."[48] He did not draw on hip-hop's hustler stylistics, as later hiplife artists would.

Panji Anoff returned to Ghana in the early 1990s, feeling limited by the music scene and British corporate media control. He wanted the freedom to develop music. "You could experiment more freely in Ghana and find an audience and musicians to work with. What I saw Reggie and others doing in London—and what he continued to do—was Americanize Africa. I wanted to make hip-hop truly African."[49] He produced the rap group Talking Drums, whose name reflected his vision of "the linguistic power of African music." They used Pidgin-language rap and local instrumentation and rhythms to bring "the multiple rhythmic styles, poetry, and instrumentations of . . . Ghanaian and African musical traditions to the global market." Talking Drums opened for hip-hop superstars Public Enemy when they performed in Ghana in 1994. Talking Drums member Kweku T remembers how opening for Public Enemy solidified his desire to be a hip-hop star. "I was still [at Ghana International School] and here I was on stage in front of this huge crowd with PE!"[50] Public Enemy's presence in Ghana inspired many young artists. Conversely, as Panji recalls, "PE were really amazed at our rap skills. When they heard some guys freestyling they were blown away." Panji remembers the show's significance, as Talking Drums experimented with highlife, neotraditional, and Afrobeat beats and Pidgin rap lyricism. "I remember watching the crowd as they listened to Talking Drums perform. At first, they were a bit slow, then they got really worked up. They felt the music; it moved them. I knew we were really onto something."[51]

Localization: Unintended Consequences of State-Sponsored Hip-Hop

In streets, clubs, and schools, hip-hop remade styles of dress, speaking, and dancing. While youth interest in hip-hop grew, state cultural institutions were concerned about preserving national cultural traditions. Throughout the 1980s the state struggled to control foreign cultural influence and stabilize the national economy. At the same time it enacted policies that promoted state privatization, opening the country to foreign commerce. The contradictions between centralization and decentralization created tensions around the moral significance of national culture. The National Theatre of Ghana opened in 1992, on the eve of the state's transition to democratic rule, with the mandate to "foster and preserve Ghanaian culture and arts."[52] However, as the state privatized, the National Theatre was identified as an institution that could raise private revenue and become self-sufficient. Theater organizers were under pressure to find programming that would fill seats and attract private sponsors (see figure 7). In this context National Theatre programming debates over whether hip-hop was African or foreign took on more specific moral implications. Ironically, amid anxiety about foreign influence on Ghanaian culture and language use, the state unintentionally supported hip-hop's transformation into a locally acceptable form.

In 1994 an annual youth performance festival called Kiddafest began at the National Theatre.[53] This program brought together artists and schoolchildren from all ten regions of Ghana, Nigeria, South Africa, the United States, and Europe for several days to perform and participate in artistic programs.[54] The annual program was so successful in gaining corporate sponsorship and attracting school and community youth participation that it spawned a regular biweekly program called Fun World. In line with national cultural programming, the aim was to encourage youths to become involved in "culture" and the arts, and by association to become good citizens.[55] In response to state and public anxieties about foreign—especially American—influence on Ghana, the organizers felt "traditional" music, dance, and drama were good ways "to teach Ghanaian and African moral and social values to youths."[56] Most urban youths were not interested in traditional performance. While attending shows and rehearsals, I often witnessed audiences taunting kids in traditional dance and drama groups with shouts of "Woa bre!" (You're tired!) for being old-fashioned and uneducated. Most performers wanted to participate in rap and hip-hop or disco dancing programs. At first, organizers were hesitant to include rap. However, they realized the potential of its popularity and created a rap segment, within certain constraints. The Artistic Director of the National Theatre explained the inclusion by saying, "Rap is an art of the African diaspora and has its origins in Africa."[57] They stipulated that participants had to rap in a Ghanaian language and to present "socially relevant and educational messages" in their lyrics.[58] The National Theatre directors ideally wanted to develop what they saw as "living"

FIGURE 7 Young rap artists performing outside the National Theatre of Ghana in 1997 with students in school uniforms watching. Photograph by the author.

modern African arts grounded in "timeless" traditional African and Ghanaian forms.[59] The inclusion of rap in the National Theatre program spoke to debates about the definition of culture and the state's role in mediating it for public consumption. The role of performance in national development was contested through the changing definitions of traditional and modern. Although hip-hop's profanity and commercialism did not fit within the institutional parameters of either modern or traditional art, it did, nevertheless, attract huge crowds of youths, and organizers hoped it could initiate them into institutional practices of theatergoing and artistic patronage.[60]

The hip-hop segments of Kiddafest and Fun World quickly became their most popular. By 1999 sixty-five rap groups were in the week-long program, with many others turned away at auditions. Organizers prescribed educational themes, such as AIDS awareness, abstinence, and "girl-child education," and banned lyrics about love and violence.[61] Performers rapped mostly in Twi, though some used Ewe, Ga, Fante, and Hausa. During auditions and rehearsals, organizers directed performers in stagecraft and lyricism. Old highlife and concert party actors and young intellectuals working at the theater encouraged aspiring rappers to draw on older performance idioms. For example, during one rehearsal an organizer shouted to an artist whose lyrics were uninspiring,

"Try using a proverb in your lyrics instead of profanity." Young artists brought cassettes of prerecorded beats to rap over. In rehearsals the resident DJ would get upset if the tape was not cued to the proper place, causing delays to rewind or arguments over using another beat. These shows became a launching point for future stars, including Buk Bak, Tic Tac, VIP, Nananom, Terry Bonchaka, Chicago, and Ex-Doe. Terry recalls being really nervous getting on stage for the first time, saying, "But being at the National Theatre gave us confidence, like what we were doing was respected."

National Theatre performers and audiences used hip-hop styles to engage class, ethnic, and urban-rural differences. While some imagined themselves as cosmopolitan and modern by adopting the image of African American rappers, others were further marginalized by the convergence of "foreign" popular culture and a space of national sanctioning. During the program, the National Theatre and its surroundings were transformed into a spectacle of thousands of youths, many in hip-hop styles. With boys dressed in baggy jeans, white sneakers, gold chains, sunglasses, and oversized American sports jerseys, and the girls wearing tight jeans and revealing tops, most Kiddafest attendees came to see rap and were uninterested in more "traditional" performances. Kwesi—a sixteen-year-old fan dressed in designer jeans, motorcycle goggles, white Reebok sneakers, an oversized T-shirt with a picture of Tupac—summed up many youths' initial relationship to hip-hop, explaining he loved American rappers, especially Tupac, because, he said, "I want to be tough like them. . . . I admire how wealthy they are and that they fight against the odds."[62]

Many youths from poorer parts of Accra and from rural villages were intimidated by the outlandish clothes and blasé attitudes of elite kids at the National Theatre. These more cosmopolitan boys and girls mediated foreign symbols and practices for more marginalized youths to interpret. Some, coming from remote towns like Wa and Bolgatanga, were amazed by the urban spectacle of Accra. One boy from the Northern Region was so sincerely impressed that he could not wait to go home and tell his friends about the people, styles, buildings, and ways of life in Accra. Other visiting students and teachers were shocked that Accra youths were allowed to behave so wildly. As one boy from the Upper East Region explained to me, if they behaved and dressed in such disrespectful ways back home, their elders would beat them. Another girl from the Ashanti Region who was attending Kiddafest as part of a traditional dance group proudly wore kente cloth and beads and danced adowa. To her, rap was foreign, not a part of Ghanaian culture, and was a bad influence on African youths, though she was certainly in the minority.

Artists and organizers unintentionally collaborated to make rap into something that Ghanaian publics could imagine as local. The National Theatre Kiddafest and Fun World rap events to some degree legitimized hip-hop. The Theatre's insistence on local-language rap and moral storytelling idioms encouraged teenagers to experiment artistically and to incorporate older performance idioms into their newfound passion. The organizers fulfilled their mandate of fostering traditional African culture while attracting youth audiences. In the process, this programming resignified hip-hop as a Ghanaian cultural practice. Young artists increasingly used local languages, proverbial speech, and traditional references in hip-hop, and found that audiences loved the music (see figure 8). As the state struggled to control public tastes, increasingly shaped by private media circulations, official ideas of culture were remade through youth culture, rather than the other way around.

But for many older folks, the inclusion of rap in national programming epitomized the negative effects of Western influence. Local rap music spurred generational debates about what constitutes African culture. Most significantly hip-hop raised questions about public respectfulness. For example, when Reggie Ossei was invited to judge a National Theatre competition, organizers found his appearance and style of speaking disconcerting. One organizer explained, "Meeting Reggie, I thought he was an African American—the way he talked and dressed with these dreadlocks and American clothes. It is disrespectful for a Ghanaian to dress like that."[63] Reflecting the views of many middle-aged Ghanaians, one member of the National Commission on Culture told me he was upset that the Theatre was holding hip-hop events. "Rap is not a Ghanaian tradition. It encourages kids to ignore their own communities and proper Ghanaian values of respect."[64]

One older radio executive from a well-known family privately expressed to me her outrage at watching a young relative on television. "The way these kids are running around Accra showing no respect to African traditions and their elders—it's disgraceful. My nephew was shown lip-synching and dancing to a rap song on television, broadcast from the National Theatre, and his mother almost died of embarrassment when people who had seen the program called to tell [her that] her son . . . was jumping around on television."[65] To some, the perfor-

FIGURE 8 Tic Tac performing at the National Theatre. Photograph by Ayana V. Jackson.

mances were mockeries, poor imitations of American music. In a society that places high value on deferential, respectful behavior, especially from youths, "jumping around" on stage was certainly not a positive form of publicity. One young gospel musician eschewed his normally reserved manner to condemn the music. "Excuse me for saying so but these rappers are fools. They spread profanity around everywhere. They want to act all American and for what? . . . If they went and stayed in a rural village for a while then they would not be so tough with their dreadlocks and baggy clothes. The villagers would not put up with that nonsense."[66] Some viewers saw performers copying African American bodily gestures as promoting disrespect, moral corruption, and even violence. These negative stereotypes about hip-hop reveal anxiety about lost local identity in the face of the genre's Americanness.

Struggles over whether hip-hop was foreign or African foretold broader moral anxieties that the music brought. Youth tastes fostered through new commercial media called into question the state's ability to dictate cultural programming and to control the national imaginary. While state cultural institutions attempted to appropriate hip-hop as an aspect of national culture in the name of youth development, rap programs at the National Theatre authenticated hip-hop as African, linking youth tastes with popular privatizing media. Through hip-hop the morality of the market penetrated state institutional ideas of cultural and moral purity.

Dressing the Entrepreneurial Body: Charismatism or Hip-Hop

The parallel appeals of hip-hop and charismatism in marketizing Africa reveal them as two sides of a moral argument about self-making. They represent opposing models for imagining success: the sacred and the profane. While charismatism promotes conservative business modesty, hiplife rejects normative ideas of public respectability. Ghanaian neo-Pentecostals and hiplifers represent a moral opposition played out in everything from lyrics and sermons to hairstyles and modes of walking. But they both celebrate "prosperity doctrines" and a morality of personal aspiration and miraculous wealth accumulation (Gifford 2004; Meyer 2004a, b). In positing bodily comportment as a reflection of personal success, they both promote decidedly neoliberal beliefs in the performative power of individual self-fashioning (Brennan 2010; Piot 2010; Shipley 2009b; Engelke 2007).

Charismatic and Pentecostal churches—as well as more traditional Christian denominations—have tended to criticize hip-hop lyrics as morally corrupting, even though most Ghanaian rappers are Christian and many first sang in church as children. As one pastor sermonized, the musicians promote "the work of witchcraft and the devil."[67] Hip-hop's style provoked particular ire, though hiplife's increasing popularity led some congregations to incorporate Christian-themed rap into their gospel repertoires. Twenty-year-old Adowa, a member of a prominent charismatic church, is critical of what she sees as youth obsessions with material possessions, linking them to foreign popular culture's influence. Two years after finishing her secondary education at elite Wesley Girls, she was unemployed and awaiting entry to university. While her goals were to become "successful in business" and "make lots of money," she dissociated herself from flashy displays of wealth and foreign styles, which she saw as immoral. "When you look at the students at University, you see all the bling they wear, playing with cell phones and spending all their time trying to travel . . . out of the country. They do a lot of immoral things. . . . We the youth need to learn, and not focus on sex [and money] like new music does."[68] While recognizing the attraction of modern styles, she also sees their danger. "Everyone in rural areas wants to come here and live the urban lifestyle. I don't know— there is nothing here. But it's true that some people in villages have still never had electric lights. We in Accra don't appreciate what we have. We need to make progress and develop what we have and not worry so much about 'out there' [in the West]." The desires of marginalized Ghanaians for modern urbanity and the idea that there is "nothing here" in Accra point to recognition of the dangers of aspirations rooted in "foreign" values. Adowa represents young aspirational neo-Pentecostals who are suspicious of popular culture's focus on the surface trappings of modern life.

Conversely, as rappers gained legitimacy, they criticized charismatics as "superficial." One rapper explains, "These pastors fool people into giving them money. They look holy but are hustlers like everyone else."[69] Ironically, rappers are sometimes described as unofficial pastors. As radio presenter Blakofe puts it, they are "preaching to and educating the public on moral topics."[70] Indeed, popular artist Obrafour takes the appellation Rap Asofo (rap pastor). Skepticism about hip-hop's moral implications and counteraccusations about charismatics' sincerity point to an emerging sphere of moral deliberation revolving around the right to identify the potentials and dangers of entrepreneurial self-fashioning (Shipley 2009b). New churches promote "prosperity doctrines" in which economic success and wealth accumulation are a sign of the Holy Spirit's anointment (ibid.). For charismatics, salvation comes through personal, unmediated relationships with the Holy Spirit (Engelke 2007), a logic akin to how entrepreneurs eschew state market regulations and rappers imagine wealth materializing through personal swagger. Charismatic styles represent a belief in success. They tend toward conservative Western suits, ties, and shirts for men and modest though elegant dresses or African print styles for women. For youths, the aesthetic contrast between hiplife and gospel represents a moral choice about how to imagine contemporary life and future possibilities.

Both charismatism and hip-hop celebrate entrepreneurial aspiration, wealth, and individual success, reflecting the national ethos as it turned away from a socialist revolution toward a market-oriented economy (Gifford 2004; Otabil 2002; Asare 1997). Meyer (2004b) has argued that the rise of new charismatic churches and a Christian imagery in popular media points to the Pentecostalization of Ghana's public sphere in which privatized entertainment, worship, and politics are reimagined through Pentecostal discourse. But Pentecostalization may be one symptom of a broader phenomenon. It is one of several overlapping, competing discourses shaping neoliberal Ghana in which the excitements of economic and cultural globalization are tempered by anxieties about the nation-state's loss of control.

Hip-Hop as Neoliberal Style

Hip-hop style provided an aesthetic template for how to be an entrepreneur. But growing interest in hip-hop raised anxieties about national identity and culture, provoking debates about appropriate public language use and comportment. It also highlighted the productive, though at times ambivalent, ways Ghanaians engage diasporic blackness. Hip-hop fantasies of black accumulation and consumption represented the possibilities and dangers of global circulation (Weiss 2009). The genre stood for the promises of American material success through a Pan-African lens. Hip-hop's early success in Accra reflected Ghana's intimate historical relationship to diasporic music and fashion, mediated through several levels of temporal-spatial displacement as hip-hop's predominantly African American symbolism was refracted through cosmopolitan black Britain and back to Accra. In the context of the city's transforming landscape, diasporic ideas of blackness took on various moral guises: for some it provided a form of authentic Africanness; others saw it as a marker of foreign modernity and wealth; while still others imagined it as a sign of moral degradation.

Yurchak (2003a) shows how young, aspiring business leaders in post-Soviet Russia focus on cultivating bodily styles and social networks as central to developing a business culture. He argues that entrepreneurship focuses on the performative aspects of economic networking. In the process of focusing on self-fashioning practices, this brand of capitalism casts mediation itself as a form of value production.

In Ghana the spirit of entrepreneurship is not new, nor is it a recognition of mediation itself as a form of value, given its long history of informal economic trade networks. Entrepreneurs have long relied upon cultivating nonstate networks to conduct business (Clark 1994). Privatization merges official and informal economic realms, linking formerly illicit market practices with a new ethos of individual wealth accumulation as a form of citizenship. Neoliberalism emphasizes the links between public presentations of self and moral value. This market logic celebrates the potential of individuals to appear successful. Bodily styles that portray the image of success provide a performative form of value creation. Older ideas of musical entrepreneurship as mediating foreign signs fit with evolving models of marketization and its popular tastes.

The process of recontextualizing foreign music and fashion operates according to a logic of simultaneity and inversion that speaks to Ghana's irreverent yet attentive relationship to cosmopolitan blackness. The value of hip-hop lies in its intimate foreignness: performers can associate it with broader ideas of modernity while using it to informally redefine what constitutes Ghanaian culture. Hiplife develops as an amalgam of musical and performative styles, maintaining hip-hop's foreign cachet, while becoming something specifically Ghanaian.

CHAPTER 3

Rebirth of Hip

AFRO-COSMOPOLITANISM AND MASCULINITY
IN ACCRA'S NEW SPEECH COMMUNITY

To celebrate the new millennium on December 31, 1999, a concert was held at Black Star Square in downtown Accra. Most of the city seemed to attend church that evening. But after services, numerous revelers headed to the massive concert. As midnight approached, rapper Reggie Rockstone mounted the stage wearing an elegant flowing white *batakari*, his long dreadlocks neatly tied back. Highlife, gospel, and younger rap artists had warmed up the crowd, but Reggie's fame and charisma made him the logical choice to headline. In front of giant illuminated letters spelling out "REGGIE ROCKSTONE" on stage, DJ Rab the International mixed and scratched on his turntables. Backup dancers in tight white outfits moved to the hard-edged hip-hop beat. Rockstone rapped in a combination of English, Twi, and Pidgin, remixing a number of his well-known hits as the crowd, estimated by organizers at 100,000 people, sang along and fireworks exploded. Organized by private radio station Vibe FM with corporate sponsorship, the concert was touted as an official millennial celebration in the capital's most prominent square. Hiplife's centrality to this privately sponsored national celebration is especially striking because, as described in chapter 2, only a few years earlier most Ghanaians understood hip-hop styles and music as foreign and morally suspect, and hiplife was not a publicly recognizable musical genre.

In the 1980s, when elite Ghanaian youths started rapping, they sounded "too American," while highlife seemed "too local" and no longer appealed to many urban youths. Musical experimentation was encouraged through the return from abroad of young Ghanaians with media skills, as well as the rapid privatization of broadcast media and new technologies of musical production and distribution. When Reggie Rockstone returned to Ghana in 1994, his code switching initially confused people—some wondered where he was from and struggled to make sense of his music—though it also provided the key to his eventual stardom. Reggie and DJ Rab's formula involved sampling highlife and Afrobeat rhythms overlay with hip-hop lyrical flows in Twi, Pidgin, and English. This music defined the generic parameters of what would constitute hiplife, providing a structure that younger artists could further elaborate. Young fans admired Reggie's confidence and fluency in both English and Twi, though his irreverence and aggressiveness appeared disrespectful and arrogant to older Ghanaians. By the millennium he was celebrated as the "Godfather of Hiplife," garnering national artistic awards and major product sponsorship deals.

Reggie is what Karin Barber terms a "culture broker" (Barber 1987), in this case someone who translates cosmopolitan black styles and performance codes across places and generations for a broad Ghanaian public. In the context of the historical movement of people, money, music, technology, and fashion among Europe, the Americas, and Africa, culture brokers such as Reggie have a foot in both metropolitan and local contexts and are crucial transformers of value that produce new forms of popular expression out of a pastiche of older ones. Reggie's music celebrates Accra through the eyes of a global traveler with local knowledge. His stories of nightlife in Accra reimagine it as a vibrant urban center of young masculine leisure linked to cosmopolitan circulations of black culture. Crucial to this are local understandings of hip-hop that transform it from a rebellion of the disenfranchised into a marker of cosmopolitan success. This new music also requires gendered narratives of success in fashioning a new popular aesthetic of masculine urban consumption. These changes occur through aligning signs of global black culture with Akan public speech practices.

Reggie is creative, irreverent, and inscrutable. To some he is a local boy who traveled abroad and transformed himself into a musical success. To others he is a Ghanaian who became too Westernized or one who never really knew his own culture. As an icon of transformation, he represents the potentials and hazards of circulation itself.

Reggie's ability to control and manipulate multiple registers is a mode of symbolic mediation that makes him an authoritative tastemaker

(Scotton and Ury 2009; Gal 2005). A new musical genre's legitimacy relies upon a performer's ability to indexically link innovative signs to established aesthetic values (Silverstein 2005). By irreverently inverting and resymbolizing diasporic signs for local consumption, young artists identify with a new Afro-cosmopolitanism. Audiences value newness and how performers connect distinct linguistic and musical codes in innovative ways. Artists legitimize these new signs by demonstrating their mastery over older contexts and referential practices (Briggs and Bauman 1992).

Reggie is the first Ghanaian celebrity in the era of privatization. While his stardom builds upon that of previous generations of musicians from E. T. Mensah to Nana Ampadu to Kojo Antwi, the frenzy surrounding his technologically mediated performative image points to a cultural shift. He is a role model for youths, demonstrating the potentials of self-fashioning and the hazards of a changing market. His unique, charismatic music marks a transformation in Ghana's musical landscape, providing aspiring musicians, media folks, and fans with a template for using fame to convert aesthetic value into material success. He models self-fashioning, itself, as a form of value creation. As Ghana's media landscape is transformed through the sale of government assets and the rise of private radio stations, television, video, and advertising firms, Reggie's story shows how personal aspiration can be transformed into fame, and how fame and notoriety can be turned into success.

With his face on billboards and advertisements for major corporations like Spacefon, Guinness, and Glo, Reggie's personal style is commodified and packaged. As Braudy (1997, 15) shows, fame is a symptom of the individualism central to capitalism's development. Individual celebrity is important in its ability to "project larger-than-life images . . . that would last longer than any specific action" (ibid.). In this sense Reggie becomes an indexical icon, a media celebrity reflexively calling forth a rising free-market public (Agha 2005b; Bauman 2002). Famous bodies become vehicles for channeling value circulations that rely on and validate a consuming public (Kockelman 2010). New radio stations and companies brand themselves using new local musicians as signs of fashionability. Here fame becomes a form of labor, made and translated into value through its circulation in images and sounds. Crucially, celebrities make themselves famous by announcing their own success. In musical self-fashioning the performative, productive aspects of language use focus public attention on the act of speaking or rapping and the potentials and dangers of travel and code switching. In highlighting performance codes themselves, being or becoming a celebrity transforms stylish bodies into condensed signs of social value and potential wealth.

Saga of the Returnee and Afro-Cosmopolitan Hip

In 1994 Reggie Rockstone and his rap partner Freddie Funkstone returned to Accra from London to perform at the second Pan African Historical Theatre Festival (PANAFEST). One night they were at the Accra nightclub, Miracle Mirage, and were freestyling in English to an instrumental track by the Fugees. Rab Bakari was in the club. A DJ and engineering student studying at New York's City College, Rab was raised in Queens and "returned home to Ghana . . . as a tourist" to explore his "African heritage."[1] He remembers his surprise at hearing the two rappers. "I was amazed. I mean, here I was in Africa and there was this guy who sounded like he was from Brooklyn." As the evening went on, Reggie switched registers, experimenting with rapping in Twi, shouting into the mic, "How many of you have ever heard of Twi fucking rap? I'll be the first one!" Reggie recalls feeling energized by a strange sense of both familiarity and newness on returning to Accra after years away. He was not yet aware of how much the underground rap scene had grown in his absence.[2]

Rab, Freddie, and Reggie's shared hip-hop idiom provided a symbolic language through which they could connect socially and musically. Rab approached Reggie and Freddie in the crowded club. "I told them I am a DJ . . . and I was blown away by their sound."[3] The next morning they met at Groove Records studio, run by George Brun. Rab began sampling funk and soul records. "They had everything, records and all the latest equipment that I was used to using in New York. . . . I started turning out beats."[4] They began freestyling verses and playing with lyrical flows, spawning what would be a lasting musical collaboration.

Rab was on a short visit to Ghana and Reggie had planned to return to London, but both were inspired to stay in Accra and experiment musically. Over several weeks in late 1994, Rab, Reggie, and Freddie were joined by Panji and others in recording sessions at the Combined House of Music (see figures 9 and 10). These sessions were a moment of excitement as musicians, rappers, and studio engineers created a new musical template. Young artists came to contribute, observe, and be a part of the scene. Local television stations recorded Reggie and Freddie rapping

FIGURE 9
Rab Bakari
in the studio.
Photograph
courtesy of
Rab Bakari.

FIGURE 10 Rab Bakari at Combined House of Music. Photograph courtesy of Rab Bakari.

and did interviews with them, adding to the public excitement around the music. Future hiplife star Sidney, also Reggie's cousin, recalls, "It was a moment when we suddenly started to feel like we could do this thing. The music felt so fresh and new, like Reggie and them had brought back a whole new perspective on life in Ghana."[5]

Sidney was inspired. "We were all so excited by Reggie. I listened to some of the lyrics; it was so amazing. I thought he was rapping in English but it was Twi. . . . He inspired so many youth to see that hip-hop was African, that we could be a part of the hip-hop community. It made us really feel modern . . . like we were part of something bigger." Sidney's initial linguistic confusion reflects the crucial stylistic innovation of Reggie's delivery: using English rhythmic flow with Akan construction. As described in chapter 2, many Ghanaians did not understand African American rap vernacular; its popularity stemmed from its formalist aesthetic. Earlier Ghanaian rappers either had sounded like they were copying American rappers too exactly or remained within Ghanaian musical idioms. But Reggie had learned to rap with an African American cadence for English-speaking audiences in London. He explained that figuring out how to give Akan rap a "hip-hop feel" was not easy. "It was hard to find rhyming words, so I would use English words to rhyme even though I was rapping in Twi. We experimented with all kinds of things . . . so Ghanaians would really *feel* the music."[6] Reggie's irreverence and confidence authorized other artists to be playful and to experiment, mixing languages and styles, rather than copying.

As a DJ, Rab's skill at finding the break—a musical section of a song between verses that could be repeated and embellished for MCs to rap over—inspired local engineers and DJs. At the same time, Rab's "hardcore, New York–style beats" expanded to include more "African sounds," sampling "Afrobeat and indigenous Ghanaian musical traditions . . . that [he] had not been aware of before."[7] Zap Mallet, a studio engineer and one of the few actual musicians involved in the initial recording sessions, would go on to become one of the most influential hiplife producers. Along with Panji, he encouraged the use of African music and highlife guitar in the mix.

For Rab, unexpectedly stumbling upon an emergent hip-hop scene in Accra was both a thrill and a challenge. He recalls, "Hip-hop did not fit with my ideas of what was African." He had imagined his trip to Ghana as "a homecoming," a way "to connect with African and African diaspora peoples in the homeland." He did not expect that hip-hop would be the medium of connection. Growing up he was "part of New York's hip-hop generation." At first he was a graffiti writer, tagging buildings and trains around Brooklyn and Queens, and later a break-dancer and DJ. He was a firsthand witness to hip-hop's evolution from irreverent street culture made by African American, Caribbean, and Latino youths to a commercially dominant genre. "In New York we would always talk about going back to Africa. . . . In hip-hop, talking about Africa was a way to connect with our history. But it was always general." According to Rab, many African Americans have a "simplistic idea of what African culture is; drumming and dancing. They aren't looking for urban style. . . . But for me, hip-hop was African culture. When I found it in Accra . . . I felt at home." The musical connection gave him a purpose: to "express the global importance of black culture and connections among black peoples everywhere." Hip-hop's spread confirmed the effects of globalization but also challenged the idea that "moving between continents . . . was only a European thing." For Rab, hip-hop provided an alternative globalization, a shared cultural idiom of musically driven exchange (figure 11).

Through its shared signs and styles, hip-hop provided a dispersed, counterpublic, projected "back" to Africa. As Warner argues, a counterpublic "is understood to contravene the rules obtaining in the world at large, being structured by alternative dispositions or protocols, making different assumptions about what can be said or what goes without saying" (2002, 56). Many diasporans from America and the Caribbean come to Africa to find personal and cultural connections, to address feelings of historical displacement and recover something lost (Holsey 2008). Yet the perceived Americanization of African culture often leads to further disappointment at the continent's lost authenticity (Ebron 2002). Other diasporans, like Rab, are excited to find African locales part of a black cosmopolitanism.

In the mid-1990s, despite growing interest, there was no market for Ghanaian hip-hop. But that would soon change. Friends in the Ghanaian music business told Reggie that to make money he should go into established gospel or highlife music. Instead Reggie and his team took advantage of Rab's hybrid New York sound and Reggie's unusual public persona that could balance Akan language use with African American vernacular styles to position their music for a local market. The opening of the airwaves created new avenues to circulate this new style in urban Accra.

FIGURE 11 Rab Bakari on the turntables in Accra. Photograph courtesy of Rab Bakari.

The Rise of Private Radio as Commercial Medium and Musical Inspiration

The privatization of media valorized individual innovation linking artistry to market competition. The 1992 constitution establishing the Fourth Republic of Ghana guaranteed that "there shall be no impediments to the establishment of private press or media."[8] Companies started focusing on broadcasting, advertising, and importing electronic technologies. Previously, Ghana Broadcasting Corporation's AM station had been the main radio frequency along with BBC and other international transmissions. Ghana Television (GTV) was the only television station, and GAMA Films was the state film organization. For several years the government did not issue any licenses for radio frequencies. Finally, in 1994 the first private radio station, Radio Eye, went on the air in Accra. It broadcast from an unknown location and its use of the airwaves was seen as a violation of government regulations.[9] It was quickly and violently shut down by the police. However, it set a memorable precedent, and from 1995 to 1997 private FM stations, beginning with Joy FM, Choice, Groove FM, Radio Univers, and Radio Gold, began broadcasting legally in Accra. Commercial stations projected a sheen of energy and newness in contrast with the grim, austere aesthetic of military discipline and postsocialist Ghana that haunted state-run programming. DJs quickly became on-air personalities, purveyors of taste, and celebrities in their own right.[10] With excitement around new radio stations came a scramble to fill empty airspace, which created room for innovation (Bourgault 1995).

Television and music videos also helped develop the new urban music. *Smash* TV, *Goldblast*, and later *Music Music* were influential entertainment variety shows that featured interviews and artists performing or lip-synching their singles for live audiences. Stations added time slots for playing local music videos, which became important media through which Accra's youths experienced the new music and style. The rise of private television and local video production crews pushed national media outlets to compete with slick, commercially oriented looks. Beginning in the late 1980s, cheap, portable consumer video technology allowed amateurs to make and distribute video films locally (Meyer 1998a). Increasingly, private media entrepreneurs produced and distributed homegrown videos and television programming. In television, a percentage of state-owned GAMA films was sold to a Malaysian company, which established TV3 in 1997. Metro TV soon came on air as the third competitor to GTV.[11]

As audience interest grew, entrepreneurs sought new modes of distribution and advertising. In the mid-1990s many young adults like Reggie and Panji, who had spent time living in Europe, America, the Middle East, or other parts of Africa, returned to Ghana. Many of those involved with the new stations and private advertising companies on air, in financing, and in technical positions were Ghanaians who had acquired broadcast skills, electronic media expertise, and interest in African American soul, jazz, hip-hop, funk, and R&B while living abroad. As mentioned in chapter 2, Paa K returned to Ghana from Britain and became program director for Groove FM, one of the first private radio stations that came on-air in 1996, hosting its *Golden Hits of Highlife* program. He also became one of Reggie's managers, organizing tours and public appearances.

Ghanaians returning from abroad felt a part of a network of global black affiliations. But many locals remained reticent about the "foreignness" of black popular culture. Paa K recalls how young Ghanaian DJs who had just returned from abroad "fancied themselves as being purveyors of black cosmopolitan sensibilities for locals. . . . After living abroad Accra could seem really parochial, but it was home, and exciting to be part of making a new scene."[12] New radio stations played a large percentage of American music, following the tastes of young DJs and radio executives. One DJ estimated they were playing 70–80 percent American music. Playlists were eclectic, including country, heavy metal, and R&B, and lacked local music as little contemporary music was being produced. As Paa K recalls, stations such as Joy FM and Groove FM sought to program the latest black music, reflecting "the excitement young people felt about making Ghana cosmopolitan. And in music modern styles had a black face."

After returning from London in 1994, Blakofe became one of the few female radio and television personalities. She remembers, "it was really exciting. I wanted to come back to Ghana and see what was happening. . . . Radio and, to some extent, television programs [that] highlighted musicians were where the energy was in the 1990s. That is where everybody turned their attention . . . You listened to hear what was new and fresh."[13] She recalls how Ghanaians appreciated "foreign" and diasporic music for the lifestyles they represented. But many listeners lamented the lack of locally produced music. The public was also hostile to some of the changes in Accra's public life, which were seen as a result of the growing influence of international media. "When I returned to Ghana, I had dreadlocks, and not many people, especially women, had dreadlocks in those days. So people would shout when I walked down the street. . . . It felt really backward. . . . Now [in 2005] Accra is really cosmopolitan."

As more radio stations competed for listeners and advertising revenue in a new, untested market, they experimented with programming. Paa K's radio show was one of the few that played older highlife, earning a small but loyal following. Most stations focused on capturing the large youth market by emphasizing the latest trends. The dominant on-air language was English, as it had been on state radio. Stations sought to capture the vibrancy and irreverence of American radio programming. Paa K recalls, "Presenters mixed in all sorts of slang, trying to sound American or British. . . . The commercial spirit where we were all competing for audiences really made everyone work hard for that edge."[14]

DJs, financiers of new broadcasting ventures, advertisers, and producers created a relatively small, new media network connected through elite school associations and family ties. For Reggie, access to media and executives at new stations was facilitated by his father Ricci, who was at the center of Accra's cultural elite. Reggie's music was unique in being both hip and local, reflecting the ethos of returnees as well as that of their local audiences. As his music spread, it invigorated Accra's music scene and gave radio stations local programming that had street appeal and was cosmopolitan. As BiBi Menson recalls, DJs and program managers wanted to project a modern urban style through their music. And Reggie provided the perfect vehicle. "Reggie was . . . unique. When he returned [to Ghana] he had this glow, like he was showing off being famous abroad. But he also knew Accra. . . . People were confused if he was local or foreign. It made an impression."[15]

Ricci Ossei, after starting one of the first high-fashion studios in West Africa, diversified, running Colour Chart Designs, a multimedia company that did everything from animation to television production. Reggie recalls that at first his father was skeptical about his music, but he was won over when he heard his son's fluent Twi rap. "When I first came back to Ghana, my dad was surprised to hear me flow in Twi. He didn't even know how well I spoke it because I lived away for so long. But he loved it."[16] Ricci was convinced that his son's Twi rap was innovative and had potential to be successful.

With Ricci's financial support, Rab and Reggie formed Kassa Records, the first label to focus on hip-hop in Anglophone Africa. Rab recalls, "We knew we had a unique sound, something to contribute to the global hip-hop community. Everyone was trying to release albums in the U.S. It was Reggie's father . . . who suggested we cater it for Africa." Rab ran the technological and managerial sides of Kassa Records. They marketed their music differently to reach Ghanaian audiences and African diaspora audiences around the world. They printed cassettes for the Ghanaian market and pressed vinyl, and later CDs, for international release. "We wanted to make music that would speak to local Ghanaian audiences but also break into the international hip-hop scene. We wanted to make it big."[17] But they struggled to integrate different linguistic and musical influences in a way that would appeal to various fans. In music production and marketing they tried to balance the specificity of local signs and language idioms with a cosmopolitan, hip-hop sensibility. As they worked to find a formula, they shaped how new Ghanaian artists and producers approached music recording, distribution, and management.

Another important influence on the Pan-African orientation of Reggie's music and Rab's business model was Dhoruba Bin Wahad, a former leader of the Black Panther Party in New York, who relocated to Accra in the mid-1990s. Born Richard Moore, Dhoruba was convicted in 1971 of shooting two Manhattan police officers. After nineteen years in a New York state prison, his conviction was overturned. Upon release he continued to work as a public speaker and political activist concerned with issues of political prisoners, white supremacy, and neocolonialism. After moving to Ghana he remained a charismatic and outspoken critic of U.S. imperialism and global inequality. He became close friends with Ricci Ossei. When Ricci suddenly died, Reggie was overwhelmed by the unexpected tragedy. Dhoruba became a mentor to Reggie, helping manage his affairs. Dhoruba's intellectual perspective on racial violence and global capitalism inflected Reggie's worldview.

Musical Transformations of a New Urban Speech Community

Reggie Rockstone's early albums established the parameters of what would become hiplife. His music synthesized hip-hop and local speech styles and rhythms imagining a spacetime both familiar and new, an urban landscape inhabited by easy-talking young men with leisure time, money, and the authority to speak their minds. His music used the authority of tradition to validate the new, and conversely the innovation of foreign styles to reinvigorate the old. Listeners were excited by the unexpected ways Reggie blended an American rap flow with Twi language usage, giving hip-hop swagger a local inflection. His fluid code switching—among Twi, Pidgin, and African American vernacular English—reflects how many urban youths in Accra communicate. In informal urban contexts, speakers mix various linguistic codes, choosing a language, as one youth explained, according to "what you feel and who you are trying to connect with."[18] Shifting registers in this manner is not acceptable in formal, public contexts (Agha 2005b; Gal 2005). But Reggie's validation of informal language use united disparate groups of young men as a community of hiplifers with a shared, publicly recognized linguistic style. His use of authentic-sounding African American vernacular confused listeners about whether Reggie was American and made them pay close attention when he shifted into Accra street slang and Twi.

In early 1996, after recording at Combined House of Music with engineer Zap Mallet, Rab and Reggie released a five-song EP on cassette and vinyl.[19] "I printed one thousand albums in Manhattan and carried a bunch of crates back to Ghana on the plane . . . to test the market, to see what formula would work," Rab recalls.[20] One track is titled "Agoo," the Twi phrase used to announce one's presence. The proper response is "Amee." This call and response, familiar to Ghanaian audiences, was repeated as the song's chorus. The track "Tsoo Boi" intermixed rapid-fire vernacular Twi and English phrasing. The song title also uses a well-known call-and-response phrasing, the old rally cry, "Tsoo Boi," which elicits the audience response, "Yei." The songs' simple, local hooks were offset by the high-energy celebratory aggression of the lyrical delivery and beats.

Though fans continue to debate whether Reggie or Panji with Talking Drums first made hiplife music, Reggie is credited with popularizing the new term in "Tsoo Boi." The lyrics announce, "Check, check it out for the hiplife / it goes on and on for the hiplife. . . . Omo feeli, Omo feeli feeli [Everybody's feeling it]." The song imagines listeners as part of a new musical celebration called hiplife. The lyrics also announce the potential of mixed-language rap to use proverbs: "Hold up, wait, twen ha merebebu be" (Hold up, wait, here I am coming to use proverbs).[21] While Reggie and Rab saw themselves as doing hip-hop with a Ghanaian flavor, others began to imagine the music as fundamentally different. Radio quickly expanded initial elite audiences to include the masses. As Rab recalls, "People were impressed with the New York sound and then later when we were doing shows in [the] U.S. and Europe and coming back to Ghana. It gave the music an international feel when most local guys felt really trapped." The tracks generated excitement on Ghanaian airwaves. "DJs were talking about us all over the country. . . . They were buggin' out," Rab recalls. "No one else was doing this kind of music so we got a lot of attention. . . . We wanted to find those old [highlife] sounds and make them hip-hop."[22] Rab also shipped CDs and vinyl LPs to DJs all over America and Europe to try to expand their market.

Rab was basically commuting, working and going to school in New York while trying to build Accra's hip-hop scene with Reggie. In his absences he sent digital audio tapes with two-hour mixes to DJs at Groove FM and cassettes of beats to help Reggie write lyrics. Rab graduated from City College in June 1997, packed up his Harlem apartment, and shipped his equipment to Ghana. "By August I was in Accra with the intention of staying and completing what we had started." With new tracks in the works, by October a full album was ready. But it had been almost a year since the EP came out. "We realized we were onto something. . . . But we had to get new material out there." The first full album was released in 1997 under two names, Rehji Ossei for Ghana and Rehji Rockstone for international markets, titled *Makaa Maka* (I said it because I can say it). "We needed to keep the [Ghanaian] public interested and figure out how to break open the foreign markets. It wasn't easy trying to balance different tastes."[23] While the album did not sell many copies, it solidified Reggie's place at the center of a new musical movement.

The second album, *Me Na Me Kae* (It's me who said it), released in late 1998, concretized the new paradigms for lyrical flow, language use, and rhythmic structure.[24] Rab recalls, "People said we had figured out the formula. We realized people wanted to hear that old West African sound, highlife, Afrobeat and all that. . . . I started digging through crates of old records to find stuff to sample." The album expresses the sensibility of a young man of leisure in urban Ghana, linking celebration to nostalgia for an older urban feel.

Rab's CD liner notes reflect their vision for a Pan-Africanist hip-hop: "Reggie Rockstone has ushered in a new revolution on the African continent. In an age where it is very easy to accept rap from Asia or Europe, he has engineered the bridge across the separation of the hip-hop diaspora. Often neglected, and not represented in the hip-hop community, the African continent now has a champion to build bridges, set foundations, and destroy all myths, hypocrisies, and misinformation about our people, culture and existence."[25] For Rab, hip-hop provided a community dialogue for connecting black peoples and could help others understand Africa as a "real" place. But he and Reggie continued to struggle to reach both Ghanaian and global audiences, "to find the right musical formula to reach different people and be successful to compete with big American stars. We had something unique to offer and we had to package it for [all] our audiences."[26]

The first single from *Me Na Me Kae* was "Keep Your Eyes on the Road." Reggie's manager, Paa K, argues that it is the first true hiplife track because it popularized rapping over highlife. However, he also recognizes the ambiguity of the genre: "the lyrics were in English, so is that hiplife yet or still hip-hop?"[27] Rab recalls making the song: "Reggie would play this old highlife [song], Alhaji K. Frimpong's 'Kyen Kyen Bi Adi Mawu,' [originally released in 1976] over and over in the room and he would just rap on it, in Twi. It was the [highlife] guitar sound that spoke to him. . . . He said I needed to do something with this track. I told him to rap in English. We already had tracks to reach audiences in the West with hard core hip-hop—now we needed to refine the formula for Ghana. Music that spoke to their experience . . . but also English lyrics. [Frimpong] was perfect. . . . It was [real] highlife. People knew the record but he was a forgotten artist."[28]

The old vinyl album they were playing was too scratched, so they went to the original recording studio to get a CD copy to sample. They got in touch with Frimpong and asked Reggie's father to speak with him for them. Reggie recalls, "He didn't understand what we wanted, so my dad could talk that old-timer speak with him. We paid Alhaji two million cedis[29] for the rights to use the track. At the time that was a lot of money. . . . I think he thought we were crazy for giving so much. I don't think he had any idea that the song or hip-hop would be so big or that it would get people interested in old-school '70s highlife again."[30]

The recognizable highlife track recalled nightlife of the 1970s, giving the song a nostalgic heft. The rhythmic reference situated the new music as local, not foreign. Rab looped the highlife guitar-layered instrumental tracks and heavy bass on top of it to enhance the sample. Zap Mallet added his own lead guitar. The song's English lyrics are scattered with local names and Twi words. The rapper appears to speak to and for a youth audience. Reggie's status as a rising star relied on his ability to claim a public voice as in this song. The chorus begins with a series of questions:

Could it be that you was never told?
To keep your eyes on the road
Who is Rockstone?
Who is Rockstone?
Do I make myself clear?
Yeah!
Do I make myself clear?
Yeah! Yeah!

Then clap your hands like there was a million mosquitos in here
Jump like you was some crazy Akrantie
Party people show me how you're feeling back there
Do you wanna party, boogie then get out your chair

The song is structured around rhetorical questions about the clarity of the speaker's words. Lyrical affirmations, "Yeah," authorize his ability to define the virtues of life in Ghana. References to visceral aspects of local life—for example, Akrantie, an animal prized as bush meat for stews, or the presence of a million mosquitos—are interwoven with a "do you wanna party" celebration mentality. Partying as a dominant trope of youth agency is used to redefine Accra as just as vibrant as Western cities that audiences admire. In contrast to highlife, Reggie's music reflexively points to the voice and process of speaking itself. As Paa K says, "Highlife musicians were more subtle in how they addressed their audience. Reggie was a bit crass and bold. Some people were offended by his directness; others loved it. But we all know controversy is good for celebrity status." Lyrics address political, racial, and social issues, moving rapidly between global and Ghanaian concerns:

I got the facts to back the superstition
Peace to Mr. Kofi Annan whatever the mission,
Forget the World Cup checkout your condition,
Economical competition before the dribbling,
The biggest crime in Africa, Skin Bleaching . . .
Jesus Christ was abibini [black African] what I believe in,
Make I free my mind this morning, afternoon and evening.

Using simple rhyming patterns, these lyrics offer a Pan-African critical perspective on daily concerns like skin bleaching, football, and Christianity. They situate Ghanaian life in the context of a global world and call for self-reflection on being black African. The song also references familiar Accra nightclubs and other in-group markers of belonging. "Yo sometimes I sit back and try to reminisce, / Shows like *Osofo Dadze* we all miss," referring to a popular TV musical soap-opera comedy from the 1970s. Nostalgic familiar references legitimize Reggie as a local narrator who can speak to and for youths. This song's poetic form creates a celebratory chronotope in which the rapper links freedom as a form of intellectual self-making ("Make I free my mind") to the familiar pleasures of Accra's urban leisure.

Rab was interested in reaching audiences, not in creating a new genre. "'Keep Your Eyes on the Road' was seen as hiplife because it sampled highlife. But I thought it was just hip-hop. . . . Radio stations really liked it. This was the one people played." Shortly before the release of the entire album, they printed promotional CD copies of the single at Citirock, a cassette duplication facility in Osu that had recently added a CD duplicator. "We wanted to use new technology to try to reach audiences all over. CDs were still expensive in Ghana . . . Most Ghanaian musicians did not have marketing strategies. . . . There were only a few business-people trying to figure out the new scene, with CDs, radio stations, international marketing, all that. We wanted to be on the forefront for the new music industry."

The second single from the new album, "Eye Mo De Anaa?," came out just after the album release. Reggie and Rab were living behind Reggie's father's house, which doubled as his fashion design studio. It was a vibrant place filled with artists and political elites. Soul, Afrobeat, and 1970s highlife often played in the background. Rab recalls, "Ricci kept asking us why we didn't use anything from Fela. He would come to the back of the house and say 'Fela . . . was the greatest, better than James Brown. You're not using him because you think it's too serious, not party enough.'"[31] Ricci gave them a CD of Fela Kuti's *Shakara*. Rab chopped up a sample from the title track and programmed kick, snare, and hi-hats on different tracks, pulling out the bass and rebalancing the instrumentation. The looped beat focused on the horns, providing a uniform sonic frame for Reggie's vocals. Reggie adapted a hook to fit Rab's beat. On the track Reggie calls, "Eye mo de, anaa?" A female backup singer responds, "Eye mo de, paa!" Reggie translates this exchange as: "Is it good to y'all?" and "It's great!" though a more literal translation is: "Is it sweet to you?" and "It is very sweet to us!" The familiar saying, rendered as a general question, draws listeners into a discussion of the virtues of life in Ghana. Twi, English, and Pidgin phrases are interwoven in a naturalistic pastiche that reflects informal youth speech patterns. The call-and-response formula lent itself to what Reggie calls "a party track. . . . People will always reply to a call-and-response groove." The common trope of sweetness ties general praise for life in Ghana to a flirtatious story about a night on the town.

> me na me kae,
> if you no like make you bore

meka nokware
barima kantinka a w'agya ne rasta
bu me se wo pastor
mengyae gyae me ho da
Twi ne Brofo rapper
meko gye me visa
London to Ghana, maybe later on America
Me tena ho da
nso ho no mu a nye me de te se Mother Africa
swear today Ghana sweet proper proper

I said it because I said it
If you don't like it piss off
When I speak I tell the truth
I am a gentleman with dreadlocks
Respect me like you respect your pastor
You won't catch me off guard
Twi and English rapper
I am going to get my visa
London to Ghana, maybe later on America
I have lived there
And it isn't sweet like Mother Africa
Life in Ghana is sweet[32]

The rapper praises his ability to shift between linguistic registers and geographic locales. Reggie's music often includes metalinguistic statements about his own prowess. Demanding respect like a pastor, Reggie paints a picture of life in Accra as a proud citizen—Ghana is sweet like no other place—while touting his ability and skill at speaking and acting with force and precision.

The album's first two singles established a pattern for sampling and looping recognizable local rhythms blended with informal mixes of vernacular lyrics. Another track, "Ya Bounce Wo Visa," is important in content because it shows how international travel and its prohibition are important to defining local identity, and in form because it invokes established moral storytelling as a legitimate form for hiplife. The slow rhythm focuses the listener's attention on the lyrical narrative. Rab used the rhythm bass line from a track by 24 Carrot Black, a 1970s American soul band, but sped it up slightly to create a different feel, using just keyboards, sound effects, and scratching. This is not a party track, but tells a moral story of frustration.

Told in Twi with few English words, the lyrics describe the hardships wrought by the Ghanaian obsession with getting a visa to travel to the West. The story unfolds through two letters to Reggie, the first written by a friend and the second from his girlfriend. Each letter describes the writer's struggles in Accra after Reggie has moved overseas, the inability to get a visa, poverty, racism, longing, anger. The song is a morality tale, drawing upon a familiar narrative structure from Ananse trickster storytelling tradition. Reggie recalls, "I wanted to write a story that would be real for Ghanaians. Everyone has visa problems. It's something rich and poor all over Africa face but no one wants to really talk about. People at home think traveling is all riches, and when people travel and come back they don't want to tell the truth that it's a struggle out there."[33] He had difficulty finding the right language to express his thoughts. "It's that art of storytelling like from back in the day. I could have written it easier in English but I worked hard on the Twi because I wanted those guys in Nsawam and Kumasi to understand the concept of the two letters. You get to the airport and your visa isn't good. Then you get over there [abroad] and it's not all you thought it was. . . . It's deep." The song begins,

> It's a struggle when they refuse to give you a visa, please.
> This is a Rockstone story, traveling is hard.
> Everybody wants to travel abroad.
> All these people lie about what happens when they go.

It posits Reggie as a wise observer, as someone who has traveled and returned who can reflect on this difficult issue.

Unlike many of his songs that rely upon simple rhyming and aliteration, the story's content dictates its structure. Partial and imperfect rhymes link Twi and English words and are unevenly spaced. Some fall in the middle of a statement while others conclude an idea. Melodic emphasis on rhymes draws the listener through the story. This storytelling form is evocative as numerous future rappers tell me that hearing this song convinced them to write lyrics, confirming the potentials of Twi hip-hop. The sad narrative recognizes the desires of travel and the frustration of being prevented from moving that young disenfranchised Ghanaians face. Listeners identify themselves with the displacement and exclusion of trying to go overseas. Hip-hop's cosmopolitanism and his own mobility give Reggie the authority to talk about locally shameful issues most do not openly discuss.

Indirectness/Directness, Respect/Innovation

Respect and indirection in performance allow a speaker to be directive of social innovation. The pervasiveness of Akan proverbs that focus on the act of speaking itself indicates the importance of proper language use in Akan public culture (Yankah 1995). Orators speak carefully, observing proper forms of address and respectful turn-taking as listeners tend to criticize even the smallest breaks in protocol (Obeng 2000). While metaphor and indirection characterize public speaking, high value is placed on a speaker's power to change the outcome of a situation through persuasive language (Yankah 1989). The aesthetic and moral polarities of directness-indirectness and respect-innovation, in some measure, define how public speaking across genres is interpreted (Obeng 1997).

The centrality of metalanguage—language about language use itself—in Reggie's music highlights the importance of reflexivity to claiming new speaking roles. The titles of Reggie's first three albums point to the act of speaking as a particularly sensitive area of public contention. His albums, *Makaa Maka* (I said it because I can say it) in 1997, *Me Na Me Kae* (It's me who said it) in 1998, and *Me Ka* (I will speak) in 2000, all use first-person forms of address, in past, present, and future tenses, to claim the right to speak (see figures 12 and 13). Frequent references to language use, demands for respect from listeners, and proclamations about his truthfulness and eloquence are metalinguistic bids for recognition as an authoritative public commentator. Reggie walks a line between respect and disrespect, arrogance and innovation. As various linguistic and semiotic registers—hip-hop, Afrobeat, storytelling, highlife, proverbial speech, Rastafarianism, Pan-Africanism—are indexed and realigned, participants' actions and words are understood within new contexts of their own narration (Eisenlohr 2006, 113; Bakhtin 1981).

In the context of hierarchies of Akan speech culture, claiming an authoritative speaking position is itself a politically charged act, especially in relation to gendered and generational differences (Yankah 1998; Nugent 1995). Reggie's bold directness in proclaiming his authority to lyrically define life in Accra diverges from indirect forms of reference and the polite turn-taking typical of older highlife and storytelling (Obeng 1997). Hip-hop voicing indexes cosmopolitan authority,

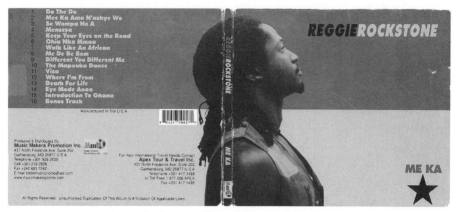

FIGURE 12 Reggie Rockstone album cover.

FIGURE 13 Reggie Rockstone album cover.

allowing the speaker to break local protocol, proclaiming his own agency in the very act of speaking.

Reggie's lyrical hooks celebrate nightlife in Accra and circulate as proverb-like catchphrases through the mouths of DJs, club goers, and radio listeners. These hooks are easily detachable, self-contained sayings that mediate between direct and indirect forms of address (Spitulnik 1996). For example, the song titles "Plan Ben?" (What's the plan?) and "Eye Mo De Anaa?" (Is it good to y'all?) both became popular phrases youths used to mark their hipness and membership in a hiplife speech subcommunity. These songs are not elaborate narratives but evoke the excited atmosphere of a night on the town; lyrical dexterity, focusing on rhyming, alliteration, reference, hyperbole, and self-praise, parallels social dexterity. At times, songs foreground the virtuosity of word control for its own sake, self-consciously announcing that speaking in and of itself has productive force.[34] Reggie's fluent vernacular English mocks the formal and superfluous use of Abrofuo Kesee (big English) common in elite public speaking, highlighting the use of informal youth language and style to claim authority. Celebratory song hooks are indirect statements about youth agency. The ability to command the storytelling form is also significant. "Ya Bounce Wo Visa" strikes audiences as groundbreaking in linking established moral tale telling with a cosmopolitan hip-hop aesthetic. References to familiar musical and speaking genres give Reggie's innovation, self-praise, and hip-hop sensibility local legitimacy. His "foreignness" allows him to directly address embarrassing local issues and provides a pleasurable disruption, keeping his audience off-balance and open to something new. Reggie's celebrity grew out of demonstrations of control in balancing innovation with respectful reference.

Nightlife in Accra: Styling the Masculine Body

Reggie's version of hip-hop provides a template for social transformation in which young men reimagine their potentials as mobile, speaking subjects. His music shapes Accra's chronotope—in Bakhtin's (1981) sense of a shared set of signs and practices that unite members of a speech community in how they imagine, live, play, and work. Reggie's music is an aesthetic condensation of his travels, presented for local consumption through his gestures, clothes, and words. In this he becomes an indexical icon, a model of how to navigate a changing urban and global landscape for young men to emulate. People have admired his ability to blur genres, creating a new sound that addresses the specific daily frustrations and desires of his audience—both elite and nonelite youths. His songs and persona celebrate the small pleasures and possibilities of Accra as a place of young masculine leisure and fantastical male consumption. For example, one song, "Sweetie Sweetie," presents a long list of playful comments on women who are flirting with Reggie. Through a chanted inventory of women, it presents a cityscape in which the rapper is an idealized masculine consumer and women are signs of wealth for agentive male hustlers.

The artist's body acts as an indexical ground for listeners to trace his musical influences in multiple directions. In his early public appearances on television and stage in Accra, Rockstone wore Timberland boots and baggy military fatigues, sometimes removing his shirt. He projected a tough, streetwise persona. For the older generation, this image caused some consternation because he resembled an American gangster. His dreadlocks were a sign of his controversial status and stylistic connections. Roots reggae had been modestly popular in Ghana since the 1970s. Ghanaians in Europe also picked up on the harder-edged image of the tough dub London-Jamaican gangster. Syncopated rhythms, patois, and imagery of Babylon and perpetual exile resonated as musical and social themes. Dreadlocks in Ghana were traditionally associated with insanity and were not worn by respectable citizens. A few musicians like Kojo Antwi had worn dreadlocks, but by the late 1990s Reggie and other returning Ghanaians adopted and popularized the style to indicate their social difference. Most aspiring hiplife artists grew dreadlocks to signal their entry into this musical world and rejection of social norms.

Linguistically, Reggie shifted between speaking English with African American vernacular, a Ghanaian inflection, and a British accent, though he emphasized the American accent when he first returned to Accra. People who did not know him were surprised that he was Ghanaian, while those who knew him as a child were surprised at his transformation. Writer Ama Ata Aidoo, a friend of his father's, was surprised when she saw Reggie on television. "When I saw Reggie rapping on television after he returned to Ghana, I didn't recognize him at first; he sounded American . . . and the dreadlocks! When I realized who he was, I was so happy to see him doing well. 'Is that Ricci's son? O my God?!'" She laughed. "He had succeeded. . . . He was transformed."[35] The dissonance between Reggie's public presentation and his origins was especially noticeable to early audiences in the moments when he shifted between rapping in Twi, English, and Pidgin. Reggie enjoyed the symbolic dissonance that he seemed to create. "I had hip-hop style which confused older folks but the kids really identified with. I looked like the people they saw in the New York videos but I rapped in Twi, so I was a hero."[36] The combination of different stylistic authenticities gave Reggie a physical bravado that defied normative ideas of appropriate behavior. His authority allowed him to reimagine earlier local rap—which had seemed like a simplistic copy—into an emotionally charged form of agency.

Reggie's music videos present a visual aesthetic of urban masculine leisure, establishing a vision of Accra as a vibrant urban world of excitement and possibility. Early videos draw on shots and sequences familiar from American hip-hop music videos of rap crews claiming urban space through partying. For example, the music video for "Nightlife in Accra," from the first album, shot by BiBi Menson, reflects a collective sensibility of youth defiance and celebration. The video follows Reggie and a cohort of youths as they playfully dance, drink, and enjoy nightlife in the streets of Accra. Reggie, Cy Lover, and others rap, while female R&B vocalist Chocolate sings the chorus. Lyrics are in English with occasional asides in Pidgin. Shots of rappers and groups of young men looking into the camera are intercut with images of motorcycle tricks, bars, flashing lights, car rims, and a roulette wheel. This party landscape shows elite youths celebrating in the streets, creating an image of carefree pleasure in a familiar space for nonelite youths to aspire to. Accra is positioned as a cosmopolitan space but one that is specifically Ghanaian.

Abraham Ohene-Djan, also recently returned from abroad, directed several music videos for Rockstone's early tracks, providing a slick, visually rich look on 16 mm film. The video for "Keep Your Eyes on the Road" is a fantasy snapshot of an elite house party, a pure celebration of carefree leisure. It begins with the camera following Reggie as he opens the door to a house party and welcomes Rab to the celebration. The video of "Eye Mo De Anaa?" shows scenes of Reggie as a bartender serving drinks at an upscale bar, intercut with shots of happy patrons drinking, Reggie chatting with a woman in his wealthy Accra neighborhood, and Reggie surrounded by dancers dressed in camouflage outfits break dancing for the camera. With low production values and inexperience prevalent in the new Ghanaian video industry, Ohene-Djan's work stood out for its visually rich production standards, further

FIGURE 14 Reggie Rockstone with D-Black in a studio in the Labadi neighborhood with Efya recording vocals. Photograph by the author.

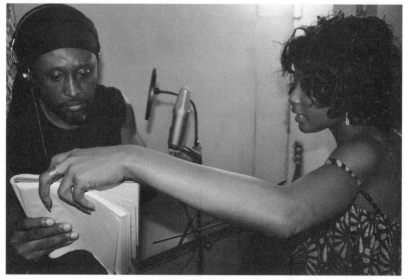

FIGURE 15 Reggie Rockstone with Efya working on lyrics. Photograph by the author.

emphasizing Reggie's image as a successful international star in the making.

Fame of Ghana: Success as Immaterial Commodity

While Kassa Records provided a business model for new musical production and distribution in Ghana and presented an image of success in its products and public images, they did not sell many albums. Reggie's music and image circulated through radio play, shows, clubs, television appearances, and word of mouth. Their success came not through selling music exactly but in creating an even more valuable abstract commodity: Reggie Rockstone, the first Ghanaian celebrity of the neoliberal era. Reggie's celebrity status—the ubiquity of his name, the influence of his music and style, the notion of Reggie as the founder of a genre, the Godfather of Hiplife—provided a model of musical and social success for young artists. Most significantly, he established a language and social persona to suit a new type of music and its related cosmopolitan, Ghana-based electronic media landscape (figures 14 and 15). Reggie's public and performance styles aligned multiple discursive registers to invoke a new kind of masculine authoritative voice (Agha 2005a). The reanimation of Akan storytelling as a public speaking form reinscribed older notions of Akan-language hegemony in an informal national public. The confident Afro-cosmopolitan sensibility that Reggie presented to young Ghanaians was premised on his ability to align disparate registers of black diasporic and local Ghanaian speech communities. Reggie's fluency in both worlds announced a new kind of national celebrity emblematic of the political-economic circulations of new-millennium neoliberalism. It was an example of potential and aspiration to a youth generation. But it was also unstable and unsustainable, as young Accra audiences aspired to cosmopolitan celebrity that they could not themselves access. Reggie's success came in his ability to represent unattainable desires; his stardom emerged through his effective reiterations of the image of celebrity itself.

In *The Fame of Gawa*, Munn (1986) argues that Gawan travelers and traders earn fame through their ability to control and channel exchange values. Positive qualities and virtues inhere in the names of successful traders. Celebrated names extend the self, circulating outward into the world, beyond the limits of the body. Outward expansiveness and exchange are highly valued, while inwardness and selfish consumption are forms of social negation. Social actors aspiring to make a name for themselves engage in exchange practices, in particular those revolving around Kula shells, canoes, and food, to extend their influence into the wider inter-island world. In the obligations entailed in these exchanges, value is returned to those who successfully externalize objects. Successful names become detachable signs, creating chains of signification that connect the bodies of their owners to the social values of the exchange practices with which they are associated.

While Munn focuses on noncapitalist exchange, her example helps explain how labor, exchange, and movement are transformed into value in Ghana's new, privatized culture industry. This occurs not primarily through abstraction and conversion into money, but through mobilizing nonmaterial wealth—value that inheres in the body as a set of qualities and experiences. Hiplife music takes on new meanings through the social circulation of artists, as they make music, and of musical and stylistic signs, as communities of interpretation debate the meaning and importance of these activities. In the performative transformation of what signs mean, participants creatively "bounce signs off" various interpretive contexts, bundling them with other signs to create new meanings through association (Keane 1997). Aesthetic values are transformed in the process of remaking sign-context relations. Speaking authority is then shaped by aesthetic value in relation to moral value. In Ghana, hiplife operates under a similar logic of the inversion and simultaneous duality of meanings, in which words or signs can refer to opposites, defining a core principle of value transformation. Local value is contested and made in externalization and return (Appadurai 1996).

Ambiguous inversions of meaning leave a community of listeners uncertain as to the "proper" interpretation of a song. Rather than trying to track down singular interpretations, authorial intents, and expert opinions on cultural meaning, my ethnographic method looks at debate, translation, reinterpretation, and transformation as forms of circulation in themselves. The idea that there is always someone else who can make an authoritative or different interpretation is itself an aspect of how people in Accra understand speech, culture, and music. Akan languages in particular rely on the idea of traditional elders as language experts and repositories of traditional wisdom. Artists and listeners are themselves part of an urban community in which people are uncertain whether others are more knowledgeable in either deep, rural traditional practices or the stylish discernments of international black music. In this context artists make claims to traditional roots—

whether they are from Asante, the North, Central Region, or Accra—in order to validate their innovative styles and visa versa.

Reggie's linguistic control projects a new kind of public speaker situated among various worlds. His unusual fluency in various local and foreign registers took advantage of local longings for cosmopolitan life and elite uncertainties about traditional expressive forms. His use of code switching—among Twi, Pidgin, and African American and Ghanaian vernacular versions of English—reflects the informal communication styles of urban youths in Accra, rather than formal Twi language use (Woolard and Schieffelin 1994). His informality indexes a speech community of streetwise young men. Hiplife, in its nascent form, addressed the daily desires and frustrations of young Accra dwellers in an atmosphere of unstable privatization, while the appropriation of familiar Akan-language speech and highlife musical idioms into a hip-hop sensibility legitimized the music for older, more conservative audiences. Reggie's ability to speak the language of hip-hop in a specifically Ghanaian way relies upon the authoritative naming and organizing of Accra as a space of leisure that is, in turn, predicated upon relegating women to sexual and visual realms. This is reflected in the lyrical focus on masculine speaking as a form of agency.

For Reggie, the experience of traveling abroad gives him local authority to interpret and transform black diasporic signs. Rab's breakbeat fragmentation of older West African songs embeds a highlife sound within a hip-hop structure. Rhythmic fragments of nostalgic tracks are detached, remade, and looped. A new sonic landscape is elaborated in studio production through layering instrumentals, references, scratching, and lyrics. The ability to disarticulate and reassemble foreign black styles within new, locally recognizable forms demonstrates popular musicians' skills of control and balance in studio production as well as vocal flows. Hip-hop's remix aesthetic reflects technological shifts as well as changes in music distribution and marketing. In transforming hip-hop into a local form, Reggie and his cohort authorize a new form of entrepreneurial subject: masculine, at once respectful of local tradition and irreverent, experienced in travel, and fluent in the art of reassembling various styles in new ways that are at once recognizable and innovative. By embracing hip-hop stardom, Ghanaian youths valorize individual celebrity for its aesthetic value and economic potential.

CHAPTER 4

The Executioner's Words

GENRE, RESPECT, AND LINGUISTIC VALUE

It is 2 AM on a Friday night in early 2000. Glenn's Nightclub, near Nkrumah Circle, is the place to go. Some people sit and drink at kiosks outside; others queue to go upstairs into the cramped dance venue, which is beginning to get crowded. Only a few months ago they played mostly American R&B, hip-hop, and pop; suddenly their playlists have mostly Ghanaian music with a few foreign hits. During a break, the DJ explains to me, "New tracks, man! Before you couldn't fill a playlist with Ghanaian songs. Now there are plenty songs that will make people boogie. They love local songs they can dance to, but also talk about their local conditions."[1] By 1999 a critical mass of hit singles by young artists filled the airwaves, coalescing into a recognizable genre called hiplife. Elaborating on Reggie's musical formula, artists searched for the right prescription for making a hit. Production software, using PC computers, aided musical experimentation by aspiring artists and producers without musical training or professional studios. Media entrepreneurs sought talented rappers to make danceable songs with local lyrical appeal that were also cool and cosmopolitan. Albums were mishmashes of various styles, with some English tracks, some Twi, some with American-sounding beats, and some with highlife dance rhythms. No one was sure what would sell, so they experimented, fine-tuning successful formulas.

Second-generation hiplife hit singles linked first-person forms of narration to various established sonic and lyrical registers, valorizing the persona of a fame-oriented self-fashioning Ghanaian rapper. This aesthetic of self-making celebrity was naturalized in the generic conventions of hiplife. Among a series of new tracks, the 1999 hit "Kwame Nkrumah" by Obrafour da Executioner exemplifies the aesthetic transformations that make hiplife a significant part of broader public discourses, giving it relevance outside of its popularity with young music enthusiasts. Merging rap and prayerlike libation chants, the song is a tribute to Ghana's first independence leader. The song demonstrates hiplife's generic transformations, in which new artists signify established discourses, giving old signs renewed vigor through their association with hip-hop styles and electronic mediation. Audiences admired "Kwame Nkrumah" for its respectful, proverbial use of language, which, in turn, validated the young rapper's hip-hop fashion and dreadlocks. Traditional oratory practices and iconic national signs gained new legitimacy for a youth generation through their parallel affiliation with hip-hop's urbane stylings. Through new associations, older signs were realigned. All of this relies on a logic of value transformation reflected in how performers balance respect and innovation.

Hiplife's emergence as a socially recognizable musical style gives general insight into how new genres are made. Initially, people judge and question stylistic changes and individual innovations in relation to established aesthetic principles. Over time, through authoritative reiterations and reflexive debates about meaning and authority, new values coalesce into a naturalized genre that participants experience and judge affectively through newly unspoken moral and aesthetic oppositions of good and bad (Briggs and Bauman 1992). Social actors claim authority by directing audiences on how to interpret words, gestures, and styles. As authoritative speakers emerge in specific contexts, they facilitate transformations between aesthetic value and social authority. They do this by working to determine, limit, and extend the contextual frames and semiotic registers through which their actions are interpreted (Kockelman 2010). In balancing respectful reference to older genres and past performances with new signs, artists like Reggie Rockstone shape the closeness and distance between signs and their referents (Bauman and Briggs 1990). A speaker can alternately defer agency or claim it, manipulating how audiences interpret their intentions (Obeng 1997). This allows an actor to negotiate authority within established genres and, in the process, remake the assumptions and predispositions of these genres for a speech community that determines what constitutes authoritative speaking; in turn the speech community is reimagined (Yankah 1995). In making performers personally responsible for the effect of their words and actions, popular cultural genres are susceptible to constant change. In valuing newness itself they both valorize and destabilize the power of individual speakers to transform the world around them through performance.

Genre is "an orienting framework for the production and reception of discourse" (Hanks, discussed in Briggs and Bauman 1992, 578). Participants reshape linguistic norms and interpretive frames, claiming the power to narrate crucial social-moral issues in the context of social transformation (Peterson 2010; Bate 2009; Dent 2009; Eisenlohr 2006). As social actors use generic conventions—shared references, communication styles, and norms of interpretation—to link signs from disparate registers, they produce new interpretations and conventions that define a community of belonging in the language of transformation itself. Reflexivity is crucial to making a new genre (Briggs and Bauman 1992). A community of listeners must recognize new conventions for them to work. In the process, a speech community self-consciously recognizes itself in these shared conventions (Warner 2005).[2] As actors define new boundaries among various expressive genres, they determine how the same sign may take on different meanings as it changes contexts.

When Reggie and other hiplifers use proverbs in informal urban contexts, they link a speech event to the authority of tradition, giving value to new speakers and the weight of tradition to their words. Proverbs alert audiences that they must actively engage in the process of interpretation and search for creative references (Agovi 1989; Yankah 1989). Many West African musical forms are explicitly multivocal, drawing on eclectic traditional and contemporary influences (Veal 2000; Barber 1987). Popular genres rely heavily on intertextual references. They are a collection of speech acts "built upon the words of others," containing "sediment of the past" in each new performance (Kapchan 1996, 55). Artists use the indexical aspects of musical signs to point to older performance registers and to draw attention to their own skills in making creative and unexpected syntheses. Audiences strain to discern the multiple references at play (Sutherland 1975). Hip-hop's aesthetic of mixing and sampling elaborates on this valorization of layered pastiche as a form of communication (Fernandes 2011). Hiplife emerges as a genre by realigning established Ghanaian styles with new and diasporic forms. As young artists experiment with various musical combinations and listeners debate the implications of the latest trends, they redefine the boundaries of what constitutes aesthetically pleasing music and, by association, the parameters of what is Ghanaian.[3]

A Critical Mass of Self-Naming Young Stars

Around the millennium, when young Ghanaians wanted to be cool and famous, hiplife was the vehicle. With the music's initial success, aspiring rappers approached the few established artists, producers, and radio presenters for mentorship and support. Social success in any endeavor in Ghana requires cultivating social networks rooted in a system of patronage (McCaskie 1995). Paa K recalls kids flocking to Rab and Reggie, begging to be taught. "There was always a group of young rappers trying to get featured on one of [Reggie's] tracks or coming around to get advice. . . . Most [next-generation] artists at one point came through Reggie's house. It reflects how people do things here . . . in traditional society." To explain this phenomenon, he used a proverb: "In Fante we say . . . 'If you climb a big tree you deserve a push.' That's how things get done in Ghana."[4] In this patronage model, successful members of the older generation are obligated to assist aspirants who demonstrate their potential. Youths strive to show their drive and ability to work hard. In this logic of investment, elders help others who will make the most of the time and money required for their success. In the future, these investments return to patrons as both cultural and material capital.

Most of the rising artists came from relatively comfortable homes with family connections of some sort, but were not cosmopolitan travelers like Reggie or Panji. As local stars emerged, poor youths looked to them as role models of financial success and social prestige. While actual musical success usually depended on having money and connections, the image of the successful rapper relied on the notion that personal hard work and individual skill would be rewarded by public validation. Hiplife styles became embodied forms of aspiration, providing a "way out" of local problems.

By the late 1990s groups of young artists were congregating at recording studios and radio stations searching for connections. Hiplife concerts at venues like Trade Fair Centre attracted large crowds to watch aspiring artists rapping over prerecorded beats. Small studios appeared, often in people's houses, consisting of secondhand PC computers with software like Cubase and Fruity Loops for sampling, beatmaking, and recording multitrack songs. At public events, funerals, and out-doorings, in markets, taxis, and drinking spots, the music quickly filled the air. Popular songs circulated primarily through radio play, television exposure, and cassette sales. Radio DJs at Joy, VIBE, and Groove led the way, promoting the music. In 1999, Peace FM, promoted as the first all Akan-language commercial station, hit Accra's airwaves. Its catchy jingles, commentary, and local playlists further developed a vibrant sound geared to a hip modern Accra. In 2000 event production company Charter House sponsored the first annual Ghana Music Awards, with several categories devoted to hiplife.

Most youths interested in entertainment wanted to rap; only a few aspired to be DJs, producers, or studio engineers. As Nkonyaa of the Mobile Boys explained, "The rapper is in front of the microphone, the one people listen to."[5] Aspiring lyricists developed an iconography of stardom through various forms of self-reference. Second-generation artists announced their star potential with stage names that combined signs of hip-hop swagger, Pan-African and reggae iconography, and tradition. Whereas being a highlife musician in previous generations had required a band and musical expertise, electronic production tech-nologies allowed a lyricist to garner all of the audience's attention. Adopting a hiplife persona showed a person's desire to achieve celebrity by speaking to a Ghanaian public.[6] Many hiplife names pay homage to figures of cultural authority, especially those valued for wise, eloquent speaking.[7] The group Akyeame uses the iconic figure of the Okyeame (pl. Akyeame), the traditional spokesperson or linguist in the chiefly courts of Akan peoples (Yankah 1995). The group Nananom (ancestors), connoting the wisdom of previous generations, was made up of three artists who on stage played the roles of Omanhene (head chief) Pozo, Nana Kyeame (linguist), and Nana Ohemaa (queen mother) from the traditional Akan court.[8] Other artists drawing on traditional iconogra-phy included Talking Drums, Obrafour (court executioner), Abrewa Nana (a wise old woman's granddaughter), Kontihene (town chief), Okom-four (traditional priest) Kwadee, and Motia (magical dwarf). Some names were local interpretations of cosmopolitan or Pan-African iconogra-phy; these included Lord Kenya, Nana King, Ex-Doe, Chicago, Sass Squad, 50 Cedis, Native Funk Lords, Black Prophet (reggae), Black Rasta (reggae), and DJ Black; other names sounded hip like Buk Bak and Tic Tac (see figures 16 and 17). As Panji recalls, "Kids took names

FIGURE 16 Hiplife star Lord Kenya. Photograph by Ayana V. Jackson.

FIGURE 17 Early hiplife group Buk Bak. Photograph by Ayana V. Jackson.

they thought were cool. . . . They were local ideas of what American rappers stood for."[9] For these aspiring rappers, self-naming connoted the ability to transform the self through the performative aspects of referencing. Taking on new personas gave individual youths the power to imagine new forms of agency.

The music of Tic Tac, an early star, exemplifies three formal features of hiplife's focus on the aesthetics of individual success: dual voicing in first-person storytelling, self-reference, and performative invocations of the idea of success. Nana Kwaku Duah, of Asante origins raised in Accra, attended the elite Labone Secondary School. He gained performance experience at the National Theatre's Kiddafest as part of a teen group, Nutty Strangers.[10] The chorus from his 2001 hit "Emma Formula" (Women's Formula) introduced his unique staccato rap to fans across the country. It posits the rapper as famous through the eyes of female admirers:

Tic Tac, all the ladies believe I am a star
They all think I have dough
They think I am tough
This is women's formula[11]

Reflecting informal urban youth speech, the chorus brings English into a Twi grammatical structure. In the line "Maa nyinyinaa believi me star" (All the ladies believe I am a star), the English verb, "believe," and the noun, "star," point to modern life and correspond to the English words, "dough" and "tough," in the following lines. The informal mixing of languages forced audiences to pay attention. Indeed, there was disagreement in what the first line was: some fans thought Tic Tac was saying "believe in my style" versus "believe I am a star." This type of indeterminacy produces more attention. Much of highlife music focuses on tales of love and loss, and gospel emphasizes the singers' faith, whereas hiplife is permeated with first-person aphoristic expressions of confidence, miraculous wealth, and instant success. Rappers often focus attention on themselves by repeating their names and by making up praise names for themselves. This song relies on a fantasy and moral warning that became common to the genre. A rapper's acquisition of cash announces his fame and attracts women, but with fame and money, the song warns, stars must be careful about the predatory nature of women who seek out successful men. This moral duality is reflected in the formal alternation between the first-person storytelling voice of the rapper and the perspective of fictional female admirers. This dual voicing imagines the rapper in a landscape of excitement and danger where success comes to those who have the courage to announce their presence.

VIP (Vision in Progress), another early, successful group, is the best example of a tough hip-hop persona combined with highlife danceability and sound (see figures 18 and 19). Its three main members—Lazzy, Promzy, and Prodigal—are from Nima, one of the poorer areas of Accra, with a high concentration of Muslims. They are unusual in using Hausa and Ewe as well as Twi. As Lazzy recalls, when they first performed at National Theatre Funworld, they were "shy, but got a lot of encouragement from . . . the people there. We are proud to represent Nima . . . to tell people about our struggles making it out of the ghetto."[12] The look that rocketed them to stardom included American-style football jerseys custom-designed with their names, baseball caps, and metal chains. One member later tattooed a teardrop under one eye. Their hardcore hip-hop look, however, contrasted with their danceable jamma beats and highlife harmonies, making it cool to dance to local-sounding beats. One fan said, "They look so tough and intimidating, like they from the ghetto. But the sound is so sweet." Their knack for making popular songs for radio and club play relies on using familiar dance beats and catchy, easily repeatable hooks. A common criticism of rap is that, as one highlife fan put it, it is "a string of meaningless phrases. Music is supposed to educate and entertain. Most rap is nonsense." Another VIP fan explained that older people take it too seriously. "It's only a rap. Sometimes there is no sense in it. . . . They just use words to rhyme. . . . They don't tell stories. They just want people to move. But they also tell you about what is important to them." For example, the chorus of VIP's track "Adoley" repeats,

> Me ye Mobile phone
> Oba ring ring ope bling bling
> *I have a mobile phone*
> *A woman calls she wants money [bling, bling]*[13]

Rather than telling a story, the lyrics provide succinct first-person statements about the rapper's success. Money and mobile phones are decontextualized signs of material success. Lyrics mix English and Twi, providing an informal register to present these signs of wealth and aspiration. Often success is represented by female desire and the third-person presence of women.

FIGURES 18 AND 19 Hiplife stars VIP backstage in 2000 and 2007. Top photograph by Ayana V. Jackson. Bottom photograph by the author.

Akan-Language Idioms

Several songs from 1999 demonstrate the crucial stylistic transformations through which hiplife gained local legitimacy and next-generation rappers emerged as individual stars. Through the use of first-person forms of narration, these songs invoked a youthful audience, providing a national chronotope centered on the figure of a young, masculine urbanite. While older highlife performers often told indirect stories from a third-person perspective, hiplife rappers make themselves the main character in their tales of travel, success, female conquest, and technology use. Primarily, these songs emphasize the artist as agentive storyteller with the authority to shape his own exploits. Whereas Reggie uses simple Twi constructions familiar to the polyglot urban contexts of Accra, younger artists pushed the formula further, elaborating on Twi and other language idioms, storytelling structures, and references to traditional life. In comparing his language use to that of younger rappers, Reggie explains to me, "I started rapping in Twi, but these cats today, they're deep. . . . They really go into the traditional proverbs, the deep indigenous culture from the villages. I use more street Twi, the way the kids talk in . . . Accra."[14] The music has been dominated by Akan-language idioms. Indeed, non-Akan artists like Samini and Okomfour Kwadee often use Twi as a lingua franca to reach wider audiences.[15] Only a few successful artists use a majority of non-Akan and non-English lyrics; notably Buk Bak and Tinny use Ga lyrics, and Traditional Rulers featuring Chicago and Ex-Doe and later Edem rap in Ewe.[16]

In 1999 Lord Kenya's "Sika Baa" (Money woman) was an important landmark for its use of rich Twi lyrical rap. But audiences were not interested in dancing to its simplistic electronic beats.[17] Many consider that year's hit "Masan Aba" (I will come back again) on Akyeame's second album *Nkonson Konson* to be the first hiplife hit that followed Reggie's formula of combining elements of danceable highlife, Twi-language rap, local humor, storytelling, and hip-hop swagger. The cover art for the cassette and CD demonstrates the logic of value transformation at the root of hiplife's popularity (see figure 20). It shows the album's subtitle, *New York Meets Accra*, repeated across the bottom of a picture of the two artists wearing shirts emblazoned with "Versace," towering over the Manhattan skyline and the World Trade Center towers. A dollar sign ($), the symbol for the local cedi currency, and a new car are placed in the cityscape as well. This symbolism reflects their musical synthesis, as well as broader generational hopes of travel

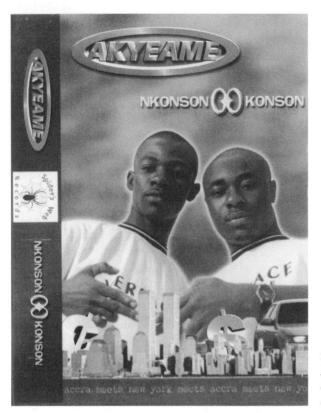

FIGURE 20
Akyeame
cassette album
cover.

and economic success. Masan Aba begins with a rhythm highlife guitar scale over simple three-pulse highlife percussion, and then bass guitar and synthesizer drums overlay a melodic highlife chorus and backing
female singers. The guitar, harmonic style, and slow rhythm recall a
danceable highlife familiar to older listeners. The chorus has a reflective melody:

> Ever since I left you
> I've been roaming and now I'm tired
> There's no one like you
> I've been walking and walking and now I'm tired
> Oh love[18]

The song is an ode to youthful searching, creating a landscape of uncertainty and possibility. The trope of wandering or roaming (*kyen kyen*)
evokes a link between the speaker's internal and external realities, a
young man searching for meaning and finding a voice. The chorus alter-

nates with long raps by Okyeame Kofi (Quophi) and Okyeame Kwame (Quoami). Quophi begins:o

> What has happened to me, I need a spokesperson, Okyeame,
> I am left alone with God
> I rushed into it and I got everything wrong
> Punish me with thirty lashes
> I can't make sense of these problems
> I have changed my life[19]

Critics' comments are reprinted on the CD, demonstrating their aim of marketing the music to both young people and their parents. Adowa Serwaa Bonsu of the entertainment weekly *Graphic Showbiz* states, "My mother loves you guys. I don't know why but it seems you're the only rap group she listens to." The high energy yet contemplative lyrics draw the listener, as one older fan told me, "to reflect on the conditions of life while also being compelled to dance." The rappers lilt lyrically through their rhymes—confessional and personal in tone—with highlife-influenced voicings and references to local daily life. Older listeners note the clarity of their tone—compared with Reggie's rapid-fire aggressive voice—which shows respect for, as an older listener said, "traditional styles from the old days."

The Okyeame is the chief's spokesperson in Akan courts. Typically, an Okyeame's ability is measured in his skillful use of proverbial oratory and rich referential language to elaborate on the words of the chief and to mediate visitors' messages to the court (Yankah 1995). In courts, linguistic mediation is a way to save face and defer intentionality in communicative situations that are potentially disruptive or dangerous (Obeng 1997). The Okyeame's power comes through his ability to mediate and channel the power of language. The group attempts to shift the authority conferred on speakers in chiefly courts to the new media. The music video, like many at the time, has little to do with the actual song, instead it is a celebration of new visual styles and technology. The video alternates shots of several women and the rappers modestly dancing as various backgrounds are superimposed, including spinning purple circles, a distant city-skyline with the artists appearing to be waist deep in water, and an extravagant marble ballroom.[20]

In the same year, Ex-Doe had a remixed hit, "Comfort," from his album *Maba* (I'm here), in collaboration with the old highlife star, Dr. Paa Bobo, adding vocals by Maggie. The track opens with highlife acoustic guitar following a basic three-chord progression before a heavy electronic bass line drops in. Ex-Doe's gritty, intense rap verses are placed over Dr. Paa Bobo and Maggie harmonizing the chorus in a lamentation of love lost.[21] Collaborations such as this demonstrate how young artists, despite their rebellious styles, show respect for and seek inspiration and legitimation from highlife stars and, conversely, how older artists seek to reach new audiences. Hiplife artist Obour (stone) explains to me that even after becoming one of the most popular artists in the country, his clearest sign of legitimacy came when, after hearing one of his songs on the radio, an elder in a rural village asked him to explain the meaning of one of the proverbs in his lyrics.[22]

As hiplife gained radio presence and cassette sales rose, successful highlife musicians like Rex Omar began to experiment with mixing hip-hop and highlife, some inviting collaborations with rap artists. This helped rappers gain more commercial viability and cultural legitimacy among older and mainstream audiences. The 1999 hit "Kokoko," recorded by young highlife singer Daasebre Gyamenah with a rap verse by Lord Kenya, was massively popular and influential in combining highlife melodies and storylines, danceable electronic beats, and rap. It also self-consciously contrasts the social persona of the highlifer and the hiplifer. The lyrics portray Gyamenah as unsuccessfully seeking the attentions of a woman. He is knocking (*kokoko*) at his woman's door to tell her, "I can never live without you." But she ignores him because he has no money. "Knocking" also refers to a man seeking public recognition of his intentions to marry a woman. Gyamenah's soft, melodic lament contrasts with Lord Kenya's entry with a confident, rapid-fire rap verse. He raps about seeing an attractive woman and wanting to meet her family. His lyrical brashness presents him as agentive and controlled in contrast to his unsuccessful colleague. While the highlifer laments economic and social frustrations, the hiplifer imagines future potential. The agonistic opposition between signs of respect and tradition and signs of newness and modernity provides a productive tension that is ongoing in hiplife.

Signifying Kwame Nkrumah

Perhaps the most influential song of 1999 was the young rapper Obrafour's first groundbreaking hit, "Kwame Nkrumah." This song demonstrates several ways in which hiplife indexically links older notions of speaking authority to the aspirational values of hip-hop. In musically recontextualizing Kwame Nkrumah, Ghana's iconic national independence hero, through a blend of hip-hop styling and traditional speech practices, Obrafour transforms himself from a secondary school student into a pop icon, seen by many as spokesman for the nation's moral conscience (figures 21 and 22). Building on the emerging parameters of hiplife, Obrafour's music brings together libation pouring and proverbial speaking as authoritative speech practices associated with traditional society, references to the central symbol of Ghanaian national identity (President Nkrumah himself), and the kpanlogo highlife rhythm. Aligning these signs within electronically produced hip-hop, revalues ideas of tradition; it naturalizes hiplife as authentically Ghanaian and elevates Obrafour as a young custodian of national culture. His respectful language use grounded the "foreign," innovative elements of his speaking and style and opened the ears of an expanded listening public, quickly elevating him to celebrity status.

Michael Elliot Kwabena Okyere Darko is from Kwahu, an Akan-speaking area in the Eastern Region, although he grew up partially in Accra. In the mid-1990s Darko was one of many secondary school students drawn to hip-hop. He considered studying law but instead pursued his music.[23] He took the stage name Obrafour, after the feared and respected traditional executioners of Akan courts, also known as court poets. Rab recalls that in the mid-1990s, Obrafour hung around Reggie's house and recording sessions looking for advice and financial help to record his own album. "He had talent. A lot of kids had developed good rap skills. We were the only ones putting out hip-hop records at the time so they had nowhere else to go. If we had had more money we would have put out and distributed all of their albums, but they had to figure it out on their own."[24] Reflecting many young Ghanaians' understanding of the importance of Obrafour's style to the music's explosion, the aspiring rapper Grey explained to me, "Reggie was the first one to really make the music acceptable, or popular rather. He showed us . . . that we could do what they were doing up there [in America] . . . but there was this Western style in [Reggie's music]. Many of [us] were not too good in that Western style. . . . Obrafour . . . showed us that we too could enter this game, that the typical youth could make it. . . . He raps in pure, typical Twi filled with . . . proverbs. He brings in the authentic Ghanaian culture."[25] Obrafour is noted for imparting

FIGURE 21 Obrafour onstage at the National Theatre, 2000. Photograph by Ayana V. Jackson.

FIGURE 22 Obrafour in the studio, 2000. Photograph by Ayana V. Jackson.

traditional moral lessons to audiences. His elegant use of Twi-language idioms, proverbs, and proper forms of speaking convinced older audiences of the music's relevance.

Obrafour began collaborating with an aspiring beatmaker, Hammer (Edward Nana Poku Osei), who had never worked in a studio before and was not a trained musician. But Obrafour liked his beats. Hammer recalls his early passion for music: "I would pound tables, make beats with my mouth. . . . I didn't research traditional music or have formal training but I knew how it should sound. I had a natural musical talent; I can hear anything and then play it on a keyboard."[26] Hammer's family was from Mampong-Asante, but he grew up in Accra, where he attended elite Achimota and Presec secondary schools. His father was a banker and his mother was a foodstuffs trader. He recalls that his childhood house in the comfortable suburb of East Legon was full of music, with R&B, soul, and Afrobeat records always playing. He says when he started making beats for Obrafour, "I had never even been in a studio before. But Obrafour believed in my ability to make music. . . . Even when the producer wanted him to use someone more experienced he stuck with me." Hammer worked with Cubase software for the Atari platform. He recalls, "It was so limiting. I had to use the sounds that were already programmed in and make them sound African." The software was revolutionary in that it allowed nonmusicians to intuitively visualize the music in different tracks on-screen throughout the process of making beats, recording lyrics, and mixing.

Old Beats, New Sounds

To put out his music, Obrafour secured financial backing from family members and from a producer. "Kwame Nkrumah" was the most popular song from Obrafour's first album, *Pae Mu Ka* (Break it open and speak, broadcast, or say it clearly), the name following Reggie's titles by invoking the act of speaking itself.[27] The song "Kwame Nkrumah" is structured around a kpanlogo or jamma rhythm. As described in chapter 1, kpanlogo is a neotraditional form of Ga popular dance music. Older listeners in the 1990s heard the rhythm as a nostalgic sign of childhood, while young listeners identified it as a sonic marker of tradition, both affirming and confining. Hammer recalls how he made the beat, which then inspired the way Obrafour imagined the song's lyrics: "I made a traditional groove with Western pattern strings and percussion. Obrafour . . . decided it would be a tribute to Nkrumah."

Hammer's beat is a digitally looped kpanlogo rhythm. It is easily recognizable and, according to Akramah Cofie, a Ga musician and dancer, "feels familiar" to Ghanaian audiences as "jamma or party music," though in hiplife mixes the beat is less prominent than with live bands.[28] The bell is more dominant in traditional arrangements, because all other instruments rely upon its rhythm. In digital mixes it is often subdued, less obvious to the listener, but giving the arrangement a familiar danceability. Many hiplife beatmakers program and loop a kpanlogo bell pattern as the primary track in a multitrack recording program to structure their music. It provides a sonic line over which they can layer other sounds and vocals. On this track Hammer contrasts the beat with sparse R&B instrumentation. Cofie explains, "Ghanaian musicians call the bell pattern a timeline because it directs the other instruments. These beatmakers are using it to make a Western sound in 4/4 time; sometimes they distort it slightly at the end of each bar to match a Western pattern or subdue it. With traditional music the timeline/bell would be well-defined . . . guiding the other instruments. When it is an electronic beat, it just sits there to make a funky drum line." Young artists manipulated electronic production technologies to adapt their parents' music to their tastes. For many adults, hearing the familiar rhythm underlying rap in the late 1990s opened their ears to the genre.

Obrafour's lyrics demonstrate respectful, indirect forms of address that contrast with audience expectations of hip-hop. His lyrical delivery in "Kwame Nkrumah" most closely resembles the poetics of libations—prayers recited by a respected elder or Okyeame in honor of ancestors. Listeners have been struck by the song's respectful forms of address, elegant phrasing, and proverbs. Lyrically, the song situates Nkrumah among ancestors and the Almighty as Ghanaians' spiritual protectors. In the process, the speaker claims a legitimate voice as narrator of the national predicament. Obrafour calls his own name, claiming the title of "Ghana rap (a)sofoo" (Rap priest), and linking his lyrics to sacred authority. His name Obrafour (Executioner) also gives his words weight through association with this feared member of the Asante court and custodian of tradition. As in libation, Obrafour respectfully offers drinks and prayers to Kwame Nkrumah, to God, and to the ancestors.

Almighty Kwame [God] receive drink
Heaven and earth, receive drink
Ancestors, receive drink

Let's pray to Kwame Nkrumah
Ghanaians
Excuse me, make way for the brand new
I stand for Ghana
I call on you Osagyefo Dr. Kwame Nkrumah[29]

In the name of Ghanaians, the rapper calls Nkrumah to receive drinks and to listen. Shifting footing, he claims the ability to both speak for and to the nation. His style of delivery invokes the rhythmic chant of libation. Obrafour directly addresses Nkrumah in the name of all Ghanaians.

Now I am coming to pour libation
Osagyefo Dr. Kwame Nkrumah, receive drink
Our forefathers, you sacrificed your soul for us

The rapper alternates voices, addressing Nkrumah as an ancestor of contemporary Ghanaians, and addressing Ghanaian society from the perspective of Nkrumah, recalling his sacrifices for modern Ghana. Obrafour's words claim authority from recognizable proverbs and national collective images. He uses traditional, respectful terms of address to structure his words, for example, by calling for the listener's attention: "Mese mesre amanfoo" (People, I beg your pardon), to call for national unity: "Monyinaa nye baako" (You should all unite), and the right to speak and reason for unity to come from shared spirituality, language, and territory: "Efiri se yete faako" (Because we live at the same place). The song lyrics chastise the nation, advising it to avoid corruption, secrecy, and indiscipline by pointing to Nkrumah's sacrifice and hard work as an example. References to Asante drummers are mixed with Christian references like "the Bible says honor thy mother and father."

The song's two verses do not narrate a story but revolve around repetitive naming practices, stringing together a loose set of references to provide moral advice to the nation, respectfully delineated into appropriate social categories. The song imagines Obrafour's audience in several ways: as a national collective (Ghanaians), a racial national collective (Africaman, abibiman), through their professions (lawyers, traders, farmers, teachers, soldiers, "royalty"), and finally as cultural-linguistic groups mentioning Asante, Fanti, Ewe, Kwahu, Hausa, Akuapem, Akyem, Bono, and Dagomba. However, references to Asante cultural practices and proverbs are the focus. The logic of calling the nation through these categories, imploring its people to take moral responsibility for social change, replicates Kwame Nkrumah's speech on the eve of Ghana's independence in 1957, in which he directly addressed various segments of society, naming them in categories of workers and cultural-linguistic groups assembled before him and calling for strength and unity. Obrafour's song also recalls earlier popular praise-songs to Nkrumah like E. K. Nyame's early 1960s hit highlife song "Kwame Nkrumah Aye," celebrating Nkrumah's leadership. The independence speech and other fragments of the first president's well-known words provide an interpretive frame, connecting Obrafour to Nkrumah's charismatic leadership.

Recognizable Akan-language proverbs are layered to reinforce the song's main point about the importance of morality, unity, hard work, and respect for national success. For example, two well-known proverbs come together near the end of the first verse shifting the emphasis from Ghana as a diverse nation to Asante cultural nationalism. Obrafour raps,

> It is very easy to break one stick of a broom,
> But it is very tough to break the whole bunch.
> Ashanti the porcupine, "When you kill one thousand, one thousand
>   more will come" is the motto.

The first proverb refers to how the strength of a broom relies on all its bristles working together. The second, sometimes seen as a central motto of the Ashanti Empire, describes the porcupine, the symbol of Asante, and the relentless fierceness of Asante warriors. The two proverbs are metaphoric calls for unity. But there is a slippage between Ghanaian and Asante references, reflecting a broader tension between ideas of Ghanaian national unity and Asante cultural and linguistic dominance of the national public sphere. Indeed, the song foregrounds one of the central political tensions in twentieth-century Ghana, between Nkrumah's Pan-African vision and his Asante critics. Obrafour claims an authoritative national voice by positioning himself between a centralized Nkrumahist vision of Ghana and a distinctly Asante cultural authority. By drawing on Akan-language ideology, hiplife artists reassert the dominance of Akan as an emblem of cultural morality that represents the nation.

Obrafour's music inserted his voice into national conversations about language and moral value by aligning youthful creativity with respectable speech practices. In an online discussion forum about political corruption and intractable fighting between Ghana's two main political parties, one writer compared the virulent insults that political adversaries publicly hurl at each other to Obrafour's style of indirection and eloquent critique. He used Obrafour as an example of proper speaking, in contrast to politicians who have "polarized" the country and degenerated into making personal attacks and insults.

> Can't our politicians and statesmen "debate" with class? I thought they are the educated ones, with the Western PhD's who are supposedly more civil. . . . Obrafour sends his messages across with "pretty," deep and wise language. He makes us think twice, listen thrice and appreciate what he says. Are our politicians failing to tackle these political battles intelligently because they are using English? What happened to the beuatiful [sic] proverbs and idioms we grew up with?[30]

To this commentator, English language use and Western education encourage foreign forms of debate antithetical to Ghanaian values. Inelegant and un-Ghanaian language use is contrasted with Obrafour's "pretty" language, exemplary of the poetic and thoughtful nature of Ghanaian speech culture. The aesthetics of good speech are crucial to moral, public accountability. Obrafour's style allowed listeners to consider hip-hop not as profane entertainment but as falling within established modes of oral circulation. Elegant, complex language makes an audience stop to ponder meaning, activating forms of moral debate and critique, making a Ghanaian national speech community.

The public ridicule that President John Evans Atta Mills faced for verbally stumbling over the word "economy" mispronouncing it as "ecomini" several times in a speech in 2009 is an example of the virtue ascribed to precision and correctness in speaking, and how it projects authority into other realms. Caught on tape, the blunder went viral, rapidly circulating through Internet, radio, and television news. It was also remixed for a song titled "Ecomini Remix" and spawned a dance, mockingly performed at a National Theatre event soon after. Imprecision opens one to ridicule and public disrespect. The lyrical depth and precision attributed to Obrafour are crucial markers of his aesthetic control and the public authority it confers. They link the pleasurable aspects of indirect verbal constructions, and the active listening they require, to respectful moral commentary on societal problems. By using "deep" and "typical" forms of Akan oratory, his music reinscribes Akan-language idioms as central to Ghanaian public life.

Their precise command of language and focus on first-person narration makes rappers indexical icons, focusing audience attention on the rapper as a conduit of symbolic transformation. Obrafour's popularity lies in how his speaking practices and self-presentation embody crucial values: hardness, precision, clarity, decisiveness, wisdom, respect, knowing your place, fluent code switching, and the ability to mediate between distinct worlds, whether they are separated linguistically, spatially, or politically. The rapper's inner virtues are revealed in listeners' scrutiny of word use. Obrafour refashioned himself from a middle-class secondary school student into a musical icon and embodiment of traditional spoken wisdom by renaming himself and projecting his name into the world through his music. By recontextualizing collective hopes of the early national period, Obrafour imagines a new space defined by individuated moral choices and hopes. Songs like Reggie's "Keep Your Eyes on the Road" and Ex-Doe's "Comfort," which sample nostalgia-inducing highlife, and groups such as Buk Bak and VIP, who draw heavily on older harmonies and rhythms, combine the symbolic force of African American youth culture with a recognizable older aesthetic of Ghanaian nationhood. Hip-hop rebelliousness gained moral legitimacy through references to tradition, while, conversely, established language practices were reinvigorated through associations with the latest trends.

The Ambivalences of Travel: The Potentials and Hazards of a "Been To"

Success brings conflict. As this genre becomes identifiable, observers excavate the past to construct historical genealogies and narratives of its origin to justify its authority and extend its reach. Aspiring rappers challenge the music's narratives to gain entry. As Reggie tries to maintain his claim as the genre's originator, others try to displace him.

In public, second-generation hiplife artists universally praise Reggie as a pioneer and founder of the genre. Indeed, the sudden emergence of numerous hiplife artists solidified his status as a national innovator. Dubbing Reggie the Godfather of Hiplife and Gyedu Blay Ambolley a proto-hiplife pioneer made them into musical ancestors of sorts, providing the genre with a legitimate genealogy. But behind the scenes, criticism is common. One rapper explains, "Reggie made it but does not want to help others succeed like he did. He is old and needs to help younger artists now instead of taking everything for himself."[31] Others see these criticisms as jealousy. Another producer expresses a common sentiment: "When you succeed in Ghana, people have that pull-him-down mentality . . . No matter what you do it is never enough . . . Jealousy, man!"[32] Hiplife is particularly prone to accusations of arrogance and counteraccusations of jealousy because of its focus on first-person forms of narration and individualism, which run counter to local ideas of collective support.

Reggie's initial success in legitimizing hip-hop in Ghana relied on his firsthand involvement with diasporic music abroad and his ability to demonstrate that Ghanaians could be cool and tap into hip-hop's swagger. However, while his cosmopolitan stance—linking Accra to an international scene—allowed his success, it also limited his ability to reach broader Ghanaian audiences. The conditions of his success were also the limits of his transformative potential. By this I mean that while foreign travel is seen as a potential form of value, returnees are also looked at with suspicion. "Been to" is a humorous, critical name commonly referring to a Ghanaian who lives abroad and returns, connoting arrogance and the incongruities that come from being away and forgetting what daily life is like in Ghana. Jealousy, frustration, and suspicion of returnees is reflected in stories—both true and untrue—of how travel's potential knowledge and wealth also raise questions about ideas of local authenticity. The negative side of the traveling subject is defined by excess. Locals feel that traveling and returning can lead to grandiose ideas of self, excessive public displays, and over-the-top consumption.

Samuel, a few years younger than Reggie, set up a local musical production company and was working in new media when Reggie returned to Ghana. He recalls some of the negative reactions Reggie got. "To me, when Reggie 'came down,' he and his minions were arrogant and pretentious, and did not know what was happening on the local scene. People resent it when someone 'comes down' and tries to take over the scene. . . . He was a 'been to' and did not know what life was like at home; coming back to tell everyone how things should be. Some people resented it or maybe they were jealous."[33] Aminata, one of the early hosts of *Smash* TV, a talk show on popular culture, points to the contradictions of going and coming home. "The same values that gave Reggie success also animate his critics. He is too foreign, too arrogant and obsessed with the idea of his own celebrity."[34] A journalist recalls how Reggie was sometimes seen as disrespectful. "As for Reggie, hmmm, I liked him but at first . . . as for him he was 'too know.' Coming back to Accra like he ran things. He did not respect. Confidence is good but arrogance? No, especially for Ghanaians who value respect."[35] The common phrase "too know" (as in "Woy3 tooo know!" or "You are too know") refers to someone who thinks they have all the answers. It is often used to describe those who do not listen to advice or who try to do things in an unconventional manner.

Rumors about Reggie were frequent. A schoolmate from Achimota recalls, "He just had that 'been to' air that rubbed peeps the wrong way. One story was that he had never actually been abroad but was raised in some village in Kumasi and was pretending." Conversely, "some people said he lived in New York for fifteen years, did not really speak Akan, and had not lived in Ghana at all except for secondary school."[36] These opposing rumors demonstrate the polarity of value between local respect and foreign potential that Reggie embodied as he gained public attention.

Observers debated the relationship between Reggie's intent and public presentation. His schoolmate recalls, "When he first came on the scene, he wasn't trying to pass himself off as some deep spiritual Asante boy. He was identifying with the West. Later on he switched. At first he needed foreign cred, then later local cred. Ultimately, the rumors originate with him and gain momentum. He tried to manipulate his image but as you know rumors take on their own life. . . . That's what I think anyway, but only he knows."

Traveling abroad is a virtue that gives those who go a set of potentials and qualities that mark their activities as successful. It is a form of externalization that can make wealth and value. But traveling also has potential hazards and threats. Ghanaians are wary of those who return. While Reggie's music established the conditions for the rise of hiplife, his ability to translate foreign styles made him a bit of an outsider with the masses. Next-generation artists, in experimenting with various musical formulas, were able to localize hiplife more naturally.

Conclusion: Blurred Genres

At a conference celebrating the fiftieth anniversary of the publication of *Things Fall Apart*, Chinua Achebe reflected on his father's generation and its creative responses to uncontrollable structural changes. "I remember as a child, elders in my village who were powerful orators; they were so skillful with the use of words they could change a situation with their eloquence. Those who were not faithful—so to speak—to their tradition such as my father became great preachers in the church, and beyond."[37] Achebe noted that African expressive genres have long been formulated in the context of outside contact in which older forms of oratory and poetics are transformed. Following in the lineages of religious and political orators, a class of young transnational African artist-intellectuals, inspired by Achebe's *Things Fall Apart*, contributed to the rise of the modern African novel in the 1960s. This genre shaped African public culture for a generation. Similarly hiplife and other hip-hop–related genres across Africa have transformed moral and ascetic conversations for the rising generation.

Numerous tracks saturating the airwaves from 1998 to 2000 announced hiplife as the distinctive, recognizable sound of a new generation. Accra youth recognized themselves in hiplife, especially in its first-person forms of narration and reflexive affirmations of youth icons trying to fashion themselves into celebrities. In moments of generic transformation, charismatic performers like Reggie, Obrafour, VIP, and Akyeame give listeners clues about how to interpret new forms of expression. As when any new style appears, audiences need especially reflexive directions to point them toward proper forms of interpretation.

As hiplife is established, self-conscious discussions about the music's parameters emerge. Radio presenter Blakofe points out to me that it is hard to define hiplife musically. "They are doing gospel music which they're rapping over—they are doing hip-hop which they are calling hiplife. I don't know who is doing hiplife at the moment. I don't know what hiplife is."[38] But the attempt to pin down its musical attributes is more important than any agreed-upon formula. After a concert, Obour reflects on hiplife's origins with fans, explaining that hiplife has two stylistic camps, artists that focus on local dance rhythms and artists that provide wisdom through lyrics that are "national treasures to the Ghanaian public." Kweku T of Talking Drums argues that the most important stylistic split is between English-language and local-language rap. Grey of the Mobile Boys thinks that the genre is divided into those who use "hard-core hip-hop beats" and those who use "that same jamma beat for every song." The formation of a genre and its public is entailed in reflexive debates and disagreements about rules and boundaries. The specific musical details vary, but as participants negotiate inclusion and exclusion the new genre's legitimacy emerges.

Hiplife is a blurred genre within which multiple established genres are interwoven through intertextual references (Briggs and Bauman 1992; Geertz 1985). It self-consciously presents a performer's ability to control stylistic eclecticism as a form of newness. As chapter 1 showed, the layering of rhythms, lyrics, instrumentation, types of speaking, and bodily styles in hiplife points to a long history of how artists shape meaning and value in West African popular forms by incorporating new things. Like highlife before it, hiplife is a social style that youths use to refashion themselves as authoritative public speakers. In the process, speakers draw on established aesthetics of speech culture and reshape them through innovative forms of reference. By overlapping different performance registers, participants are positioned to imagine new spatiotemporal frames (Hanks 1996; Bakhtin 1981). In the heteroglossia of this blurred genre, metatalk about origins and the boundaries of the genre are themselves crucial to its existence (Bakhtin 1981). Debates about style and definitions of genre are themselves constitutive of new forms. In claiming the right to public voicing previously reserved for adults, a new generation of musicians imagines their own celebrity and success. This is a cyclical process in which each generation reinvents its relationship to diasporic styles to mark its rebellion against, and difference from, older generations, inevitably understood as old-fashioned and "colonial."

Hiplife is musically diverse and characterized not by a particular rhythm or lyrical pattern but rather by a performative electronic orchestration of Akan-language practices with diasporic hip-hop. New public stances require a performer who can self-consciously shift between multiple social registers. In this process, linguistic and bodily controls are qualities that point to the potentials of self-fashioning. Reggie's initial popularity is based on a structural disposition to value diasporic/African movement and transatlantic exchange. Reggie's version of hip-hop/hiplife inspired a generation of new artists and media folks. But his style was too close to hip-hop. It was only when hiplife inverted hip-hop, when it could mirror and reinvent the productive affinities of diasporic expression, that hiplife became a locally acceptable form.

Hiplife is an inversion, simultaneously diasporic and African, foreign and local. It reimagines a spatiotemporal landscape for its youthful community of interpretation (Munn 1986, 14). For Ghanaian youth, locality is defined through symbolic parallels between traditional life and diasporic cosmopolitanism that intersect in the middle space of urban Accra. Hiplife unites and objectifies these symbolic forms and displays them for contemplation and reinterpretation. The music voices ambivalence toward the free market, particularly for African subjects on the margins, providing models of how to transform the values and authority of traditional speech culture into value for local and global consumption (Tsing 2005). Through the transformation of diasporic hip-hop into local terms, hiplife became a way to reobjectify established moral narratives of the nation as a popular aesthetic and then convert them into new moral and economic value.

These four chapters have sketched a broad picture of how hiplife emerged as a genre and became significant to national public discourse. The second half of the book examines how the genre takes on new forms of urban and transnational media circulation in shaping an entrepreneurial aesthetic.

CHAPTER 5

Scent of Bodies

PARODY AS CIRCULATION

This chapter focuses on how parody and humor are key to value transformations in hiplife, driving lyrical circulation and the conversion of
musical aesthetics into broader forms of public recognition.[1] Provocatively ambiguous songs excite listeners, encouraging them to repeat
lyrics and play with their interpretations. Humor drives circulation; audiences make new parodic connections, further accelerating songs' flow
across various social realms. As audiences speculate and elaborate on
lyrical meaning, the process of interpretation drives movement. Parodic
humor is by no means new in Ghanaian public life, but hiplife infuses it
with a bravado that gives credit to the musician as individual originator
of successful music while eluding blame for making disrespectful, direct
criticisms. Chapter 4 describes how Obrafour and other young artists
balance references to overseas, black diasporic registers with traditional
forms of expression to give their words new authority. The parodic mode
is one way that speakers realign direct forms of address and self-
reference, shaping authoritative public commentary through its elaborate, controversial circulation.

In this chapter I trace the trajectory of two parodic songs as they
circulate across urban Accra. I follow the humorous political discussions on a tro-tro (minibus) heading toward Accra sparked by "Vote for
Me," a 2000 song about winning presidential elections by making absurd promises to the electorate. I also map the circulation of "Scenti
No," a hit hiplife song about bodily smells, as it moves from humorous,

irreverent political critique to legitimizing marker of populist approval in relation to the 2004 presidential elections. In highlighting these musical exchanges, I describe how artists try to harness rapidly changing media technologies to reach audiences. Hiplife circulates across urban spaces in electronic and proverbial forms, weaving together an evolving Ghanaian popular imagination. This genre is built upon a culture of circulation in which the authority of words and people relies upon the ability to control public perceptions of authorial intent. Perceptions of the intent of a speaker or singer are central for defining the meaning of words and their correct and incorrect interpretation. As described in chapter 1, irreverent highlife songs such as Ampadu's 1967 "Ebi Tie Ye" and Ambolley's 1973 "Simigwa Do" caused public controversies around authorial intent and moral messages. Debates about authorship and interpretation are productive of a community of interpretation. In urban Ghanaian contexts, audiences are predisposed to find dual meanings, humor, innuendo, and obfuscation—in contrast to American popular audiences, for example, who tend to make literal assessments of public words. Ghanaian artists, DJs, politicians, and advertisers try to make fame and money by appropriating songs and phrases, reshaping their references and driving their circulation across new contexts. Audiences and everyday citizens find pleasure in these plays of words and power.

Parodies are effective when they make unexpected inversions, or incomplete transfers of meaning between two types of things that are related and not quite opposites. Inexact inversions reveal humorous tensions. Phrases circulate in their incompleteness and openness to new interpretations. Artists become well known when their songs take on a circulatory life of their own, interjecting into public moral and political debates without appearing to be directly involved. Artistic innovation and successful marketing strategies rely upon a speech culture that values the rapid circulation of provocative song hooks.

Songs that parody visceral bodily desires and actions involving eating, sex, money, and grooming transfer meaning and value from one social realm to another and from one kind of body to another. This logic relies upon a metaphoric inversion between a private individual body and a public social body. The movement of bodily fluids and the fluidity of bodies mark a moral geography in which private desires threaten to become public indiscretions. Oppositions between ingestion and expulsion, production and consumption, provide visceral ways to indicate the high social value placed on public control and the shame that comes with revealing private indiscretions.

Bodily expressions and desires are a parallel poetic terrain upon which ideologies of individual choice and consumption are marked as decidedly masculine. While I elaborate more fully on the gendered aspects of entrepreneurship in chapter 6, the following examples show that a masculine public persona is articulated through tropes of sexuality and grotesque or excessive bodily consumption. The moral legitimacy of an individual microphone-wielding speaker is produced and contested in parodies of politicians, pastors, and other public figures and humorous discussions that songs provoke. Central to hiplife is the connection between self-fashioning and marketability. In humor, youths fashion themselves as free-speaking. At the same time, their aspirations rely upon converting ideas of personal freedom and expression into marketable music.

Whereas centralized states demand that their citizens are regulated through government institutions, marketization fragments authority, valuing individual initiative and personal desire as core principles of an entrepreneurial citizen-subject. Musical expressions of individual success valorize self-fashioning over collective good. Inhabiting bodily and lyrical forms of authority, even in parody, allows young Ghanaians to remake themselves as aspiring, individuated speakers. Popular musical circulation provides a realm of free expression in which subjects performatively enact the principles of self-making that define the privatized state. In copying and elaborating these principles, musicians push self-fashioning to its extreme such that earlier forms of humorous storytelling become increasingly exaggerated parodies of themselves (Boyer and Yurchak 2010).

Popular lyrics circulate and are reanimated in a variety of daily contexts linking face-to-face interactions to broader social registers. Social actors use parody to point out the interplay between public control and private desire. Humor is a highly reflexive mode of production that relies on the performative aspects of value making. Satire drives musical circulation, and circulation produces new forms of value. While demonstrating the power of words, the circulation of songs across social spaces also shows the tenuous nature of linguistic and moral value and the need for speakers to constantly maintain their authority or risk public ridicule.

This chapter examines how a distinctly Ghanaian liberal subjectivity emerges in the dispositions cultivated through hiplife, specifically in relation to electoral politics. Here a self-sovereign subject is precariously situated both within and against the state. Popular music constitutes neither a simplistic realm of opposition to the state nor a realm for the incorporation of difference into civic and corporate institutions. Rather, this popular music provides a formal arena through which youths appropriate official channels of communication and signs of power into an alternative imaginary of individuated power, manifest in the ability to claim public voice. This occurs, however, within a context in which the state continues to struggle to control legitimate speaking and social movement.

Eating the Elections: Popular Parody of Political Agency

Popular music instigates public debates. The hiplife song "Vote for Me" by Native Funk Lords (NFL) provides examples of how lyrics become easily circulated discursive fragments, structurally predisposed to provoke oral and mass-mediated political-moral debate (Spitulnik 1996). The song is a parody that provokes humorous political talk, reflecting the mechanisms that inspire rapid circulation of words and ideas across mundane social spaces. Hiplife lyrics, like proverbs, Ananse trickster stories, and highlife songs before them, circulate by word of mouth across public domains. Hiplife is often explicitly described by musicians and listeners as "telling stories and using proverbs in ways that draw on the speech culture of Ghanaians, especially the Akan linguistic traditions. . . . A crucial part of this is the play of interpretations."[2] Interpretations drive oral circulation. As a proverbial phrase or nested set of proverb-like sayings moves across audiences, it provokes reinterpretations, riffs, and debates about meaning. Public discourse around songs commingles the pristine, the grotesque, and the absurd (Bakhtin 1986). The public negotiation of proverbial meaning sets the terms through which everyday Ghanaians fashion themselves as moral agents. Hiplife becomes crucial to this domain of public moral discourse.

One typical afternoon not long before the 2000 elections, travelers waited at a bus stop for a car to downtown Accra. The radio played "Vote for Me" as I climbed into a rusted fourteen-seat tro-tro (minibus). The rattling engine competed with the shrill radio blasting electronic beats and Pidgin rap as we made our way from the outlying area of Adenta past tire sellers and metal shipping containers converted into food stalls toward downtown Accra. The driver's mate leaned to collect bus fares as he balanced precariously on one foot; the other holding the van door closed. The morning rush was over and the torn plastic seats gained some relief from the constant pressure of overcrowded bodies. With the brief freedom of the open road and a breeze blowing through the windows came a casual intimacy in this mobile social space. Banter about daily events provoked by the popular music of the day or key phrases from current events debated on radio news and call-in programs is an important aspect of public life in Accra. The imminent end of President Rawlings's nineteen-year rule and the upcoming presidential elections in December 2000 brought both anxiety and excitement. People were increasingly willing to talk publicly about political differences, though often in comical or oblique ways. A young man seated next to me chuckled as he listened to "Vote for Me's" humorous lyrics in Pidgin English clearly aimed at the upcoming presidential elections. He said to no one in particular, "It's true, Ghanaians! We fool, oh." I asked him what he was talking about. He replied, "Look, we believe any promises politicians make. We never remember that these were the same things they have always said, until they actually get into power. Then they forget what they had been talking about and chop [eat] the money."

Overhearing our conversation, the driver joined in. He explained how he supported the outgoing President J. J. Rawlings when he first came to power in the 1979 coup. Then, J. J. had espoused moral discipline, and was critical of the corruption of African elites and Western economic exploitation. As I have described, even as Rawlings called for economic self-determination (after he gained power again in the 1981 coup) in the face of currency fluctuations, drought, fuel shortages, and the sudden return of a million Ghanaians from Nigeria, the state was forced to accept IMF and World Bank loans in exchange for privatizing state enterprises and accepting Western ideas of democratic governance. Elected in 1992 and 1996 as democratic president of Ghana's Fourth Republic, Rawlings continued to call for state-based discipline and local control of economic resources though the policies of his government moved in the opposite direction, encouraging foreign investment and open markets, divesting state interests in numerous industries. The tensions of this transition were played out across public life. The 1992 and 1996 elections were relatively peaceful, though accusations of corruption and rigging were prevalent (Nugent 1995).[3] Rawlings had promised to step down after two terms as per the constitution, though this was uncharted territory. Ghana had never had a peaceful electoral

PLATE 1 A barbershop in Accra in 1997. Photograph by the author.

PLATE 2 Rockstone's Office before the crowds arrive. Photograph by the author.

PLATE 3 Reggie Rockstone performing. Photograph by the author.

PLATE 4 Jubilating hiplife audience in 2000. Photograph by Ayana V. Jackson.

PLATE 5 VIP onstage. Courtesy of Ghanamusic.com.

PLATE 6 Mzbel promotional image for Red Lipsticks Concert 2011. Courtesy of Ghanamusic.com

PLATE 7 DJ Black live on-air at Joy FM. Photograph by the author.

PLATE 8 Reggie Rockstone and D-Black performing. Photograph by Capture photography.

PLATE 9 R2Bees in concert. Photograph by Capture photography.

transition of government. State credibility was tied to civic evidence of democratic governance, of which the most visible sign—for both local and international political analysts—was conducting free and fair national elections.

As we discussed the upcoming elections on the tro-tro, both the driver and the man next to me seemed ambivalent about the main political hopefuls: Rawlings's current vice president, John Evans Atta Mills, from the National Democratic Congress (NDC), and the opposition leader, John A. Kufuor, of the New Patriotic Party (NPP). Indeed, it seemed the political climate in Ghana was dominated by nostalgia—a reckoning with past hopes and failures—that tempered most working peoples' aspirations for the future. After a silence as we stopped to let passengers on and off, the driver reflected on twenty years of political aspirations and traumas that were just becoming part of the public reckoning with the national memory of Rawlings's regime: "J. J. tried to change things. When he came, he tried to help we, the grassroots people. Junior Jesus, hmm. Now, Rawlings has grown fat. . . . How? He can't fit into his military fatigues. Look at the price of petrol! He has been corrupted by being in power too long. . . . Ghanaians need a change. Ghanaians, we are suffering. . . . Vote for me, hmm!"

The description of the politician's body as "fat" represents a metaphoric inversion of the perceived economic and moral suffering of the nation and the people at the grassroots who had believed in his antineocolonial agenda but did not, in practical terms, benefit from state reforms. In this suddenly pointed discussion on a public bus, the driver's personal lament bespoke disillusionment, not simply with specific politicians but with the possibilities of the Ghanaian state itself as a viable political and economic collective and the moral relationship of specific agents to it.

"Vote for Me" was one of several songs on the radio that addressed politics, though most of the others were more oblique. These lyrics are an explicit parody rapped from the perspective of a presidential candidate:

Vote for me, I want chop president (2×)
Vote for me, I go make you vice president.
If I come power everything goin' be alright
Be you see what I dey talk e no be no lies
This one I know fit take, no controversial
Several times you suffer, no rescuer

Kenkey price come down no more suffer[4]
Appreciate educate school, form better plan
Come see different sense inside one man
No more promise and fail, no delay
I fit say I show you self you go proud

With the chorus "Vote for me, I want chop president," the song offers an ironic critique of the political process in Ghana. The rhymes are placed over a typical, sparse electronic beat but the song is unusual in that it is all in Pidgin English. The song describes all the beneficial things that the singer will do if he is elected president: provide cheap food, schooling, and hospital fees; kill all the mosquitos; invite tourists and investors to Ghana; and arrange for free visas and easy flights. Recalling the promises of independence and Pan-African unity, samples of Prime Minister Kwame Nkrumah's speech on the eve of Ghana's independence on March 6, 1957, and the jubilant shouts of the crowd on that night are mixed into the background of the song. Nkrumah's haunting voice proclaims again and again, "Ghana . . . Ghana . . . Ghana is free forever . . . is free forever." The cover of the cassette itself recalls the moment of Ghana's independence. The three members of the musical group stand on a platform surrounded by microphones, wearing traditional clothes from northern Ghana and striking the same poses as in the famous images of Nkrumah and his ministers addressing the newly liberated nation at midnight (see figure 23). The rappers also wear sunglasses and make hand gestures recalling familiar hip-hop stances of defiance. This rich layering of familiar, contemporary, and historical symbols and the humorous, ironic tone of delivery emphasize the discrepancy between bold promises made by charismatic politicians and daily realities. As Ghanaians headed to the election polls, the song reflected a common ambivalence, historicizing state politics with both nostalgia and regret. Historical references indexically linked past political and speech events to the current elections, providing a set of contexts for new conversations and political positions to emerge (Irvine 1996).

The lyrics position the rapper as an imagined political candidate making a campaign speech. English is the language of state politics such that the use of Pidgin, rather than formal English or another African language, positions this song closer to the form of a political speech while emphasizing its subversive quality as Pidgin is associated with the

FIGURE 23 Native Funk Lords cassette album cover depicting the group reenacting the independence day speech of Ghana's first prime minister, Kwame Nkrumah.

uneducated and bawdy side of Ghanaian life. The rapper boasts about the power of an imagined political actor to fulfill the desires and relieve the social ills of the nation, and humorously mocks the promises of immediate progress that politicians make when running for office. Eddie Blay, a member of NFL, recalled, "We made the song to be critical of the political process in Ghana and to show the hypocrisy of politicians who always say they will do things and then don't follow through. But we were also just having fun."[5] As in many popular realms, "having fun" can be a most potent form of critique.

The central metaphor of the song revolves around "chop," a common Pidgin term that means to eat or consume (Bayart 1993). It refers most directly to the consumption of food but is commonly used to refer explicitly or in parallel reference to the consumption of money and resources, and the male sexual consumption of women. Metaphors of eating have long been critical aspects of political debate in Ghana and across Africa and point to familiar public discussions of state excess and corruption as well as the historical impotence of postcolonial African politics in the face of foreign influence. The explicit multivocality of "chop" indicates how this verb links the active processes of consuming and figurative ideas of self-transformation. This resonates with the process of voting in that many Ghanaians saw this election as the first in which they were given a real choice. Electoral uncertainty and excitement stirred up all sorts of stories about the dangers of authority and potentials for future prosperity. Equating voting with consuming (chopping) allowed for assessments of the actual transformative possibilities of the elections and the populace's role in them.

Returning to the tro-tro, the initial exchange between two people around the song on the radio, in the confined space, spread to all in the car, elicited nods of agreement, and started a humorous conversation among former strangers. The comments I reproduce here point to several key features of hiplife music and its incitement of public discourse. The conversation continued sporadically after the song ended before a series of advertisements for air conditioners and churches and the station call for Radio Gold. As the car took a detour into East Legon with its luxurious homes and hotels, a professionally dressed woman in her thirties, who had said little up until then, chimed in with a final humorous commentary on the song. Warming to her audience, she spoke Pidgin, punctuating her words with hand gestures indicating she was about to take the parody to another level: "If I be president, I go keep the money well but I go chop small [take a little bit of the money]. If someone is president by all means he go chop the money. If I go out, I go use Benz car with air condition. I go flex. But if I go to work I go use abongo car. Chorolorry car [an old broken-down car]! People go think say, I no get money but I go chop um small small."

Several people smiled at her description of personal fantasy that stood in for serious political commentary. The woman humorously inhabited the role of president in a way similar to the rapper in "Vote for Me." By linking her speech from the backseat of a tro-tro to the speech of the rapper as a fictional leader, this female speaker embodied a moral critique of political authority. She affirmed that it is common sense for anyone in a position of power to take money while also acknowledging the moral imperative not to have this revealed in the public domain. The humor in her statement revolves around the same axis as the ironic tone of the song, that is, the disparity between public performance and private action. The song creates a metaphoric parallel between personal corruption of the leader and the corrupt of the body of the nation. By the mid-1990s Rawlings was the butt of jokes, perceived as hypocritical as he grew fatter and could no longer fit into his military uniform, formerly a sign of his moral discipline. As inequality increased under his policies of privatization, he continued to talk about sacrifice, state power, and national unity. The radio play of songs such as "Vote for Me" allowed Ghanaians to publicly negotiate new narratives of national political failure and trauma, using formal elements of humor and indirection to address the obligations and possibilities of an individual leader in the face of obvious and overwhelming structural inequalities.

In "Vote for Me" new musical circulations reshaped how Ghanaians talked about personal choice and changing state authority. This song humorously brings into public discourse traumatic failures of the state to achieve the promises of independence. The rapper states:

> If I come power everything goin' be alright.
> Be you see what I dey talk e no be no lies.

The politician's blatantly impossible promises and his repeated insistence that he is not lying highlight the contradictions of the privatizing state and fears of the duplicitous nature of leadership. The power of words and the efficacy of talk itself are stressed in describing the affinity between trickery and public figures. Politicians' charismatic talk masks their immoral hustle. Through double-voicing public words and private desires, this song stresses the dilemmas of individual aspiration in the context of changing ideas of sovereignty. Discussions around the song call into question the effects of public speaking. In parodying political hope, "Vote for Me" confirms that while speakers promise liberation, language's seductiveness is structured by personal aspirations that undercut collective progress.

In 2000 hiplife music offered newness and subversion. The tensions between state centralization and privatization were embedded in the mobile phrase "vote for me." This song parody points to the "societalization of the state," in which official state discourse is drawn into the realm of public opinion (Habermas 1996, 432). Humorous discussions initiated by the radio broadcast of a song parodying national elections link state transformations to popular culture. The freshness of deregulated private radio opened up public spaces for critical engagement around politics, music, and the politics of speaking itself. The music's edginess thrilled listeners as it also invoked nostalgia for glory days of highlife and

FIGURE 24 Eddie Blay and Kweku T on-air at Vibe FM. Photograph by the author.

independence's idealism. This musically inspired conversation indicates how hiplife music in urban Ghana mediated the changing nature of political discourse in a moment of uncertainty and transformation.

By 2008 this music from 2000 was seen as "old school." Eddie Blay, formerly of NFL, and Kweku T, formerly of Talking Drums, presented a weekly radio program on Vibe FM playing hiplife and American hip-hop (see figures 24 and 25). As musical elder statesmen, they invited new artists to discuss music on the air. After one show I asked Eddie how he recalled his early hit. He reflected,

> Back in the day, it was new. No one knew where the music was going. We did it for fun and to make a statement. . . . We made "Vote for Me" as a political statement to talk about corruption, to say we had a right to say what we wanted to say. Now it is more acceptable. . . . It is more commercial. Some of the kids are making money, which is great, but there is not really enough money in the system to be really successful. Everyone is hustling, but the original message isn't there anymore. . . . Did we lose the edge?[6]

Eddie made a successful media career as a radio presenter, moving from Vibe FM to YFM to XFM, and television host for shows like *Football Academy* on Metro TV, a popular reality program on which young foot-

FIGURE 25 Eddie Blay and Kweku T interviewed outside an album launch at the club Boomerang. Photograph by the author.

ballers compete to win a tryout with an English Premier League football club. Kweku T tried to revive his English-language rap career, after becoming a contestant on the first season of South Africa's *Big Brother Africa* reality show. Increasingly, as privatization was normalized, realms formerly controlled by the state were transformed by dispersed media and commercial tastes. The excitement around free expression in the first years of democratic rule was linked to developing private radio and new public voices. But it was also a vehicle for developing new commercial tastes, blurring the lines between critical voicing and market making.

Privatizing Publics

Private radio not only shaped musical tastes but reconfigured public life more generally. In the months leading up to the December 2000 presidential election, songs and radio call-in programs calling for peaceful elections, political change, and public accountability were a prominent new feature of the political landscape throughout the country. As Radio Gold Programme Manager BiBi Menson recalls, "The 2000 elections showed how much Accra had changed. We had so many stations on air that they became the main way people talked about politics. In the 1996 elections it had been mostly newspapers and state-controlled media."[7] Private radio was suddenly available as a medium for political discourse, though it also linked public opinion around politics to public commercial tastes. The election of John Kufuor's New Patriotic Party (NPP) in 2000 was the first electoral transition of a Ghanaian government. The NPP government continued state liberalization, though in the popular imagination the 2000 transition was a crucial shift from state-centered approaches toward acceptance of free-market–oriented governance.

Private radio stations became central to a flood of political and social commentary unmediated by the state. On-air interviews and call-in shows addressed urban problems like water shortages, power outages, political corruption, sexual indiscretions by local clergy, fake spiritual healers, and family grievances. During popular weekly programs, hundreds of people gathered outside radio stations to present their cases (Shipley 2009b). In emergencies radio hosts alerted police and fire services, calling on-air for them to remove dead bodies, search for armed robbers, or rush to burning buildings, mitigating the government bureaucracy's poor communication. Especially with the proliferation of mobile phones, radio programs were at the center of public dialogues around political and social issues. It was not unheard of for members of parliament, criticized on-air, to call from their mobile phones to make immediate rebuttals.

In state circles, economic progress was assessed through middle-class growth, connections to multinational corporations, and creating conditions conducive to foreign investment. While a small middle class flourished, growing inequality relegated a large segment of the populace to impoverished neighborhoods within and around Accra. New private infrastructure overlaid a state-centered postindependence vision of the capital, which in turn had been built on an older colonial administrative capital. The emerging business-oriented cityscape encroached on the informal commercial and dwelling spaces where the majority of the city's people were caught between various competing visions of Accra. Private banks, multistory glass-and-steel offices, shopping malls, traffic lights, highway overpasses, luxury hotels, and glossy billboards advertising luxury goods, hair products, and mobile phones appeared across Accra. Luxury cars drove on fashionable main streets, running alongside dented taxis and tro-tros. New luxurious multistory houses and planned developments sprang up in new suburbs.

As in much of contemporary urban Africa, growing class polarization became increasingly visible through the city's new infrastructure. Wooden shacks with pirated electric wires, shared outhouses, and hand-carried water stood in the shadow of multistory houses with satellite television and central air conditioning protected by private security forces. "World-class" tourist facilities arose as unemployment grew. Impoverished families struggled as basic resources like water and electricity were privatized. Dirt lanes, open gutters, tightly packed mud-brick and wooden shacks, compound houses, tin roofs, foodstuff sellers, dressmakers, tailors, barbers, car mechanics, lottery kiosks, drinking spots, and chop bars that characterize the daily lifeworlds of most people were pushed to the margins by a vision of Accra for a small, growing economic elite. While the city appeared to develop modern civil infrastructure, prices for food and fuel rose. The masses increasingly struggled to find work that would cover basic living expenses. Poor neighborhoods like Nima and Labadi and ever-expanding suburbs were often discussed by young inhabitants in the language of ghettoization gleaned from hip-hop lyrics. In this changing urban context, popular culture took on the appearance of a neoliberal business practice, promoting the hopes of individual stardom over moribund visions of national collective progress.

Shifting Music Markets and Rise of the Digital Single

Three interrelated shifts shaped music's and public life in the first decade of the 2000s: a technological shift from radio to digital file-sharing; a financial shift from focus on cassette and CD sales to courting corporate sponsorship; and an emphasis on hit singles rather than albums. Artists began releasing albums and mixtapes online not to make money but as advertisements to gain recognition so that they would be invited to perform at live shows and to participate in marketing campaigns. Popularity increasingly relied on a hit single getting regular radio play and its video getting TV and Internet views. More often, tracks circulated solely as digital MP3s via flash drives, Internet, and mobile phone Bluetooth file sharing among DJs and fans. Even the poorest youths listened to songs on their mobile phones; while radio remained important, it was no longer the primary point of access to music. These changing financial and technological conditions of the informal music economy shaped postmillennial hiplifers' struggle to translate sound and style into fame and fame into wealth.

By the turn of the millennium, hiplife commanded an estimated 40 percent of the music market. But even top artists who became quick celebrities around town privately admitted that they struggled to turn fame into financial profit. Producers invested in promising artists' music, bribing DJs and television programmers to play songs and videos for publicity. They printed albums on cassette and CD, distributing them through small shops and market vendors. At the peak of physical market sales between 2001 and 2005, moving 30,000 to 80,000 cassettes was seen as successful.[8] But it was still difficult to turn a profit. CDs remained too expensive to sell in volume, and bootleggers quickly undercut profits selling duplicates for much less. The Musicians Union of Ghana developed a hologram label to place on official copies, but profits remained slim and producers struggled to get returns on their investments. Furthermore, even well-known artists often received lump sums for the rights to their music and did not reap rewards for sales.

Profiting from live shows was difficult as promoters had to keep ticket prices low to bring in young audiences. Many musicians had only one or two hits, not enough music to put on an entire concert, so event organizers often put numerous artists together for showcases, with each performing a few tracks. Since a majority of rappers used computer-generated beats, most shows did not have live bands. At concerts rappers usually lip-synched recorded versions of their hit songs. Crowds came to live events, paradoxically, to hear the hit singles they knew from televised, radio, or digital play, rather than seeing the live show as the main musical activity in and of itself. The digital forms were the originals rather than the copies. Artists feared deviating from recordings because audiences explicitly came to hear the hits and the spectacles of technological precision they represented. Live performances affirmed the electronically circulating imaginary built around an artist's words and image. For young audiences, hiplife shows were spectacles of electronic sound and style. As one young audience member at a Trade Fair concert explained to me, "We come to be part of the scene. . . . I listen to the music but I just want to see the rappers that I hear on the radio with my own eyes."[9] Face-to-face interactions referenced circulatory technology rather than the other way around. Hiplife concerts were not sites of improvisation but were important in referencing the origins of the music in electronic production and as signs of the modern spectacle of technology and media. Presence at live performances, then, was confirmation of a circulating, ephemeral electronic original.

As chapter 4 describes, the music industry's fictive kinship network functions by successful artists and producers mentoring—and profiting from—protégés. While most second-generation artists were relatively elite and used private resources to fund their music, with their visible success numerous impoverished urban youths saw them as models for their own middle-class aspirations. Aspiring hiplifers have expressed to me both hope as well as anxiety and frustration at these mentoring relationships. Outside small and large studios and radio stations, hopeful youths congregated in large numbers looking for patronage from established producers and artists. Live shows, studios, and radio stations became social hubs for what James Ferguson (1999) describes as a prevalent, highly mobile, class of jobless urban youths. Without state narratives of hope for the masses, hiplife provided them with a possible road to local fame and access to foreign wealth. Many hiplifers aspire to be rappers but only a few make it—about several dozen rappers became well-known in the first years of the millennium out of thousands of youths who tried to do the same.

Beatmaker and producer Hammer has been perhaps the most successful at finding new talent and recognizing how to use changing technologies to market artists. After his success producing Obrafour, Hammer received numerous offers. "Kids kept coming up to me asking if I could produce them. I would come to the studio [and] they would just hang around my car waiting for me. But I only wanted to work with the best,"[10] he explained to me. Hammer, always on the lookout for talent, would ask unknown rappers who approached him to freestyle in order to test their skills.

Recording one evening at Hush Hush Studios in 2004, Hammer was surrounded by about thirty teenage boys and a few girls. From the mixing board, he directed the artists to go outside to rehearse verses and then enter the recording booth to lay down vocal tracks. Despite having a recognizable signature sound, he was always experimenting with new beats, sound, and styles, trying to figure out how to market each artist. That evening he spent hours trying to replicate fontomrom drum sounds using the keyboard with preprogrammed beats, pounding on keys to mimic the deep rumbling rhythmic patterns of the large Akan drums. Despite the dominance of local languages in hiplife, he also experimented with reintroducing English rap.

In the mid-2000s Hammer produced a series of compilation CDs with each track featuring a different unknown artist. Each rapper paid a fee to cover the studio time and expenses. "I wanted to identify the best talent out there and see how the public would respond to them. . . . The singles from the compilations that were successful, I would work with those artists." The compilation albums were effective at testing the market viability of different artists and musical combinations. In this manner, he developed numerous future stars: Tinny, the best known Ga rapper; Edem, the first hiplifer to rap fully in the Ewe language (see figure 26); Sarkodie, who is known as Ghana's "fastest rapper"; Kwaw Kese, who Hammer nicknames Abodam (Crazy Person) and shapes his persona and lyrical style to match the image of a crazed outsider unafraid to say taboo things.

50 Cedis, Motia, and other rappers with tracks on the compilations, despite prodigious talent as lyricists, did not seem to appeal to audience tastes and Hammer did not pursue further recording with them. Motia, from the Central Region, raps in Fante and uses rich proverbial language and a unique, slow delivery. At age nineteen, his eloquence impressed everyone who heard him freestyle, though producers worried that his style was "too deep" for urban audiences. Motia freestyled for Reggie, who advised him, "Simplify your lyrics . . . and come up with hooks the audience can remember." For Motia, being a successful rap artist was a way "[to] support my family. I want to be remembered as having been a success through my own hard work. . . . As a young man I cannot rely on others. I have to do it myself."[11] Motia was frustrated by what he felt was a lack of support for his unique talent, and he continued to seek support to make an album on his own, buying studio time to record tracks with young producers when he could afford it.

Around the same time other influential beatmakers, most notably Jay-Q and Appietus, popularized electronic jamma dance rhythms. For several years Jamma artists dominated the hiplife sound, with the most popular tracks striving for infectious pop danceability and light, hook phrases. Hammer took note of these popular trends but also maintained his sound with simpler hip-hop beats that emphasized and supplemented his artist's lyrical dexterity.

Hammer's real genius has been his ability to brand artists for the market. He relishes his behind-the-scenes persona, shaping the musical landscape while remaining relatively unknown to the public. "All the musicians know what I have done, shaping hiplife, but many people don't recognize me or know I am behind the sound of so many of the most popular artists."[12] He is also a careful observer of technological

FIGURE 26 Beatmaker Hammer (center) and his protégé rapper Edem (left).
Photograph by the author.

change. When CD and cassette use declined, he was quick to exploit the
potential of digital and video promotion on television. "A few years ago
you released an album and tried to promote it with a single; but you had
to invest in making copies and marketing and distribution. Now you
make a single and you take it to radio stations and get them to play it.
You make the video . . . and take it to TV3, GTV, TV Africa, Metro, and
you pay them a fee to put it in their regular rotation of videos. . . . If
you have a hit your name will get out there and you will become popular and people . . . corporate sponsors and stations and promoters will
invite you for shows. . . . That is where the money is now. Corporate
sponsors and shows. Later, after your single, you can put out the album.
But with downloads, that is not where you make money these days."
While physical sales were still the focus in 2003, only a few years later
artists and producers focused on making and promoting hit singles and
finding sponsors. Artists, producers, and managers recognized success
in the language of corporate marketing, and increasingly, the state
itself followed these public tastes.

Parody of the Body and Accra's Culture of Circulation

Sidney's hit song "Scenti No" is an example of how the circulatory logic
of Ghanaian speech culture is reinvigorated by new production and

marketing techniques, in the process inserting popular culture into state political discourse. A song's ability to package and transport a sonic feeling is made in various stages. A musician establishes the authority to place words, beats, and melodies in listeners' ears by invoking origins and connections that imply previous success. This is done by controlling seemingly minor narrative devices that give potential listeners and promoters clues as to how to interpret the music. Humorous songs with vivid provocative images, easily repeatable phrases, and sexual or grotesque imagery are rapidly diffused, first via radio play and later digital file sharing, and then inserted in daily conversations, political talk, song remixes, and so on across social life. Circulation, travel, and movement are not only central tropes in songs but are crucial to the processes of musical production and the ways that musicians and producers struggle for success.

Sidney Ofori explains to me that he took the name Rap Ninja because of his lyrical dexterity. He later took the name Barima, a respectful term of address for a man. He was born in Accra, though his paternal hometown is Akwatia in the Eastern Region. He attended elite schools, including West African Secondary School in Adenta. While in school in the early 1990s, he began singing dance hall and raga and rapping—all in English. He was part of the first wave of artists to blend traditional imagery and African languages with hip-hop. Sidney started his musical career with NFL before forming Nananom with two schoolmates. He explains to me that Nananom refers to ancestors or elders, and they chose the name to show their respect for tradition.[13] According to Sidney, they popularized the growing trend of groups using traditional names. After recording "Agoro" (Play/Games), a track on Reggie's *Makaa Maka* album, their first album in 1998, *Nana Kasa* (The chief speaks), and their second album in 1999, *Nana Nono* (The chief is cool/Where it's at), reimagined the speaking authority of the chiefly court as hip and stylish, in line with artists like Obrafour. As cultural critic and academic Esi Sutherland-Addy argues, hiplife makes youths believe that "they have the right to speak in public whereas traditionally youth are supposed to sit down and show respect to their elders."[14] But Sidney's solo work took hiplife's formula a step further by actively seeking out controversy to find his audience. At the end of 2002 Sidney released his third solo album, *Scenti No!!* one of the biggest-selling hiplife records of its era (see figure 27).[15] The title track was the most popular song in Accra for many months and could be heard ubiquitously on radio, in nightclubs,

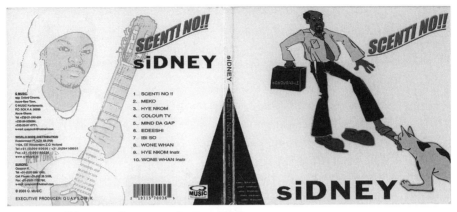

FIGURE 27 Sidney CD album cover for *Scenti No!!*

and drifting through the air of public spaces. The title means "the scent," bringing an English noun into an Akan grammatical construction.

The song is a humorous discussion of bodily smells and their underlying implications. In describing the song's intent, Sidney told me that one evening he was backstage at a performance and a band member commented that someone was sweating profusely after performing, exclaiming, "Scenti no!" The phrase struck Sidney as a great hook for a song, and he started to realize it was a socially important message. Sidney describes the song as a "hilarious and informative moral comment on sanitation and personal hygiene in line with the vice president's campaign on public indiscipline, pollution, and choked gutters."[16] In numerous public interviews and private discussions, he used this same formulaic description of the song's message to deflect criticism he later received about his intent as an artist and political commentator. The song begins with childish laughter and parodic official-sounding parade music, framing the song as explicitly humorous. The beat is simple and danceable within a contemporary highlife idiom.

> The scent, the scent
> Is everywhere
> When the honorable removes his shoes
> it's the socks
>
> Look, if I don't say it, who will?
> Controversial, first class
> We also hear it

Your armpit is full of boils
And yet you claim is pimples
Even the honorable black snail uses body spray
This is the modern world
No way
To remove your stinky shoes here, my God
All the kids in the 18 run away
You've bleached your skin and the scent
When you drink akpeteshie
And you don't paste the following day
The smell of delicious soup drives through
your nose when you pass by that house
The scent of a trotro mate's armpit
When the honorable removes his shoes
It's the socks[17]

The song's metalingual statement, "Look, if I don't say it, who will?" uses a first-person form of address to performatively call into being the young musician as a legitimate social and political critic. Hiplife in social circulation focuses listener attention on metalanguage about the possibilities of public speaking. In making direct moral critiques, the rapper claims authority as both animator and author of his words (Goffman 1981). This reflexive invocation of the right to critique contrasts with more oblique lines that string together a series of scenes of public smelliness as metaphoric commentary. The song describes daily activities that are humorously and embarrassingly haunted by bodily smells and public unseemliness. Graceful bodily comportment and control of public emotion are highly valued in Ghanaian societies (Yankah 1995). While cleanliness and containment of bodiliness are markers of modern life. Stinking feet are hidden beneath the respectability of shoes; drinking *akpeteshie* (local gin) is noticeable through bad breath; overreaching to collect money on a bus reveals smells; profuse sweating causes armpit boils; clandestine skin bleaching emerges beneath the facade of beauty. These activities make the body vulnerable to scrutiny in public. The song contrasts modern commodities, actions, and moralities—brushing teeth, using body spray, wearing proper shoes— with the uncontrolled bodiliness of local existence—drinking, sweating, desiring—and its dubious morality. Sidney pokes fun at people who do not take care of their bodies in proper modern ways by saying even the traditional snail uses body spray in the modern world of contemporary Ghana. The lyrics move across various realms of urban life from transportation to cooking to politics to hygiene, showing how corruption and immorality are insidiously rotting every social realm. The stinking body stands in for putridness of the social whole.

The song reflects the links in the Twi language between smell and orality that demonstrate a poetics of synesthesia. For example, the phrase "mati wO nka" means literally "I hear your smell" and is a common way to describe the sensory feeling of someone noticing a smell. It also points to the importance of hearing and speech in ordering and assessing the social world. The chorus of the song, "Scenti No a gye be bia" (The scent gets everywhere) imagines smells as physical markers that define how people experience space. The song maps out good and bad smells as the listener moves across the city. The humorous, proverb-like statement "Honorable apoofii koraa use spray" (The Honorable black snail uses body spray) pokes fun at those who do not understand modern hygiene habits that mask the unpleasant aspects of the body. The snail is considered a dirty animal. The insertion of references to animals to reflect various human traits and their movement between realms is familiar from Ananse storytelling and creates a critical narrative of a particularly Ghanaian modernity.

At their most titillating, the lyrics describe someone as "Honorable"—a term taken to refer to a member of parliament—who removes his shoes, revealing stinking socks. Government officials saw this reference as a disrespectful political attack and took action against the song. Though there are no direct references to corruption or politics, in public discussions, it was assumed that the song was a more or less indirect critique of political corruption. The album cover depicts a man wearing a tie and carrying a briefcase on which "honourable" is written (see figure 27). The man attempts to maintain his dignity as he struggles to pull his leg away from a large dog that has clenched its teeth onto one of his socks and is slowly pulling it off. The Honorable is mocked for public loss of control in revealing smelly socks beneath his respectable veneer.

"Scenti No" became the most popular song in Accra for many months. Young and old were singing it and quoting it, inserting its title into other conversations. Following older traditions of public rumor and proverbial talk, the title acted as a proverb in its detachability, potential to provide indirect and metaphoric commentary, and ability to quickly reference multiple registers in the song and in new contexts. The song's pithy vignettes led to many serious and frivolous public discussions on how the stench of armpits, socks, bad breath, and so on permeate daily life, and the unspoken serious implications of this truth, as insidious smells viscerally evoke hidden moral corruption.

In the market near Madina Old Road just north of Accra, I witnessed an example of how this song's title acted as a form of humorous citation, providing moral and personal critique cloaked in popular frivolity. A woman who looked to be educated and of some means was shopping for food. She was carefully selecting plantains, yams, and tomatoes. She began to argue with the market woman over what she saw as the inflated price of these items. As the woman moved past the point of normal bargaining and became irate, the trader became more obstinate and maintained her prices. The woman gave up and paid, though she almost flung the money at the market woman. She drew herself up, paused for effect looking at the gathered crowd, and intoned, "Hmmm! Scenti no!" She was met with laughter from the crowd and angry insults from the market woman as she turned her back and walked toward her car. Her quick reference to the song reframed her role in the interaction as that of a victim and a critic of moral corruption instead of one who failed to bargain successfully in the market.

Another example of the song's reuse shows the varied ways that moral belonging is linked to bodily comportment. People across ethnic groups and social status, across realms of everyday life in Accra, use the phrase "Scenti no" to point to transgressions of sexual, moral, or political boundaries. In Adenta, a sprawling suburb of Accra, there is a drinking spot in a small wooden shack attached to the outside of a compound house. On Sunday afternoons they serve special meals of fufu and goat light soup. One evening as the sun set, young men and a few women from the area strolled over to sit in small groups to chat and drink Coke, Fanta, Star beer, and Guinness. An old television and a radio competed from behind the counter with the sounds of evening prayers from the mosque down the block. A young man named Kwesi emerged from the house's gate dressed to go out to meet a woman for a date. He had put a lot of time into looking sharp and wore bright white basketball sneakers, baggy camouflage trousers, and an oversized Nigerian-made basketball jersey with a Los Angeles Lakers logo. Immediately he became the center of attention as well as the butt of jokes. His friend said,

Hey, wey you dey go, New York or Accra self?
My friend, this be Africa.
Why you dey dress like some American yoyo boy?

[Where do you think you're going . . .
You know you're in Africa, right?
Why dress like a trendy American?]

In the midst of this friendly teasing, someone shouted "Scenti no" and everyone fell about laughing. Someone else dramatically went up to him, pretended to smell his feet, and said, "Abong wa ha" (It smells/stinks here), provoking further laughter. Kwesi smiled and said, "You're just jealous of my look." He drank a Fanta Orange and then walked down the road to catch a tro-tro toward Accra.

"Abong wa ha" is a corrupted reference to a hit highlife song from 1998 by Daddy Lumba called "Aben Wo Ha," which literally means "It's cooked here" or "The food is ready." This song was popular because it was understood by most people as a metaphor for sex. The phrase "Aben wo ha" was heard all over Accra, usually in emphatic reference to something exciting. In several newspapers and radio call-in programs the ubiquitous saying was transformed into "Abong wa ha" (It stinks here) as a pithy reference to corporate and state corruption scandals in the news at the time. Kwesi's hip-hop style of dress provoked these comments, not because the other youths would not dress in such a manner, but rather because his flashiness stood out as a self-conscious expression of confidence drawing public attention to his means and ends, where he came from, and where he was going, literally and metaphorically. Difference produced suspicion expressed in parody. His style invoked a moral geography and an indirect conversation about the difference between New York and Accra. This quick scene, with its densely multivocal references, points to how the circulation of shared signs, even in agonistic ways, produces community affiliations. The song title foregrounds the transgressive aspects of seemingly mundane activities. When Kwesi was teased for dressing in hip-hop styles, by simply saying "Scenti no," the pleasure of word play acted as public moral critique. The joker invoked a moral geography within which a stylish modern look could easily reveal itself as a façade hiding private indiscretions. This popular phrase became shorthand in Accra for a set of broader conversations.

The combination of humor, indirect political commentary, and electronic circulation accelerates discussions of moral impropriety. Hiplife artists take on the role of social commentators or mischievous moral advisors. Literally dragging politicians by their socks into the realm of the everyday, this song makes profane the untouchable body of the politician (Mbembe 2001). The struggle to contain and reveal bodily excess is the medium of political critique. As Mbembe (2001) and others have shown, the prevalent links between vulgarity, consumption, and excess in postcolonial African politics represent an instability that lies just beneath the surface of spectacular displays of public control (Geschiere 1997; Bayart 1993; Bakhtin 1986; Elias 1978). Grotesque and humorous representations of the body in "Scenti No" invoke images of decay concealed behind public facades. These become critical engagements with embodied notions of morality, consumption, and containment across national and transnational spaces.

Bodily scents made urban life into a visceral map, bringing politicians out of the elite space of government and into an everyday realm. The notion of a virtuous citizen became the point of articulation for Ghanaians to examine politics in contentious ways. It also led the government to attempt to protect its citizens from exposure to the very same critiques. Several MPs who saw the song as offensive and profane brought it to the floor of parliament for discussion and tried to have it banned in a court of law. As Sidney put it, "The minister was even on television and in all the newspapers and wanted to take me to court but many Ghanaians defended me." This of course made the song even more popular. Surprisingly, President Kufuor took Sidney's side in defending the song. In fact, the president endorsed it in a speech he gave at the National Theatre and reinterpreted the metaphor of a smell spreading all over the country to refer to himself and how his political success had spread throughout the nation.

In mid-2004 President Kufuor's NPP party approached Sidney to buy the rights to "Scenti No" to use for the upcoming reelection campaign, to be held on December 7, 2004. The song became the centerpiece of a national television advertising campaign. Using the beat and the basic lyrical structure, they had another rapper redo the lyrics to focus on President Kufuor. With scenes of the president smiling at crowds, with campaign fervor, the new song played in the background:

The scent, the scent
President Kufuor is here
President Kufuor is here
The NPP is everywhere.
The scent of development is everywhere

After Kufuor's successful reelection some even said the song helped encourage the youth vote. As one political commentator said, "The song
implies that the president's scent is everywhere; that wherever you go
there is development, construction, and political progress. . . . Here
Ghana democracy is about making consensus." This revoicing linked
political progress to a supposedly "hip" urban aesthetic, recontextualizing the political critiques of the original song. The multiple levels of appropriation, however, made it difficult to discern sincerity from irony.

Because of the success of the government's campaign to reappropri-
ate a widely dispersed public critique of politics as a sign of moral unity
and political strength, the NDC opposition party decided to follow suit
and approached Sidney to buy the rights to another song, "Colour TV,"
on the same album. This song describes how the narrator sold his color
television and bought a black-and-white one. Sidney claims the song
was written about a lost love. The NDC was interested in the song because they saw the metaphor in political terms. To them, the lost color
television represented the nation's loss of former President Rawlings
of the NDC party and the black-and-white television reflected the impotence and absurdity of the NPP government. This, in fact, reflects a
controversy in June 2004 when the NPP government put black-and-
white photographs on Ghanaian voter registration cards. This caused a
huge public outcry and nostalgic editorials in the press about how conditions were better under Rawlings's regime. People around the country
were outraged. Reflecting how a seemingly small issue takes on great
symbolic value, one young voter remarked, upon returning home from
the registration station in suburban Accra, "This government must be
fooling. How can they issue these old-fashioned pictures? What is this, a
return to colo [colonial] days?" After the NDC approached Sidney with
an offer for the song, the NPP made him a counteroffer to prevent him
from selling the rights to the opposition. According to Sidney, the NDC
did in fact buy the song though it was never used in an advertisement.

As Sidney's relationship to political campaigning and his concerts
around West Africa under the rubric of UNESCO's anti–child soldier

initiatives demonstrate, popular culture has the attention of state and nonstate organizations in struggles over public opinion for the growing masses of urban youths across African cities. Institutional appropriations of hip-hop idioms have influenced policy and reshaped local and global understandings of Africanness. UNESCO in particular has funded many Ghanaian and Nigerian popular artists to play for anti–child soldier campaigns, clean water initiatives, and youth civic participation promotions in Liberia and Sierra Leone and around the subregion.

The circulation of "Scenti No" across various public and media spaces links daily urban life and conversation to the realms of politics and the possibilities for youths to gain a public voice. Sidney's recognition of what makes music circulate is tied to his personal business success and marketing savvy.[18] Indeed, Sidney studied for a marketing degree at International Professional School in Accra. Linking the logic of business marketing and branding with the circulatory aspects of Ghana's speech culture, he explained to me, "There are so many rappers out now that you have to compete. Now you need a new image; back in the day it was easy to talk about traditional things. You have to put some serious marketing into your songs. Use some lyrics Ghanaians will remember. Talk about daily life and the real environment people know about."[19] Word play, then, is not only about public critique and the pleasure of speaking but also about economic competition in the marketplace. The productive affinity between salesmanship and lyrical aesthetics marks hiplife as an ideal popular genre for privatizing Ghana.

In the circulation of "Scenti No," new public configurations and speaking positions are established. The song and its circulation reflect established patterns of Akan and West African political culture in which "the pattern of formal speech interaction involving surrogation and verbal mediation . . . underscores the search for consensus in the art of persuasion—the aim of the interaction [being] to engage the support of the audience" (Yankah 1995, 19–20). Proverbs, and easily detachable and mobile song lyrics, become indirect ways of discussing moral, political, and philosophical issues and of attempting to reach agreement. One rapper explained to me his view of why songs tell such oblique stories rather than addressing moral and political issues directly: "Ghanaians don't like to insult someone directly, but spread rumors, talk about them. Then smile to their face. They don't like conflict . . . so we make jokes instead." The ambiguity and "semantic indefiniteness" of proverbial speech provide comfort through indirection, although they become points of public contestation (Yankah 1995, 42). In debate, community affiliation is forged through disagreement over meaning. Many songs following "Scenti No" provide a repeatable and detachable proverbial hook connected to a humorous moral story. Audiences, publics, and other performers pick up the phrase to indirectly point to previous arguments and imagine new social stances.

In the lead-up to the 2004 presidential elections, "Scenti No" was reframed, transforming from a proverb-like joke that served as a metaphor for the malodorous spreading of state corruption to a campaign ad praising the virtues of President Kufuor's NPP spreading across the nation. The NPP recognized the power of popular expression, public circulation, and joking. Rejecting earlier state discomfort with critical voices, they appropriated the idea of free expression itself, parodying themselves by co-opting a song critical of politics. Whereas in 2000 the state was uncertain how to handle private media such as call-in radio and informal critical discourse, by 2004 political parties were cognizant of the need to incorporate public sentiment into representations of politics and tuned in to the links between the political body and market tastes.[20]

Conclusion: Humor and Circulation

With hiplife's maturation as a genre, parody initiates popularity of song lyrics as well as various recontextualizations of songs. Bawdy phrases provoke talk about appropriate and inappropriate behavior, in the process focusing public attention on aspiration and desire. Parodies reveal tensions by inverting the expected relationships of inside and outside, bodiliness and control. Effective hiplife songs are often driven by ambiguous, titillating phrases that are taken as metaphors for taboo subjects. Parody emphasizes the reflexive aspects of style and communication and point to questions about value transformations: how audiences assess the elegance of words, who has the authority to levy criticism, how notoriety accrues to those who drive oral circulation, and what economic potential comes from this fame. Many songs follow this formula. Rappers claim speaking authority through self-proclamation, while they defer authorship and intent by crafting imagined characters and ambiguous stories with humorous overtones. This logic facilitates recirculation of and elaboration on titillating phrases. Through lengthening chains of reference, animators defer responsibility for critical words while claiming the growing public relevance of speaking. As circulations speed up, critiques proliferate in new contexts.

Hiplife relies on a logic where electronic technologies and dispersed affiliations elaborate upon older oral forms of Ghanaian proverbial speech culture. Old formulas for public circulation of proverbial speech that rely on humor and parody proliferate across multiple media as the market elevates notions of personal taste into styles that shape public life more generally. The sincerity that permeates discourses of privacy and individual consumption at the core of the new liberalized state provoke Ghanaians to pry at this public facade to see what lies underneath. With a sort of fractal logic, musicians can successfully poke fun at public control and use this parody as a form of value and control itself. Parody as a style of transformation relies upon stories of inversion: public-private, inside-outside. Parody requires elegant, precise language usage that plays with the line between respect and innuendo. Virtues like precision, respectfulness, and indirection all rely upon bodily and linguistic control and a performer's skillful manipulation of the appearance of intent. Bodily smells are out of control. They betray intents, revealing inherent bodily immoralities. The pervasiveness of bad smells is both subtle and uncontrollable; it is not an overt violent gesture. The metaphor points to what Munn calls a negative form of value transformation, which is nonagentive, undermining the public control of those aspiring to modern life, who are betrayed by the locality of their bodies. Skillful speakers, politicians, and businesspeople gain success through control of their words that then extends their influence into the world at large. Artists like Sidney become famous through music that is widely circulated. Warnings about embarrassment reveal the genuine threat of public shaming to someone's reputation. Ghanaian audiences are careful observers of style and of little flaws in public figures' presentation.

A politician's ability to manipulate public morality and a musician's ability to comment on it performatively delineate the shifting boundaries of modern Ghanaian life. By making fun of excess and hidden indiscretions that threaten to reveal success as a superficial façade, lyricists and public commentators provide a reflexive language to critically engage with the changing nature of public power (Mbembe 2001; Bayart 1993). Representations of the consumption of sex, food, and money are salient in drawing the line between public and private acts, a line crucial to the liberal citizen-subject. Individuated bodily consumption becomes the terrain upon which Ghanaians debate dichotomies of public-private morality at the center of the emerging neoliberal national public.

CHAPTER 6

Gendering Value for a Female Hiplife Star

MORAL VIOLENCE AS PERFORMANCE TECHNOLOGY

As she left the stage at the end of a hiplife concert in the city of Kumasi, famed female rapper Mzbel was groped and pulled into the crowd by rowdy students. Popular sentiment after the event sponsored by the Kwame Nkrumah University of Science and Technology (KNUST) on October 1, 2005, claimed the well-known artist provoked the audience's frenzy with her sexualized performance. Mzbel defended herself in a radio interview, stating, "I cannot be blamed for my own assault."[1] Refusing to be intimidated over ensuing months, she continued, as another rapper said to me, "wiggling her waist in skimpy skirts." One year later, on September 12, 2006, armed robbers broke into Mzbel's home in New Gbawe on the outskirts of Accra, sexually assaulting her and one of her dancers and stealing a cache of American dollars, clothes, and electronic equipment. Following this robbery and assault, a media frenzy ensued in Ghana and among Ghanaians in America and Europe through radio call-in programs, Internet blogs, newspaper articles, and online postings. Accusations flew, with speculation that the attack was an inside job committed for personal revenge on the artist. Others thought the motive was jealousy at her success. Some argued that she was asking for trouble by unapologetically dressing in sexually revealing clothes and using provocative stage displays. Some said that she deserved to be raped for acting in sexual ways and not heeding the warnings of the earlier onstage attack. In the language of public discipline, one Internet posting proclaimed, "She has not behaved like an African woman. This will teach her a lesson!" Others were appalled at the violent events and called for the criminals to be punished. This sentiment was often posed in terms of fame and gender, asking, "How would you feel if she were your sister, girlfriend, or mother?" An entertainment journalist lamented, "Is she paying . . . the price of fame . . . ? She knows what her fans like and she steps up her game by giving them more of what they want. If she deserved to be attacked because of her talents then it is very alarming."[2]

Strikingly, these attacks inverted the narrative of her hit song "16 Years," which portrays a young, sexually provocative girl who is chased by an older man. In the song's video the man is ridiculed and brought to court. After the real attack on Mzbel, the public seemed more concerned with her moral culpability than that of the perpetrators. In 2007 an exuberant Ghanaian entertainment story described Mzbel as "the most sought after female Ghanaian musician in the world," contrasting with the view of many who see her lyrics and dance styles as too transgressive for public presentation by a respectable African lady.[3]

Of course, public disciplinary violence against women and criticism of female pop artists for being provocative are neither new nor unique to this context. But this violence is somewhat surprising to local and foreign observers because women in Ghana do not appear to face fierce public inequality as in many locales around the world. In this case, sexualized violence was justified in collective, moral terms. While this sort of public attack is unusual in Ghana, it points to other episodes in which successful female entrepreneurs have been punished for social-moral decay during moments of economic transition. Most notably, after Rawlings's first coup in 1979, his AFRC government stripped market women naked and publicly whipped them in punishment for hoarding commodities and acting immorally at the expense of the nation. These exceptional cases reveal how gender organizes local understandings of moral and economic value. In examining hiplife's social significance, Mzbel's example raises a number of questions: How is entrepreneurship a gendered concept? How can a Ghanaian woman be both modern and moral, financially successful and socially respectable? Do anxieties about female aspiration and agency—rather than sexuality per se—set the conditions for her attacks?

The musical success of and subsequent violence against Mzbel is not primarily a question of sexuality but rather of the gendering of speaking authority (Gal 1990; Hill 1987). While blaming a woman's moral failings for sexualized violence against her is common in many locales, this case shows how gender defines the limits of popular public morality in Ghana's transition to privatization. I argue that the transformation of aesthetic value into speaking authority and fame for hiplife musicians is predicated upon representing women as objects of consumption and exchange. Male artists claim agency by critiquing women for the ways they manage the transitions between modern and traditional life. A female performer self-consciously wielding her sexuality, then, provokes anxieties around how an autonomous subject looks and how she controls value and meaning under free-market conditions. The attacks on Mzbel transform negative value. That is to say, they are disciplinary inversions of how young male artists seek fame and fortune by spreading their words across social space.

Mzbel was the second successful female hiplife artist. Most women in Ghanaian music sing gospel.[4] Hiplife's first female star, Dorcas Opoku Dakwa, performed as Abrewa Nana (a wise old woman's granddaughter). Her stage name is a reference to the notion that women are bastions of traditional wisdom. It recalls for audiences an idea that female wisdom comes from the domestic sphere and is not expressed directly. As scholar Esi Sutherland-Addy notes, "When male elders in a chief's court, for example, cannot find a solution to a problem they would consult an old woman who in the house or market actually is the wisest and most knowledgeable."[5] Abrewa Nana's first two albums, *Sagoa* in 2000 and *African Girl* in 2002, provided a mix of ragga-inflected rap, melodic vocals, and clean electronic reggae-influenced dance beats (see figures 28 and 29). She has a strong stage presence, de-emphasizing female sexuality by wearing baggy outfits, loose dresses, jeans, leather jackets, kangol caps, and so on. Her husky vocal delivery and subtle dance steps convey toughness and understated confidence. Abrewa Nana appropriates the forms of speaking ushered in by male hiplife artists, in contrast to Mzbel's sexually provocative style. Her lyrics de-emphasize her sexuality and she did not receive the kinds of public criticism that fueled Mzbel's problems.[6]

Women in Asante, and across Ghana, have been central to the development of trade routes and a market economy since at least the early twentieth century (Allman and Tashjian 2000; Clark 1994).[7] Women not only have maintained economic autonomy in the domestic sphere but have been innovators in the development of West Africa's market

FIGURE 28 Abrewa Nana cassette album cover.

trade networks (Guyer 2004; Allman and Tashjian 2000). However, women's economic success was often met with suspicion before and after independence. Indeed, in a variety of colonial and postcolonial contexts around the globe, women's economic and sexual autonomy has been seen as a challenge to economic-juridical orders (Povinelli 2002).[8] Neoliberalism's removal of local political autonomy raises anxieties about masculine economic control.[9] Female entrepreneurship is at times seen as a threat to social order, as the sexualized female body becomes a fetish of social control.[10] Violent responses to female sexuality—as metaphoric of female agency—show how women are often seen as the bearers of tradition and all that it represents. Critiques about public female sexuality are, in fact, gendered judgments of public speaking authority and individual economic accumulation.

Mzbel's provocative performances and the violent, ambivalent reactions to them become ways that publics contest moral norms. As hiplife's technological platforms evolve, radio call-in programs, digital music files, televised music videos, and Internet conversations mediate participants' relationships to competing national and transnational moral communities. Through these circulatory technologies individuals are recognized, misapprehended, and disciplined. Female sexuality

FIGURE 29
Abrewa Nana
showing off
advertisement
for a show.
Photograph by
the author.

provides a set of institutional relations that point in one direction to a visual language of liberal individualism and in the other to the constraints of traditionalized notions of moral discipline.

Mzbel's attacks occurred in the context of public anxiety about disorder and violence in Accra. Anxieties about rising crime correlate with state privatization that for some equate freedom with moral indiscipline and discourses of cultural loss (Comaroff and Comaroff 2006). Figurations of the entrepreneur and the artist, the hustler and the innovator, overlap in popular debate about the meaning of violence and, as Mzbel's case shows, are highly gendered. Moral ambivalence toward women's agency fixates on their perceived susceptibility to foreign influence. Debates about female fashion and sexuality repolarize public imaginaries of traditionalized and modern realms while simultaneously despatializing these notions. Hiplife ignites debates in which the language of moral authenticity blurs with discussions of economic entrepreneurship. Sexual sovereignty implies the ways that ideologies of entrepreneurship and self-expression rely upon a masculine subject as the agent of liberal freedom. Male sexual desire is translated into notions of accumulation and consumption. Female sexualized ambition, on the other hand, marks the contradictions of this confluence and in some measure shapes current transformations of public life.

Contradictions between images of success and lack of work opportunities are reflected in growing moral ambivalence to women as active producers of value rather than signs of it. Sexualized violence against Mzbel raises questions about the gendered nature of public life and how ideas of traditional African womanhood are mobilized during a time when autonomous individual expression is celebrated. Transformations of aesthetic value into economic value rely upon a highly gendered idea of public speaking. Female attempts to claim public authority show the limits of how words circulate and translate across social realms.

As discussed, the circulation of controversy is central to how hiplife music permeates public life. The case of Mzbel shows how urban circulations are integrated through rising digital technologies, connecting various parts of the nation to a transnational Ghanaian moral public. In other words, overlapping conversations facilitated by radio, mobile phone, and Internet media magnify moral disjunctures that link urban Ghana with broader Ghanaian publics abroad. Ironically this dispersed public coalesces around divisive moral ambivalence toward public female speaking authority expressed in terms of sexuality. Sexualized violence against a popular female singer shows the limits of gendered agency under conditions of liberalization. Women are often blamed for instability in moments of economic transition. Hiplife reinvents traditional proverbial oratory to challenge older ideas of acceptable youth behavior in the language of individual ambition. But ambivalence toward a female artist reveals the gendering of this reinvention. Mzbel's sexualized persona, and the public violence that it seems to justify, align older forms of gendered moral authority with a highly performative notion of individuated free-market value production. The physical and discursive attacks on Mzbel reflect the entrenchment of gendered forms of structural inequality in the name of liberalization and individual freedom and raise questions about how women can inhabit the role of self-fashioning subject.

Female Bodies and Public Moral Judgment

Humorous warnings to men about the dangers of female sexuality, and to women about being too provocative, are often central themes in hiplife lyrics. Controlling female sexual circulation is crucial to musical and bodily aesthetics and to the making of economic value. Some songs provide morally polarizing stories that make fun of women for acting in ways deemed un-African. Others demonstrate artists' ability to attract and consume women through their verbal skills in talking to or "rapping" a woman, as in "me ma no raps" (I gave her some raps). Shifting between titillating critiques of public sexuality and flirtatious praise for proper Ghanaian inner core values, hiplife songs often focus on women as objects that mark value. Women are symbols of success. Lyrical hooks provide metaphors and innuendo for a community of listeners to reflect on morality. In hiplife's iconography, women are objects of male desire whose presence indicates male success. Female bodies become barometers of control and transformation. Changes to a female body stand in for transformations of the broader social body and are taken to be matters of public concern rather than private taste. Personal style and audacious speaking practices have the potential to transform a young boy into a successful man. Numerous songs are predicated on women as the objects of their stories that reveal moral truths about men; they are meant to be markers of success, consumed for male pleasure or, conversely, potential threats to value accumulation. They are not supposed to be tellers of tales.

Tic Tac's 2000 hit "Philomena" pokes fun at a woman for improper grooming. The song teases a woman named Philomena for having too much hair under her arms and between her legs and for adopting habits that are deemed disgusting and indicate moral degradation.

Philomena, there is some [hair] here and here and here, oooh![11]

The sung chorus is accompanied by the rapper pointing to his underarms and crotch and then throwing his arms up for emphasis, saying, "Ooooh!" It became a common joke, repeated all over town in reference to many things relating to sexuality, impropriety, bodily disgust, and the transgression of boundaries. The embarrassment of revealing bodily secrets in public drives this song's message about personal control and self-image. It became a coded way for young men to critically address anxieties about female sexual agency, uncleanness, and moral impropriety and the adoption of "foreign" habits by women. For more conservative elements in society, this song demonstrated the moral absurdity of hiplife. The coded nature of the chorus—humorously indicating, rather than directly naming, the hair or the part of the body being discussed—uses innuendo as social commentary. While the meaning of the song was widely understood in this vein, its humorous ambiguity muted the dangerous force of these public verbal communications. This song's examination of female bodily impropriety as foreign style reflects a key preoccupation of hiplife. From the perspective of religious and government critics, songs such as this show the profanity, moral degradation, and foreign pollution of hiplife and the younger generation (Collins 2012). However, from the perspective of many youths, these songs are themselves critiques of foreign moral behavior.

Sidney's 2002 hit "Abuskeleke" also critiques female bodies but is framed as a humorous warning to young men to avoid the distractions of young women. The catchy song title quickly became a catchphrase shouted at women around town as moral criticism for wearing revealing clothing. In the proverb-like oral circulation of this song, male consumption is metaphorically linked to business investment and personal success. This song helped establish the relatively new musical genre of hiplife within the realm of public banter in which the threat of female seduction provides the moral counterpoint to youth agency. The song describes women as threats to male progress. In informal public spaces such as markets and bus stations, trendy styles and reflexive discussions of them become crucial aspects of how moral value is contested. Fragmenting and circulating songs humorously critique female agency by transforming styles into signs of social order and disorder.

Interviewing Accra traders in 2002 about gospel, highlife, and hiplife music provided examples of how this type of song is relevant to making and policing a gendered public.[12] Tema Station is a main tro-tro (minibus) and taxi station abutting one of the largest markets in central Accra. Like transportation centers across Africa, this taxi depot is a bustling center for trade and gossip as people move around the city and on long journeys to more remote locations (Kapchan 1996; Clark 1994). Ga, Twi, and Fante mix with Hausa, Ewe, Pidgin, and English languages in a sonic pastiche familiar across Accra's public spaces. Drivers and their mates, passengers, out-of-work men, wandering youths, and workers congregate in the flux of daily life. Girls carrying trays of water sachets, oranges, or chewing sticks call to people as they get into their cars. Shoeshine boys wander between the buses and vans looking for customers. Men gamble and relax in the shade of kiosks. Women display baskets of foodstuffs, tomatoes, yams, and plantains outside of the gates of the lorry park with increasing density along the sides of the roads approaching Makola, one of the main markets in the city. Music plays from cassette and video sellers, newspaper stands, and taxis, mixing in the air with conversation, gossip, bargaining, and shouting drivers' mates calling passengers to various destinations.

Kwame, Adjei, Kudjoe, and Patience are between fifteen and seventeen years of age and are native Akan speakers. Kwame and Patience sell handkerchiefs, baseball hats, socks, and undershirts, all hanging loosely from the edges of several umbrellas where they sit. Adjei sells coconuts from a wheelbarrow, and Kudjoe makes change for people, giving 800 cedis in coins for every 1,000-cedi note he receives.[13] They speak little English and all left school during primary school. The boys often dress in oversized shirts and baggy trousers, basketball and urban sports fashions, and the girls wear tight tops and jeans. Vendors walk through the markets and transportation stations laden with hangers full of secondhand clothes and Nigerian- and Chinese-made knockoffs emblazoned with the names of well-known American artists like Eminem and 50 Cent and designer labels like Nike and FUBU.

When I ask these teenagers what they think of hip-hop, Kwame's response shows the significance of African American life to Ghanaian popular imaginations. He says, "Mepe Omo yoyo life no." (I like their yoyo life.) He explains that "yoyo life" refers to black American lifestyles, fashion, and flashy mobile phones. "You know they are cool." Amid busy commuters and shoppers at Tema station, we discuss the latest in hiplife. As a young woman walks slowly past us wearing particularly tight jeans and a tank top and stylish sunglasses, one of the boys watches her, turns back to us, and, smiling, chuckles "Abuskeleke." Everyone laughs in agreement. Sidney's new song had become wildly popular that year and had, over a matter of months, become a term of everyday usage. The major form of circulation for "Abuskeleke" was through radio and club play. It then proliferated by informal oral means. People of all social standings throughout urban centers began invoking the song title in reference to women dressed in Westernized and sexually revealing fashions. By inserting the term into another speech context, a speaker invokes a moral position critical of female temptation.

The song describes women who dress provocatively and use sexuality to get what they need. Musically, it is built around a danceable highlife rhythm and melodic backup singers. Sidney begins by stating the proverb-like title and its meaning: "Abuskeleke, when the money finishes, she is still there." Two verses then expand on this theme:

I will pour it on you, love
What is money, I need your love
I will give you something you haven't seen, Boahema
Abuskeleke, money finishes before I'm full
Happiness is in the pocket, so let
money speak for you, women are
devils, they will just dance in your
face to get your attention
Abuskeleke, money finishes, but she is still there[14]

The song offers a twist on older metaphors of power through consumption (Bayart 1993). In line with common interpretations of "Abuskeleke," several of the boys explain that this song is a moral lesson for men. It is a warning that men should not chase women and spend all their time and money looking for pleasure and momentary sexual gratification. The chorus warns men that eventually money will run out, but there will always be more women to chase. The most provocative images in the song's video intercut a man turning out his empty pockets, a sexually dressed woman pouting and fanning herself with dollars, Sidney lying on a bed alone holding his head with money scattered around him, and stylish women dancing while men shout the song title at them. Women will use their sexuality to get what they want, leaving men unable to maintain themselves. The song calls for discipline in the face of feminized temptation. Moral ambivalence drives discourse surrounding the song in that it celebrates the very practices it denounces. Its meaning is not fixed, but in circulation it becomes a point for talk and debate, relying on a poetics of moral ambiguity to provoke audiences (Anyidoho 1983). "Abuskeleke" calls forth a moral nationhood revolving around moral choices and female bodies. Individual desires are never satisfied and you can easily spend your life chasing their unattainable satiation. Men, as agentive individuals who control value, should be wary of women, as objects for consumption, who represent the ephemeral nature of success and threaten to take control of the production of both material and symbolic value. The sexualized female body becomes a fetish, threatening male economic accumulation and moral good. However, female sexuality is simultaneously a celebration of self-fashioning, style, and the freedom that hiplife and its African American referents prescribe for urban life.

Rumors around origins of the word "abuskeleke" show that controlling authenticity is often at the root of verbal authority. A number of youths told me that "abuskeleke" is a little-known "traditional" Akan word referring to a woman's buttocks. It was further explained that the song originated when Sidney overheard the term in a market in Kumasi when an older market woman used it to criticize a younger woman displaying her body in public. He realized it would make a good song. This origin story shows a cultural logic in which traditional knowledge legitimizes gendered criticism of consumption and morality.

When I later talked to Sidney about this song, he explained that he was in a bar in Takoradi near the border with Ivory Coast and met some Ivorian guys who used the term "abuskeleke" to tease a woman nearby. They told him the meaning of the Ivorian word and he decided to use it. According to Sidney, the term, then, was not Ghanaian at all, and its genealogy remains uncertain. He explained the meaning of the song in terms of economic and moral transaction, using the language of investment to frame sexual desire: "The song is all about good investment; about how to spend money wisely. It is also advising the men about their character. It is a story about a battle of the sexes. The man thinks he can use money to get whatever he wants. He can buy drink and women and whatever he desires. He is not in love but is just chasing women for fun. The woman replies, that you can bring all your money and it will eventually run out but she will still be here."[15] As with much hiplife, the song's critiques are framed with humor and celebrations of the sexual temptation of which it warns.

The song's popularity and sexual and moral references quickly attracted public controversy, with many conservative politicians and religious leaders calling its lyrics inappropriate and profane. The minister of tourism and the MP from Nkawkaw asked parliament to ban the song for profanity and for promoting public conflicts between men and women. The attempt to ban the song was unsuccessful. But Charter House, the private media company running the Ghana Music Awards, was encouraged not to nominate the song for any awards. The effect of controversy was, as in other cases, to increase the song's popularity.[16]

Songs like "Abuskeleke" provide a reflexive language through which Ghanaians consider the possibilities for individual success and the dangers of desire. The potential of female agency is circumscribed within masculine desire. As public cries of "abuskeleke" aimed at scantily clad young women became common in buses, streets, college campuses, and markets across urban Ghana, women began to reply to street-corner critics by stating with poise and disdain, "I'm aware" (meaning that they did it on purpose). This direct reply was often taken with shock, amusement, and, significantly, male silence, as this female response was based upon claiming intentionality and inverting the innuendo. This statement is understood as a declamation of sexual, and by extension public, agency by young women. By claiming intentionality in doing the things they are criticized for, women appropriate and recontextualize critiques. Thong underwear and tight garments came to be called "abuskeleke" as a noun, as in the phrase, "I am going to wear my abuskeleke." Several hiplife artists subsequently released songs addressing the phrase "I'm aware" as an inappropriate declaration of femininity. For example, in 2005, TH4 Qwages song entitled "I'm Aware," on their album *Wongye* (You can't get what I have) ridiculed young girls as unprincipled for showing off and for their self-conscious acceptance of "foreign" values over Ghanaian principles of modesty.

"Abuskeleke" invokes a speech community through divisive moral debate. Fashion becomes the language of both individuated expression and disciplinary conformity with each side claiming the other is being "un-African" (see figure 30). Declaring "I'm Aware" is a reflexive acknowledgment of female intentionality through fashion and all it implies. Being "aware" means that one is not only conscious but reflexively conscious. It is a strategy to claim the right to name an activity and the ability of a performer to direct the terms of performance. This proclamation points to female dress as an explicitly performative way to claim public recognition (Agha 2005b). The moral ambiguity ascribed to female practice is tied to how authority is appropriated and reclaimed within specific urban contexts.

This song shows that music's circulation relies upon the ambiguity of dual meanings, manifest in face-to-face communications and driven by radio and digital mediation. Aspiration appears to Ghanaians, not in relation to national progress, but in terms of individuated masculine consumption of feminized value as it appears in personal interactions and informal spaces. Style as agency reinvents a classic gendered op-

FIGURE 30 Fans at a hiplife show. Photograph by Ayana V. Jackson.

position where the containment of female sexuality produces the ideal of a masculine public subject. But overconsumption or the impossibility of control and containment threatens to overwhelm masculine self-fashioning, and so becomes subject to warning and ridicule. As Mzbel's case demonstrates, gendered consumption defines the parameters of individual success.

Digitizing Moral Ambivalence: Mzbel and the Business of Hiplife

Mzbel's fame called into question hiplife's focus on the objectification of female sexuality, raising questions about the potential and threat of female sexual and economic agency. In the late 1990s after completing secondary school, Belinda Nana Ekua Amoah, known as Mzbel, began working at state and private radio and television stations producing youth entertainment programs and advertising. While an assistant producer at Hush Hush Studios, she wrote and recorded several tracks that attracted attention, releasing as her first album *Awoso Me* (Shake me). Hammer, who made the beats for a number of her tracks, recalls, "She was always quiet and respectful in public." He remembers her public image evolving. "There was a need for more sex appeal in hiplife music to help the industry grow. Especially because there were so few women onstage. . . . She could be marketed as a sexy and strong role model for young girls; be like the Lil' Kim of Ghana," he said, comparing her to the controversial American rapper known for provocative expressions of female pleasure.

The title track of Mzbel's breakthrough second album, "16 Years," was one of the biggest songs of 2005–2006. The lyrics describe an older man who pursues a sixteen-year-old girl. Sung from the perspective of the girl discovering herself as a sexual being, the song emphasizes the girl's playful exploration of styles of dress and the public display of her body. The older man is portrayed as a predator. The girl encourages him to look at her but not touch. The song's provocative, irreverent imagery drove the artist's popularity, as it entered into daily conversations about style and urban life. It introduced Mzbel to the public as a controversial persona and foreshadowed later accusations of immorality and valorizations of her bold self-expression. While she was vilified by conservative critics for promulgating foreign styles, she was celebrated by some female fans for her determined self-expression. According to one young female fan, Mzbel is a "good moral role model for young girls. . . . She shows girls that they can strive to be stars, and can be anything they want to be, and make something of themselves." Reggie's manager Paa K recalls that the intended meaning of the song differs greatly from how most people interpret it. "'16 Years' makes a statement about underage sex and the molestation of young girls. Most people who listen to hiplife music don't listen to the lyrics. . . . They hear the chorus and make their own interpretations."[17]

Mzbel uses a mixture of simple Akan and Pidgin English. The informal lyricism reflects her background growing up in urban Accra, drawing on informal code switching and urban conversational genres.

> I be sixteen years, I be this way oh.
> If you touch my thing I go tell mommy, oh.

According to Reggie Rockstone, the song is "a moral warning for men to leave small girls alone." This song affirms the right of "women to wear whatever sexy clothes they like without being harassed."[18] Mzbel's verbal directness and informality entail a critique of the gendered nature of formal Ghanaian public speaking, which values elegant indirectness (Anyidoho 1994). In particular, young women do not often "have the right to speak in public."[19]

The song's music video received a lot of attention on television in Ghana, but Internet traffic is increasingly determining hiplife's trends. Mzbel's song received a lot of traffic when it was posted on the popular entertainment site Ghanamusic.com. Founded in 2001, this Web site became the premiere online site for Ghanaian music and entertainment. Ghanamusic.com not only reports on entertainment but its influence helps determine which musicians become stars. It is used both by people in Ghana as well as those around the world interested in the latest music and style trends in Ghanaian music. It maintains an extensive online catalogue of videos, stories, profiles, and event exclusives.

The "16 Years" video begins with Mzbel applying lipstick in her bedroom mirror. She puts on a miniskirt and white leather knee-high boots. The camera cuts to her strutting with confidence through the streets of Accra followed by confident female dancers. The images emphasize expensive accessories like mobile phones, sunglasses, and purses in the making of the modern girl as she comes to sexual adulthood and moves across the urban landscape. Castro, a male hiplife rapper, makes a cameo on the track, flirtatiously dancing with Mzbel on a basketball court. His rap verse warns men not to be tempted as she is too young. Locations like a new petrol station and basketball court portray Accra as a modern space for carefree girls to navigate freely. Mzbel is comically pursued by a heavy-set middle-aged man. He tempts her to ride in his new truck and tries to seduce her. She pushes him away in mock outrage. He is taken to a law court where Mzbel sings from the stand while he sits helplessly in handcuffs as the crowd in the courtroom jeers at him and the parents of the young girl point accusingly. The video cuts between two narrative progressions: the courtroom trial of the old man and the playful and seemingly unknowing sexual movements of the young girl and her friends around the city. The girls appear overtly seductive but unaware they are cultivating male pursuit. They are portrayed as having the right to self-expression, implying that they are dressing for themselves and not to seduce men. But to the old man, the girls are intentionally seductive. In the chorus Mzbel repeatedly implores her attacker to leave her alone.

Bra Laryea make you no do me so,
Bra Laryea make you no mess me up.

A jeering crowd in the law court insults the old man for his immoral behavior. It represents the shaming communal justice of Ghanaian society against taboo actions like sex with young girls. The alternating narrations in the video point to public debates about morality and publicity that have been central to hiplife's first decade, which intensified in gendered terms after Mzbel's appearance on the scene. The lyrics imply that the girl is pure, but, at the same time, she cultivates attention. "I be innocent," she emphatically proclaims as she pouts and sucks on a lollypop. In the video, the law court and state protect free self-expression for the young girl while the old man is unable to contain his desires. However, in the real violence against Mzbel, she was the one being shamed for being morally uncontained. Public female sexuality is the point of articulation for notions of communal social containment and individuated desire as Ghanaians consider what constitutes modern life. As both "16 Years" and "Abuskeleke" show, the disciplining of female sexuality and the control of male desire mark anxieties about progress and autonomy. Mzbel focuses on the relationship between seeing and being seen in negotiating the moral rights and obligations entailed in daily life. The lyrics proclaim,

> Look at my jeans and skirt, I am free, I'm aware
> Brother, look at my buttocks and my chest
> This is like a television you know
> Check me out but don't be silly[20]

The song and its video emphasize that being seen is an important aspect of public femaleness and that woman have a right to dress to display their bodies without giving an invitation to engage in sexual activities. The female body is made analogous to a television in its visibility: both mediating pleasure and desire and an object of desire in itself. Here the female body controls public space by channeling male desire, reconfiguring women's obligations to be objects of masculine consumption. By infantilizing her sexuality, Mzbel appropriates the dangerous taboo of sexualized children, playing on the ubiquity of this fantasy. It is this moral ambiguity that makes the song so provocative. She is simultaneously and self-consciously celebrating (saying, "I'm aware") and condemning the consumption of female sexuality. Public critiques emerge as she claims female agency through these oppositional fantasies.

This duality reflects how gender and class intersect with ideas of culture for non-elite Ghanaians. While sitting with friends on the veranda of a drinking spot and supermarket I frequent, Mzbel's video comes on the television on a Ghana Television music-video show. The proprietor, Comfort, shakes her head. "That girl does not know how to dance properly! Look at her shaking all over the place." Comfort is a twenty-seven-year-old seamstress and foodstuffs trader and also a member of a cultural dance troupe.[21] Her assistant and several patrons watch television in the shade of her awning, chatting and drinking on a slow afternoon. Comfort's critique of Mzbel's dance skills reflects the local importance of bodily precision to discourses of public respect. Watching the video, she also reflects on a common belief that elite consumption of foreign popular culture is eroding sexual mores and cultural knowledge. "People don't grow up in the village now in the traditional way; everyone is in the cities or overseas. Now you can't just put a cloth on or beads and come outside. Now the boys and girls are looking at [new] styles and are attracted to them. . . . The people who have been to school, [and] their families have money—they don't care about traditional culture and language. They think they know about the world. They have book learning but they don't have wisdom. They just follow foreign styles without thinking about what things mean. The traditional people, the workers who have not been to school, they like these styles, but they also have a deep understanding . . . of the [traditional] African ways of doing things, of understanding through proverbs. So we are not as fooled by foreign ways."

From the perspective of Accra's underclass, elites are further removed from traditional life. "Culture" can stand in for both morally correct, traditional values and for negative, backward ignorance. Displays of foreign, disrespectful dress and uncontrolled bodily movements are at the center of these concerns. At the same time, poor workers desire the wealth and mobility new styles connote. Young traders at Tema station talk of admiring American "yoyo life," though at the same time they are ambivalent about changing gender roles. While elites consume desired "modern" products, they are criticized for not being "African" enough. This seamstress's comments demonstrate a strand of public discourse marked by lament and the desire for retraditionalization. Young urban women are caught in the tensions as traditional respectability and modern forms of (sexual) expression become moral polarities (Mbembe 2001).

Discerning fans, particularly young women, ascribe to Mzbel's song a moral critique of male sexual predation. For many audiences, however, the sight of a petite young woman such as Mzbel dressed in scanty clothes overwhelms this critique, evoking anxiety, anger, and desire. Hiplife music and fashion entail reflexive debates about meaning and misinterpretation as they circulate through urban spaces and technological media. Public female dress and sexual expression are metonyms for the threat of female economic agency to both "traditional" culture and hypermasculine hip-hop-inspired entrepreneurship.

Mzbel follows a similar formula as her male colleagues, like Sidney and Tic Tac, in garnering fame by making sexually provocative music that circulates widely. She is talented at assessing audience tastes and embodies the musical and marketing skills of an artistic entrepreneur. "16 Years" tantalizes fans by glamorizing the visual display of sexualized young girls while simultaneously condemning male sexual predation. As the video and song gain popularity among Ghanaian audiences, the increasingly rapid interplay between urban face-to-face and electronically mediated publics seems to magnify the moral tension of the song. But while hiplife success requires entrepreneurial skills, its symbolic logic relies upon the objectification of female sexuality. The free-speaking rapper-entrepreneur is posited as a male-consuming individual. Entrepreneurship is masculinized, predicated on the consumption of female value, while at the same time threatened by it. When Mzbel tries to appropriate this logic through an "I'm aware" aesthetic, she threatens dominant masculine circuits of value circulation.

Public Shaming and the Violence of Recognition

In the "Fact-Finding Committee's Report on the Alleged Manhandling and/or Harassment of the Hip-Life Artiste, Nana Akua Amoah (a.k.a. Mzbel)," University officials in Kumasi moralistically describe Mzbel's role in the street carnival where she was attacked on stage. Rendered in empirical, almost ethnographic detail, the report pinpoints what officials see as the crucial causal elements of the "Alleged Manhandling."

> As the peak of the week's celebration, the Art Society on Saturday 1 October 2005 held a socializing event in the form of a street carnival (musical performance) at the Royal Parade Grounds. The street carnival began from 5 PM to about half past midnight. The reason for the change from the traditional socializing at the premises of former College of Arts to the street carnival at the Royal Parade Grounds

was to give students the chance to socialize amidst musical performance by popular Ghanaian hip-life artistes.

This change in venue is significant in that it located the event away from the campus in an informal urban space. It is noted that "about 20 minutes before leaving for the programme," Mzbel had "Don Garcia (wine) while her dancers shared another box of the same drink." The dancers' dress is seen as visually tempting and linked to the audience's growing agitation:

- Mzbel . . . was dressed in a white unzipped long-sleeved minijacket on a glittering pink bra, a pair of white "track" trousers and a pair of white sneakers.
- Her dancers were each in a red-checkered cap, a white sleeveless blouse and a red-checkered mini-skirt with white underwear and a white sneaker.
- Occasionally, the crowd hurled some items to the stage. Most of the crowd in front had camera phones with which they videoed the underneath of the dancers.

The report uses a narrative of seduction to describe the performance:

- Immediately after Mzbel's performance and while on stage, her dancers turned their backs to the crowd and shook their buttocks. Also, Mzbel partly bared her breasts to the crowd. Whereupon, the crowd cried "one more" or "last one" to which Mzbel responded by baring, again, part of her breasts to the crowd. The crowd got more aggressive in their cries for "one more" or "last one."

The artist is transformed into an object over which the crowd fights for control:

- With the crowd holding or pulling Mzbel's legs, some of the organizers, some students and the MC (Nii Mantse) also begin pulling Mzbel back onto the stage. . . .
- This "tug-of-war" results in her trousers being pulled down to about mid-thigh level as told by a section of those on stage.
- In the course of the struggle, Mzbel screams and yells. She also loses her mini-jacket; eyewitness[es] claim so and videotapes show so.
- Those on stage finally succeed in pulling her back onto the stage, and she lies there for a while sobbing.[22]

The report emphasizes Mzbel and her dancers' performance as immoral while the violence against her is narrated with empirical distance. It implies that through escalating levels of sexual enticement they actively incited the crowd into a violent near-riot. In conclusion the committee recommends, "on behalf of the University community and the undisciplined students . . . an unqualified apology to Nana Akua Amoah (a.k.a. Mzbel) for the unfortunate incident which happened to her." But it also states, "In the event of any musical show/performance on campus in the future, only decent artistes must be considered." The detached description of the violence against the artist was based on recorded videotape and camera phone images as well as eyewitness accounts. The facts of the assault are not questioned though the moral implications are contingent upon the acceptability of Mzbel's performance.

After Mzbel was attacked, she publicly condemned the violence against her, criticizing KNUST, one of the premiere universities in Ghana, for allowing this kind of action and not reacting strongly enough. Despite the fact that the event was not on campus, the university wanted to handle the incident as an internal matter having to do with the rowdy nature of young university men. University officials reviewed video images of the assault and eventually expelled three students. In a series of widely quoted radio interviews, Mzbel argued that the university's response was inadequate, that legal action needed to be taken, and that it was unacceptable to blame her for inciting her assailants. In the process of publicly defending herself, she declared on Peace FM that "our University students are useless" and "uncivilized."[23] The University Students Association of Ghana responded by saying that the assault against her was unfortunate, but that was no excuse for her to insult Ghanaian students. They called on her to apologize for her remarks, which she refused to do.

This exchange marked a shift in public opinion, as previous supporters called for Mzbel to rein in her immoral act. Less than two months after the attack, Mzbel performed again in Kumasi, this time with heavy security, wearing the same outfits and doing the same songs she did for the university program. This also was seen by some as a provocation, showing a lack of respect and arrogance in the face of the shaming violence she had brought on herself.

An article titled "Watch it Mzbel," replicated across several Web sites, advised Mzbel to take heed of growing public criticism of her immoral actions. It argued that, people have been outraged by the get-up that the young musician presents on stage and have gone as far as to blame her for deliberately inviting trouble onto herself by wearing body revealing clothes. . . . Now the debate has so raged that it has become important that Mzbel takes a second look and tries to balance her vision of herself on stage and the social environment in which she performs. . . . Our advice is that Mzbel should guard against the possibility of losing the goodwill that had been so forthcoming for her in the aftermath of the unfortunate incident at KNUST and turn it to her good advantage.[24]

Mzbel and her management purportedly filed a lawsuit against the university, asking for 600 million cedis in damages for "her mistreatment." As Radio Gold Programme Director BiBi Menson explained to me, even those who supported Mzbel within the music industry felt she should heed public warnings about her behavior for her own good in light of "Ghanaian cultural values." He recounted how shy Mzbel was in person and marveled at how that contrasted with the public firestorm around her.

Another article, citing a phrase heard on the airwaves and in conversations in the streets, complains, "'Oh! Mzbel won't close her legs, [or] her mouth.'" For media observers, her outspoken criticism of the attackers in radio and newspaper interviews and her continued sexual displays indicate "the fast degenerating stagecraft of Ghana's female hiplife sensation." She is seen as lacking the proper control for not "checking her behavior" in response to violence she invited upon herself.

> It is ridiculous how some Ghanaian artistes copy blindly the lifestyles of foreign artistes only to be victims of their own blindness. . . . Mzbel should know that fame is a reputation that has to be protected with all humility and dignity, also the fact that she is a woman and not any other woman but a Ghanaian woman, should always ring a bell and put her on track. The time has come for Mzbel to start living up to the name Nana Ekua Amoah, which sounds more African and as a matter of fact Ghanaian. Only then will she start retracing her steps to the civilization of the modern Ghanaian woman whose slogan is simply "decency."[25]

In this statement, reflexive discussion focuses on the cultural conditions of the right to speak, understood in terms of gendered morality and authenticity (Lee and LiPuma 2002, 193). Mzbel's performances are seen as misrepresentative of Ghanaian womanhood. She is criticized for being stubborn, undisciplined, and un-Ghanaian, and for not heeding the moral warning the attack represented. Here, women stand in as signs of tradition. The "modern African woman" is an ambivalent figure defined through her "decency" and control. Moral indignation over indiscipline revolves around the visual presentation of uncontained female potency in public places. Mzbel subverts assumptions through perceived appropriation of masculine forms of self-control. In asserting her individuality, Mzbel incites anger. Her continued outspokenness and refusal to be humble and act like a decent African woman continued to invoke moral outrage. Unlike hiplife artists using traditional names for performance, Mzbel's cute English nickname—a combination of Miss and Belinda—contributes to the perception that she is not "living up to" or properly representing her Ghanaian heritage.

Assessments of indiscipline link market behavior to the aesthetics of bodily comportment. Particularly in times of economic transformation, female power and agency are often seen as threats to social well-being. As Comfort described in criticizing Mzbel's dancing as uncontrolled, in Ghanaian societies, moral order is manifest in poetic values of bodily and linguistic containment and precision. Esther, a member of the National Dance Ensemble and an expert on Asante traditional dance, explained to me how the attack on Mzbel could be partly attributed to how her dance aesthetic was understood, especially in Kumasi the capital of Asante. "She doesn't really dance. She just jumps around. It has no meaning and is not beautiful to local people. It is just some undisciplined sexual display."[26] Her "Western pop music choreography" is anathema to the "language of Asante dance" and bodily communication. Professor Mawere Opuku, also from Kumasi and the founder of the Ghana Dance Ensemble, says that Akan courtly dances such as Adowa, Frontomfrom, and Kete are noted for their subtle symbolic meanings.[27] Aesthetically they do not rely on large gestures, as do dances from other parts of the subregion, but rather have a grammar of small, controlled hand, foot, and facial gestures. Through these dances, proverbs are communicated and power is allocated (Yankah 1995). Dancers subtly praise and insult their audiences. The aesthetic precision of Asante dances reflects social order through the control of bodily expression. In contrast, Mzbel's performance could be seen as "vulgar and insulting" to those with "traditional sense."[28] Her movements read as foreign and imprecise. She becomes vulnerable to insults because her performance marks her as outside of public norms.

The circulation of discussions about Mzbel's attack shows how the language of cultural authenticity and tradition can be used to reject new popular forms as foreign and female aspiration as immoral and un-African. Reggie's manager, Paa K, who is from Cape Coast, explains, "This attack probably would not have occurred in any other place; partly because of the rowdy nature of the university boys there, and partly because of the history of Asante pride and public discipline. I mean, many Ghanaians don't even realize that Kumasi is so hierarchically organized. Socially everyone has their place and [they] are punished for not conforming. Traditional people across the country have responded critically to her but nothing like what happened [there]." In the eyes of many non-Asante Ghanaians, established national perceptions that Kumasi is a bastion of traditional culture are reiterated in opposition to perceived foreign influence.[29]

While for Ghanaians at home, Mzbel's performance is a sign of the nation's modernization whether it be threatening or titillating, for Ghanaians abroad, violence against her reinforces Ghana as a place of tradition with all the ambivalences that entails. Nii is a dancer from Accra who lives in New York. He describes growing up poor in Accra as "good preparation" for the struggles of surviving as an illegal immigrant. He uses mega-Web site Ghanaweb.com, which consolidates stories and videos from various online Ghanaian sources, to keep up with news from home and to sometimes post comments on stories. In a small South Bronx apartment in conversation with a group of Ghanaian friends, he turns from his computer and asks, "Have you seen all the stories about recent violence [against Mzbel]? Ghana has really changed since I left in 2000."[30] He disagrees that this would only have happened in Kumasi as it is a sign of broader moral issues, though he thinks Asantes' disrespect for other Ghanaian peoples is made clear by the manner of the attacks. "Mzbel's attack could have happened anywhere in Ghana. It is shameful that we do not act in more modern ways. The Asante are especially tied to tradition. They think that they are the only ones who have tradition and culture and don't respect other Ghanaians." For Ghanaians abroad, the music and the attacks represent the familiarity of home as well as distance from it. The attacks on Mzbel traditionalize Ghana in the eyes of those who have left even as they comment on the unusual nature of the events. Continually updated Internet news provokes a nostalgic nationalism and a sense of being part of ongoing conversations even if from afar. For people such as Nii, national and cultural affiliations appear as technologically managed lament.

Cultural, national, and transnational affiliations coalesce into a neoliberal moral public caught between competing claims of cultural tradition and modern potential. Mzbel challenges hiplife's liberal male subject by positing a female authoritative performer. Her symbolic and material access to foreignness threatens traditional moral order. The public shaming of an undisciplined subject is an attempt to contain "un-African" moral values that guide her actions. The need for bodily containment is a crucial aspect of the poetics of public action. The aesthetics of indiscipline invoke an emotional response that excuses violence against the performer. The violence reveals the contradictions of competing moral economies.

The public attacks on Mzbel transformed her claims of female sexual autonomy into disciplinary shaming. Public opinion contested whether Mzbel's outspokenness precluded her claiming the legal and moral status of victimhood. Her assault reveals the tension between violence as legitimate traditionalized discipline and violence as unlawful disorder. It also shows a moral ambivalence prevalent in how youths navigate public life. Debates about whether Mzbel is a victim of violence or a provocateur of sexual desire show how hiplife provokes the gendered expectations of public life. As a highly visible self-made celebrity Mzbel attracts both established forms of ambivalence toward female sexual and economic autonomy, as well as new versions of these moral debates in the language of entrepreneurship and aspiration.

Sexual Violence and Consuming Foreignness

In September 2006 armed robbers broke into Mzbel's house in Accra, taking thousands of dollars and electronic equipment. According to reports and testimony, she and one of her dancers were robbed, held at gunpoint, and assaulted before the robbers fled. She had just returned from publicized performances abroad and it was known she would be paid in foreign "hard currency." According to one news account, "This time around it had nothing to do with her sexual appeal or any of her sensuous provocations on stage. It had all to do with the dollars she earned and returned with from a United Nations contract in Liberia."[31]

While commentators speculated about the robbers' motivation, the artist's public humiliation in Kumasi set the discursive conditions for unsympathetic responses to this attack. There were two versions, both hostile. For some it was about the jealous taking of dollars, as both material and symbolic forms of foreign value, from a celebrity. This version fit with increasingly violent stories of armed robbery and indiscipline in Accra. For others it was a continuation of moral punishment for her illicit behavior.[32]

The story of the second attack emerged in a very public way. The immediacy of call-in radio brought the issue to life for listeners. Radio DJs often use live calls and text messages from listeners to create immediate dialogues around current issues. As Ghana Boy, a comedian and musician, recalls, "Early in the morning after the attack Peace FM called her live, on air. She was crying but she denied being raped. But you know Ghana news; at times it is true, at times it isn't. Especially with entertainers you don't know what to believe. But I am not sure it was right for the DJ to put her on the spot for everyone to hear. It was later on she admitted she had been raped."[33]

Public suspicion fell on those closest to Mzbel who might have cause to be jealous of her success. Rumors circulated that Mzbel's half brother, with whom she had had an argument, sent the robbers to punish her. A computer engineer, he was "arrested on suspicion of master minding the raid when Mzbel told the police that one of the robbers claimed they were sent by him."[34] He vehemently denied involvement. The police inquired whether her boyfriend in Britain had some reason to try to punish her. Some questioned whether her manager Goodies might be indirectly involved. Others said critics were punishing her for continuing to dress and act provocatively even after the university assault and the societal warnings it should have given her. Mzbel had not learned her lesson about public indecency and was being disciplined for her lack of traditional dignity. As a friend in the music industry recounted, Mzbel attempted to withdraw from public scrutiny and continued to deny that she had been raped as the attention only exacerbated her trauma. She contemplated leaving the country and quitting the music business.

Radio call-ins and text messages read on air by DJs as well as Internet comments were full of judgments about the incident. In these public, electronically mediated conversations, fans and critics explored the possible reasons for the attack, all of which pointed to bodily violence as disciplinary action against a woman for inappropriate public activity, whether sexual or economic. Notably, it appears that Ghanaians living abroad were on the whole more shocked by the violence and more willing to condemn the attack. Mimi Victor, posting online from the United States, was outraged: "Hmmmm. Those animal [sic] in human skin deserve to be casrated [sic] when caught."[35] The role of the media itself in the incident became a point of debate. As one article argued, "The media has made it almost criminal to be a successful female artiste. She isn't hiding behind the 'gospel' façade to express herself and that's wrong in the eyes of the very people who use her music to hype their radio shows. Her song '16,' directly addressed our system of sexual exploitation, which most young women deal with almost on a regular basis. Funny thing is, she never thought for a minute she would live those realities of the hit track."[36]

By being visible as a success and as a sexual icon, Mzbel made herself vulnerable. Some felt she was "paying for the price of fame."[37] In Web commentary, radio call-in talk, and informal conversation, many applauded her rape in graphic terms. Others blamed the artist in more spiritual terms. One Web author concluded that the attack was ultimately due to her "demonic" clothing styles. Another called the rape "a punishment from God." Still another, while decrying the violence, maintained that Mzbel "MUST REPENT." She continued, "I humbly appeal to Mzbel to refrain from any conduct, which make people hate her in public. She should try to associate well and respect all and sundry because as a musician, she needs to have public respect/support." Another chastized, "you should know that you dig your own grave when you stand in public and expose the very thing that need to be hidden by nature. Next time lie low."[38] Here the artist's choice to publicly reveal her sexuality and her success makes her vulnerable to attack; her active self-exposure—her "I'm aware" attitude toward self-expression—is disrespectful. Even some who support her feel she brought the violence on herself by being provocative and not heeding warnings. For many the use of "foreign" modes of expression, while seen as transgressive for young men, is unacceptable for women. The outpouring of violent sentiment online and in public talk highlights rape as a social disciplinary measure.

An Internet posting in support of Mzbel criticizes the duplicity of Ghanaian public. It emphasizes that youth culture dominates public life, linking business aspiration to popular style. Here the connections among free expression, choice, and consumption are made in the language of female sexuality. Osaberima writes on Ghanaweb,

> Ghanaians should understand that Mzbel is an entertainer who has her own style. She is bold enough to express her sexuality with her hot lyrics. Thats her trade mark. If you enjoy her song, buy her CD, if you don't appreciate her song, don't buy it. If you like her show, attend her concert, if you dislike her show, dont go. This is a matter of choice. We cry about freedom and democracy and yet we wanna impose our so-call moral issues on others—thats' double standard Ghanaians. If Mzbel wanna perform in her thongs, so be it.[39]

Mzbel's supporters defend her actions in the language of consumer choice and artistic free expression as characteristic of modern society. As one male rap artist explained to me, "Most Ghanaians cannot accept someone like her because she just expresses herself, does not mind what people say. It makes men angry to be ignored." Sexualized violence enacts masculine anxieties about uncontrolled modernity and changing forms of productivity.

By tracing the phone numbers of the stolen mobile phones, Mzbel identified her attackers at Labadi Beach and assisted the police in apprehending them. Her stolen laptop turned up for sale at a local hairdresser's salon in the hands of a known neighborhood hustler. When her manager seemed unsupportive, she dropped her record label and began managing her own affairs. As another artist told me, "She is strong; she seems to have come of age through this tough time. She will not let people take advantage of her anymore." Mzbel continued to travel and perform.[40] As an interviewer commented, "Mzbel hasn't changed much since that horrid attack almost two months ago. Things have pretty much returned to normal and she's now taking full control of her business dealings." Her willpower and control in the face of disorder continued to inspire her fans. To Esther, a nineteen-year-old aspiring dancer and singer, Mzbel's ordeals reveal the star's inner strength. "She does not mind what people think. She does what she wants and loves to be determined. She is a good role model for us girls."[41]

Six months after the attack, Mzbel is backstage at a major national celebration, the President's Show, held March 6, 2007, in honor of the fiftieth anniversary of independence. Her continued popularity is evident as Mzbel and her dancers prepare for their performance, dressed in schoolgirl miniskirts, pigtails, tight T-shirts, and scarves emblazoned with slogans proclaiming Ghana's independence. An exuberant crowd fills the old streets of Accra just outside the gates of the Kwame Nkrumah Mausoleum. Around 2 AM, fans go wild with excitement as Mzbel and her backup singers are announced amid performances of other hiplife and highlife stars. Before she goes onstage, I ask how things are going. In her quiet and determined voice she tells me that she will continue to "be herself" as her dress and performances are expressions of "individual style and creativity." The attacks make her more adamant, refusing to be intimidated into changing who, she says, "I really am." As one of the most popular artists of the moment, she mounts the stage at the all-night concert near the climax of the event. Her hit song "16 Years," with its infectious jamma dance beat, has the crowd jumping.

Watching from the side of the massive stage ten feet above the packed street, I see the young, rowdy crowd sway and sing along: "I be sixteen years, I go be this way oh." Standing with me is Reggie Rockstone's manager, Paa K. He reminds me that contradiction and controversy drive public discourse. "She has had a hard time but Mzbel is bold. She raises moral issues in her music. People took it the wrong way and thought she was [just] being provocative and sexual. They lost the deeper message of the song." But it is the duality of her public presence as both moral message bearer and sexual provocateur that gives her such popular resonance. This duality mirrors the paradoxes of Ghana's youth-oriented public sphere.

Onstage, Mzbel and her dancers continue with her signature choreographies (see figure 31). Her performance at the fiftieth anniversary is significant because in these celebrations the state is particularly concerned to represent itself for international eyes as a model of liberal reform and a stable place for private investment. At the same time, the state tries to show it is in tune with popular tastes by staging this concert for local non-elites. This show, which includes the most prominent musicians in the country, is the president's attempt to provide free popular entertainment for the masses in the midst of celebrations that are aimed for the most part at elite audiences and visitors. In doing so, it replicates the contradictions at the heart of its current valorization of the free market. One of the most popular artists and crowd draws is a woman who has been vilified in the media in the language of traditional cultural values for acting un-Ghanaian. For the state the

FIGURE 31 Mzbel onstage at outdoor concert with DJ and backup dancers. Courtesy of Ghanamusic.com.

concert is a presentation of popular styles. But this music presents a moral ambivalence built around polarities of locality and foreignness, tradition and modernity, cultural belonging and self-expression. For youths within Ghana, the violence against Mzbel reflexively marks female sexual expression as simultaneously standing for cultural containment and modern aspiration.

For Ghanaians abroad, these incidents foreground the contradictions of moral belonging. The perceived immediacy created by digital mediation brings forth an awareness of the incoherence of the dichotomy between tradition and modernity and the literal and metaphoric distance of home. Back in Nii's apartment in the Bronx, a group of Ghanaians in their thirties are listening to a mix of current Ghanaian popular hits and American R&B music. Their responses corroborate the strict moral reactions to anyone not maintaining their "proper" social place. When Mzbel's "16 Years" plays, everyone sings along to the chorus. As has been true for highlife and hiplife music across the decades, without need for introduction or discussion the song indexes a shared political and moral landscape predisposed to provoke debate and discussion. Enjoying the song, two men in particular begin talking about Mzbel's rape. The event is positioned within a discourse of foreign influence and failing moral discipline. Kwame describes these contradictory and conflicting moralities:

> This foreign influence is too much. People forget their culture and will do anything for money. . . . Something should happen for these people to learn some sense. But when the consequences come no one is prepared. . . . I know it is a bad thing that happened to [Mzbel] and no one deserves that but I don't know why I don't feel for her. . . . Gone are the days when the traditional court had power. We had our taboos which prevented the girls to dress like that. . . . I think from this incident a lot of people will learn a lesson about how to act and dress. My last trip to Accra I was in Madina market [in a peri-urban area north of Accra] when I heard a shout go up from all the boys around. There was this university girl wearing tight shorts revealing her buttocks. All the boys started yelling and insulting her. It was shaming. But even though it was embarrassing . . . she asked for it.[42]

For Ghanaians abroad, Ghana remains the location of tradition in two contradictory ways: first, in their lamenting the loss of traditional culture, and second, in perceived failures of Ghanaian modernity. The worst aspects of violence are described by the social embarrassment and shame they connote. Kwame condemns the violent reactions to female displays in Ghana while he understands them as signs of traditional values. At the same time, he is repulsed by his own affinity with this form of discipline. This moral conundrum shows how people struggle to identify a particularly Ghanaian modernity. The ambivalence of affiliation for Ghanaians living "outside" is reinforced through the interplay between distance and closeness that this incident provokes. Electronic media change the significance of formerly intimate local activities, such as the attacks on Mzbel, as they circulate across dispersed national communities.

Conclusion: Sovereign Sexuality and the Contradictions of Female Entrepreneurship

One perceived effect of economic privatization in Ghana, as well as locales like Brazil and South Africa, has been an increase in violent crime, armed robbery, and sexual assault (Caldeira 2006; Morris 2006). As the Ghanaian state shifted away from policing indiscipline, which it did in the early 1980s when Rawlings came to power, toward fostering a civil society conducive to private transactions and free-market penetration, new market freedoms were accompanied by anxieties about lawlessness. After the 2000 elections, new freedoms of expression and movement were at times seen as freedoms from collective morality. Guntoting robbers openly attacked petrol stations and private houses, which would have been unthinkable a few years previously. In 2005–2007 there was a series of random killings, armed robberies, house break-ins, car thefts, carjackings, and drug-related crimes across Ghana. Anxiety about violence and indiscipline rose, shocking many who contrasted Accra's public order with Lagos's perceived lawlessness.

Some saw these outbreaks as extreme responses to years of state oppression of free expression. As Alhaji, a radio presenter at Radio Univers known for his criticisms of corruption explained to his listeners in the lead-up to the 2000 elections, "Some people think that individual freedom means they can do and take whatever they want. . . . For some Ghanaian youths, democracy and freedom are associated with lawlessness and personal gain. They think that being an entrepreneur means making money any way you can."[43] One older commentator lamenting Mzbel's attack blamed growing violence on the fact that the Ghana of his youth had a "strong work ethic" but was taken over by "undesirables whose only aim is to amass wealth and results through violent means."[44] The line between official and unofficial violence—disciplinary order and criminal disorder—blur in the valorization of the entrepreneur (Comaroff and Comaroff 2006, 292–293). In this sense, violence is a symptom of the contradictions faced by Ghanaians in an era that links the hustler and the entrepreneur. It places the burden of youth aspiration on the morality of market-oriented aspiration without providing resources for the possibility of business success (Ferguson 2006; Ong 2006). For proponents of liberal economics, the rise of violence and disorder that has often accompanied the turn to liberal democracy can be seen as a failure of the state to protect private property and foster free-market activity (Harvey 2005). For others it is a logical extreme of liberal political economy in which value is meant to emerge, not from productive work, but from the desire for success or the needs of the market itself. In this logic, violence is a reflection of the entrepreneurial spirit inculcated in people who are not given the material or structural support to enact its promises. The correlation between lawlessness and liberal democracy shows the tension between entrepreneurship and cultural-national affiliation. Valorization of individual success blurs the role of law in regulating Ghanaian citizenry.

The turn to the global free market seems to have brought forth anxieties about how to control value that emphasize gendered hierarchies in Ghanaian public life. Ghana's economic liberalization in the 1990s valorized the entrepreneur as the preeminent national citizen. This figure is refracted through the lens of neoliberal popular culture that blurs the line between value production and personal style. Music epitomizes both material and symbolic aspects of entrepreneurship as young men use the microphone to claim the right to speak in public. The figure of the hiplife entrepreneur is predicated on the privatization of state media and electronic and digital circulation. Hiplife blurs entrepreneur, hustler, and lyrical artist, orienting them around masculine self-expression.

Hiplife music imagines a gendered urban landscape in which the consumption of value is masculinized and value is feminized. In circulating song fragments, metaphors of gendered value shape how a dispersed Ghanaian community judges appropriate public speaking. While artists control words and fashion a worldview through their music and personal style, female voicing threatens hierarchical ordering of value. Modern female bodies that tantalizingly reveal flesh and claim voices threaten a public moral order built upon visible signs of respect, hierarchy, control, and order. The movement of hiplife music across the urban landscape reveals the close relationship between visible sexuality, desire, and economic value. Public shaming of women is a moral intervention, containing economic and symbolic value in the face of modern change and market uncertainty.

In examining how Ghanaians responded to the rape of Mzbel, the tensions within male entrepreneurship emerge. Artistic self-expression is fostered by hiplife's valorization of publicness and celebrity in highly gendered ways. Hiplife reimagines the masculine aspects of both hip-hop and public speaking traditions of West African oratory in a contested language of sexual consumption. Young men and women in Accra use style to mark their identification with global racial marginalization refracted through this African American imaginary. For local youths, these styles represent affiliation with a cosmopolitan modernity. Hip-hop's hypermasculinity, bravado, and hustler aesthetic provide a language for black entrepreneurship (Rose 1994). The music authorizes young, uneducated Ghanaian men to invent an authoritative public presence in the language of global blackness.

As "Abuskeleke" and "16 Years" demonstrate, hiplife relies on contro-versy and contradiction to animate public circulation across urban and technological publics. Changing forms of mediation magnify moral conflict from the immediacy of urban rumor circulation to the disper-sal of multiple electronic and digital forms. Mzbel and Sidney both link self-expression to entrepreneurship in the popular imagination, though with different effects. Hiplife artists embody ideologies of free expression, creating possibilities for youth mobility while simultane-ously inculcating disciplinary aspects of market tastes. Liberal subjec-tivity is manifest across social roles, blending business entrepreneur, robber, self-fashioning artist, and media-savvy fan. Considering hip-hop as a liberal project, it blurs the line between entrepreneurship and hustling, such that individual aspiration also reopens the possibilities of violence.

The circulation of popular controversies is particularly effective at connecting dispersed urban and transnational Ghanaians through a moral ambivalence. Youths affiliate with public life through disjunc-ture. A public emerges not through consensus but rather in productive, sometimes violent contradiction. Within a youth-oriented public, the circulations of opinion produce a divisive community of interpretation convened around debates about music, style, and sexualized violence. Transnational Ghanaians affiliate through dispersed participation in local acts of disciplining and debates about what constitutes traditional morality. The retraditionalization of the public sphere places the moral contradictions of violence onto the bodies of women.

In her novel and epic poem *Our Sister Killjoy*, Ama Ata Aidoo de-scribes the experience of a young woman going to Germany to study abroad and how she unwittingly becomes the object of various male and female fantasies at home and abroad. The novel points to the moral dilemmas arising from the contradictions of attempting to be black and female, African and modern, of traveling abroad and returning to Ghana, of being African in the West and Westernized in Ghana. Aidoo's work shows the particular vividness of the sexual fantasies projected onto African women's bodies.

Fetishizing female sexuality and then disciplining it are central to the formation of civil order and related ideas of individual rights-bearing subjects in liberal societies (Warner 2005; Berlant 1997; Fou-cault 1990). For a Ghanaian transnational public, the sexualized female body becomes a fetish for economic entrepreneurship and its dangerous potential. Female sex is both potent and dangerous, in need of containment. Violent responses to women reproduce them as the bearers of tradition. Gendered piety is opposed to "foreign" fashions and lifestyles. In hiplife, female sexuality as an object of consumption stands for male economic success and aspiration, though females' attempts to control their own sexuality are met with violent criticism in the name of tradition. Gendered violence marks the limit of individual choice in the face of cultural belonging. Anxiety about female sexual expression shows the tension between desires for foreign consumption and the reemergence of a traditionalized moral order.[45] While the attacks on Mzbel are unusual, they point to a history of discomfort with women being in control of economic activity especially in moments of social transformation.

Subjects are caught in the contradictions between traditionalized morality and modern consumption, social obligation and free expression. Hiplife depends on a discourse of sexual consumption and the moral controversy it provokes. Sexuality becomes a form of self-regulation in which desire translates into aspiration and aspiration becomes value. Moral contestation over female sexuality is metaphoric for conflicts over free-market principles. Sexual sovereignty describes how hegemonic notions of individual success and aspiration define the limits of public life in the language of sexual morality. Public expressions of sexuality become the terrain of moral structure rather than a horizon of freedom and choice (Povinelli 2006; Foucault 1990). With the hegemony of the entrepreneur, the redemptive potential of self-expression for African lifeworlds is bound to the reinscription of a traditionalized, gendered political-economic subject (Mbembe 2005; 2002). Ideologies of choice and self-fashioning are internalized as disciplinary strategies of the entrepreneurial spirit.

Moral divisiveness in Ghanaian public life often revolves around perceived dichotomies between traditional culture and urban/foreign values. Hiplife, as I have argued, reshapes how young, urban Ghanaians rethink the way cultural, racial, and gendered identities authorize speaking practices. The language of freedom, then, is also one of self-discipline and moral judgment. Self-sovereignty in a neoliberal state refers to the production of the interiority of the subject in the language of market-based principles (Giroux 2008; Comaroff and Comaroff 2000). In the popular imagination, individual consumption and aspiration are presented as productive of value. Aspiration is the external projection of inner desires defined in moral terms rather than rational economic ones. Celebrity hiplifers convert aspiration into value, though, as Mzbel's case shows, this relies upon a highly gendered logic.

In 2012 Mzbel herself recognizes that her struggles paved the way for other female hiplife artists. "People didn't understand me because what I was doing and wearing seemed new to them. Now people wear worse stuff and it is not surprising anymore because people are used to that now."[46] But I think the relative acceptance of female performers and the normalization of celebrity culture in Accra is not about the Ghanaian public sphere's turn to a Western moral modernity but rather that the immediate postmillennium years in Ghana were a period of transformation during which rising notions of entrepreneurship and private popular media provoked anxieties. Hiplife's images of celebrity, celebration, and success promised to transform desires into reality. In some measure, these fantasies of freedom—free markets and free moralities—created a backlash in which the signs of female sexuality at the center of masculine fame and value production also became signs of threat. A few years later both these promises and anxieties seemed much more distant and normalized.

CHAPTER 7

No. 1 Mango Street

CELEBRITY LABOR AND DIGITAL PRODUCTION AS MUSICAL VALUE

How does an artist as entrepreneur convert musical labor into fame and economic value? On October 2, 2010, London-based Ghanaian musician Mensa Ansah, better known as M3nsa, launched his album *No. 1 Mango Street* with a small concert event at Rich Mix, a culture-art center off Bethnal Green Road in East London (see figure 32).[1] The album's title refers to the address in Accra where M3nsa grew up. His music is perhaps best described as alternative hip-hop mixing rap and Afrobeat, neosoul, and R&B. Some observers say he is at the cutting edge of hiplife. He sings and raps in Twi, Fante, Pidgin, and English with different tracks aimed at different audiences in Ghana and abroad. M3nsa's music, more than that of most Ghanaians who started out doing hiplife, crosses genres and audiences. He is gaining a following among Ghanaians and Nigerians abroad as well as multicultural hipsters and alternative hip-hop heads. Hard to categorize, his music moves through underground circuits of neosoul, Afrobeat, and hip-hop. The long-distance exchanges that went into making the album—as well as its explicit themes of work and travel—reflect what Rab Bakari calls the "tricontinental status" of young Africans. The development of the album involved collaborations with musicians, producers, video makers, and Web designers across Europe, America, and Africa over several years. M3nsa wrote many of the songs in London. Returning to Ghana, he recorded and reworked a number of tracks. He did the final mix for most tracks in New York. He performed and shot music videos across

FIGURE 32 The back cover of M3nsa's album *No. 1 Mango Street.*

three continents. Carrying his tracks as Pro Tools files on a portable hard drive, he continued to adjust and add to the song mixes as he encountered new collaborators and honed his sound. The digital sound files accrued value and depth through his travels. Collaborations with various artists expanded the music's generic influences and referential registers. M3nsa struggled to maintain financial and artistic control over his musical products, as growing recognition of his musical talent in the African music world meant that collaborators and small-scale music business entrepreneurs (middlemen) attempted to use his potential success to buoy their own search for fame.

The album launch was advertised through Facebook groups and Ghanaian music and global alternative black music Web sites. Significantly, the physical album was not for sale to correlate with the album launch. M3nsa printed only a few hundred CDs to give to fans, DJs, and media for publicity. While some of the songs had been circulating for free online for almost a year, others were not available at all. Before the launch, M3nsa made the tracks available for sale at online music sales giant iTunes for a few days, as he told me, to "experiment and see how they would do on the market" before taking them down. For artists like M3nsa, entrepreneurship links pleasure and work, lifestyle and success. Artists struggle to use social networks to convert musical value, pleasure, and leisure into buzz and celebrity, and to market personal stories as tales of celebrity success. The potential of digital music to be endlessly replicated offers marketing opportunities but also causes anxiety among artists and producers about controlling products and making profits (Stokes 2004).

The collaborations, labors, and travels that went into producing and circulating M3nsa's album show how musicians make value in an industry increasingly based on dispersed production techniques and digital, nonmaterial products (Meintjes 2003). For young artists, the potentials of success revolve around creating music that circulates without the financial, geographic, and institutional constraints of material form (Peterson 2010; Charry 2000; Erlmann 1999). Making music is a lifestyle choice, which denotes a way of engaging with daily existence as much as it is about producing a specific artistic product. In other words, it is pleasurable and productive in itself—or at least it is supposed to be. But being a musician also provokes a lot of anxiety about how much musical products are worth, how to reach an audience, and how to make money (Hart 2009). The curious, yet not uncommon, practice of launching an album when an actual album is not available points to questions about the conditions under which artistic labor, travel, and collaboration are converted into economic value as artists try to circulate their music and their name to transform music into fame.

For musicians all over the world, the challenges of making and selling music have changed in recent years (Dent 2009; Wallach 2008; Guilbault 2007; Stokes 2004). For independent Ghanaian artists without institutional backing, the process involves passion and hard work, social networking and business savvy. Electronic beatmaking software, multitrack PC-based recording and mixing, and digital file sharing have made it possible for an individual artist to make ambitious music without enlisting live bands. New production technologies also help artists elicit new audiences and disseminate music across the Internet and through mobile digital music players.

The rise of private radio, new electronic recording studios, cassette and CD distribution networks, and television shaped the ways that hiplife circulated across a Ghanaian public in the years before the millennium. By 2007, however, cassette and CD sales plummeted as digital MP3 files became the musical medium of choice. Files were copied and circulated to DJs and audiences with phones capable of transferring and playing digital music. Online social networking, in particular, changed how musicians and producers strove to control musical circulations and reach out to audiences and how listeners imagined music's relationship to identity and geography (Miller 2012).

The spread of digital file sharing and PC-based music software has led to a global crisis for record labels and musicians no longer able to make money from selling physical products (Collins 2009a; Bhattacharjee et al. 2007). It has also led to new possibilities for aspiring musicians to make music and imagine themselves as part of a global community of artists. Digital technologies have opened new possibilities for independent musicians to live and work transnationally, play with conventions of genre, and reach new audiences. But these artists struggle to find new ways to convert artistic labor into audience recognition and economic value. Underlying the work of transnational musicians like M3nsa are profound shifts in broader dynamics of labor and value and how African youths reimagine dispersed communities of affiliation through musical labor.

The work collaborations that went into M3nsa's album reflect forms of exchange and labor-value conversions characteristic of the Ghanaian music industry and its intersection with global informal music circulations (Kapchan 2007; cf. Klein 2007; Goodman 2005; Stokes 2004). As Keith Hart (1973) points out in the context of Accra's urban trade networks, informal economies are not opposed to official networks but rather define a terrain in which those on the margins appropriate social networks for economic gain across various alternative realms. Artists use the language of exchange for making music. Musicians bring an idea of the free market to a network of personal affiliation to transform music and publicity into celebrity; the value of celebrity, then, can be transformed to access new audiences, economic realms, and corporate sponsorship.

Returning to Accra to Record: Pidgin Translations

In August 2009 M3nsa took time off from work in London, returning to Accra to focus on his musical career full time. While he had returned to Ghana every few years to visit family, this time he was focused on his musical work, reviving his networks of friends and associates as both business possibilities and social connections. His musical talents provided a way for him to reengage with Ghana. He said, "I hadn't come back as much, but as I am trying to make moves in my music career, I am reconnecting more. That is in some ways what this album is about."[2]

M3nsa comes from a family with impressive artistic credentials and connections maintained across several generations. M3nsa's mother taught him to play piano when he was eight, encouraging him to perform in church at a young age. His father is a musician, Ebo Ansah, who for a time played guitar for British-Ghanaian Afrorock crossover band Osibisa in the 1970s. Filmmaker Kwaw Ansah and fashion designer Kofi Ansah are his uncles. His cousin Joey Ansah is an actor and martial artist with credits including *Batman Begins* and *The Bourne Ultimatum*. M3nsa attended prestigious Adisadel College in Cape Coast, where he met a number of future collaborators—in particular, Wanlov the Kubolor, Bosco, and Gibril da African. As chapter 2 elaborates, connections made through elite secondary schools were crucial to the first generation of hiplife artists. While the music spread more widely to nonelite urbanites (chapter 2), children of an urban cultural elite remained central to the genre's development of the genre.

As a teenager in 1999, M3nsa was part of a young hiplife group called Lifeline Family assembled by a producer to take advantage of the new musical trend. They were best known for their massive hit single, "Wo Sisi Ye Wo Ya" (Your waist hurts), which playfully teases an old man for trying to dance with a young girl.[3] The song has Twi lyrics and a highlife dance-oriented electronic beat. For several years it was a favorite at parties and clubs, attracting cheers and laughter when it came on, with listeners singing along and dancing while holding their backs in mock pain and pretending to use walking sticks. Years later M3nsa recalled his early music with some embarrassment: "It had a really cheesy highlife beat. But it was funny and people could dance to it."[4] It had a "local" sound that did not match his later work's cosmopolitan neo-hip-hop sensibility. Lifeline Family did not get paid for their work. "The producer presented it as an opportunity for us as aspiring artists to get exposure. I am not sure he knew what he was doing but was trying to make some money from us. Hiplife and new technology were changing the music industry and these guys were trying to figure out how to get involved." M3nsa's attitude reflects broader understandings of the financial realities of being an artist and the ways that managers rely upon and manipulate talent. "When you are an artist you know you are being exploited sometimes but you do it anyway because you want to make the music or act or whatever it is. If you don't agree then you won't get to do it." The song's popularity garnered television appearances and radio play, though the group did not last. But M3nsa did make new connections in the music industry. He followed up with a solo album, *Rapublic*, with the hit "If You Don't Know" featuring hiplife stars VIP, which was nominated for several awards in 2007 at South Africa's Channel O Spirit of Africa Music Awards. The album led to recognition of his talent within hiplife circles.

M3nsa then made the beats and produced Reggie Rockstone's 2004 album *Last Show*. Despite the boost that connections to Reggie's status as hiplife's godfather provided, soon after he relocated to London to expand his musical horizons. He recalls, "I always maintain my connections to Ghana but there was a limit to how far I could take my music if I stayed and worked with Rockstone in Accra." As described in chapter 3, in 1994 Rockstone was compelled to return to Ghana when the limits of hip-hop as a global musical form constrained his musical career in London. A generation later, Ghanaian artists such as M3nsa who want to pursue music have new options due to changing global perceptions of black music and new technologies of production and distribution. With his family spread among Los Angeles, Accra, and London, M3nsa remains based in North London with his wife, an R&B singer of Nigerian descent with whom he sometimes records, and their young daughter. He worked for the London Underground's Information Services, though he took a leave to devote himself full time to making music. With touring, digital sales, and teaching occasional music lessons and courses, he is trying to make a living from it. "This is my time to really make it internationally," he tells me.

In Accra, at his family's Mango Street house, M3nsa turned his room into a makeshift recording studio with a PC computer and microphone. For M3nsa, coming back to Ghana is a mixture of seeing old friends and figuring out how to push his musical career to the next level. He is consciously trying to balance the personal pleasure of making music with making a career of it. While he has recorded and produced numerous tracks over the years, it has been almost a decade since he released a full album. He explains, "I want to get this one right, to reach the next level of popularity." But figuring out the formula for success involves much more than making popular, well-crafted music; it involves making oneself into a celebrity. With *No. 1 Mango Street* M3nsa is trying to differentiate himself from older hiplife. The genre's stylist evolution from highlife samples to minimalist electronic jamma beats to a self-conscious eclectic pastiche of hip-hop, Afrobeat, and R&B sounds and rhythms follows the technological shift from sampling LPs and cassettes to early beatmaking programs to infinite computer archives of beats and sounds.

M3nsa's artistic persona reflects the tension between pleasure and work in living as a musician; music is business but it is also an experiential lifestyle. In this tension, artists strive to connect with other artists and new audiences, getting their name out there. M3nsa is respected by other musicians and has a number of national hits. But he is not a recognizable star. Much of his music has not reached a wider public. Like most young artists, he has suffered from a lack of management. "I am like a lot of artists. I have a short attention span," he tells me. "I can work all night in the studio. I will endlessly change a song even . . . after I finish an album. Or I might get bored with songs and just move on to a new project. I have trouble following through with promotion, distribution, and all that business side of things, but there are no good managers out there so I am forced to try to do it myself."

The new album's title track reflects on the artist's youth as a lost point of origin but one that maintains his purpose as he pursues future goals. He recorded it in his makeshift Mango Street bedroom studio. It is a lament questioning the nature of home and ideas of return reminiscent of Osibisa's Afrorock anthem in a minor key, "Welcome Home." For M3nsa, returning to Accra and recording provided a way to reflect. It entailed a "mix of frustration and joy at being home; seeing it differently from when I was a kid now that I was older; social life in general. But I realize that I have changed not them. . . . The process of making this album has been . . . metaphoric of trying to find myself." With English lyrics floating across trip-hop rhythms, M3nsa sings,

> Retracing my steps don't mean I'm going backwards.
> I was distracted, now I'm looking for my way home.
> That's where my Ma is; it's where my heart is; where it all started.

M3nsa works intuitively as a musician. Rather than worrying over the technical aspects of production, he relies on his musical skill to capture and convey raw emotions. He programmed the beats and recorded the vocals. "I did it in one take and it just felt right" even though his voice is a bit off-key and recorded with an inferior microphone. He explains, "Its [vocals are] raw, which reminds me of the meaning of the song. . . . You can't go back to how things were but you can look for those old connections." The recordings' flaws remind him of the place and process of recording; while digital files are infinitely repeatable exact copies, they also are nonmaterial indexical icons of the recording locale and experience, replicating its flaws and relative production values. The recording in itself points to the artistic journey the track represents as well as the juxtaposition of digital copying and transportability with the particularities of locale. After recording the song, M3nsa carried the digital file with him and sent it around, playing it for other musicians, who commented on it and made suggestions about adding bass lines, drum tracks, and so on.

For several tracks he enlisted friends to add vocals. M3nsa explains, "Most people on the album I know personally from my childhood and around. Samini adds ragga vocals to 'Biribi W'om.'" Emmanuel Samini was raised in Accra, though his hometown is Wa in Ghana's Upper West Region. At first he used the stage name Batman before Africanizing it to Samini. He had a major hit with the hiplife love song "Linda" in 2004, which launched him as a musical sex symbol with his blend of reggae, hip-hop, and R&B. He gained continent-wide recognition and became an emblem of African music for European audiences. He has been a favorite at the rising number of awards shows that publicize new global music connections, being nominated for MTV Europe's Best African Act in 2007 though losing to Nigerian hip-hop star D'Banj, as well as being tapped for awards by Ghana Music Awards, MTV Base Africa, and MOBO UK. He was one of the most prominent artists sponsored by mobile phone company MTN, which made him one of their 2010 World Cup representatives. He and M3nsa were childhood friends. M3nsa explains that not only is Samini a good singer but putting him on the album takes advantage of his current celebrity. "He is famous across the continent now . . . but he grew up down the block. We are old friends." M3nsa explored using various beatmakers and producers but ended up doing a lot of the production work himself. "I am a proper musician, unlike a lot of kids in the Ghana music business. I use live guitar and trumpet and other instruments on the album as well as electronic beats and I am a producer myself, so I don't have to rely on anyone."

Musically, he was impressed by MA Peters's beats, whom he had taught production skills before leaving for London. Initially working with Rockstone and artists in his circle including the Mobile Boys, MA makes beats for many of Accra's top rappers as well as underground aspirants, though he does not get much public recognition. He is a regular fixture around the scene, at radio stations, clubs, and studios where musicians and industry insiders meet. He is quiet and observant though has a sharpness. Often he will sit smiling in a club surrounded by people dancing to his beat. "I like it when people don't know it's my music. It gives me an edge." Like many beatmakers, he makes beats on his PC at home and copies them onto CDs or a flash drive to bring into the recording studios that are tucked away in spare rooms of houses across the city where rappers and singers lay down vocal tracks. M3nsa was inspired by his sound. "MA is one of the hardest working producers in Ghana. He has no musical training but he makes great beats. Most rappers don't understand what he is trying to do. . . . That is to my benefit. He is a true artist, doing it for love of the music. MA gave me a bunch of different beats to listen to. I picked ones I liked to use. He had the beat for 'Biribi W'Om,' the track I did with Samini, for years but no one else recognized it."

Late one evening, several rappers, beatmakers, and friends finish their drinks at a quiet bar in Accra's Cantonments neighborhood, piling into cars to reconvene in a recording studio in a small room in a Labadi-area private house. Reggie Rockstone and a young female vocalist, Efya Awindor, take turns in the sound booth laying down vocals. They sing from notebooks full of handwritten lyrics, editing and amending their verses and choruses based on how the progressive takes sound upon playback. The song "Blame It" ends up on Rockstone's new album *Reggiestration*. Up-and-coming rapper D-Black, also featured on the track, and others observe and occasionally offer their opinions on lyrics and flow, though usually younger artists stay quiet. D-Black explains that learning music production requires spending as much time as possible in the studio with experienced people: "I watch how the producer works with the musicians. . . . the technical things, how they use the different tracks and levels and double up on vocals to make it sound rich. . . . It's a great chance to learn for my own music."[5] Rockstone directs the proceedings, commenting on how he wants the lyrics to be laid down over the beats. MA sits calmly observing. He has his hard drive with beats on it, but in this studio he is a guest watching while another producer controls the proceedings from the computer and monitors. While he loves the music, he also sees it as serious business, sometimes working all night making a beat. "It looks like just fun but it's hard work. You have to have skills with the [computer] program and know how to bring in different sounds." After recording, listening to, and discussing several verses, the group heads to Rockstone's recording studio not far away, where MA plugs his drive into the computer and opens Pro Tools to pre-view some beats he has made and plans with Rockstone which ones might work with various lyrics for songs in progress. At the end of the night, after working intensely on music while joking and arguing, every-one heads home around 4 AM.

M3nsa recognizes the relationship between work and pleasure in-volved in this type of music production. "People are starting to appreci-ate music as a business. Making beats is not just fun. It is a way to get out of a bad economic situation, to be a celebrity. But, if you see that as your main goal that is a problem. But if someone makes a beat, you have to pay them for their work. Some rappers will promise to pay people who help them but then don't follow through. MA has been working for many people for free with the hope that connections and success will lead to bigger things."

The informal exchange network of musicians and beatmakers relies upon friendship and camaraderie among musicians. Accra's popular musical world is small, divided into a few shifting camps of artists re-volving around a star rapper, vocalist, or hot producer. Most rappers know each other and call upon whoever is trendy at the moment to feature on their tracks. Young artists hope their connections to estab-lished artists will bring experience and exposure, though the intimacy and overlap of friendship and work can lead to conflict and misunder-standing. MA and Reggie have had several heated conflicts over appro-priate compensation. Indeed, one time MA hid the hard drives and re-fused to give Rockstone his tracks until he was paid. Eventually Reggie gave him some money and they began to work together again. MA says, "Reggie thinks I should just work for free for years. I can't live on prom-ises. If he makes money I expect my cut. . . . even if it comes from something related to the music."[6] Rockstone says he isn't making money from selling the music and feels that MA should appreciate the connections and fame that he has provided him. "If it wasn't for me no one would know him; I am the one who brought him on the scene."[7] Friends and collaborators often debate the value and exchangeability of various kinds of labor, how much the meticulous work of program-ming beats and mixing sound tracks is worth in relation to writing and recording lyrics or in terms of the value of celebrity. Since in many cases no physical record is being made and sold and money is made indirectly through live shows and sponsorship, it is hard to calculate worth and easy to accuse artists of hustling for personal gain, forgetting their compatriots once they become famous. Collaborations for artists like M3nsa and beatmakers like MA with bigger-name stars like Rockstone and Samini are made through fictive kinship networks, in which musicians treat close associates as family. Value is added by associating with better-known artists but how that value is converted and who should pay for it is sometimes unclear.

For M3nsa, MA provides beats and some production work and when M3nsa makes money from a show or sales later on, he pays MA so they maintain a close working relationship. "With MA I will work with him and then give him sometimes half of whatever I get. He will sometimes say, 'No, you take more.' We both want to maintain the relationship to be successful." Work is not necessarily paid for up-front, nor are there often formal arrangements; labor is seen as an investment in connections and future possibility and its worth is often negotiated after the fact. Maintaining social relations is important for success in this context. As M3nsa explains, "We are all in this together. If you succeed, then everyone will eat!"

M3nsa's closest musical collaborator has been Emmanuel Owusu-Bonsu, a longtime friend and Pidgin rapper known as Wanlov the Kubolor. "Kubolor" is Ga for street urchin or vagabond and reflects his views on music and life. Born in Romania of Ghanaian and Romanian parentage, he came to Ghana for school, attending Adisadel College where he became friends with M3nsa. After studying and living in Texas and Los Angeles, he returned to Ghana. Focusing on music, he released his first album, *Green Card*, in 2007. He developed a distinct style, accessorizing his long dreadlocks by wearing African-print cloth wrap skirts, T-shirts with stylish designs or humorous slogans, or sometimes going shirtless and barefooted at all times. With sunglasses and sometimes a Palestinian scarf around his neck, he contrasts sharply with prevalent styles for rising rappers, who opt for baggy or skinny jeans or crisp suits suggesting hip-hop hustlers. In his satchel slung over one shoulder or knapsack, Wanlov carries copies of *Green Card* on CD to sell. His unconventional appearance and hilarious, irreverent Pidgin-language rap delight audiences, though they cause some to dismiss him as "disrespectful."

FIGURE 33 M3nsa and Wanlov performing at Bless the Mic event at Coffee Shop, Accra. Photograph by the author.

Kubolor and M3nsa develop their individual projects separately but have formed a long-term collaboration, humorously dubbing themselves the FOKN BOIS (see figure 33).[8] Together they made "BRKN LNGWJZ" (Broken Language), which appears on the *No. 1 Mango Street* album. The track introduces their style of bawdy Pidgin rap filled with elegant and irreverent innuendo. Wanlov begins by asking M3nsa, "They no really know wan identity so. How you go describe yourself?" Each rapper takes turns rhyming long lists of actions and things that define him. M3nsa's lines include calling himself "The slangs Pidgin Cockney talker, the only time I watch sports is when Ghana's playing soccer watcher." In his lines, Wanlov describes himself as "The last African hippie hopper. The pro Gypsy non-tippsie risky rapper, the murderer, the hahahaha joker." The duo began working with Panji Anoff under the rubric of his Pidgin Music production company, reviving some of his earlier musical experiments. M3nsa and Wanlov also collaborate on *Coz Ov Moni*, directed by King Luu and produced by Panji, which Panji described as "the first West Africa Pidgin hip-hop musical feature film." It follows a day in the life of two friends as they dress, bathe, eat, chase someone who owes them money, steal clothes, swim, chase girls, and party. The entire dialogue is sung in Pidgin. Working with Wanlov on the film project, M3nsa explains to me, "inspired me to take this album seriously. It pushed me to the next level." Panji, Wanlov, and M3nsa are making music for an alternative vision of hiplife. Panji says, "Reggie wanted to make things too much about hip-hop. . . . Many of the young programmers and rappers who followed were taken in by electronic sounds. I have always felt hip-hop could bring African music, sounds, and the poetry of our languages to the world in more original ways. That is why I founded Pidgin Music. It has taken ten years but we are finally making the kind of music I wanted to do."[9] When I ask Wanlov why he raps in Pidgin, he explains, "Everyone understands Pidgin. It is beautiful and makes people come together." To him, Pidgin is a form of translation, a way to speak across various audiences and demographics. When Reggie, Panji, and others returned to Ghana in the mid-1990s, they reshaped local music and invented hiplife by remixing styles from abroad. Ten years later next-generation musicians raised on private radio and hiplife attempted to remix the established formulas linking Ghana to transnational contexts in new ways.

Reflecting in London: Traveling Hard Drives and the Value of Foreignness

M3nsa returned to London after six weeks of recording and shooting in Accra, carrying with him a number of tracks in various states of completion on an external hard drive. There he worked with his live band developing his songs. M3nsa explained to me that developing the music in London would give it a fresh appeal for Ghanaian audiences. "You know Ghanaians, they will see something as valuable if it is from 'outside.'" At the same time he was concerned that since he was living "outside" he would be seen as out of touch with street life and current trends in Ghana. The production of *No. 1 Mango Street* takes advantage of the various ways in which travel is a form of value conversion, transforming movement into self-expression. For West Africans who have not traveled abroad, Western locales add an aura of distinction. For London hipsters, traveling and recording in Ghana give M3nsa exotic authenticity. In both places, attempts to convert movement into value raise questions of how value is exchanged across incommensurate aesthetic and economic registers.[10]

Traveling allows M3nsa to reflect on the role of context in shaping a musical aesthetic in terms of both production and audience. "It's funny, how things sound different depending on where you are. I was more at peace listening to tracks in London. I had some distance. Being in Accra was so intense and creative . . . continually working, and then I needed to reflect on what I had done. When I would listen to something I recorded in Accra when I was back in London, I would hear the same song differently." In London, M3nsa uses musicians to lay down instrumental and vocal tracks over the raw lyrics and beats, refining and layering the music. Throughout the process of finishing a song, M3nsa continues to circulate unfinished digital tracks for friends and artists through Facebook and Dropbox, getting critical feedback from a variety of sources. Songs whose melodies and arrangements he conceived of through digital beatmaking he translates into live music, orchestrating his new songs for a small live band with drums, keyboard, and bass for London audiences. M3nsa has achieved crossover appeal, which has eluded many African musicians. He plays for urban hipsters at stylish venues like Jazz Café. "White, black, Indian, Bangladeshi, Caribbean all come to hear me play. My style appeals to a lot of people. I get these white guys coming up to me saying, 'Dude, you're funny,' even when they don't understand the lyrics. That's the key to crossing over; either they understand the song or they feel the beat."

A number of artists of Ghanaian and Nigerian descent have been central to shaping mainstream British hip-hop (cf. Bald 2004; Hesmondhalgh and Melville 2001). In the 2000s, Lethal Bizzle, Dizzee Rascal, Sway, and Tinchy Stryder were four of the most successful UK hip-hop MCs helping develop Grime.[11] All were born in Ghana or are first-generation British-Ghanaians. Whereas M3nsa experiments with linking Ghanaian and international audiences, these artists orient their music toward an urban black British public. After achieving success, however, Sway began to musically engage Ghanaian topics and experimenting with rapping in Twi, releasing a song called "Black Stars" to celebrate Ghana's hosting of the 2008 Africa Cup of Nations football tournament. In 2010 he traveled to Ghana and did a number of collaborations. He worked with 1970s highlife/Afrobeat musician and hiplife originator Gyedu Blay Ambolley. Titled "Shepherds Pie," the track opens with Ambolley chanting the chorus, "Shepherds pie, fish and chips, face the wall, kokonte Makola," over a kpanlogo beat before Sway raps. He also collaborated with Ghanaian R&B singer Richie on a track called "Intoxicated." Despite winning Best UK Hip-Hop Act at the BET Hip-Hop Awards in 2006 and being signed to Akon's Konvict Muzik, Sway is not well known outside the UK. Sway and M3nsa also worked on a collaboration that would benefit both. M3nsa tells me, "He is doing really well [in his UK music career] but he says that he feels incomplete without his own people's acceptance. . . . Through a collaboration I can help him reach that audience because he knows I can rap in multiple languages and bring in a Ghanaian sound. And he can give me broader exposure in the UK market." While Sway tries to find a way to engage Ghanaian music through his successful UK hip-hop style, M3nsa's relative success belies his continued attempts to figure out who his audience is and how to translate his eclectic style and image into a marketable sound that might reach multiple fan bases.

New York Mixing for a Professional Sound and Added Value

In November 2009, M3nsa came to New York to shoot a music video for the title track and to find a place to mix his *Mango Street* tracks. He explored several small mixing studios in the New York area that offer package deals to independent artists, eventually deciding to work with Ed Reed even though he charges a bit more than some studios. M3nsa thinks Reed is more experienced and his musical artistry is on a different level than many engineers who cater to underground musicians. Reed charges $1,200 to mix and master twelve songs, spending approximately half a day on each song. He agrees to do an extra song as the album has thirteen tracks.

In Reed's studio, which fills the basement of his semidetached house on a quiet street in Staten Island, M3nsa sits in front of the mixing board, punching his BlackBerry and listening to Reed adjust track levels. Reed most famously worked on Naughty by Nature's 1991 crossover hip-hop hit OPP, and now works as a producer in a number of top Manhattan studios. For independent clients, he works out of his well-equipped basement. M3nsa's short dreadlocks and dapper, urban style contrast with Reed's old-school tattoos, sleeveless jersey, and backward baseball cap as they pore over Pro Tools tracks (figure 34). M3nsa continues to Tweet, update Facebook, and SMS. "Man, so much goes into getting this album finished. It's hard work. I can record an album over a weekend; it's all the other stuff. Now I am focusing on Internet and social networking presence, distribution. The music and mixing are the easy part."

Ed Reed won his first Grammy in 2008 for a live Latin jazz recording at the Village Vanguard, but he has a long history working with hip-hop artists, from Stetsasonic to Queen Latifah. The Grammy sits in a glass case above a piano, stacked drums, and guitars. Naughty by Nature's platinum record for OPP shines down on the monitors and mixing

FIGURE 34 M3nsa and Ed Reed in Reed's Staten Island, New York studio. Photograph by the author.

boards. We talk as he keeps his eyes trained on his mixing board. "I work in million-dollar studios in Manhattan but for independent projects and young artists I love working with them as well and can get a professional sound here in my personal studio." The tracks were made in Pro Tools and imported as separate files. As a producer himself, M3nsa is careful with media management, providing Reed with easily importable separate files for each track on each song. He is able to develop his skills from this new collaboration. "I wanted to work with Reed because he has so much experience working with different musicians. I can really watch him and learn a lot."

For the title song, "No. 1 Mango Street," there are forty separate tracks, a relatively small number. Reed imports the multiple tracks. "I EQ them, mix them, add effects that I envision, arrange them." Ed tells me that for small jobs he is committed to helping young artists, but he does have to work without the luxury of resources. "It's faster than I would do for a professional job. You want time to mix a song, take it with you, listen to it in different places, in the car, at home, and see how it feels. But we are a bit more constrained with time so we do the best we can. With my equipment, though, we can get a professional sound equivalent to anyone out there today." Reed is dedicated to music and has found a way to make a living at what he loves. As I watch, Reed and

M3nsa discuss the layerings of sounds, the song's arrangement and effects. They play a ten-second segment of the song, comment on it, and remove or adjust the sound until they both agree. It is a painstaking, repetitious process. Reed comments, "It's not easy. People think being in the studio is glamorous. It's hard work. . . . Imagine listening to the same track for eight hours straight!"

M3nsa recognizes the importance of a proper sound mix for shaping music's feel. For most aspects of the album, M3nsa relies on friends and connections. But he feels the sound mix is the most important area to invest in financially. Mixing adds value, musical polish, and emotional power to a track. He is impressed with Ed's studio and his craft. But as they work together, he notices that Ed's sound is "a bit old-school. . . . We have to learn to listen to each other to get the sound that I want for the final record. . . . Ed has that 1990s hip-hop feel. It's a bit wet compared to the sound now." In the 1990s pop and hip-hop used heavy reverb and compression. M3nsa explains, "Reverb gives music a wet sound. These days Jay-Z and these guys are using a dry sound. I like a more raw feel. Tracks on this album like 'Anaa?' have a . . . grimy sound. 'Fanti Love Song' uses reverb to create a gentle soothing sound on the ears."[12] Aesthetic dryness equates to a feeling of crispness and precision, whereas griminess imparts reverberation and fullness to the music. Mixing gives new feeling to each track. "A mix will define the music and determines the mood . . . its emotion. . . . It puts the track in a different class or genre."

Early Ghanaian hiplife producers working on PC computers learned the art of mixing tracks by trial and error and by listening to old records and new American hip-hop. M3nsa recalls, "At first [hiplife] was so blown out, but producers learned over time and raised the quality of music production. That's one thing that made Reggie and Rab stand out at first—the quality of their sound." One aspect of hiplife's distinctiveness is the way it is mixed. According to M3nsa, its distinct sound is "characterized by heavy drums and bass line and loud, dry vocals sitting heavily in the mix. Everything else sits in there softly." Ghanaian artists worry about how the technical quality of sound compares to international standards. Since most producers in Ghana lack top-quality equipment, many musicians who record there try to mix and master their music in America or Europe. M3nsa recalls his early tracks as a hiplife artist with embarrassment. "Our music was not subtle. The beat was too bright, and the lyrics just too heavy . . . brittle."

Every day for two weeks M3nsa travels two hours from New Brunswick, New Jersey, where he is staying with his schoolmate and musical collaborator Bosco (known in music circles as Kwabena Jones) and his wife to Reed's Staten Island studio.[13] As the mix reaches its conclusion, M3nsa is pleased. "If you listen to my record next to Jay-Z's or Beyonce's the quality is comparable. Unlike some artists, I am a musician and concerned about the craft of the sound." Reed is not happy with the quality of the vocals on the title track and with the fact that they are out of tune. M3nsa rerecords some of the tracks at Bosco's house to reinsert in the final mix but is still not satisfied. "I am still not happy with that track. I liked the raw version I recorded in Accra. Whenever you try to redo something, you lose that spontaneous feel that made it right, you know?" He would continue to rework the track, as the vocals did not seem to fit properly into the mix.[14]

M3nsa, Bosco, Rab, and I sit in an Irish bar on 14th Street in Manhattan one evening discussing how Ghanaian music gets categorized by artists and audiences and how M3nsa will market himself. In 2001 Rab returned from Accra, to work for Universal Music Group. He was frustrated with the limits of Ghana's music business. "I felt I did all I could there and needed to come back to New York to see if I could push African hip-hop to the next level from this end."[15] He continues to work with Reggie and to promote rising Ghanaian artists. We consider how to release the music and reach audiences with a budget of a few thousand dollars—at most. The success of Brooklyn-based hip-hop artist Blitz the Ambassador's independent album *Stereotype* in mid-2009 provided a template for other underground and cross-over musicians to emulate. Like M3nsa, Blitz (Samuel Bazawule) was raised in Accra and was part of the early wave of teenage hiplifers, featured on the hit hiplife track from 1999, "Deeba," rapping in English on the mostly Twi song. He left Ghana to attend Kent State University then relocated to Brooklyn to pursue music. Blitz cites personal encouragement from Chuck D of Public Enemy as crucial to his music's Pan-African political messages as well as his lyrical style.

Unable to get a deal with a major record label, he organized his own publicity. Blitz recalls how one day while selling his mixtapes in front of Virgin Records in Union Square in Manhattan, he met his future manager and business partner James Bartlett.[16] For Blitz "sitting in meetings pitching my music to executives felt terrible. But I couldn't do it on my own. James and I built a team. . . . Graphics, web design, everything to get the music out." Blitz put together a live band reflecting his blend of hip-hop, primarily English rap and Afrobeat orchestration. The musicality differentiated him from other rappers trying to make it in New York. "We built up a fan base by performing live shows with the band." Blitz's publicity places his Ghanaian roots and his music within a hip-hop genealogy. As his Facebook description reads, "Born and raised in Accra, Ghana, Blitz the Ambassador grew up to the sounds of Afro-Beat, Highlife, Jazz, and Motown. But when his older brother introduced him to Public Enemy's classic album, *It Takes a Nation of Millions to Hold Us Back*, as a young boy, he was changed forever. 'I had never heard young Black people express themselves in that way before,' recalls Blitz."[17]

In the lead-up to the album launch of *Stereotype*, Blitz had several short humorous Webisodes shot with a character wearing a suit and an old cassette ghetto-blaster as a head; the album cover features this character shooting itself in the head. Through various connections he was able to get the music video for the album single "Breathe" onto the MTV2 Web site. With buzz from live shows and online videos, Blitz's album went to number 9 on iTunes hip-hop sales. With critical praise, market recognition, and the flexibility to appeal to hip-hop, jazz, folk, rock, and world music fans, Blitz and his band would be picked up by programmers for music festivals around the world. With the release of his next album, *Native Sun,* in 2011, his position in this circuit was solidified. Blitz has hit on a formula for making it in the strange landscape of global music. "We make some money through digital sales but mostly through live shows in Europe. People don't know me in New York but at festivals in France and Germany we will play to 50,000 people."[18] With only friends and no major marketing or label backing, this success inspired other independent musicians.

Rab thinks M3nsa's music is harder to brand but has broader potential. "Blitz has a great template for success. But he is straight up hip-hop; he is not marketing himself as Ghanaian or African. M3nsa is harder to market in the U.S. as he is not doing world music, he doesn't sound like African music, he is not really hiplife; he can reach a broader audience and cross over if we can figure out how to market it."[19] Rab wants M3nsa to be less informal in doing collaborations, arranging rights, and organizing online marketing and sales. Watching how artists achieve success these days, he explains, it is important to "look professional" and have a "media strategy" and coordinate online content so that consumers can easily find artist information, watch videos, and find out where to buy tracks and merchandise. M3nsa has a more improvisational view. While he is dedicating himself full time to the music and the goal is to make music and make money, it must be in an uncompromising manner. As M3nsa describes with regard to the single "Adjuma": "It's about desire. I want to make a living at this; make money. But riches won't make me happy. Love, family, friendship, man."

Rab has been e-mailing to try and arrange the rights to use a sample from Nigerian-French singer Aṣa, which M3nsa has already included. He explains, "Aṣa is a big-time Nigerian singer and we are in the process of negotiating the rights to use her vocals for 'No One Knows Tomorrow.'" Rab is concerned that in leading up to the album's release M3nsa should maximize his music's potential impact and avoid any problems. "You have to have all the content ready so when people hear the single they can buy the album." As Rab points out, a lot of young artists make the mistake of releasing a song and not giving an online audience more material. For M3nsa, as with Blitz, selling music online will hopefully lead to name recognition and invitations for live shows. Whereas a few years ago cassette and CD sales were the main money-making mediums, with online sales and the circulation of MP3s, artists have returned to focusing on live shows. M3nsa plans to coordinate the release of *No. 1 Mango Street* with shows in Europe, America, and Africa. "Money is not in record sales. Endorsements are crucial these days and playing out at shows and then getting booked for the next gig if you perform well." But it all starts with an Internet audience and music-marketing savvy.

M3nsa completes the mixing and mastering, circulating among collaborators the almost-complete songs for contemplation via an online file-sharing site, Dropbox. He flies to London already planning a new collaboration with British rapper Sway for the following day. "Making music is a lifestyle. I have so many tracks that I am working on. Beats that I have had for years, just waiting to use. I have a track that I did with my dad that I almost put on this album. But I am never quite satisfied with the final products, which drives me to keep making more music."

M3nsa thinks his music is positioned well to reach international audiences. He describes the sound of *No. 1 Mango Street*:

Afro-funk is the school from where I am from. Grimy hip-hop with a jazz feel. It is a break from old Ghanaian highlife, but draws on that sound. . . . I put a hard, driving song to open the album. I have gotten good responses from African American listeners. African American hip-hop is important to me. Heavy drums, my flows, how I chop up the breaks comes from an American sound. When African American musicians hear me they say, "Wow, you have sick flows! Is this Fela?" But man, there are so many other African musicians out there; Americans think everything African is [Nigerian Afrobeat pioneer] Fela. But even if they can't understand the lyrics they like the flow and funky music. I got so much interest because it's a fresh sound. I'm not just doing the same old thing with rap.

M3nsa must present his travels differently for different audiences in order to attempt a musical balancing act: for Ghanaians his status abroad gives him credentials but he has to prove he is still in touch locally. For international audiences he must provide authentic Africanness. For the hard-core hip-hop crowd he has to show an American or even a UK hip-hop fluency. His music slips between easy generic definitions, with each track invoking a multitude of styles. At one point, M3nsa's Facebook page described his music as "Hiphopish-Soulful-Highlifey-AfroBeatish-Tones," and his place of origin was listed as "Accra by way of North London through LA," showing his blending of place and style. Thinking about his musical trajectory, he wonders, "Maybe my music is still hiplife. I wouldn't mind calling it that. . . . I wish people would not try to constantly define and separate styles."

With digital technology, releasing an album no longer includes the physical act of manufacturing and marketing albums. On Facebook and Twitter, M3nsa has a loyal following of thousands of fans: Ghanaians abroad, Ghanaians at home, and knowledgeable global music hipsters. But M3nsa and his team of collaborators are trying to expand their online following. Rab is working as a digital content specialist for Universal Music Group. He is especially concerned with helping rising artists reach new audiences through their digital presence. We discuss designing a Web site dedicated to the new album and getting the songs onto iTunes, Amazon, and other pay download sites through third-party distributor CD Baby. He explains to M3nsa, "We need to create as much online buzz as possible. If we create as many links as possible to your Web site it will help it come up in searches and start directing traffic our way. We need to constantly update the content so that people come back and follow what you are doing. Web videos, blogs, new photos of events, free downloads to keep people interested." Rab is worried that M3nsa does not have enough content to maintain audience interest and implores M3nsa to post more photos and write short blog entries. They plan to print a thousand physical CD copies of the album for U.S. distribution. "Sales are online these days," he explains. "The actual CD is more like a calling card, for sale at shows and to get your name out there. But the real numbers are digital downloads."

In the song "No One Knows Tomorrow," M3nsa samples and loops vocals by Aṣa, providing a neo-African soul aesthetic as background for his lyrics:

> When I wake in the morning I know I'm blessed as a man can be.
> Never forget my ancestors, gone.
> I know they watch down on me. It's inspirational.
> I am charged with aspirations and dreams to follow,
> and leave behind my life troubles and all my sorrows.
> And live today,
> because no one knows tomorrow.

The song posits a carefree individual living in the moment. The Pidgin English lyrics, well-known artist sample, and light melodic rhythm are aimed at an eclectic audience. M3nsa arranges to shoot the video for the song in Atlanta, to be directed by Sam Kessie, a young Ghanaian filmmaker. She invests money in making the video, as it is an opportunity to show her visual talents. "Since M3nsa will reach a wider audience it will help people see my work and hopefully lead to other jobs."[20] Artists of all sorts seek inspiration and recognition through collaborations. Being an artist in this moment requires the artistry of making connections as much as it does musical, vocal, or visual talent.

Representations of Work in Accra

Back in Accra in December 2009, M3nsa releases "Adjuma" (Work) as the album's first single.[21] He times this with Farmer's Day, a national public holiday celebrating farm labor and the nation's agricultural legacy. The "release," again, is a digital affair mostly entailing online and radio promotion. He circulates the track as a free digital MP3 download to Ghanaian DJs, other musicians, fans, and Accra club owners. M3nsa explains, "I know a lot of the DJs and presenters so I use those connections to get my music out there." It receives heavy airplay across Accra, garnering critical acclaim. M3nsa goes on air at various stations for interviews about the album. He explains to me that the song explores "people's everyday hustle . . . what normal people have to do to survive." Okyeame Kofi (formerly of the hiplife group Akyeame) discusses and plays it on Adom FM. M3nsa makes appearances at XFM with Eddie Blay in the evening and with Naa Adjokoor on her morning show. Julz, a Ghanaian music promoter based in Toronto who runs Ghanamixtapes.com, an "Online Ghana Music Community," is in town looking for new artists and features "Adjuma" on a mixtape compilation online release.

DJ Black promotes the track on his weekly Saturday night *Open House Party* program on Joy FM. M3nsa is a guest on the show, a regular stop for musicians to showcase new music, freestyle, and talk live on air. Later, DJ Black remixes the track and recirculates it online. Kwadwo Ampofo, known as DJ Black or Toontoom (Akan for black), has been one of the most influential radio DJs playing hiplife, beginning in the late 1990s when he worked at University of Ghana's FM station, Radio Univers. At Joy FM since 2001 he has also gained an international reputation across Africa, performing in DJ competitions like the Sprite Channel O Emcee Africa Battle in 2008 in South Africa and spinning for Channel O and MTV Base television stations in Johannesburg during the 2010 World Cup. At the Joy FM studios M3nsa puts on headphones and adjusts his microphone opposite DJ Black. While he talks to M3nsa, Black scans music playlists on his MacBook Pro, which is connected to the station computer, mixer, and scratching turntable, planning his selections, checking online requests, and monitoring his Facebook status. When he gets the signal to go live, he shifts to a light familiar tone and begins the bantering on-air interview:

> **Black:** What up, what up M3nsa? Officially welcome to the Open House Party. It's been a long time coming. I know it's been difficult getting out of Number One Mango Street.
>
> **M3nsa:** Ah, man.
>
> **Black:** It must be a difficult street.
>
> **M3nsa [chuckles]:** Adjuma no edoso. [It's a lot of work.]
>
> **Black:** But tell us the story.

The conversation quickly merges into an improvised version of the "Adjuma" track.[22] With the beat bumping through his headphones, M3nsa finds his pace and marks his lyrical entry with a mix of greetings, self-proclamations, and subtle jokes.

M3nsa: Hey man, listen man. Check it check it check it out, yo. Mo ncheckin' me out yo.

Black: [laughs]

M3nsa: Sounds so good, challey. Should I? Or maybe I should?

Warming up and calling for audience attention, M3nsa plays with word reversals. He subtly reverses "Check it out" from a call for listeners to a humorous statement of his lyrical prowess, mixing Twi and English in "Mo ncheckin' me out yo." Black laughs as M3nsa pointedly describes the purpose of his visit to the radio station, stating, "You all are checking me out." Freestyling, M3nsa intones a slowed-down version of the song mixed with improvised lines.

M3nsa is back again to drive the world insane.
Everything I do is a result of hard work—I don't ever complain.
Working hard with these two hands washing these plates and these pans.
So I can shedda [dress] myself maybe buy some brand new shoes and pants.
But you don't understand.

"Adjuma" describes the duality of how labor defines contemporary life. Its lyrics implore listeners to recognize the daily struggles of working.

We don't have a life, all we do is work.
When we go to sleep, we dream about work.

The song provides a lesson on labor that is relevant to the contemporary music industry, stating that work provides the possibilities of life but also its limits; with the free market comes the potential for small-scale entrepreneurs to succeed through their own labor, but at the same time keeps them in place as laboring subjects. The song points to the ways in which work dominates everything, even your dreams. M3nsa's lyrics state that no matter your profession—trader, carpenter, football player, doctor—labor is hustling. The notion of hustle in popular usage has a dual morality, defining both life's possibilities and its constraints, legal aspiration and illicit value accumulation. This is an apt description of the development of small-scale electronic music production and Internet-based distribution networks that challenge the music industry's control of taste and of economic value as well as the use of African music as a place-based marker of local identity.

M3nsa made the beats and produced "Adjuma" himself. Whereas the album's title track focuses on the problematics of return and adopts a sincere tone, "Adjuma" examines work with an ironic quality. M3nsa describes the song as a "parody. . . . I don't like to preach. I want to get a message across with humor. [My] music focuses on little daily concerns; funny little things that are part of our culture. People know exactly where it's coming from but it also has multi[ple] influences from all over. . . . I want them to sit down and listen to the songs but you have to give them funky style for youth and foreign audiences so that they will take time and listen to the messages."

The song begins with the title repeated with staccato reverb. This loop is an explicit reference to the opening of Lil Wayne's 2008 hit "A Milli." Musically, it is stripped down and, as M3nsa explained to me, has "that southern crunk sound." He chose this as the first song for release because, he said, "I want to show people what I can do. People say, 'M3nsa's been away from Ghana for so long.' I want to remind them that I know local life, street life, slang and all that."

M3nsa conceives of making music as a part of everyday life, and this song in particular shows the overlap between musical content and form. He does not write songs in a linear fashion; rather he imagines them holistically. He explains to me, "I wrote [the song] 'Adjuma' in my head and laid out the beat the same day. I was on my way to work sitting on a [double-decker] bus going from North London and the concept came to me; I pondered it at work that day. I kept thinking about this dirty south crunk vocal and then the beat came into my head. . . . I hate an MC who is preachy. I wanted to get my message across without judging."

From his YouTube account, mightymensa, the artist posts the song's music video on YouTube on December 3, 2009. It is compressed as an MP4 video for easy upload to Web sites and for downloading to mobile viewing devices. It is linked to his Facebook fan page, Myspace, Sonicbids, and various Ghana music sites. The YouTube copy promotes the album, "First music video off M3NSA'S No. 1 Mango Street Album, due out in the new year 2010!! ADJUMA captures the very essense [sic] of what the hustle is, for the average Ghanaian! Enjoyable to watch and inspiring."[23]

The video opens with sped-up shots of M3nsa standing on an overpass staring at the camera as people rush to work. They blur past while he remains still in the background. M3nsa raps the chorus,

What be your hustle? Eh? What be your main thing?
What you dey do with your muscles? ibi carpentry or painting?
Mankind for eat! So be like all be the same thing!
Whether you be lawyer, doctor, or you dey push truck for Kaneshie!

The song links various labor practices across class, describing them all as ways to eat and survive. M3nsa describes the lyrics: "When I say 'What be your hustle? What be your main thing?' I don't mean selling drugs. Everyone's got a hustle, being a doctor or whatever. It means being an entrepreneur, doing what you have to do to survive." The lyrics both celebrate and lament the need to work to survive.

The music video for the song was shot in markets and roads around Kaneshie in central Accra. Day laborers and traders look into the camera, repeating endlessly the mantra "Adjuma, Adjuma, Adjuma." As their images are chopped and looped, workers appear to endlessly repeat their task—construction, carrying loads, selling food. The camera captures smiles of complicity on workers' faces that they share with M3nsa, the camera, the viewer. The song switches between languages: Twi, Fante, Ga, Pidgin, and English. For M3nsa this is not a conscious choice but one that represents how he inhabits the world. He explains, "If I knew what I dreamt in, I would write only in that language. I think back and forth between them naturally. If I feel a language or a particular word gets out the emotions I am looking for in a lyric, I go for it."

In December and January, with Panji and Wanlov's help, M3nsa promotes his music in Accra. He pays for a local company to print a thousand CDs of an EP version of the album, titled *Small Mangoes*. But they printed the cover wrong and many of the discs were blank. Though M3nsa hoped to have them for the holidays, by January 15 they were not ready. He quarrels with Panji because he replaced one of the song mixes M3nsa did in New York with his own mix of the song. "Panji liked his version better but he didn't even tell me he replaced his mix before the files were sent to the CD printer." M3nsa and Wanlov hang out at Panji's house in his loftlike second-story studio, as an editor color grades and pieces together the scenes from their film *Coz Ov Moni*. They are happy with the edit and the rich color and depth of the high-definition footage. They discuss how to get it to market. Wanlov says, "We have to sell it cheap and fast to beat bootleggers." He is concerned about the speed at which local bootleggers copy new products, saying they should print five thousand VCD copies fast and sell them cheaply at four cedis each before anyone can copy it.[24] It is better to sell more quickly than to charge a high price and sell a few slowly, he argues, because if you charge more someone will copy it and undersell you before you have a chance to make back your money.

M3nsa and Wanlov do numerous performances across Accra over a period of weeks. M3nsa explains, "Since I am not around all the time some people think I am out of touch, so I need to reach out to the public and show them what I am doing." They perform with a live band at Reggie Rockstone's new club, Rockstone's Office. They rap over prerecorded electronic beats at a regular hip-hop showcase called Bless the Mic held at Coffee Shop. They make several appearances at the Accra Shopping Mall near Tetteh Quarshie roundabout, where there is a small billboard advertising the music. M3nsa places the EPs on CD for sale in a few venues anticipating the full album.

London Album Launch

Back in London M3nsa organizes his resources to officially launch *No. 1 Mango Street* in October. Although M3nsa is busy with various projects, coming back to Accra for the official premiere of *Cuz Ov Moni* at Ghana's National Theatre on May 15, 2010, he expands his collaboration with Wanlov into a full-length FOKN BOIS album. He enlists London-based PR people for advice. He exchanges work by a Web designer for piano lessons. As I mention, he puts his tracks on iTunes for a week "to test the market" but takes them down again. There are numerous stories and announcements on arts, hip-hop, African music, and London-area culture Web sites about M3nsa's music. He performs live at BBC radio studios.[25] He sends out links to his Facebook community. He prints a few hundred CDs and T-shirts for the launch. Late in the game, M3nsa decides to rerecord the album's title track and is finally happy with the results. His cousin, musician Ryan Ansah, adds a light jazz guitar riff that floats over the beat. The lyrics are smoother, embedded in the mix. He explains to me, "I just wasn't happy with the way it sounded. I redid the whole thing myself and mixed it to match the tracks we did with Ed Reed."

The October 2 launch is a success. As usual the crowd loves his live band's performance. It increases his Internet presence, but there is still no album to sell or online digital tracks available. After the album launch, M3nsa receives attention, garnering positive reviews from a number of online music sites that turn into more calls for radio appearances and live shows. On October 13, 2010, he opens for hip-hop legends Arrested Development at Barbican Hall in London. On November 9, 2010, his gmail status update promotes his latest outing, performing with rising Nigerian Afro-soul star Nneka. "Tonight EVERYONE is heading to 02 Shepherd's Bush Empire, as I support an old friend Samini and the Amazing Nneka! . . . http://fb.me/JjoYzTlQ." On November 29, 2010, M3nsa's Facebook update announces the release of the first single from the forthcoming album: "'No One Knows' single out on iTunes TODAY, Monday 29th November 2010!! First single to be taken from the forthcoming 'No.1 Mango Street' album VIDEO COMING SOON!! AWW." When I send him a message teasing, "How many first singles and releases can your album have!?" he writes back jokingly, saying, "Don't worry this is only the second first single!" Interest grows as he heads to Hungary to perform and record for six days, shoots two television spots in London in one day, then flies to Los Angeles, Atlanta, and New York to perform and record music videos. He is nominated for a 2010 MOB Award. "Things are heating up," he tells me. "I have gotten more interest from all sorts of fans who really appreciate my music. . . . The blend of hip-hop and live band is speaking to fans." Atlanta-based Ghanaian video director Sam Kessie shoots videos in Brooklyn for "Fanti Love Song" and in Atlanta for "No One Knows Tomorrow," The latter gets attention on non-Ghanaian music Web sites like Okayafrica, MTV Iggy, and Hip Hop Chronicle, which post short reviews of the album and links to videos and online sales.[26]

Again, M3nsa puts the tracks for sale on iTunes and other Internet music shops, though he continues to struggle with finding ways to turn the growing critical acclaim and recognition into a financially viable career. Rab remains critical of M3nsa's strategy, asking, "Why spend all sorts of money shooting videos and 'releasing' albums that you don't back up with marketing?" The emotional links between ideas of home, family, music, and business rise to the surface for M3nsa as he and his wife have their first child in early 2011 in London. The lyrics for his song "We Go Rock" use the dominant idiom of financial investment to convince a woman to emotionally invest in him. His wife, Nigerian singer N'didi, adds her vocals to the track.

It no be coincidence I find you here.
It be my fate oooo.
You be my destiny, make I try to show you the best in me.

Make your first deposit, invest in me;
if you go bank in me it go pay, ooo.

These lyrics link music making to emotional passion to financial investment in an apt metaphor for the fast-paced hustle that being a contemporary artist requires. Over the next few months investments seem to pay off as M3nsa and Wanlov gain international recognition, increasingly performing across Europe, and planning for future collaborations.

Conclusion: Pleasure and Labor

Transnational African rappers like M3nsa defy groundings of genre and place, instead drawing on multiple local and foreign musical registers for legitimation. Genres, locales, identities, and styles become a pastiche of signs in which making music is simultaneously a lifestyle, an artistic process, and a business strategy. Collaboration, as musicians such as M3nsa conceive of it, involves working with beatmakers, singers, producers, videographers, and digital media workers in making and distributing music. It becomes an idiom of sociality and value conversion that links ideas of self-expression to economic sustainability. An artist performatively produces himself as a celebrity or spokesperson through authoritative circulation of his music online and through live performances. Individual artists use influence, skill, and charisma to marshal their social networks in order to position themselves in relation to a more formal entertainment industry, literally making a name for themselves. African music—in both its growing global popularity and significance for Ghanaian youths—resonates, as pleasure, business practice, and diasporic refraction intermingle.

There is pleasure in the process of making music, traveling, performing, aspiring to fame, collaborating, and planning for success. This musical process is driven by aspiration and improvisation, remixing previously meaningful signs into new configurations that point to new possible futures. Living the life of a musician is a form of self-fashioning. M3nsa's songs evolve as he records and remixes and adds pieces to tracks in different locales. He began as a hiplife artist but his music has surpassed easy generic categorization. M3nsa's style is eclectic and appeals to a variety of audiences within Ghana and abroad, in addition to typical hiplife listeners. In its symbolic work, however, it is still hiplife, in that it regrounds Ghanaian youth in linking specific Ghanaian images, language practices, and rhythms to cosmopolitan networks of black identities in music, travel, and fashion. But thinking of hiplife in terms of this lifestyle and locale, M3nsa still defies expectations, living and working in more expansive ways. With the rise of online digital file sharing, the relationship between musical aesthetic value and economic value takes on new tensions. Artists struggle to control how their work and lives are symbolized and how their names travel, symbolically associating their labor—and by association their public selves—with authoritative signs in the cyber and geographic locales through which they circulate.

Making music of any kind involves various kinds of labor from many different people. Rapidly changing technologies of production and distribution instantiate social relations, meanings, and values distinct from those made through live recording and performance-based music (Miller 2012; Stokes 2004). Whereas popular musicians of past generations needed the leadership and musical skills of a bandleader, turn-of-the-millennium hip-hop artists require the skills of an entrepreneur, a branding executive, and an Internet/social media expert. An artist must piece together the musical, production, marketing, and distribution aspects of making music. The process begins with lyrical fragments and digital beats. Artists carry beats, instrumentals, and vocals as digital files between home recording setups, private studios, Web designers, and Internet upload sites scattered across cities and continents. Musicians strategize on how to use travel and connections to imbue their musical products with distinction. Music production, promotion, and distribution for M3nsa's album involves bartering and negotiating with beatmakers, DJs, producers, promoters, and video makers dispersed across three continents, incrementally adding labor and value to a digital product.

M3nsa's experience shows that labor input from many different people is required to make a musical product. Sometimes they sell this product, sometimes they do not. Sometimes it takes the material form of a CD or DVD but many times it circulates digitally, sometimes for free. Artists want to circulate their work in order to make a name for themselves and gain some level of celebrity that will lead to more work, sponsorships, and possibly large-scale deals. Various collaborators and artists are aware that they are contributing work to making something. Some say they are doing it out of love for the music or artistry. Others hope to earn money in the future. Still others do it in exchange for some other skill that the artist can provide them. These exchanges define a loose network of place-based and artistic kinship that weaves in and out of connections to family in Ghana, schoolmates, white hipsters, hip-hop heads, or Ghanaians abroad.

Most participants are uncertain about the value of their work. Karl Marx (1993) points out that there is a crucial temporal delay between the selling and use of labor and paying for it. Workers are only paid after they have completed their job, pointing to the ritual contingency that defines exchanges around labor relations and the importance of temporality to value. Artistic collaborations rely upon an investment of labor in which participants usually do not know when or how they might be remunerated and artists themselves are not sure of how they might attract an audience and gain more fame. Temporal lags often involve the mediation of institutional forms like online sales agents such as iTunes that quantify exchanges and extract capital while appearing to leave things in the hands of the artist. Exchanges and calculations among artists maintain personal and artistic relationships over time through shared potential, risk, and debt. Artistic exchanges are motivated strategies, investments in future potentials. The logic of the commodity form is here subverted so that it embodies the history of its production in the person of the artist—where classically it is abstracted through exchanges between commodity and money forms, assuming an abstract universal exchange value. Artists like M3nsa make enough money to continue to make music, to travel, and to dream of fame, but usually rely upon more regular work to survive. The uncertain exchanges of labor and value that go into making music focus artists on "hustling" to find the right formula to convert music into celebrity and celebrity into economic value.

While artists like M3nsa desire audiences to appreciate their music for its artistic value, they also recognize that they must convert musical value into popularity as a product in and of itself. This version of celebrity as it circulates relies upon a valorization of leisure that requires intensive labor to maintain (Braudy 1997). Self-fashioning artist-entrepreneurs work hard to cultivate public desires for effortless leisure and celebrity. Success is imagined to come from converting musical value into celebrity. Celebrity leads to economic success. In collaboration, movement, and technological circulation, artists try to add value to their musical products and personal brands.

International Ghanaian popular music such as M3nsa's shows how youths negotiate changing notions of travel and labor. Young African cosmopolitans, traveling and living, build upon the circuits of older, multidirectional African diasporas. International African musicians rely upon an informal entrepreneurial charisma in which pleasure and labor become intermingled, especially through the rapidly changing role of technology in popular music. For a segment of more elite Ghanaian artists, rapid and frequent travel between Ghana, Europe, and America has become normal. Musical production is often rooted in both the symbolic and social aspects of international travel and imaginings of place. Aspiring artists link the pleasures and labors of music through changing technologies to leverage themselves into positions of celebrity. Popular hip-hop music does not simply provide a liberatory project for global black youths, as some scholarship of black music implies, but rather instantiates a set of labor relations built upon new technologies of music production and dissemination. For both artists with access to international travel such as M3nsa and youths struggling to make it in the music industry in the streets of Accra, music making is about entrepreneurship, driven by changing media and business forms.

CHAPTER 8

Ghana@50 in the Bronx

SONIC NATIONALISM AND NEW DIASPORIC DISJUNCTURES

Popular music is central to how Africans in Europe and North America imagine new spatial configurations that recall home while making new worlds in the language of diaspora. But choosing which diaspora is complicated in that Ghanaians identify with African American society or black British life while at the same time maintaining the specificity of recent Ghanaian global movements. Africans in the United States must contend with a different set of race and class histories than those moving to Britain and Europe. Older Ghanaians coming to the United States seeking economic opportunity maintain Ghanaian community ties, often planning to return home eventually. But for youths these connections are less clear. A generation of Ghanaian youths born in the United States and those relocated as children who have fading memories of Ghana struggle to balance new racial and cultural affiliations with home cultural and national forms. Ghanaians abroad maintain affiliation through churches, restaurants, and African shops that sell foodstuffs, beauty products, and videos. Community events such as out-doorings (naming ceremonies), weddings, funerals, and picnics are important. Highlife used to be the soundtrack for Ghanaian events abroad. However in the 2000s the soundtrack shifted to hiplife. The latest Ghanaian music recalls familiar nightlife and pleasures while bringing the latest news from home.

For a segment of Ghanaian youths abroad, hiplife provides a mobile form of sonic nationalism that highlights the disjunctures of distance that diaspora entails (Campt 2012; Edwards 2003; Hanchard 1999; Gilroy 1993). To them Ghanaian music is not about shiny newness but rather nostalgia. Musical style marks home. It provides a mobile, sonic structure, a soundscape for navigating a foreign landscape while maintaining what it means to be Ghanaian. Accra's sounds represent belonging for urban dwellers and memories of home for those who have left and even for youngsters with secondhand memories of home. With sonic nationalism, I refer to how hiplife viscerally calls forth Ghanaian identity through bodily action. Bodies in musical contexts are oriented through a poetics of sound invoked in rhythm, language use, gestures, spatial organization, and culturally specific uses of media (Peterson 2010; Dent 2009; Fox 2004; Feld 1990). Hiplife provides a set of movements and linguistic practices that at once mark an Afro-modernity, cosmopolitan belonging, and a nostalgic recollection of home (Edwards 2003; Ferguson 1999; Hanchard 1999).

Hiplife concerts and parties in the United States are central events for the citation and celebration of a dispersed and sometimes ambivalent nationhood. Ghanaian musicians are regularly brought by ambitious promoters to Britain, Holland, Germany, and sometimes Canada and the United States to perform for Ghanaian audiences. Hashim Haruna organizes hiplife events for Ghanaian communities in the New York area. He has brought top artists from Ghana including VIP, Tic Tac, Samini, Ofori Amponsah, M3nsa, and Reggie Rockstone. In the context of concerts at Gaucho's Gym in the South Bronx celebrating Ghana's fiftieth and fifty-first anniversaries of independence from British colonial rule, Ghanaianness is marked within and against broader black affiliations. Cultural nationhood in this case is produced and stretched through the transnational circulation of hiplife music from Ghana toward Ghanaian communities abroad as a marker of authenticity and homeland (Pierre 2012). Nationalism is not about identifying with the geographical space of the nation-state. Rather, nationhood defines a moral-cultural core providing individuals abroad with potential tools both to be successful and to maintain identifications with dispersed networks that point home (Buggenhagen 2010; Ong 2006; Stoller 2002).

Artists in Ghana's hiplife industry travel back and forth from Ghana to the United States providing a new language for mobile African youths to identify with African American imaginaries while maintaining specifically Ghanaian community affiliations. Instead of being solely a form of nostalgia or a way to maintain an inwardly focused community outside the boundaries of home, Ghanaianness in the Bronx provides a language through which people aspire to individuated success (cf. Tsing 2004). The Ghanaian diaspora maps out a space "between" that is productive and ambivalent. This space emerges in certain material technologies of music and its accompanying stylistics. Hiplife music is transmitted through electronic media, transposing temporal simultaneity for spatial distance. For Africans living abroad, feelings of displacement and disjuncture negate cultural and national continuities but also produce new, reflexive ways to identify with a dispersed collective. An important way young Ghanaian diasporans mark their belonging to African and black communities while at the same time differentiating themselves from broader forms of racial and cultural communality is through an ideology of individual artistic expression.

Ghanaianness is increasingly experienced through popular entertainment, which is accessed and circulated through mobile phones and social networking. Through mediating digital technologies, text messaging, entertainment Web sites, and rapid file sharing, Ghanaian affiliation is made into an increasingly transnational musical culture. Music entrepreneurs, artists, and promoters create economic, technological, and artistic networks linking Ghanaians at home with those abroad, facilitating circulation between the two. Aspiring youths imagine themselves as part of a networked community of musicians and members of a cosmopolitan world in which travel and flexibility promise wealth and celebrity. The speed and ubiquity that cyber-movements promise, however, lay bare the physical restrictions on bodily movement that national borders and limited economic resources pose. In linking Ghanaians at home and abroad to broader ideas of African diaspora, hiplife music emphasizes the productive disjunctures of distance. That is, globalization is not simply about speeding up movement but, rather, radically modulates the velocities of people, digital material, and money.

For young Ghanaians, a hiplife concert in the Bronx reimagines a small, local event as continuous with both proximate networks and with broader national belongings. Space is important here in three ways. First, spaces of performance align participants with new imaginaries entailed in the bodily experience of a musical concert's sights and sounds. Second, Ghanaians dispersed across the United States use concerts and parties to connect with a diasporic Ghana. Third, Ghanaians abroad imagine the movements back and forth to home in the language of this music.

Ghanaian popular culture provides a language for Ghanaians in urban America to both identify with and differentiate themselves from the African American community, as blackness and Ghanaianness are sometimes aligned and sometimes contradictory for youths living in the United States. Ghanaian parties and music events enact bodily forms of sociality, speaking, humor, parody, and dress to carve out a specific space in New York's nightlife for representing Ghana. African immigrants to the United States are racialized within a multicultural black working-class cultural imaginary (Pierre 2012). At the same time, they struggle to maintain a feeling of Africanness that is not encompassed by American ideas of race or black culture. Through hiplife parties and concerts, Ghanaians publicly enact their difference from broader ideas of blackness and mark their specific potentials for achievement and success. The bodily and sonic forms that mark Ghanaianness delineate a subject who can successfully travel and earn while maintaining a Ghanaian moral core (Stoller 2002). For a generation of youths who either came to the United States as children or were born in the United States to Ghanaian parents, hiplife marks tradition, cultural belonging, and pride. For aspiring American-based Ghanaian rappers and DJs, the music is a way to both identify with home and make connections in a broader cultural language. Reggie Rockstone, among others, is an icon to these youths, who identify with his form of cosmopolitanism, which marks an ability to be both authentically Ghanaian and to blend in with broader diasporic communities. For some, hiplife inspires them to learn their "local" languages. For others, it becomes a way to think about continuity and disjuncture between home and the racialized daily landscape they inhabit.

Hiplife events are shaped by an ideology of public speaking and acting that emphasizes the self-fashioning aspects of indexicality (Gal 2005; Hill 2005; Silverstein 1976). Participants and audiences are predisposed to examine dress, language use, comportment, and stage presence as a mix of traditional references and new aspirations (Bauman and Briggs 1990). By proclaiming success through movement, artists and promoters imagine a landscape within which aspirations are contextualized and grounded by references to home (Kockelman 2010; Keane 1997). Drawing on hiplife's ideology of self-making and reliance on first-person narratives, rappers become indexical icons both pointing to and enacting the forms of agency necessary for aspiring Ghanaian youths to maintain cultural affiliations while subscribing to a mobile global aspiration. The body of the hiplife star performer centers these forms of identification made through a complex blending of passion, ambivalence, intimacy and distancing. For Ghanaian youths, aspiration has its own culturally specific aesthetic that is highly mobile, though tied to a set of familiar bodily forms, linguistic patterns, and moral polarities. In this chapter I ask: What are the visual and sonic aspects of dispersed nationhood? In the Bronx, what makes a party or concert a Ghanaian event and how do its contexts, music, and bodily forms of expression demarcate a sonic landscape of affiliation beyond spatial identification? In these contexts, how does travel—circulation itself—operate as an aesthetic?

Bronx Localities, Ghanaian Technologies

At sunrise Reggie Rockstone arrives at Kotoko International Airport in Accra ready to board a plane for New York. He is headlining a Ghana@50 Golden Jubilee concert advertised for Ghanaians across the East Coast of the United States in celebration of Ghana's fifty years of independence. The concert is to be held in two days, March 10, 2007, at Gaucho's Gym in the South Bronx and will feature other Ghanaian hiplife artists based in London and New York. In 2002 Reggie performed at famed downtown Manhattan club CBGB, catering to American alternative and hip-hop crowds. Now he is focused on the Ghanaian community. Rockstone, seen as an elder-statesman by twentysomething promoters and artists in the United States, is advertised as the star attraction. Promotion includes postcards and posters circulated by hand and put up on walls but is dominated by online and text message advertisements circulated through personal networks (see figure 35). With long neatly kept dreadlocks, dark sunglasses, a pinstriped blazer, and a black dress shirt unbuttoned to his chest, he waits with a small entourage as Delta Airlines officials deliberate over his passport. Rockstone tries to use his celebrity status to expedite the process but after long discussions, they refuse to let him get on the plane. With deferential respect to his status as a public figure, the ticket office official says, "Look, Uncle Reggie, we all know you and respect you but it is against airline regulations and we cannot put you on the plane. You will be turned back in New York because your papers do not match requirements." Reggie was born in England and travels on a UK passport. It is valid, but according to new strictures since 2005, U.S. immigration requires all passports to be equipped with a computer-chip tracking device. Rockstone calls the

FIGURE 35
Boogie Down Nima promotional poster for Bronx show.

New York promoter, Hashim Haruna, who had bought the plane ticket, to ask if he can do anything from that end. Hashim begins frantically calling every few minutes to find out what is going on.

We climb into a taxi, trying to decide whether the U.S. or the British Embassy will be more helpful. We decide to rush to the U.S. Embassy to see if they can clarify the situation. Since I am a U.S. citizen, we are able to make our way through the sea of Ghanaians lined up outside waiting to be called for their visa interview. Several hundred applications for U.S. visas are processed every day for a nonrefundable fee of $100. Applicants and their supporters fill the streets surrounding the visa section. Others have set up businesses based on this traffic, selling everything from food to passport photographs. As Reggie and I enter the embassy, Ghanaian security guards smile with excitement and ask Rockstone for complimentary copies of his CDs as we empty our pockets at the metal detector. The U.S. passport–holders' affairs office is upstairs away from the throngs.

On the stairs, an old man waiting for his passport recognizes Reggie and greets him: "Rockstone, how are you. You look great; like you are living well."

"Thank you, Wofa [Uncle], I am trying." Reggie replies calmly despite our frenzy to get to the visa officer.

"You should help an old man who has no money."

"Another time—I am late to catch a plane."

Behind bulletproof glass, the embassy official explains that the bigger problem is that his passport has been flagged in the computer. It will be necessary for Rockstone to be fingerprinted and processed by the FBI and Homeland Security computers in the United States, which will most likely take at least a week if there are no complications. She says that she cannot say why his passport has been flagged but that there is nothing she can do once he is in the system, but maybe he will be lucky and they will get the visa in time for him to get to New York by the weekend. Rockstone explains to the American woman, "Look, everyone here knows me. I even was at the U.S. ambassador's house last year to perform to promote good relations with Ghana. Isn't there something you can do?"

The agent speaks with a flat bureaucratic tone. "Mr. Rockstone, I have been told by the Ghanaians in the office you are very famous. But once you are flagged in the computer there is nothing we can do. Good luck." Reggie is told that he needs to follow regulations and initiate the process of applying for a visa by registering online to set up a visa appointment, download the forms, go to Standard Chartered Bank to pay the one hundred dollar application fee, and return with all of his paperwork and payment receipt on the appointed day. One of his assistants pulls up outside the embassy in his beat-up Toyota to drive us to the bank. He comments, "It's like 'Ya Bounce Wo Visa' part two!," referencing Rockstone's track from years earlier in which he criticizes the racist tactics of Western embassies in restricting visas for Africans. In the car we debate why he has been flagged by U.S. immigration. Rockstone laments that in 2000 he was paid to perform several shows in the United States but went in with a tourist visa. Immigration discovered that he had the wrong visa that did not allow him to earn money and detained him for a lengthy period. "It's because of Dhoruba's connections that you are in their computer," says another friend crammed into the car's backseat. He is referring to Reggie's friend and manager, Dhoruba Bin Wahad, a former member of the Black Panther Party who lived in Ghana from the mid-1990s. As chapter 3 describes, after nineteen years in New York State prison, his conviction for shooting two New York City police officers in 1971 was overturned. Upon receiving a settlement from the state of New York, Dhoruba moved to Ghana, becoming close friends with Reggie's father, Ricci. He remained an outspoken lecturer and political activist critical of U.S. racial politics and global imperialism. Dhoruba was Reggie's mentor and manager. "Yeah, I am sure D. is on the FBI or CIA list or something." Reggie replied. Dhoruba returned to live in the United States in 2007 with his wife and baby son. People teased Dhoruba that his boy would become a revolutionary because he bore a striking resemblance to Kwame Nkrumah and was born on Ghana's independence day.

In the car, we speculate about what it means to be "flagged in the computer" and its possible causes. The power of immigration restrictions relies on a lack of transparency, promoting speculation, paranoia, and fear. It inspires creative attempts to circumvent border policing: everything from U.S. visa lottery scams to suspect marriages to making sacrifices at traditional shrines to having church congregations pray for your visa (Piot 2010). Speculation about the motivation of visa officers is a form of vernacular ethnography, deploying psychoanalytic reasoning to uncover the logic of how and why American and European officials make seemingly random, flip decisions about people's immigration status that then shapes their lives.

Hashim Haruna keeps calling Reggie on his mobile to find out if he got the visa. Hashim is nervous and wants to know that everything is being done to get him to New York on time. The success of his major event in New York relies on Reggie. We drive back to the airport so that I can try to make the flight and Reggie can try to get his visa application in as fast as possible. I rush to board the flight at the busy airport thick with tourists, dignitaries, and artists attending fiftieth-anniversary celebration events. I wait at customs with American R&B superstar John Legend, who is leaving, and we watch Stevie Wonder arrive for a performance later that evening. When I land in New York, Hashim texts me, "Whatz up, RR coming? Call. Hash." I tell him I think it is doubtful considering the tenor of U.S. immigration policy. There is one more flight he could conceivably catch if all the paperwork and authorizations go as smoothly as possible. No one is hopeful.

As he prepares for the concert, Hashim and I meet in the Bronx to talk at his sister's African restaurant and market where they sell videos and personal care products as well as food. He is a quiet, serious young man with an eye for detail. As described in chapter 2, Hashim grew up in Accra's Nima neighborhood dominated by peoples from northern Ghana. He was passionate about hip-hop from an early age and was friends with members of celebrity hiplife group VIP. "We loved hip-hop because we saw it as music of the ghetto and we lived in the rough part of Accra. . . . When we started listening to hip-hop; there was a guy who would DJ in the neighborhood and always played the latest music from America."[1] His parents were relatively comfortable, though his family left the country seeking economic opportunity. "My parents wanted me to have a good education and chances to better myself which was hard to do in Ghana at the time." He came to the Bronx in 1995 with his parents after his first year of secondary school.

"It was hard at first being in America. People looked down on Africans, so I hid who I was in school, but I was good at soccer so I made friends." Hashim attended community college and now works as a technical assistant at a Bronx medical center. "It wasn't until after school that I got back into hiplife music that I had been into in Accra. When I reconnected with VIP and saw that they had become big stars in Ghana, I knew I could do something to make this movement global." Under the name Boogie Down Nima (BDN), Hashim promotes hiplife-oriented entertainment events in the New York area for the Ghanaian community. Ghanaians in the United States maintain connections to Ghana and keep up with current tastes through concerts, cultural fairs, and picnics, which feature the latest artists.

Ronny Boateng is a hiplife DJ who frequently works with Hashim. He also lives in the Bronx and works full time in shoe sales in lower Manhattan. As DJ Ronny he spins for Ghanaian parties and shows and plans to promote Ghanaian artists and music. He explains to me why hiplife is important for Ghanaians abroad. "Living in America can be isolating. Ghanaians want to feel comfortable and listen to music that is familiar to remind them of their culture and make them proud."[2] He grew up in Kwahu, moving to Accra in 1998. In 2000 he left Ghana for the Bronx. "Hashim was my senior in school. There were only a few Ghanaians or Africans in our school. This whole music promotion thing started small. Now Hashim is getting big. When he would throw house parties I began to build up my DJ skills and develop a personal style." He is passionate about making and promoting music. "We all have full-time jobs, which stops us from moving quickly. But the music is what we do."

Ghanaians in the Bronx congregate in neighborhoods on specific streets and apartment blocks.[3] For Ronny, this provides a sense of community in the midst of the city. "Ghanaian groups here revolve around churches, African stores, and music events and parties. The area near Yankee Stadium and 168th Street is a little Ghana neighborhood. There is a movie mall, Ghana school, food shop, music shop. There is even a Ghana police officer who speaks Twi when he patrols the area. We feel at home." Hiplife is a growing part of these identifications. Churches and businesses provide community centers. Music, in its digital and physical circulations, emphasizes mobility.

A few older promoters have controlled the organization of musical events for the U.S. Ghanaian community since the 1990s. After several years of organizing parties and promoting hiplife artists and DJs in New York, Hashim has developed a reputation for catering to younger Ghanaians in the United States. But so far most of his events have been on a relatively small scale with intimate venues and audiences of several hundred. Hashim recalls, "I got a reputation when Tic Tac came to New York and I was able to get him to come to the party I was promoting. Because he is such a big star, people started to take notice of me." Ronny notes the rising interest in Twi rap among first-generation Ghanaians, "In the Bronx a lot of [Ghanaians] are rapping. A few years back only a few were. . . . Now many kids are growing [up] who have never been to Ghana but their parents are from there. They only understand a few words and are trying to rap in Twi a bit and English with hiplife and highlife beats. We did a talent show at Lehman College a while back . . . a lot of them came to show their talent. Some are good and some are not but they are trying."

Now, relying on Reggie's celebrity status, Hashim hopes to raise his profile and "push hiplife popularity in the United States to the next level." For weeks he has been hyping the show on Facebook and Myspace; Ghanaian online sites like Ghanaweb.com and Ghanamusic.com, which consolidate news and entertainment articles; and through Ghanaian friendship and community networks across the eastern United States. Hashim explains, "The show is [a] celebration of Ghana's independence for Ghanaians who cannot make it home for the events in Accra." It will also feature Wanlov, Bright formerly of Buk Bak fame, and a number of aspiring Ghanaian rappers and DJs based in the United States. Rab

Bakari will be a guest MC. Hashim is expecting Ghanaians from all over the East Coast and is afraid that if word gets out that Reggie is having trouble getting to New York, no one will come. He is also nervous that if Reggie does not show up, he will be accused of lying to boost ticket sales, ruining his hard-won reputation as a reliable events manager with connections in the entertainment industry. Reggie is worried because he has come to be seen as an elder in the business; he has not done many full-length live shows in recent years. "I don't want to develop a reputation for not performing," he tells me. "All I have is my reputation and the public's respect for what I have done for Ghanaian music. But you know how the industry is—people will start talking and say, 'He sees himself as too important to show up.'" His manager, Paa K, is worried about Reggie. "He was shaken by his visa experience with the U.S. Embassy. He asked me, 'Why me? I am just a musician.' But I told him, 'No! Music is politics.'"

Hashim had hoped that Reggie would make the Friday flight and arrive for the show. The U.S. Embassy suggests his visa might be ready in time. Reggie goes to collect it, only to find that his passport is not ready and that nothing can happen over the weekend. As soon as Hashim calls and discovers that Reggie will not make it for Saturday evening, Rab suggests that Reggie send a personal video that can be shown to the crowd apologizing for his absence and explaining that he intended to show up and it was not the performer's or organizer's fault that he was not there. After all, "If there is one things Ghanaians will understand it is troubles with immigration and visas," Rab jokes.

An assistant shoots a video of Reggie in his studio on Saturday afternoon and takes the tape to Busy Internet, which is one of the newer and best-equipped Internet cafés in Accra that has high-speed connections. It is a local meeting spot and place to conduct business of all sorts. Late in the evening, groups of teenagers congregate there to surf the Internet for jobs, music, pornography, research for school projects, e-mail friends abroad, start overseas romances, and send Sakawa and 419 scam e-mails (cf. Burrell 2012). Busy Internet has also become a site for outsourced jobs, at one point taking a contract to process New York City parking tickets among other things. The café workers help to download Reggie's video from tape to digital file, compress it, and then copy it onto Pando, a download file-sharing program. They e-mail us a link to the file, though Rab and I are unable to download it. We talk back and forth with the technicians at Busy Internet as they try to re-compress the file and reupload it. It is past midnight in Accra and getting close to the scheduled time for the start of the Bronx show. We are finally able to download the file using YouSendIt, another file-sharing program that is more compatible with the older computer being used to send the video clip. We convert it into a QuickTime file, and import it into the video editing program Final Cut, quickly adding titles that mark its date, time, and location: "Reggie Rockstone Ossei, Accra, Ghana, 5:30 PM 9 March 2007." Copying the video clip onto a small hard drive, Rab and I rush to the venue.

Gaucho's Gym in the South Bronx is a modest warehouselike building on a dark commercial block with an open African market on one end and fenced empty lots across the street. Known for boxing, basketball, and local sporting and community events, the venue consists of an open basketball court with removable bleachers and balcony seating. As we arrive around 9 PM a sound crew is dragging speakers from a rented truck and finishing setting up the sound system, small stage, and mixing boards. Hashim wipes the sweat from his face as he directs the crew in the final preparations. He has invested thousands of dollars promoting the show, renting the venue and sound and video equipment, hiring the DJs, and paying artists' appearance fees and travel expenses for Reggie from Accra and M3nsa from London. Hashim keeps a close eye on the crew and bouncers running the door. "Not everyone ends up paying full fee because they have connections or something." As advertised online, the gate fee is $40, though it is reduced to $30 for those wearing "traditional" clothes, since the show is being billed as a national independence celebration. Hashim means traditional wear in a loose sense, "They could wear a fugu [Northern smock] or lace or T-shirts with Nkrumah on them. They don't have to be dressed only in "cloth" like [people wear] in Ghana. This is New York. But their clothes should show they are proud to be Ghanaian." Here, Ghanaian cultural identifications are marked through fashion but in a loose manner from a nostalgic distance rather than in attempting to replicate appropriate manners as they would be in Ghana. Invoking tradition both brings ideas of home closer as well as reinscribes distance between Accra and Gaucho's Gym.

Of course, it is rare for young people in Ghana to wear traditional clothes to a party. As the crowd grows, there are few people in "traditional" Ghanaian dress despite the discount offered. The minority of attendees in their thirties or older are wearing more formal dress shirts, suits, and party dresses, in line with modern fashion trends and how people dress at parties in Accra. For this group, attending a Ghanaian party is a way of nostalgically experiencing home, though not as a locale of tradition. For some, the Ghanaian community acts as a lived extension of life in Ghana. One older guest told me, "I mostly attend events in the Ghanaian community in the U.S. That is where my family and friends are."[4] For the mostly younger crowd, however, while Ghana is home, it is not immediately familiar. I ask one teenager, whose parents moved from Accra when he was young, why he is not wearing "traditional Ghanaian dress." He says, "I grew up in New York and don't have any African clothes." Dressing for parties reveals broader conflicting identifications of a young generation of people of Ghanaian ancestry whose sense of bodily comportment are American. Publicly this is manifest in terms of dress. Older Ghanaians lament the fact that the youths may not even know their "mother tongue" and cultural and moral values of their people. They often express ambivalence about the ways that youths accept and blend into American life and African American community and homogenous notions of racial identification.

DJs have been spinning a mix of contemporary Ghanaian highlife, hiplife hits, and current American R&B and hip-hop as people filter in. Eli Jacobs-Fantauzzi, a longtime collaborator of BDN, VIP, and Hashim, is filming the event for future broadcast. He plugs into the soundboards to record sound and to the video projectors to output live video.[5] Two large video screens display recent music videos by Papa Shee, a hiplife artist associated with BDN. Around 11:30, performances begin with young Ghanaian rappers from New York rapping in Twi. The crowd congregates around the makeshift bar, which consists of a folding table with several bottles of Hennessy cognac and trash cans full of ice, beer, and soft drinks around the edges of the basketball court. As the rappers begin, the audience surrounds the two-foot-high, eight-by-fifteen-foot platform stage. Through distorted speakers, the young rappers experiment with Twi rhymes and struggle to keep on beat. The crowd does not find a groove and is unenthusiastic about the unknown artists. They are not rude though and try to act supportively of the young performers.

The crowd reaches capacity, about twelve hundred people, at around 2 AM. Hashim wonders aloud whether the crowd feels the event is a concert or a party. The experiential difference between the two is significant, because a concert implies people have paid to hear a specific musician, whereas a Ghanaian party would be a social event to foster connections among friends and to meet other Ghanaians, reminding them of home. Here heritage is represented by hiplife. Hashim is nervous that when people find out that Reggie did not make it, they are going to become violent and demand their money back. While advertising touted Rockstone's presence, when a young man begins to protest that the star has not shown up, Hashim tells him pointedly that it is "a Ghanaian party, not a concert. It is for the community to celebrate independence, not a concert focused on one performer." He tells the DJs and crew not to say anything about Reggie but still word leaks out and crowd members keep asking whether it is true that Reggie could not get a visa.

Various musicians mount the stage as the night progresses. After local Bronx-based Ghanaians, well-known artists from Ghana begin to perform. Wanlov raps in Pidgin with a stark, humorous style. Buk Bak's Bright does a powerful set rapping and singing his group's highlife-style tracks over electronic beats. The crowd is exuberant, singing along. M3nsa performs a brief set. His songs are lyrically intricate, mostly in English, and are not known to the crowd. With heavy distortion and the speakers echoing and bouncing off the metal ceiling and around the basketball court, it is hard to distinguish anything except the most recognizable songs. It is not a place to listen carefully to new sounds but to enjoy familiar tracks. After waiting as long as possible, Hashim must announce to the crowd that Reggie is not coming. He instructs that the two-minute video that Rab and I have downloaded and quickly edited be projected on the two ten-foot screens. Since I have just been in Accra, he asks that I take the microphone and act as a witness for the crowd. Moving awkwardly between Twi and English as a humorous distraction, I explain that I was with Reggie several days earlier in Accra and that indeed the U.S. Embassy had inexplicably refused to grant him a visa. The goal is to deflect blame away from the promoters and artists and, rather, have the audience—many of whom have firsthand experience of rough embassy treatment—identify with Reggie's frustration at being stopped from traveling abroad. The swelling crowd is hushed and watches as the video shows Reggie in Accra wearing a T-shirt with Kwame Nkrumah's face with his long dreadlocks falling down his shoulders and sunglasses and standing in front of a Ghanaian flag. Speaking Twi he begins, "People, I beg you. It is not my fault; it is not the promoter's fault; it is not Kwame Nkrumah's fault. The embassy bounced my visa. I wish I was there with you to celebrate . . . one love."

The crowd murmurs in disappointment and uncertainty, but it appears that major unrest has been avoided. Audience members over the course of the evening have transformed the basketball court as concert venue in the South Bronx into a Ghanaian space of leisure and entertainment. The informal selling of drinks and Nkrumah T-shirts and the open space to dance and converse seem to make the event into more of a Ghanaian party than a concert relying on Reggie's presence. This event's success required remaking the gym as a Ghanaian space within which familiar forms of casual sociality could be reenacted far from home. In this context Reggie's nonappearance demonstrates connection and familiarity through absence and disappointments associated with international movement. Travel prohibition, ironically, supports metaphors of connection rather than dislocation. Digital media are central to the reformulation of the immediacy of hiplife affiliations by speeding the movement of images such that there is a simultaneity to Reggie's absence and presence. This disjuncture is reminiscent of other daily struggles of diasporic Ghanaians.

At 6 AM the promoters promptly shut off the sound system and turn the lights up as the crew immediately gets the gym ready for the day's athletic activities. The crowd disperses into the street as the sun rises. For a few hours artists and audience are transformed within the space of a Ghanaian musical party where skills as lyricists and understandings of the canon of hiplife songs mark them as members of a diasporic Ghanaian community. Now in the growing morning light, the crowd heads home through the South Bronx, to the subway at 149th and Grand Concourse. Those with cars show off outside the venue before hitting the road for long drives to destinations as far away as Connecticut and Maryland.

The concert maintained a life of its own online. Eli's concert footage is edited and within a few days posted on YouTube under the title "Ghana's Golden Jubilee [sic] Concert—NYC."[6] The electronic dialogue between various posts reflects some of the crucial conundrums faced by diasporic Ghanaians. Some use video clips such as this that are circulated on social media, music, and video sites to find new music they like and query like-minded viewers about their interests.

> **Shawty2greezy:** does anybody kno the name of the artist & song that plays at 02:55 to 04:00?
> **Donazaa:** Buk bak—kakachofa (ginger)

These postings inspire an outpouring of pride and recognition of Ghanaianness in a shared set of signs and debates around an expert knowledge of the music:

> **Ajoabemma:** i just have three words to say I LOVE GHANA!!
> **Nomenad:** Go Ghana the motherland. From Kpetow V/R

They also open fissures around how moral actions reflect national pride, showing the tension between being born in Ghana and living abroad. Feeling nostalgic raises questions about both returning home and identifying from afar through an emotional sense of absence:

> **Runganomahuni:** if you love Ghana wht are you doing in the Diaspora, go bak there then, waste of SPACE
> **Amyhrs:** wha is wrong with one showing patriotizm to where they come from?
> **Runganomahuni:** the bottom line is love it and cherish it, so why not stay there, thts the big question love. WHY?
> **1MaRiSs1:** becuz most ppl are born somwere else and want 2 feel as if there in there motherland thats why
> **Akuabawaah87:** I wish I was their!!!

As is typical of online forums, many participants feel freed from the constraints of face-to-face interaction to state pointed, contradictory opinions. Invocations of broader African diasporans' racial affiliations are made in the language of partying and music:

> **Cutieama94:** ay! aso aso aso! ay ghana fwo! [Ghanaian people!] ay party big ay! ya'lls got da gud music
> **Surinamerr:** i love surinam :D but ghana too

Some first-generation Ghanaians lament their inability to speak Twi fluently, driving their desire to understand the music:

> **Mamie4784:** damn i wish i speak better twi!!!

And comparisons are made between different Ghanaian enclaves abroad:

> **1MaRiSs1:** idiidnt miss anythign!! cause back in holland whe have are own ghana fiesta!!! XD
> **Queenplove:** honestly yall know to throw a party in new york better then Chicago

These online exchanges show concerts and parties as points of reference for negotiating how to imagine self in relation to the absences experienced in living abroad. Place, language, and nationhood become emotional nodes invoked in people's reactions to popular music. The pleasure of listening to familiar songs opens sensorial and affective relationships for a dispersed, electronically mediated Ghanaian diaspora. For a younger generation, Ghanaianness is at times defined through tropes of movement and its prohibitions. It is a narrative of both possibility and lament. Possibility emerges in the growing ease of circulating images, dialogues, music, and so on across a dispersed set of locales. Lament comes as self-recognition in the structural, bodily, and emotional constraints on coming to the United States and on returning home.

A Bronx-Ghanaian Poetics of Performance

The following year's 2008 fifty-first anniversary independence celebration hiplife concert at Gaucho's Gym in the South Bronx reveals two dichotomies that define a cosmopolitan Ghanaian landscape: first, nostalgia/absence versus innovation/possibility and second, blackness/Americanness versus Ghanaianness. Regarding this second dichotomy, as I describe, there is a productive symbolic tension at the core of hiplife—and indeed much Ghanaian popular music throughout the twentieth century—in juxtaposing blackness and Ghanaianness. It reflects how recent African immigrants experience the contradictions between the United States's ideologies of race and citizenship (Kelley 2003; Goldberg 2002; Robinson [1985] 2000). African settlers coming to the United States are caught in violent dynamics that constitute structural racism and processes of racialization (Pierre 2012; Holsey 2002). Generational and technological changes lead to new attitudes about being Ghanaian or West African in diaspora rather than being incorporated into broader American and African American publics. Younger Ghanaians often choose to emphasize being Ghanaian, whereas even five years ago they were more likely to hide this fact. In hiplife we can see how Ghanaians identify with and against African American racialized imaginaries. Artists mix references to African American forms of affiliation and Ghanaian political and cultural community. For audiences, these juxtapositions invoke a dynamic of simultaneous distancing and familiarity, intimacy and alienation.

Ghanaians as a minority within black communities in the Bronx, Maryland, Atlanta, and so on affiliate with the particularities of Ghanaianness through the music's sonic and bodily aesthetics. Hiplife appears to the casual listener as a subgenre of rap, though to insiders its specific musical and lyrical references and bodily movements are reflective of a Ghanaian cosmopolitan moral subject. Hiplife music places a high value on local cultural knowledge, subtle linguistic and bodily signs of respect, and references to familiar places, schools, and histories that connect artists and audiences as a dispersed sonic community. At the same time, as audiences in the United States dance and sing along to familiar songs, local Ghanaian knowledge and its bodily expression magnify the distance from home and articulate with a broader Afro-modern collectivity. Ghanaian diaspora involves an ambivalence of identifying with the cultural-linguistic features of home while placing them within a genre recognized as part of a broader black diasporic world.

After promoting the fiftieth anniversary show, Hashim continues to organize musical and party events for the Ghanaian community in the New York area, looking for innovative ways of bringing young people together. He strives to find the right combination of venue, location, entertainment, and advertising to regularly attract sizable audiences and be financially successful. In August 2007 he organized hiplife performers, including Mzbel, for the annual Ghanaian Picnic held in upstate New York, one of the biggest U.S. events for the Ghanaian community. This event was also marred by several artists having trouble getting their visas on time. Hashim's efforts are changing the look and feel of Ghanaian community events that a few years earlier were dominated by the tastes of the older generation. He says, "I love this music; [I am] trying to make a difference for people . . . bringing them their culture." In November 2007 he co-organized a party in Manhattan aimed at more affluent professionals. He advertised primarily online and through mass text messaging. A text advertisement from Hashim:

November 21th Wednesday. BDN Pro/TrueKings Ent.
Present Pre-Thanksgiving Jumpoff A Fall Affair
for grown and sexy to be held @Deweys Flatiron 210 5th a
venue bet. 25 and 26 street. Ladies free b4 midnite
$20 afta gents $10 b4 midnite $20 afta. 21 and
over id a must Doors open @ 10pm. Dont miss out.

Relying on digital media and intimate networks within the community, one of Hashim's texts extorts people to "forward to all Ghanaian friends. Reasonable prices. Reasonable location." The venue, Dewey's Flatiron, is a dual-level bar filled with flat-screen televisions and low-slung seating. The DJs spin American hip-hop and urban music, switching to Ghanaian music as the night progresses. With only a few hundred people in attendance, organizers are a bit disappointed with the turnout. This is partly attributed to the Manhattan location and lack of celebrity attractions.

For the 2008 independence show, Hashim and his BDN Productions plan another concert at Gaucho's Gym on an even bigger scale, capitalizing on the previous year's momentum. While the fact that Reggie did not show up as advertised the previous year damaged Hashim's credibility, the ambition of the show still helped his reputation as a promoter. "It showed we can do this kind of hiplife event for a big audience," he explains. The 2007 show was groundbreaking in bringing hiplife to the Bronx on a large scale. This time, as soon as Reggie and VIP (the headlining acts) arrive from Ghana, they go to WBAI FM on Broadway and 115th Street to do a live on-air interview assuring fans that the stars are really in New York. Tic Tac, the other headliner, is already in the country for other events. VIP group members are staying in the Bronx with friends, while Reggie is staying at his manager Dhoruba's house in Irvington, New Jersey. Dhoruba is still getting used to being back in the United States after living in Ghana for so many years. Reggie and Dhoruba catch up on political and musical affairs, visiting friends throughout the tristate area.

The day after the musicians arrive, I stop by to chat with DJ Ronny at Shoemania in Union Square, where he is overseeing the preparations for the concert. Customers clamor to buy discounted fashion footwear while sales attendants, working on commission, rush with walkie-talkies to find requested sizes and styles. Ronny greets me saying, "Hey, your man has made it this year! People better show up for the concert!" As we walk to get lunch at a nearby Caribbean restaurant, he exclaims, "Hashim is hustling, man. He wants to be sure everyone knows that Reggie and VIP are really here this year. We want this to be a huge show!" They have shot video of Reggie at the airport to post on Facebook to provide more evidence that he really has arrived in the country. The interview on radio the previous night was helpful, but as Ronny says, "Ghanaians don't really listen to FM because we don't have a station. It's more about Facebook, Myspace, and texting. That's how we connect."

FIGURE 36 Nana NYC at Gaucho's Gym before the show. Photograph by the author.

I go to Gaucho's early to check out the setup while Reggie, Dhoruba, and Rab prepare for the show. I meet Nana NYC, a Bronx-based aspiring rapper, who is one of this year's opening acts (see figure 36). He recalls the previous year's show. "It was the biggest Ghanaian hip-hop event ever in the U.S. Before that there were fifty or a hundred people at shows or parties. Hashim is really promoting and showing respect for this music. He is making it big for us here in America." Nana was born in Ghana to parents from Kwahu. He came to New York with his family as a young child and grew up in Parkchester in the Bronx. Currently he works as a security guard and a part-time waiter. But he sees these jobs as a way to support his goal of becoming a successful rap artist and entrepreneur. He says that he has written over two hundred rap songs, mostly in English, though he increasingly mixes in Twi language. He recalls that, like many kids from Africa growing up in the United States, he was teased for his foreignness.

> I rap in English because I grew up here. . . . But when I was young it was tough being from Ghana. I got good grades. But everybody would pick on me. Black, white, Jamaican, whatever. It was like some Puerto Rican kid [I knew]. They wanted to hide where they were from, that they were

new here. Now we young Ghanaians have to be brave to do it first and be proud to speak our language. Now even Ghanaian elders respect Twi-language rap. For us who were not raised in Ghana, it is a sign of respect for our culture to try to rap in Twi even if we are not fluent.

According to Nana, the fact that Reggie did not show up in 2007 will make some hesitant to come in 2008. "Reggie is the bridge that connects young Ghanaians to Ghana. We grew up with his music. He is the big draw. He is an elder in this business. Because Reggie didn't show up [for the 2007 event] it was disappointing. A lot of people will not come because they don't believe the stars who are on the [advertising] poster will be here." In the popular imagination Rockstone has completely transformed from a threat to Ghanaian national culture, when he first returned to Ghana in 1994, to an embodiment of linguistic and cultural tradition. In an ironic reversal, early hiplife from the 1990s represents traditional values and language use for youths to emulate. For young adults, Rockstone's music reminds them of home and childhood. Nana performs with a young Jamaican woman backup singer, who has never been to a hiplife show before. She tells me that she likes the music, but explains, "it is really different than the hip-hop I listen to or if you go to a Jamaican event [in New York]. I don't really know how to dance to this music, though I could learn."

Hashim has hired Imagination, a company that produces corporate and entertainment events, to implement an ambitious production design for the show. At one end of Gaucho's Gym is an elevated stage, three times the size of last year's, surrounded by several giant projection screens splashing a light show on the walls. Three well-dressed representatives from the Ghanaian consulate arrive and are given folding chairs and are seated close to the stage, constituting their own VIP section. Sitting comfortably among scantily clad young women and men in baggy jeans, they are thanked by the MC as community elders.

The Ghanaian urban landscape in New York revolves around neighborhoods—including Grand Concourse in the Bronx and Flatbush in Brooklyn—where there are many West Africans and Ghanaians. Gaucho's is well situated and Hashim hopes to attract an even bigger crowd than last year. The show brings together a diverse group of Ghanaians from across the New York area and the United States. Various economic levels, types of workers, students, and linguistic groups are represented, aligned through the poetics of this event and a shared discourse of

FIGURE 37 Bright of Buk Bak performing at Gaucho's Gym. Photograph by the author.

hiplife. Hashim, aside from the headliners, takes advantage of the presence of well-known artists. Bright from Buk Bak has moved to the Bronx and his partner Ronny is visiting from Accra (see figure 37). They are trying to revive their music career after a long delay since their last hit album. M3nsa and M.anifest are both in town and will perform as well as back up Rockstone. From all over the East Coast people are in town, staying with friends for the weekend. Top hiplife artists, as well as contemporary highlifers, are part of an international circuit in which performers based in Ghana earn a substantial part of their income by traveling to perform for Ghanaian communities, mostly in European centers such as London, Amsterdam, and Hamburg. In the United States, artists are brought in to cater to Ghanaian audiences in the New York area as well as in Atlanta, Georgia; Worcester, Massachusetts; Alexandria, Virginia; and so on. When artists visit the United States, promoters try to set up a tour with multiple shows and appearances around the country in areas with large Ghanaian communities. As another promoter tells me, "Once you cover the cost of the plane ticket, everything else is profit. We take the financial risks. We have to be sure to pay the artists properly so that it is worth their while. But you know—you lived in Ghana for a long time— this one be Ghana business matter. There are no contracts or official papers. It is all done between friends. We are all hustling, you know?"

DJ Sam Q (Sam Quaye), a former heavyweight boxer, is at the show. He is one of the most respected Ghanaian DJs in the United States.

Now in his thirties, he was born in Accra and came to the United States in 1990 to further his education. There is a big population of Ghanaians in Chicago, where he is based, but to his mind it is not cohesive. He plays regularly for non-Ghanaian and Ghanaian crowds around the country, catering to different audiences. He explains, "You have to be able to read the crowd to DJ well. The role of the DJ is to judge what music a crowd wants and to make the speed of each track correspond to its mood. . . . For non-Ghanaians I will mix in everything, hip-hop, R&B, dance. [For] Ghanaians I play our local hits more." But he says that hiplife is his passion. "Hiplife is helping kids in the U.S. learn what it means to be Ghanaian. We can go back to our roots; learn native language and local music." The use of "local" to describe Ghanaian culture is common, showing how cultural practice is spatialized. Locality marks not a geographic location but a person's closeness or distance from a set of practices.

The celebrity microphone-wielding rapper is the focus of the performances. But the poetics of the event also revolve around technology. The prominent display of electronica—video and still cameras, mobile phones, sonic digital effects, lighting, microphones—mediates ongoing interactions among audience, artists, technicians, and organizers, becoming part of the spectacle. The elaborate decks and mixing boards are stage right. A technical support crew runs the soundboard and amps. Unofficial video and still photographers crowd the sides of the stage, flashing their cameras. Eli again organizes the official video shoot coming from his home in California for the event. This year they have a small mechanical camera crane feeding images to the two fifteen-foot projection screens on each side of the stage. Multiple DJs trade off spinning and dominate one side of the stage with assistants milling around the decks. Rappers' support crews and backup singers crowd the sides of the stage. Throughout the show the crowd is busy taking pictures on mobile phones and digital cameras held high over their heads. Between performers and at the end of the show, audience members even mount the stage to take pictures with their arms around the stars. All of this activity is part of the pleasurable, intimate spectacle.

Hashim has orchestrated things well. Sam Q will DJ for Tic Tac and M3nsa. DJ Ice will spin for VIP. After local artists warm up the crowd, Tic Tac performs several of the tracks that made him a star in the late 1990s, including "Philomena" and the more recent hit "Kangaroo." He hypes up the crowd.

"Yeah! What's up New York! Put your hands in the air!"

Tic Tac was one of the first early hiplife stars to recognize the importance of marketing and has sought out collaborations with international artists such as Tony Tetuila of Nigeria, as the subtitle of his 2003 album states, to "go international." As he finishes, the DJ plays the beat to VIP's hit "Besin" as they run onstage, singing an abbreviated chorus. The crowd roars with recognition, shouting along the lyrics,

Besin, wonim se wowo high heels,
Besin, wonim se wokita nice fingernails,
Besin, wonim se wodo VIP a
Besin, wonim se wo beebia bo so a,
Obaa Yaa, Bbbrrraaa Bbbrrraaa Bbbrrraaa Bbbrrraaa.

Come and follow me, you with high heels,
Come and follow me with your nice fingernails,
Come follow me you who love VIP.
Come everyone of you
All you women, Bbbrrraaa Bbbrrraaa Bbbrrraaa Bbbrrraaa.

The song follows hiplife's popular formula of positing a masculine speaker confident in seducing women. The use of English nouns within Twi constructions indexes differences in language ideology where Twi usage points to participation in a broad Ghanaian public and English words focus on desires for modern commodities and lifestyles, marked most visibly by explicit displays of female bodies. In the context of a performance in the United States, English familiarity helps draw connections for unfamiliar listeners to Twi language constructions. The rapper's poised vocal control is affirmed in his ability to capture the attention of female fans. Women in the front row laugh and yell the lyrics back at the group as VIP's members coolly grasp their microphones and roam the stage.

VIP's performance demonstrates the dual aspects of hiplife in indexing both a black cosmopolitanism and a Ghanaian particularity. This opposition is particularly noticeable in the contrast between their sonic references and their visual presentation. Their fashion style is very hip-hop. Lazzy stands out with aviator shades and baggy jeans, holding the microphone low, flirting with women in the front row. The whole crew has oversized VISION IN PROGRESS T-shirts with red, gold, and green lettering with hoodies, caps, and oversized beads and jewelry.

As one young female fan, who moved to New Jersey from Accra when she was a child, told me, "They are tough and their look is really hip-hop. They make us proud to be Ghanaian." Bronx-based rapper Nana NYC invokes the link between hip-hop and a populist underclass sensibility. "VIP is from Nima, which is the ghetto in Accra. That is where real music comes from. That is why they are such powerful performers." Like most groups they rap in Twi, although they also use Hausa and Ewe. Their use of English and Pidgin is sparse in the music, though in spoken asides to the crowd they use English almost exclusively.

One of the video cameramen for this event is Kwesi Boateng. KB is from Kumasi, has lived in the Bronx since 1998, and now drives a taxicab. His brothers and mother moved back to Ghana but he sees himself as dual, belonging to both American and Ghanaian worlds. "Hiplife is American life blended with Ghanaian culture. We Ghanaians are good; we do not segregate ourselves like some groups when they come to this country, but we know who we are. I grew up listening to reggae and all forms of music. Now hiplife is international but it is also distinct to us." He often works with Hashim and is particularly interested in shooting music videos and hiplife visual styles. "We want to create a specific look that expresses what the music is about for us." KB works the camera in front of the stage as the artists perform. The visuals are projected onto the giant screens on each side of the audience, replicating and amplifying the performers onstage.

Moving through their most popular numbers, the DJ spins their signature track, "Ahomka Wo Mu," and the crowd jumps as one. In contrast to their gangster look and their initial hyping of the crowd, VIP's sound emphasizes highlife's smooth rhythms, harmonies, and controlled precision. Their movements are driven by a contained danceable highlife beat. Their stagecraft here is similar to their performances in Ghana or anywhere else and revolves around a basic set of coordinated highlife dance steps that quickly excite the crowd. The three artists stand in a spread-out triangle and move in sync to the jamma beat. And while their rap lyrics are delivered with the bravado of hip-hop, the lyrical content and the rhythmic sensibility of their songs recall for some Ghanaian listeners the simplicity and circumscribed, familiar struggles of life in Accra. VIP's songs recall an older highlife's chronotope: Accra life with its hustles, hopes, and tragedies. As Paa K, Reggie's manager, once told me, "For our parents, highlife was specifically Ghanaian and urban. It was about the hopes and failures of their life. It was about home. And even when they were far from home and in some predicament, highlife was the sound of Accra and makes you smile and say 'yes, this is who I am.'" This is not an intellectual identification but one embedded in the bodily forms of shared familiar movement, repetition, harmonizing, and lyricism. Singing with smooth harmonies, the performers punctuate the tracks with shout-outs and machine gun–like staccato rap, reminding the crowd of their multiple fluencies.

The nostalgic highlife-oriented aspects of hiplife are emphasized when these artists perform in the Bronx. Recall that initially Ghanaian rap artists used highlife beats to help the music resonate with older, mainstream audiences who saw hip-hop as foreign. In the Bronx, highlife rhythms and harmonies serve to evoke home for young listeners. The youthful crowd, many of whom have lived most or all of their lives in the United States, nevertheless identify with being Ghanaian. The crowd responds viscerally to the highlife-driven beats of VIP in contrast to what DJ Rab describes as the "New York–style beats" of Reggie and other rappers. The crowd dances and jumps with a dual familiarity: first, it recognizes VIP's musical and fashion success in merging hip-hop and highlife, their masterful ability as transformers of values and signs. Second, highlife provokes nostalgic recognition for past generations' foundational styles. Specifically around anniversary celebrations for Ghana's independence, highlife recalls Pan-Africanist hopes of early independence Africa. In the hands of this young generation abroad, Pan-Africanism is a national history that also speaks to individual struggles to find economic success. For many Ghanaians, living in Europe or America is understood as an economic necessity shadowed by longing for home. One young man at the concert, who is based in New York, expressed a common sentiment: "Ghana is sweet if you have money, but if you have no money you cannot stay. I plan to make money and then return some day."

At one point, VIP stops the music and gives shout-outs. "What's up New York! What's up New York! You know why we're here and you know who brought us here all the way from Accra, Ghana!

"Ampa, Ampa. [True, True].

"We like to give a big shout-out to my man Big Hash. Hashim, where you at?"

The growing significance of hiplife among Ghanaians in the United States reflects the changing ways popular culture links familiar signs to broader dispersed forms of identity. I am referring to the way in which the now-ubiquitous genre of hip-hop becomes a vehicle for specific forms of Ghanaian affiliation. Hip-hop spread around the world as a poetic structure that emphasizes multivocality through dense musical and bodily reference. Within this genre, pleasure and debate emerge from the ability of rappers, DJs, and audience members to make referential connections between samples, beats, and lyrics and older forms of musical expression, popular culture, and markers of political (often class and race-based) struggle. Hiplife as it circulates and is consumed in the context of U.S. Ghanaians opens up a dialogical relationship between Ghanaianness and blackness in the language of popular entertainment. It represents nostalgia for language and culture, though it also delivers nationhood in a technological form that aligns modernity with culture in the making of a dispersed Ghanaian public. For youths of Ghanaian origin, daily experience involves negotiating perceptions of racialized identity by peers and education and work institutions. Hiplife enfolds African American critical discourse on race and power into what it means to be Ghanaian in America.

Reggie's Celebrity in Spectacle and Repetition

VIP's and Reggie's songs are familiar to a majority of the crowd. The pleasure of dancing and singing along is created by the copresence of audience members and performers, which allows them to share and refashion what it means to be young, proud, and Ghanaian. Participants recognize themselves as part of a global Ghanaian diaspora within which they maintain personal connections to home through familiar musical references. At the same time, the music's hip-hopness links Ghanaian identity to the varied landscape of black cultural cosmopolitanism, making it one node within a varied field of black communities in the Bronx.

The crowd reaches its peak by 1 AM. It is mostly twentysomethings and as Hashim estimates perhaps 95 percent Ghanaian. Despite the bigger production and high-powered performances, the crowd is only a bit larger than the previous year. DJ Ronny says that some people stayed away, still not trusting that the artists would actually show up (see figure 38). The use of Internet technology as a primary form of advertising has meant that, contrary to expectations, Ghanaians outside of the New York area are better informed than those living locally. Physical proximity has led to less communication for many. Ronny explains, "Ghanaians out of New York are actually here more because

FIGURE 38 DJ Ronny at Gaucho's Gym. Photograph by the author.

they were following online and knew the artists were in [the country]. New Yorkers who did not come because they did not keep up will be disappointed to have missed it!" People are decked out in stylish nightclub wear accessorized with sunglasses and jewelry. Women wear tight jeans, short skirts, and pushup halter-tops, while men are decked out in stylish open-necked shirts, oversized jerseys, and baggy pants or skinny jeans; urban fashion allows mixing and matching. Some women are dressed in tailored Ghanaian cloth. A few older couples and gentlemen are dressed in suits and ties.

Tina has lived in the United States since she was in grade school and now attends community college in Virginia. She brings her two close African American friends to the show. One likes the show while the other hates the scene. Both are surprised by its vibrancy, modern feel, and specificity (see figure 39). "I had no idea this kind of thing went on, that Ghanaian music was like this," says Kiesha. "This sounds like hip-hop a bit but everything is off key and slow and really boring. I don't like the way people dance to it. It's slow and I can't understand the songs," says Kim. Tina says she loves Reggie. She is waiting at the side of the stage to take a picture with him. Even though she is twenty years old now, and was only ten when his most popular album came out, she

FIGURE 39 Audience members at Gaucho's Gym sing along and take photographs of the performers. Photograph by the author.

idolizes him. While she does not speak Twi regularly or very fluently, like much of the young crowd, she sings along to all of his songs with both English and Twi lyrics.

DJ Ronny, a relative newcomer to the Ghanaian music scene, feels honored to DJ for Reggie. To him, "Reggie's presence means a lot to New York kids. He is an icon that shows us we have the potential to succeed." M3nsa has flown in from London for the show. He performs a short set with M.anifest. M.anifest, who is in town from Minneapolis, came to the United States to attend Carleton College and works for a nongovernmental organization to support his nascent hip-hop career. His music mixes English and Pidgin rap, as in his recent hip-hop version of Fela's Afrobeat classic "Gentleman."

M.anifest's music eclectically mixes live music and rap. During the show, M.anifest explains to me the difference between the setup of a Ghanaian show and an American hip-hop performance. In American hip-hop, the DJ is often center stage as a part of the performance, promoting more interaction and improvisation with rappers and other musicians. He says, "I am used to directly communicating with the DJ and musicians. With Ghanaian events often the DJ is down on the side so the MC has to follow his breaks . . . how he spins. . . . It makes it harder to interact with and respond to the crowd's energy. These shows are more about people knowing the songs and responding to that."

M3nsa and M.anifest stay onstage and help call Reggie to the stage (see figure 40). Reggie is dressed in a pale pinstriped suit and white open dress shirt. His long dreads are neatly tied back. "One, two . . . make some noise! I beg DJ bo nyum [play the song]! New York!" And from the crowd: "Big up RRReggieeee! Be hyei [Look]! We *know* you!" A common praise name for Reggie is shouted: "Osseikrom President, twelve years!" Interjected comments and interactions between performers and crowd are moments of affiliation and disjuncture. Reggie is masterful at reading the crowd, exciting them with the music, and picking moments to stop and speak with them. At one point between songs, he stops the DJ. "Hold up. Hold up. Family, family. Abusuafuo, Me nehu wu akye! [My family, I have not seen you in a long time!] He invokes the crowd's connection to home through the music and by recognizing and making reflexive his role as a star who links these worlds together. In a sense, the crowd becomes Ghanaian by watching these stars and conversely by being seen and recognized by them. Later Reggie announces his role as community observer through photography, announcing, "I want to take a picture of the whole crowd so I can show it to my people back home. Someone, give me a camera! Everybody, if you know somebody back home, they're about to see your ass! You ready! You ready?! Be somebody!"

During the performance, audience-members continually take pictures with digital cameras and mobile phones, some even climbing onstage to do so. The spectacle of technology is part of the live excitement of the show. Digital images also begin chains of signification that can circulate through texting photos immediately, posting on Myspace and Facebook, and sending to people in Ghana. The highly visible activity of documenting one's presence by taking pictures with celebrities affirms attendance and aligns the self with success by proximity to fame. For BDN the cameras and large screens that repeat and magnify the stage are part of the spectacle of the show.

Reggie follows a common and effective formula for getting the crowd involved. As he sings the song's chorus, he points the microphone at the audience to encourage them to sing along in unison. Participants on and off stage align in collective recognition by simultaneously singing tracks that recall fond memories. Repetition is an important aspect

FIGURE 40 Reggie Rockstone and M3nsa performing at Gaucho's Gym. Photograph by the author.

of how performers hype the crowd, teaching the audience how to act and emphasizing unity of experience through the music. When Reggie begins a chorus of one of the hits he did with M3nsa, "Me Nesesa Da," M3nsa reflects his own excitement onto the crowd by calling for it to be repeated. "Oh shit! One more time, one more time," M3nsa interjects after Reggie does the chorus a cappella with no beat. On the recorded track a woman does the chorus, followed by Reggie rapping in Twi and M3nsa in English. It is slow in a minor key with a Spanish guitar sample. In concert they repeat the chorus over and over, first with no beat and then with a different electronic beat with more drive than the album. M3nsa reiterates key lines and hypes Reggie throughout.

While good-quality amps and equipment are used, the sound is highly distorted, as the sound designer cannot manage the reverberations off the open metal roof and back wall of the gym court. Lyrics are hard to hear. Unless the audience knows the song it is difficult to understand, and the crowd loses interest. Excitement, then, stems from nostalgia and recognition for older hits recalled from growing up. Often DJs will stop, repeat, and loop the opening beats of well-known tracks to raise the level of the audience's anticipation. DJs and MCs also vocally emphasize parts of the beat that the crowd responds to. This sort of repetition and foregrounding has a metapragmatic effect, directing the crowd when and how to get excited by the music.

With well-known tracks the musicians at times change the beats and timing under familiar lyrics and strip down the layers of recorded music to a simple rhythm, pump up the volume, and echo the chorus through the room. Distortion focuses the listener's ear on the bare, familiar aspects of lyrics and dance beats. Pauses that the DJ inserts into the flow punctuate for the crowd their synergetic movements. Unexpected silences highlight absence and in the process makes lyrical flow more spectacular in its synchronicity, volume, and rhythm. The spectacle's emotional power relies on activating and making collective familiarity. In blurring the subtlety of the recorded tracks, the symbolic power of rapping/speaking/claiming agency are highlighted. Distortion and repetition are metapragmatic elements of this live event that make the act of performing, and being famous itself, a formal marker of collective pride.

Mistakes and miscues also contribute to the concert's sonic feel. At times the beat drops out by mistake at hiplife shows due to a DJ's mistake or an electrical problem. It is especially noticeable when the high-volume distorted sounds suddenly disappear completely, making the audience, if only momentarily, all too aware of the vacuous space around them. These faults often inexplicably interrupt a performance. As with the 2007 event when people complained that Reggie did not show up, there is an aspect of electronic and organizational failures that people identify familiar instability. Technological equipment breakdowns index communal struggles. Absence and frustration index belonging in the familiar ways that artists and audiences complain about problems.

Reggie holds a place of special reverence in the youthful Ghanaian imagination. One of Reggie's more recent hits tells a story of betrayal based on a true story of an affair between Reggie's best friend and his first wife. The chorus of the song is in the voice of his betraying friend, sung by highlife crooner K. K. Fosu, who implores, "Reggie Fa nebo me ne chere me, Wai?" (Reggie, will you please forgive me my sins?) The song's video, shot by Abraham Ohene Djan, won an award for Best African Music Video at the South African–based continental Kora Music Awards in 2004. In the Bronx, as Reggie begins to sing this chorus, his voice is immediately drowned out by the crowd shouting it back to him.

A master of timing, he stops singing and holds the mic out to them, smiles, and listens as a thousand voices implore, "Reggie, forgive me my sins!" In the recontextualization of this lyrical snippet, Reggie, as rap icon, is implicitly transposed to a figure with the potential to transform audience members. His star-celebrity aura is almost palpable as the crowd moves closer, as if his presence will somehow rub off on them if they are close enough. The presence of the artist has the power to transport listeners to a familiar place through his recognition of them. His recognition animates and legitimizes the pleasurable forms of communal identification for Ghanaians abroad. The fact that people were so upset at Reggie's absence shows the importance of his presence as a sign of home and of the potential of transformation.

This concert carves out a familiar place within a foreign country. Repetition of familiar dance steps and lyrics invokes an embodied national pride. Crowds glow in the simultaneity of singing along and repeating familiar choruses while jumping with the rappers to highlife-inflected rhythms. Musical copresence elicits pride in "local" Ghanaian language use. Whereas in the 1990s rapping in African languages was seen as backward and un-hip, and African immigrants in the United States and Europe were ashamed to identify as African, hip-hop unexpectedly reauthorized African practices and languages as points of pride for Africa and U.S.-based Africans. African cultural practices have been given new life in defining the unique ways in which Ghanaians can situate themselves as aspirational subjects and maintain their cultural specificity. Though, of course, what constitutes Ghanaian cultural traditions is continually being reassessed. Twi rappers are indexical icons pointing to and embodying the hybrid combinations of Afro-cosmopolitan Ghanaian identity.

An incident at the end of the evening showed how state violence and segregation of space in racial terms continue to haunt the movements of black peoples. After the concert, Dhoruba drives Reggie, Accra radio DJ Naa, and me into Manhattan. Dhoruba pulls his old Ford sedan with New Jersey plates to the curb as I get out on Broadway. Suddenly a police cruiser pulls alongside. I stand on the empty street corner waiting, trying to make the police aware I am watching, as an officer asks for Dhoruba's license and registration. After a long delay, they discover that, unknown to Dhoruba, his license has been suspended. We watch in shock as he is placed in handcuffs and taken to the back of the squad car. Dhoruba commands us to call his lawyer and explain what has happened. Naa gets behind the wheel as I get back in the car and we follow the cop car to the nearby 221 Precinct. She laments, "When they saw a white guy get out of the car they assumed drugs were involved, because we didn't do anything." I call Dhoruba's lawyer, famed civil rights attorney Robert Boyle, to explain that Dhoruba has been arrested for a minor cause after an unsolicited traffic stop. He listens carefully suddenly alert. "Uh oh. That's the same precinct where the two cops Dhoruba was accused of shooting in 1971 were based. Don't let him out of your sight. If they discover who they have in custody this could be really bad. I am on my way." We sit in silence watching an officer process Dhoruba. Boyle is renowned for having defended political prisoners in American jails and countering systematic efforts by U.S state and federal organizations to criminalize radical and progressive political organizations. Boyle was instrumental in securing Dhoruba's release from prison in 1990 upon recognition the FBI had manipulated evidence in his trial. But that is not how the police would see it.

Reggie, Naa, and I wait in small chairs as the officers in front of us at the central booking desk fill out paperwork and Dhoruba sits in the cell behind us. As we wait nervously for Bob, Reggie tells stories about police brutality from his London days. Finally Bob arrives and, after much bureaucracy, manages to secure Dhoruba's release. Amazingly, the precinct officers had not accessed Dhoruba's record. Around 8 AM we leave the station. We go eat pancakes at a nearby diner. Dhoruba and Bob, undaunted by the evening's activity, recount the years of legal battles it took to overturn Dhoruba's original verdict.

While Reggie and younger hiplife musicians evoke Pan-Africanism through musical and bodily styles, flashes of capricious state violence remind us of the longue duree and myriad fronts in the struggle against perduring conditions of racial inequality. Dhoruba tells us of how the FBI's Counter Intelligence Program (COINTELPRO) manipulated the legal system and provoked infighting, seeking to destroy American political organizations fighting for racial and class-based justice like the Black Panther Party, issues he has lectured widely on since his release. He sits back in the booth and puts the evening in historical perspective: "now there is no Black Panther Party to protect our interests. It is a different era, but nothing changes." We never found out why Reggie's passport had been flagged by U.S. immigration computers nor why the

New York police, conversely, did not find Dhoruba in their computer. But the Bronx concert as a space for celebrating around diasporic connections and disjunctures is put into stark relief by Dhoruba's detainment, a reminder of the ever-present possibility of state violence.

The next day at Dhoruba's house in New Jersey, Reggie, Rab, Dhoruba, and I reflect on Reggie's visit to North America. He is surprised by how much attention he gets. "I never expected the kind of reception I got. Everywhere I go, people [are] shouting my name. So happy to see me. All these Ghanaians who been away from home for so long. It means a lot to them if I can remind them of Ghana and their roots. And now there are all these young kids here rapping, trying hard. They don't even speak Twi but they're doing it and mixing languages and all. It's amazing." Before leaving the country, Hashim arranges one final appearance for Reggie at Zodoo's, a Francophone African nightclub also in the South Bronx. After the show around 4 AM we go to a nearby Ghanaian restaurant to eat *wache*, a local Ghanaian dish, accompanied by dried fish, beans, and dried *garee*. There are several customers, taxi drivers getting off work, clubgoers on the way home.

As Reggie walks in, he is recognized by the proprietor and the surprised customers who gather around him for photographs and questions: What is he doing in the United States? How are things going? How is Ghana? What I find striking is the immediate intimacy people feel toward the Ghanaian star. They feel they know him, and his presence confers upon each of them a personal set of connections to the mobility and privilege that they assume celebrity status entails. Reggie enjoys and takes seriously his role as an icon for young Ghanaians. "They look to me for hope that they can make it. It is not easy for the youths today and they see what I have done and want to be successful too but want to do it in a way that is uncompromising; that is true to who they are, their culture. I try to show them that they need to remember where they came from always and keep in the struggle; never give up." Reggie greets the small group and answers their queries before we settle in to eat.

Conclusion: New Sonic Collectives

Shared forms of recognition are made in moments of intimacy—whether in celebration, violence, or simple greetings—in the midst of complex transnational lives. Sonic nationhood is composed in disjunctures of movement and the ways that youths use the cultural dimensions of displacement to reimagine new continuities. Loss and nostalgia are productive of new potential value. Creative entrepreneurs like Hashim observe their communities, inventing opportunities for connection and profit. Language, music, movement, and video intermingle in highly mediated concerts in which audiences and performers imagine themselves as agentive within and against broader forms of black affiliation. The aesthetics of these events emerge in the sum of their spatial, musical, and visual aspects defined as hiplife. Shared sensory and emotional experiences invoke a sonic community. Artists and entrepreneurs speak within a national idiom but locate this nationhood in shifting locales and nonmaterial forms.

The ways that Ghanaians abroad produce locality—make themselves at home in diaspora—are changing (cf. Ho 2006; Appadurai 1996). Globalization itself has changed from the 1990s to the 2000s, manifesting in the new ways music and people move and how media technology is used to imagine and connect life at home and abroad. While each successive generation has its own experience of home, travel, and globalization, the persistence of structural inequality for black peoples reinforces shared forms of displacement.

The making of hiplife involved youth imagining hip-hop as a representation of American blackness and transforming diasporic aesthetic values into Ghanaian ones. Now hiplife returns to the South Bronx—the purported birthplace of hip-hop—transporting Ghanaianness to America.

Ghanaians abroad are dispersed within broader African American and immigrant communities with competing popular cultures and networks of affiliation.[7] Theories of race and African diasporic cultural ideologies must take account of the internal nuances that intertwine culture, blackness, and nation for first-generation immigrants. For young Ghanaians, diaspora reorganizes itself around mobile principles and sonic bodily experiences. Ghanaians in America note that they have tended to blend in with African American life especially in the face of particular negative stereotypes about Africans. As one audience member at Gaucho's states, "Unlike Nigerians, we Ghanaians like to blend in with society around us. We don't like to stand out and make a fuss." In contradistinction, hiplife shows and parties provide ways for youths to identify specific cultural-linguistic idioms nested within a broader Afro-cosmopolitanism. For outsiders and first-generation Ghanaians, hiplife is understood within a broader hip-hop genre shaping their expectations of this music in relation to American racial and popular idioms. For some, this makes the music disappointing and its bodily and linguistic references uninteresting. For others, it inspires them to learn Ghanaian languages and gain the cultural knowledge to claim Ghanaian heritage.

Young Ghanaians raised in the United States listen to hiplife and find pride in their cultural heritage. They identify with home, differentiate themselves within a black diasporic world, and learn Twi through this popular idiom. As some of them, like Nana NYC, subsequently return to Ghana, they earn respect for being from abroad. For Ghanaians traveling or being prevented from traveling, music delineates a symbolic register of mobility and constraint. Ghanaian community is not a geographic designation or a homeland, but instead a set of aesthetic principles that make movement more or less possible.

Rockstone's Office

ENTREPRENEURSHIP AND THE DEBT OF CELEBRITY

This book has traced how artists and publics make musical value and use celebrity as a form of currency to convert aesthetic into economic value. These processes reveal a resonance between the aesthetics of music and of entrepreneurship. This is most apparent in how value is made through various kinds of social circulation and how artists struggle to harness the potentials of mobility as changing technologies reshape what and how people, things, and signs move. For young Ghanaians, the musician-entrepreneur is a self-fashioning figure who succeeds by harnessing pure aspiration. New musical audiences are called into being as artists reinvent older forms of verbal eloquence in the context of a commercial digital-media landscape.

Aesthetics is usually concerned with beauty and examining the formal visual, literary, tonal, or compositional properties of artistic works in intellectual terms (Eagleton 1990, 13–17). Instead, I have used it to demonstrate that formal properties of texts must be understood in social contexts that shape the affective, embodied tastes and values of audiences and artists. These pragmatic relationships that make meaning are subsequently themselves reshaped in the contexts of meaning-making. Aesthetics is a rubric for linking formal musical, visual, and linguistic properties to technological, spatial, temporal, and political-economic registers through experiential practices that make and maintain them. I have shown how hiplife is defined by an aesthetic of entrepreneurship in which a pervasive market-oriented ethos shapes the experience of music focused on making rappers into celebrity artists. This artist-entrepreneur becomes an indexical icon pointing to and embodying business success envisioned through social-musical style.

Hiplife's entrepreneurial aesthetic is built on several main qualities: first-person accounts and self-making; linguistic and bodily control; newness; blended genres; new technologies of circulation; and celebrity value.[1] High value is placed on an artist's ability to publicize himself or herself through morally titillating rhythms, words, and bodies that operate in highly gendered ways. In doing so, artists reflexively redirect how audiences value music and concomitant social identities. Through hiplife, youths imagine success through individual performance virtuosity. The focus on individual voicing makes personal success into a virtue. The figure of the rapper as a cosmopolitan traveler allows these artists to ensnare and control disparate and marginal words, symbols, and values. In the process, an aesthetic of individualism shapes disenfranchised youths into free market–oriented subjects for making, circulating, and consuming value.

Linguistic precision and bodily control are critical to hiplife success. The ability to self-fashion requires an aesthetic of control in which artists are celebrated for verbal eloquence. The ability to use words poetically focuses audience attention on a speaker's authority. Hiplife lyrics and fashions are assessed in a rapper's ability to shift between the indirect, proverbial persuasiveness of Ghanaian speech culture and the direct in-your-face bravado of American hip-hop.

Artists and audiences also value the newness that comes from the pleasures of combining multiple genres in unexpected ways. Generic juxtapositions ground innovative styles in past authority by blending them with references to older genres and texts. Aesthetic value relies on how a speaker makes new styles by balancing traditional, respectful forms of address with irreverent foreign forms. Rappers dazzle audiences with their ability to control these blends. In the process, speakers claim the authority to narrate the social transformations of the age. Artists strive to control oral, urban, and technological forms of movement in making connections to other artists, producers, audiences, and sponsors. New electronic technologies of circulation allow hiplifers to create a self-image and disperse it across local and transnational markets.

All of these aesthetic virtues link entrepreneurial skills to musical ones, making celebrity a currency in and of itself, a medium that generates musical, linguistic, and economic value. In the context of the free market, musical work appears as service-oriented labor, relying on circulatory forms of consumption to make wealth. But artists struggle to determine how to define the value of their labor. Musical products accrue value through newness, but this newness is carefully groomed to appear to have links to the past. Popular culture's constant need to remake itself reflects the ways that, in a capitalist system, profits must always grow. Making hiplife requires work but also the appearance of leisure and effortlessness. The blending of work and leisure under neoliberal conditions has implications for how people imagine successful living.

With the growing global hegemony of free-market economics in the 1980s and 1990s, Ghana was, from the perspective of the IMF and World Bank, a success story, instituting Western-style democratic reforms, privatizing state resources, and establishing a climate for entrepreneurship and service-industry development. Accompanying subjectivities emphasized a universal rights-bearing citizen. Public discourse celebrated the fantastical power of the individual to make wealth, erase historical inequality, and promote cultural difference through the processes of circulation itself. The entrepreneur became a central figuration of power who made prosperity through words, improvisational skills, and comportment. However, the language of universal, individual potential also highlighted the constraints Africans faced in harnessing flows of productive capital for their benefit.

Links between entrepreneurship and musicianship are not just metaphoric. Corporate mediation became increasingly crucial to hiplife's entrepreneurial spirit as artists tried to brand themselves and their music to reach youth-oriented markets. Social emphasis on business and market-driven individualism inflect musical aesthetics and practices. The aesthetic practices that make good music also make good business. They both rely on the performative aspects of personal aspiration necessary for ceaseless self-promotion and self-production.

The celebrity body bundles, condenses, and focuses public attention on the potential of individual success. Crafting the image of the successful celebrity engaged in leisure celebrations is a form of labor that generates value for products, symbols, and practices by association. The celebrity transforms public anxiety about economic and political instability into individual potential and hope for the future. This idealized modern citizen–speaking subject provides a semiotic node around which

Ghanaians assess the economic and moral potential of social activities—often in highly gendered ways. But success is accompanied by questions about the relationship between surface appearance and deeper meaning, musical value, and economic potential. The value of music relies on celebrity as a medium, a currency that directs audience tastes and structures of feeling. Making audiences believe in success brings fame and, hopefully, fortune. But fame must constantly be renewed. Participants continually struggle to add new value to personal brands and musical products through material and symbolic affiliations that promise power and success.

Diasporic Celebrity as Entrepreneurial Value

Ghanaian musicians and audiences have expectations of global black celebrities that speak to hiplife's Afro-cosmopolitan aesthetic that I have been detailing. Ghanaian artists see transnational hip-hop collaborations as a way to add value to music; but divergent interests between diasporic artists and local life create anxiety about connections and often reveal cross-Atlantic disjunctures rather than Pan-African solidarity. Hip-hop mogul Jay-Z's 2006 Accra performance demonstrated how the unstable dynamics of diasporic disjuncture and solidarity are exploited as entrepreneurial ways of adding value.

Symbolic networks linking business to music come into play when prominent international black artists perform in Accra. Events management companies periodically bring international hip-hop, dance hall, and R&B artists to Ghana, including Ja Rule, Shaggy, Beenie Man, Wyclef Jean, Busta Rhymes, Eve, and Rick Ross. Reggie Rockstone and other rappers recognize these visits not simply as chances to listen to music but as opportunities for collaboration that enhance local credibility and provide the opportunity for international exposure through association with these stars. Reggie explains, "When someone is coming to perform in Ghana, the promoters call me and other younger guys to perform with them. People see me as the Godfather, so they have to show me respect in my town. And I take advantage of that to get some exposure. It's good business." When Beenie Man came to perform, Reggie got him into the studio to record a track and included his protégés, the Mobile Boys. Beenie Man, 2Face Idebia (from Nigeria), and Reggie recorded another collaborative piece as well.

The discrepancy between global perception and local life was highlighted in 2006 when the United Nations and MTV teamed up to appoint

Jay-Z honorary Global Water Ambassador. This project intended to bring global attention to the problem of inadequate clean water for impoverished peoples around the world. In the name of humanitarianism, Jay-Z toured countries in Africa—including Ghana, Nigeria, Kenya, and South Africa—and around the globe. He opened new borehole wells and posed in promotional photographs with impoverished villagers. A Web site dedicated to the project featured photos and blog entries by Jay-Z on his impressions of the different locales. Donations could be made to support clean water. United Nations Secretary General Kofi Annan introduced the project and, like a number of recent African humanitarian and education programs, it was framed by a prominent African American's "return to Africa." For hiplife artists, music fans, and the local media, the ostensible purpose of the visit to promote clean water was incidental to the fact that a hip-hop icon would be performing in Accra.

Jay-Z's music and personal trajectory epitomize the business of hiphop. He gained prominence as a rapper in the early 1990s, producing a consistent string of hit tracks over more than a decade. His business and marketing savvy led to his appointment as CEO of Def Jam Records. The mainstream business success of Jay-Z—along with Sean "Diddy" Combs and Russell Simmons—demonstrates hip-hop's shift from association with images of the street hustler to the figure of the rapper as entrepreneur in the popular imaginary. Jay-Z's rise from street hustler to rapper to corporate chief executive is emblematic of the politics of neoliberal entrepreneurialism that pervades hip-hop's commercialization. The local promotional firm and organizer of the Ghana Music Awards, Charter House, handled Jay-Z's visit to Ghana. He was booked to perform at the upscale Conference Centre in Accra. Ticket prices approached $75. For his Nigerian concert, tickets were $125. On-line, Jay-Z blogged about being in awe of Africa, its warm people, and its endemic economic problems. Local hiplife artists, including Reggie Rockstone, were contacted to perform as opening acts for the visiting star. Jay-Z—or at least his handlers, as no one was able to actually communicate with him directly—refused requests to meet with any local musicians and the star sequestered himself in high style. Reggie tried numerous channels to reach him but was ignored. "He comes to my town and refuses to even meet with anybody. It's disrespectful." Reggie boycotted the performance. Some criticized him for putting on airs while others defended him for standing up to an international celebrity.

"I mean, he comes here promoting clean water. We know we got water problems! Who is he telling? It's people in America that don't know what is going on. . . . He hasn't seen anything for himself. We are living here; he just comes and thinks he can talk about people without meeting them." While at first the Ghanaian media celebrated Jay-Z's visit, the disjunctures between the stated purpose of promoting clean water, his concert, and the refusal to make himself more available led to criticisms of his lack of interest in the real Africa. As one local entertainment reporter explained to me, ticket prices for the concert were so high that the event was inaccessible to most people. Controversy erupted as to whether the local promoters had taken advantage of the situation or whether Jay-Z's promoters were trying to make money under the auspices of a humanitarian tour.[2] With the expectation of forming real connections comes the disappointments of different agendas and unfulfilled promises. Visiting diasporic stars are celebrated for their music and personal success, though assessed in terms of a logic of exchange and how they can add value to the local scene. As I have argued, hiplife's legitimacy as a genre relies on the incorporation of diasporic black styles to continually reinvent the music's newness while maintaining links to older forms of Ghanaian public culture. Local hiplifers sought to make personal contact with Jay-Z as a potential collaborator but were rebuffed. His trip was more about the mediations of development discourse and corporate image that relied on diasporic musical affinity to promote other agendas. The promised affinities of his presence were inverted and became an instance of failed recognition, maintaining him as a distant icon of both hope and disappointment.

Other diasporic musical connections have translated into more productive marketing opportunities. With the rising influence of corporations on Ghanaian public culture, an artist's ability to align with celebrity and cosmopolitanism becomes a form of value production on multiple levels. To inaugurate the launch of their network in Ghana, Middle East mobile service provider Zain sponsored a concert on November 22, 2008, featuring Haitian American superstar Wyclef Jean at Accra's Ohene Djane sports stadium. Local artists Obrafour, Tinny, and Kwaw Kese, among others, opened, followed by Nigerian 2Face Idibia and international R&B star Mario and singer Eve. Despite high expectations, the show was a disappointment. As one hiplife fan noted, "It was too expensive for any local people. The stadium was empty. . . . The mics did not work, and the artists were behind a fence." Despite the concert's organizational failings, Zain's launch of service in December 2008 was a success in gaining local market share.[3]

Unofficially Wyclef's visit provided a more intimate set of exchanges. At the Zain-sponsored concert, a frustrated Wyclef climbed over barricades to sing directly to a small crowd, much to their delight. He also spent time with numerous local artists. Reggie organized a studio session with local beatmakers and rappers, and a small video crew improvised a green screen backdrop for a shoot. "We got everyone together and just made it happen. You can't miss an opportunity," Reggie explains. They wrote a song and made a music video with him in a few hours; "Glad," with Wyclef, Reggie Rockstone, 2Face, and Kwaw Kese circulated online and later ended up on Reggie's double album *Reggiestration*. Both Kwaw Kese ("War") and D-Black ("Wonderful World") also enlisted Wyclef to feature on songs for their albums. As D-Black described to me, "It gives you cred to have done a track with someone like Wyclef . . . and it helps with online searches. . . . People find you through their name." As corporations use music as a form of branding, local artists take advantage of opportunities provided to them to gain prestige by association.

Investing in the Office

With hiplife's growing public relevance, banks, food and drink corporations and, especially, mobile phone companies sought out artists to brand their products as fashionable. Artists have, in turn, reinvested corporate prestige and resources in new projects. As the first and most prominent celebrity of the privatization era, Reggie recognizes the power of musical branding. "I am not in this game to make money, but if I can support myself and my people and promote the music, then I will use the system to do so," he explained to me. Reggie's reputation as the Godfather of Hiplife makes him an ideal corporate spokesperson. Early mobile company Spacefon (now MTN), which went on-air in 1996, honored him through their marketing campaign with a Spacefon Legend Award in 2003. Two years later, Reggie became the face of Guinness in Ghana, appearing in a series of prominent billboard ads and television commercials (see figure 41). In 2008 he received a large cash payment from Nigerian mobile phone giant Globacom. This was one of Glo's many extravagant marketing investments in high-profile Ghanaian celebrities over several years, during which they paid numerous artists to appear in billboard and television advertisements. They even sponsored

FIGURE 41 Reggie Rockstone advertisement for Guinness used for billboards, posters, and news media. Photograph by Eric Don Arthur.

the Ghanaian football Premier League. Glo's move to sponsor artists was part of a trend among the major mobile phone service providers—at the time MTN, Zain, Tigo, Kasapa, and Vodaphone—of buying artist loyalty by paying lump sums for appearance rights and branding opportunities (see figures 42 and 43). Artists under the pay of one mobile provider were often forbidden from performing with those sponsored by rival companies. Accra fans, musicians, and DJs became intensely aware of which artists were sponsored by which mobile phone companies. The heated rivalry between mobile service providers was conducted through artistic proxies.

Artists have tried to use sponsorships for their own purposes. At the end of 2008, with money he received from Glo, Reggie Rockstone bought a nightclub lounge called the Office. At the time, Reggie told me, "I have to diversify. . . . This is a good investment in the future." At first the club provided a comfortable, discreet drinking spot tucked behind the Japanese embassy that catered to a bourgeois crowd for after-work drinks, food, and music into the night. Reggie embellished the club's name to Rockstone's Office and remodeled, putting in floor-to-ceiling windows so people on the patio could look in at the corner office, with its computer desk, CEO chair, and mini-bar serving as a small VIP section. A cocoa pod logo adorns the club name on the lighted sign above the door. "The cocoa pod is a sign of money and success and it is very Ghanaian. Cocoa is what made us wealthy back in the day."

During Christmas holidays its first year, the Office took over Accra's nightlife. Reggie explains, "The holidays are when all these cats come

FIGURE 42 Reggie Rockstone and Gyedu Blay Ambolley posing at an Accra boxing gym during an advertising shoot for Nigerian mobile service provider Glo with a South African video crew. Photograph by the author.

FIGURE 43
Advertising poster for an Okyeame Kwame (formerly of Akyeame) show sponsored by mobile service provider MTN.

back to Accra after living abroad to see family and just show off—so that is when people are really spending money. These brothers would roll in with cash trying to show off. I called in my connections and everyone came to my spot. Everyone knows me, so this was the place to be. We almost shut down . . . other clubs around town." It was packed every night for weeks, as sharply dressed patrons jostled to get in. Reggie's wife, Zela, took over managing the Office's calendar, sustaining the club's long-term popularity with a marketing strategy. According to Zela, "You have to brand each night to attract different crowds . . . keep it fresh." Reggie's stage charisma translated well into the role of club impresario. Late in the evening as he dresses and leaves the house, he says, "I have to go to the Office," chuckling at the double meaning. He recalls, "We always tried to look successful, even when we were broke; now I am finally making money. The music doesn't sell but I can make my fame work for me now." Rockstone's Office is a physical manifestation of Reggie's years of personal, family, and musical connections. He uses Twitter, Facebook, and texting to publicize events and cultivates an endless stream of musicians, journalists, students, photographers, and filmmakers. The club has an air of established success, a place at the center of Accra's growing celebrity culture. Catering to a slightly older crowd, in 2010 they built an addition to the Office called Grand Papazz, which serves as an elegant VIP lounge with leather booths. The appeal of scarcity sells memberships. Reggie says, "Everyone wants to be in here. So we keep it exclusive." He calls on connections enticing celebrities with free liquor to make appearances. On any given night, you might meet business leaders, embassy workers, musicians, international football stars, fashion industry people, or Nigerian artists. "People are excited to be around stars. . . . They will always see someone here." Reggie has translated his celebrity status into sustainable commerce.

As epitomized by The Office, the links between musical and entrepreneurial aesthetics are increasingly explicit. As capitalism requires ever-increasing profits for survival, popular artists must constantly reinvent their music and themselves to remain relevant in a service-oriented market. Up-and-coming artists seeking to make names for themselves must be particularly adept at incorporating new sounds and looks and exploiting changing technologies for publicity. Desmond Blackmore, known as D-Black, exemplifies the new entrepreneurial image. As a student he began helping Reggie manage musical and business affairs. Reggie says that D-Black's talent is "his ability to connect to people. He knows how to work the network. He was the kid who listened and paid attention to how the game is played. At some point he realized it wasn't that hard; he could do it himself rather than managing others." While still studying at University of Ghana, Legon, D-Black[4] cultivated his English-language rap skills. His musical style is GH rap, a subgenre oriented toward straight-up American hip-hop beats and lyrics.

D-Black sees music through the eyes of a marketing executive, confiding to me, "There are a lot of artists who are more experienced rappers than me, but I know how to get myself to the fans and to the awards shows and try to reach South Africans, Nigeria, the U.S.; I see myself as a businessman. . . . I am CEO of Black Avenue Muzik, not just a rapper." Even before becoming well-known he referred to himself in promotions as a "hip-hop mogul." D-Black represents the prevalent new business-casual corporate look. Fresh and neat—more boardroom hustler than political activist or grimy street gangster—wearing suits and crisp white-collar shirts, high-fashion jeans and printed T-shirts, and smoking cigars (see figure 44).

D-Black's recognizable business savvy becomes a valuable commodity in itself. One of Accra's hottest video directors, George Gyimah, of Phamous People Philms, shot two music videos for D-Black at reduced rates because he "knew D-Black would promote them well and give me good publicity." D-Black sent these videos to the BET Awards organizers in Washington, DC, who, word had it, were looking for a Ghanaian artist to include in their Best International Act: Africa category for 2011. He was nominated for the award. Another Ghanaian rapper unable to get international attention marveled, "He isn't that popular in Ghana, can't rap that well, and has barely any music out, but he has created this image of success in a short time."

Other young artists, while their sounds are completely different from D-Black's, also rely on a corporate image. Groups like Ruff-n-Smooth, 4x4, and R2Bees, for whom hiplife from the early 2000s is "old-school," make dance-oriented pop hiplife with some rap, R&B, and mostly Pidgin lyrics aimed at reaching beyond Ghana to bigger markets in Nigeria and across the continent. For example, R2Bees's marketing description on their Facebook page and across music Web sites explains that the name is short for Refuse 2 Be Broke. As one member reiterated in a radio interview, "refusing to be broke is not a crime."[5] Older artists VIP, Tic Tac, and Okyeame Kwame made comebacks at the end of the 2000s

FIGURE 44 Promotional image for D-Black and Kweku T.

by latching on to what these young artists were doing, changing their sound and their clothes to reflect the new corporate look.

Some of the changes in Ghanaian music reflect broader global transformations of the music industry. African American hip-hop innovator DJ Jazzy Jeff notes that in the American context, "the new hip-hop group is a rapper, a producer, and a video production guy. . . . It's not about getting your demo to a major label or live parties either, . . . it's about branding yourself and getting your music to new audiences online."[6] But Ghanaian artists inflect changing technological conditions in unique ways. At home and abroad they refract a longer history of informal "economic life lived under conditions of volatility" in which economic actors struggle to translate value across incommensurate registers and spaces (Guyer 2004). As Jane Guyer argues, West African systems of exchange emerged over centuries of trade in unstable conditions where multiple variables were simultaneously in play. In this context traders and economic middlemen struggled to make wealth by linking West African systems of exchange to global networks, trying to bring together incommensurate regimes of value (Bohannan 1955, 56–57). This meant transactions relied upon personal charisma rather than routinized, depersonalized economic structures for successful conversions of value. Whereas Guyer's analysis of West African market economies posits market traders in some measure as performers, I have examined

FIGURE 45 A photographer and a trader outside Rockstone's Office. Photograph by the author.

performers as market traders who make aesthetic and economic value in a service-industry economy (see figure 45). An ideology of market exchange dominates how artists link the labor of music making to the pleasures of leisure and celebrity. Hiplife stars are transformative figures animating the potentials of entrepreneurship through self-proclamation as a performative currency of success.

The Debt of Celebrity

As I have argued, celebrity is a currency that transforms aesthetic into economic value, but through the logic of its exchange debts are incurred. For Marx, the commodity was the crucial form through which labor was circulated and transformed into the more abstract value-form of money. For contemporary Ghanaian musicians, celebrity plays that role. Money as a pure abstraction is supposed to wash its users clean of any residual social debts incurred in exchanges (Graeber 2011; Simmel 2004). This is of course the only way that monetary systems are idealized as all forms of social exchange involve debts, obligations, and uncertainties embedded within their logic. Indeed, celebrity as a medium of value transformation entails continuing obligations driving the process of exchange and the making of value in new contexts.

Debt produces wealth by deferring its potential into the future. As with money, the abstraction of value in celebrity is a promise of future value, not value in itself. Entrepreneurship, in this sense, is the ability to take advantage of the performative aspects of value making. While hiplife artists struggle to package themselves and find a market, the image of success becomes both currency and product, and music one way to make it. Marx's (1993) theory of circulation posits that the conversions between money, commodities, and back into money with added value (Music-Celebrity-Music') are not only how labor is abstracted and made highly mobile, but also how real relations of production and conditions of labor are hidden. In this process of abstraction, magicality inheres in the commodity form, which becomes a fetish that masks labor relations, and the surplus value that constitutes profit, with consumer desire for the commodity. The process of exchanging commodities for money accrues value that, in turn, produces new desires and needs through circulation. New commodities must be made to fulfill these new desires. Likewise, celebrity becomes a fetish, a nonmaterial form of desire that stands in for labor and material wealth. Ghanaian artists make exchanges in which debts accrued in music production and business networking create both musical value and new connections that attract future potential collaborators and sponsors. New musical and marketing opportunities add value to the public image of success (Music-Celebrity-Music'). In the process, the fashions and musical sounds associated with celebrity must be continually updated to fulfill desires for newness.

In *Capital*, vol. 3, Marx shows that the productivity of debt and circulation are central to surplus value and profit. Marx argues that capitalism's need for increasing profit is its driving force. Debt is a form of value circulation that extends the ways commodity production makes value. Money is an abstraction of labor that is the promise to pay, not an actual payment (Marx 1993, 525). This abstraction provides the potential to make a profit purely through circulation. For example, as Marx points out, as labor is abstracted, valued, and sold, there is a temporal lag between workers selling their labor and getting paid for it: labor is only paid for after it is used. This time gap between work and payment creates a debt with the potential to circulate, adding value as it replicates itself. Money allows the performative potentials of credit and debt to produce new value while claiming to represent a more concrete, "real" material value. Money represents social relations but it is also a deferral of promised investment return, creating a debt relationship with future promise. Paying off debt means incurring new obligations, requiring endless reinvesting with hopes for wealth and stability deferred to the future. Debt is always an incomplete transaction capped by the promise of future transactions. An economic investment is not only a bet that the value of something will go up in the future but, crucially, a gamble that the transaction itself will proliferate. Investments are not based on an intrinsic value but are performative social acts that make the product, service, and the process of investment itself valuable. This relationship between value, investment, and debt characterizes the economic and social transactions of Ghanaian musical work.

Within the Ghanaian music community, labor debts are crucial in forming collaborative relationships that project past affiliations and present obligations into future potential, structuring relations of value and, in fact, creating wealth. As Roitman argues, the ontological status of debt is foundational of social relations; debt is productive and "cannot be reduced to a problem of exchange" (2003, 213). For example, the intimacy of "successful" collaborations between Wyclef and artists in Accra with their songs circulating on YouTube and music Web sites contrasts with the "unsuccessful" Zain concert that brought him to Ghana. Jay-Z's refusal to meet local artists and conferring on them celebrity value through association contrasts with his tour of Africa as a proponent of clean water deemed successful from the perspective of international institutions. For Ghanaian artists, their claims to membership in an Afro-cosmopolitan hip-hop community entail obligations of successful artists—especially African Americans visiting Ghana—to use their fame to showcase local talent and in the process produce it as recognizable. Debts, whether personal or cultural, are imagined through shared histories that then in fact produce these connections.

As musical self-fashioning appears to be a viable pathway to success, numerous young people claim to be artists and producers, and to some, the image of successful celebrity outweighs what it is supposed to stand for. As Reggie joked, "Today, everyone is a rapper or runs a record label. What does that mean? There are no records and no labels." Another artist quipped, "[There are more] awards shows for music videos and hip-hop than there are artists. . . . There isn't much music even coming out . . . but people want to have an image of a big music industry." A socialite who runs a blog about Ghanaian and Nigerian celebrities tells me that going out in Accra "is about being photographed having fun rather than actually enjoying yourself." If everyone aspires to be an industry insider and a star, the line between production and consumption blurs, where being a musician or producer is a lifestyle focused on celebrity aspiration.

Successful musicians like Rockstone, Obrafour, and VIP invoke for aspiring youths the promise of the self-made man, or in Mbembe's (2002) sense, the potentials of "self-writing." But this leads to anxiety about the uncertainty of valuation. In this context, the self-made man is a masculine speaking subject who, in the face of large global forces of capital and punitive border security, appears to control his own path. Young Ghanaian artists and producers in Accra, London, and New York use music to forge new economic and affective networks of movement. Nodes of deterritorialized community are fashioned through informal exchange networks that spring up following the circulations of music between Ghana and abroad. For disenfranchised youths in Ghana, images of successful circulation fuel desires for movement and frustration at being held in place. For youths living abroad, hiplife maps a specifically Ghanaian nationhood in relation to the ambivalent connections and disconnections to Ghanaian and broader African diasporic worlds.

Young Ghanaian artists engage in a complex set of labor exchanges and travels in order to attach value to their names. They make music in order to make celebrity. They struggle to convert work into music and music into celebrity because, in a rapidly changing and globally dispersed music world, celebrity gives value to circulating images and sounds. Labor and value relations are objectified and circulate in ways seemingly contrary to what one might expect under conditions of informal entrepreneurial production. Artists do not use informal networks to create autonomous alternative systems but instead replicate and internalize images of corporate power as signs of belonging. Celebrity branding is the currency of a postmaterial music industry. As Ghanaian artists like D-Black aspire to corporate patronage, they engage in forms of self-branding in which they adopt the sheen of major-label corporate artists with the hopes of accruing the success this image implies. In order to continue making music and being invited for live shows and collaborations, musicians must cultivate a community within which their name can be associated with a set of authoritative musical values and public images.

Instead of corporations mediating the relationship between consumers and producers, musicians are facilitating the relationship between corporations and publics. An artist-driven music industry that taps directly into public tastes collapses and inverts the capitalist distinctions between work and leisure, labor and aesthetics, pleasure and production. Music becomes a form of entertainment and a lifestyle. It relies on an idea of free-market entrepreneurship in which labor is imagined as unalienated, and businesspeople seek out favorable labor conditions. Artists are owners and workers and consumers.

Entrepreneurial musicians appropriate and reconfigure formal realms and official sensibilities for their own purposes. As they attempt to draw the global and the corporate into their intimate worlds, artists and audiences are appropriated for corporate marketing and branding purposes. As an ideology of the free-market spreads, it undermines itself by authorizing those on the margins to appropriate market techniques outside of the centralized control a free market requires. New configurations of entrepreneurship posit self-images of business prowess as forms of social mediation that promise value. In these contexts, work is not an institutionally mediated exchange of labor-time for abstracted value in the form of money. Rather, work is the marketing of self-image. And value comes increasingly from the image of success. In neoliberal economies, labor focuses on making abstract shiny things like celebrity experiences, tourist excitement, customer service, and youth pleasure. Entrepreneurs and consumers struggle to quantify and value these experiences as forms of labor. The question is decreasingly about capitalist appropriation and exploitation of workers but rather labor's seeming desire for self-alienation.

Artist-entrepreneurs rely on an aesthetic of musical and bodily control to convert both the pleasurable and alienating aspects of a highly mobile world into new forms of linguistic, moral, and economic value. They foster networks of artistic kinship through relations of production and circulation but fight to convert these networks into success. Artists release free online tracks to spread their name and talents across the digital world to those who will celebrate their lyrical eloquence. While a few artists transform musical value into other forms of wealth through the conversions of fame, most remain both hopeful and anxious about the potential connections the music will bring.

Celebrity is a form of currency that incurs productive forms of debt. The debt of celebrity is like desire—always a lack needing to be fulfilled. It traps its beneficiaries in their own objectified desires for fame and dictates that they work endlessly to maintain the image of success, confidence, and leisure. Maintaining fame necessitates endless new fashions and new hustles.

NOTES

Introduction

1. This was one of the first programs inspired by the popularity of *American Idol*, which was rebroadcast on Ghana Television. Numerous reality TV series showing competitions to find musical stars emerged, including: *Stars of the Future* on GTV, *Icons* and *Mentor* on TV3, and *West African Idol* out of Nigeria.
2. Grey, private interview, January 2005.
3. Reggie Rockstone, private interview, January 2005.
4. Translated from Akan by the author with assistance from Grey.
5. Reggie Rockstone, private interview, June 2005.
6. Mohammed Ben Abdallah, private interview, February 1999.
7. Estimates are that about 50 percent of Ghanaians are native speakers of an Akan language and almost everyone understands some.
8. Anonymous market trader, private interview, February 1998.
9. Grey, private interview, January 2005.
10. Scooby Selah, private interview, January 2005.
11. I released a feature documentary film on the origins of the music, *Living the Hiplife* (Third World Newsreel, 2007), and a second feature on Reggie's visit to perform for the Ghanaian community in New York, *Is It Sweet: Tales of an African Superstar in New York* (Third World Newsreel, 2013).
12. Esi Sutherland-Addy, private interview, July 2005.
13. These include Africanhiphop.com, Afropop Worldwide, Nomadic Wax, okayafrica.com, World Hip Hop Market, Clenched Fist Productions, and Akwaaba Music.
14. U.S. cultural attaché Accra, name withheld, private correspondence, January 2005.
15. For more on black music and style as embodied practices that engage gendered, raced, and class hierarchies in black communities, see Pough et al. 2007; Sharpley-Whiting 2007; Cooper 2004; Perry 2004; Maira 2000; Guillory and Green 1998.
16. For Munn space and time are inseparable and mutually constitutive. Spacetime refers to how a cultural-symbolic system situates social actors in relation to both temporal and spatial registers. People make themselves in social spacetime, and in the process make the experiential spacetime within which they are situated.

17. Pragmatist Charles Peirce (1992) argues that signs work through three basic properties: iconicity, indexicality, and symbolism/abstraction. Rather than structuralism's emphasis on the internal logic of sign systems, Peirce's emphasis on triads highlights the importance of context and practical relationships among social actors in making meaning. The iconic aspects of signs operate through resembling or reflecting that which they are representing. The indexical aspects of signs work by pointing to their object. The abstract aspects of signs rely upon collective understandings of signs' meanings. The indexical aspects of signification are particularly significant in making and contesting social registers in that actors can actively maneuver the ways that signs point at other signs.

18. DJ Ronny Boateng, private interview, March 2007.

19. Nkonyaa, private interview, January 2005.

20. One hundred million cedis was about $10,000 as of June 2005.

21. DJ Black, private interview, June 2010.

22. One well-known producer charged young artists between 800,000 and three million cedis per song ($90 and $325) as of June 2005.

Chapter 1

1. The study of Ghanaian music of various sorts has been central to the development of ethnomusicology as a discipline and debates about the relationship between music and socio-historical context (Friedson 2009; Avorgbedor 2008; Agawu 2003; Agovi 1989; Chernoff 1981; Nketia 1962) Agawu (2003) points out that ethnomusicology in Africa has tended to emphasize the search for purity in musical performance and favored musical texts as conveying meaning in and of themselves rather than providing rich contextual understandings of music and its social meanings. Visits and musical interest from high-profile rock musicians and producers like Brian Eno, Mick Fleetwood, Paul Simon, and so on. played an important role in promoting Ghanaian and African music in the world music scene and encouraging musical tourism to the country (Collins 2009a).

2. The first gold record by a Ghanaian highlife artist was T. O. Jazz's 45 rpm golden disc in 1968 on Philips, *Aware Bone Agu Manim Ase.*

3. In the 1870s West Indian troops were brought to fight the Asante Empire. Jamaican soldiers stationed in Lagos were influential contributors to what would develop into juju music in the 1920s and 1930s (Waterman 1990). Regimental brass bands merged with local rhythms evolving into konkoma and adaha, popular Akan coastal brass band music (private interview, John Collins, January 10, 2004, Accra, Ghana). The British used konkoma's popularity to recruit Gold Coast soldiers for the army in the lead-up to World War II, and konkoma instrumentation and styles influenced postwar highlife guitar band musicians (Collins 1996, 5).

4. Louis Armstrong's two visits to Ghana as well as those by many less well-known jazz musicians were influential on local musicians. In the context of Cold War politics, the U.S. State Department took advantage of a global interest in black music for diplomatic purposes, sending jazz groups on tours

of Africa throughout the 1950s. In the battle for superpower influence across Africa, African American music became propaganda in an attempt to counter Soviet arguments that America was a racist society (Von Eschen 2006; Guillory and Green 1998).

5. Bob Vans, private interview, February 1999. See also Cole (2001, 143–144); and Collins (1996).

6. The new nationalist fervor surrounding Nkrumah was celebrated through popular highlife songs. One tune nicknamed Nkrumah "Showboy" because he was seen as a master of drama and public charisma

7. American W. E. B. DuBois, Trinidadian Pan-Africanist George Padmore, and other prominent diasporic artists and intellectuals moved to Ghana after independence helping shape the new nation. A small but significant African American community developed in Ghana. Later visits by prominent figures such as Frantz Fanon, Mohammad Ali, and Malcolm X further highlighted Ghana's place in the global black imaginary as central to conversations about Pan-Africanism, civil rights, anticolonial struggle, and structural racism. The tensions between Ghanaian national interest, Nkrumah's focus on anticolonial movements, and black internationalism contributed to growing national disdain for the first president and the eventual Western involvement in his overthrow in 1966.

8. Concert party veteran and television producer Nana Bosompra explained to me that sometimes musical and theatre groups praised whoever was in power in their music and plays in order to gain support. "Some of the groups supported the CPP [Nkrumah's party] or were just appeasing him and when he was overthrown in 1966 they just supported whoever was there [in power]." Nana Bosompra, private interview, March 1999.

9. Goldfinger, private interview, March 1999.

10. Spurred by wealth from Nigeria's oil boom, in the mid-1970s over one hundred independent Yoruba theatre companies toured western Nigeria, supporting a number of paid performers (Barber 2003, 1–2). Collins has compiled a list of over 240 actively touring guitar bands and concert parties in Ghana from the late 1950s to the early 1980s, peaking in popularity in the mid-1970s (John Collins, private correspondence, November 1999).

11. Mr. Y. Bampoe, private interview, February 1999.

12. Paa Kwesi Holdbrook-Smith, private interview, December 2009.

13. *Daily Graphic*, March 3, 1971.

14. The 1966 Festival of Negro Arts in Dakar initiated a series of international festivals to celebrate black cultural unity hosted by African states. Other events, including James Brown's 1970 Lagos concert, the 1974 Rumble in the Jungle boxing match between George Foreman and Mohammad Ali and the accompanying soul concert in Kinshasa, and FESTAC 1977 in Lagos, linked nationalist celebrations, "traditional" performances, and Pan-African culture spectacles. They endeavored to garner international attention, create political and economic networks, and define local legitimacy by symbolically linking African cities to a global black imaginary (Apter 2005).

15. Edith Boateng, private interview, September 2002.
16. Mary Yirenkyi, private interview, November 1999.
17. *Daily Graphic*, March 3, 1971, pp. 10–11.
18. At the time, under Kofi Busia's Second Republic of Ghana, Black Star Square was called Independence Square to minimize the public memory of Nkrumah's legacy.
19. *Daily Graphic*, March 13, 1971, p. 5.
20. Concert footage was edited into a film called *Soul to Soul*. There is no narration, simply groups performing in Black Star Square over the course of the evening, preceded by a few scenes of African American performers interacting with Ghanaians.
21. Mary Yirenkyi, private interview, November 1999.
22. Nana Ampadu, private interview, February 2000. Also see K. Yankah (1995), A. Anyidoho (1994), and K. Anyidoho (1983) for discussions of Ghanaian oral traditions and their relevance for contemporary urban life.
23. Gyedu Blay Ambolley, private interview, March 2007.
24. Except for adowa and possibly sikyi, these styles do not predate highlife but are neotraditional hybrids evolving in ongoing dialogue with highlife and with West African coastal and diasporic musical forms (John Collins, private correspondence, December 15, 2010).
25. Kpanlogo's basic bell-pattern rhythm provides the structure for jamma music, used in Accra social gatherings and football celebrations.
26. Lincoln said he developed kpanlogo's musical style based on an Ananse story his grandfather told him about a man who used trickery to find out the names of three girls, one of them named Kpanlogo, so that he could meet the challenge of their father, the chief, who had stated that whoever learned their names could marry them (Collins 1996, 110).
27. Transformed 5 pulse played in 4/4 meter is ubiquitous in Cuban rumba, Brazilian samba, and calypso.
28. This was also confirmed in later informal conversations I had with the musician, though Collins's more formal interview captures the essence of Ambolley's position succinctly.
29. Akramah Cofie, private interview, October 2008.
30. Anonymous, private interview, October 2008.
31. Reggie Rockstone, private interview, December 2008.
32. For many Ghanaian musicians, visits to Europe and America have had the effect of "Africanizing" their music. For example, Guy Warren played dance band highlife in Ghana and found limited success as a jazz drummer in the United States. He increasingly moved toward reintegrating "the sounds of Ghana, and thinking about Africanizing jazz, you know? That's when I came back to Ghana." He returned, changed his name to Kofi Ghanaba (literally, "child of Ghana"), and fused the individual musicianship of jazz with the sounds and styles of various Ghanaian drumming and spiritual performance traditions (Kofi Ghanaba, private interview, December 1998). See also Feld 2012.
33. Anonymous, private interview, January 2004.

34. Thompson's ground-breaking 1973 article, "An Aesthetic of Cool," argues that across West African contexts high value is placed on an actor's bodily sense of control, composure, and mastery of emotions and of the world around him. Coolness links external physical appearance to inner emotional control and moral purity of belief and purpose. In examining rituals, art objects, and criteria of aesthetic judgment in West Africa, Thompson argues that similarities in aesthetics between West African and African diasporic peoples across the Americas can be explained by understanding a "lexicon" of coolness that is of African origin. While Thompson focuses on African aesthetic forms as points of origin, I am concerned with West African forms as themselves historical products often relying upon eclectic influences from the Americas.

35. See Saidiya Hartman (2007) and Maya Angelou (1991) for literary accounts of African American journeys in Ghana.

36. Part of James Brown's influence on generations of musicians was the fact that his performances were highly interactive; his stage shows indexically invoked the active participation of the audience; he cared about how energetic audiences were and adjusted his music accordingly.

37. Mamdani (1996) on twentieth-century African politics, Mbembe (2002) on urban life and African subjectivity, and Mudimbe (1988) on African philosophical discourse all argue that, despite recognition of complex histories, discourses of Africa and Africanness continue to tend toward the polarities of romanticism and exotic culture, on the one hand, and degraded, failed modernity, on the other.

Chapter 2

1. Anonymous, private interview, February 2007.

2. Clement Sangaparee, "The State of Ghana before June 4th 1979," GhanaWeb, March 22, 2010, www.ghanaweb.com/GhanaHomePage/features/artikel.php ?ID=178877.

3. Paa Kwesi Holdbroke-Smith, private interview, February 2005; Panji Anoff, private interview, December 2004.

4. At first Rawlings's government included a number of artists. The playwright Asiedu Yirenkyi became Secretary of Tourism and Culture, though was replaced by Mohammed Ben Abdallah. The writer Ama Ata Aidoo was made Secretary of Education, and the poet Atuquai Okai was Mayor of Accra.

5. Mohammed Ben Abdallah, private interview, September 1999.

6. Mohammed Ben Abdallah, private interview, April 1999.

7. Amed Ibrahim, private interview, January 2010.

8. Anonymous, private interview, January 2005.

9. Ibid.

10. Amed Ibrahim, private interview, January 2010.

11. Babylon Disco, Black Caesars, Keteke Club, and Cave de Roi, among other clubs, played R&B, disco, and the latest African American records.

12. Adjetey Sowah, private interview, March 1998.

13. Anonymous, private interview, December 2009.

14. Ama Ata Aidoo, private interview, October 2005.

15. Amed Ibrahim, private interview, January 2010.

16. Mohammed Ben Abdallah, private interview, April 1999. J. B. Danquah, Joe Appiah, and other independence-era public intellectuals were alternately lauded and teased for speaking with (pseudo) British posh accents. One memorable aspect of Nkrumah's public speaking was that, as one retired school teacher recounted, "he sounded Ghanaian. . . . He did not put on some foreign accent. He had studied abroad like the rest of them [the independence leaders] but he spoke to the people in a language we understood, not trying to sound foreign" (Anonymous, private interview, January 2006). His refusal to speak with foreign intonation was seen as a rejection of a colonial mentality.

17. Indeed select secondary schools built on the English public school model have been crucial to forming political, intellectual, and artistic networks since before independence.

18. Anonymous, private interview, January 2005.

19. Panji Anoff, private interview, December 2005.

20. Kelvin Asare Williams, private interview, October 2002.

21. Anonymous, private interview, January 2005.

22. Reggie Rockstone, private interview, December 2005.

23. BiBi Menson, private interview, January 2005.

24. Ibid.

25. Ibid.

26. Nii Moffat, private interview, December 2003.

27. Akoto, organizer of rap and hiplife programming at the National Theatre, private interview, December 1999.

28. PLZ stood for Party à la Maison and, later, Parables, Linguistics, and Zlang.

29. Reggie Rockstone, private interview, December 2005.

30. Freddy Funkstone, private interview, June 2011.

31. Reggie Rockstone, private interview, December 2005. For more on how London, African, Caribbean, and South Asian youths used music as a public language of community identification in 1980s and 1990s, see Bald 2004; Hesmondhalgh and Melville in Mitchell 2001, 106.

32. John Akomfrah, private correspondence, March 2011.

33. The group, led by Rodney P and Bionic, had several minor hits notably "London Posse" (*Big Life*) in 1987 and "How's Life in London?" in 1993, which received MTV airplay in America. Their style mixed reggae rhythms and dub flows with bass-heavy beats, scratching, and beatboxing. They rapped with working-class London accents mixed with Jamaican patois, presaging the rise of grime and other British hip-hop styles a decade later.

34. Reggie Rockstone, private interview, December 2005.

35. Panji Anoff, private interview, December 2005.

36. Ibid.

37. Paa Kwesi Holdbrook-Smith, private interview, November 1999.

38. See Tina Campt (2012) for examinations of the relationships among photographs, image-making, and black European subjectivities.

39. John Akomfrah's 1986 experimental documentary film *Handsworth Songs* captures the experience of black and Asian immigration, aspiration, and racial violence in Britain during the 1980s.

40. Hashim Haruna, private interview, March 2007.

41. The Notorious B.I.G. and Tupac Shakur's success, wealth, and sudden violent shooting deaths at young ages made them particularly popular across Africa. Images of the two slain rappers became common across Accra and other urban centers, representing both the possibilities and dangers of black masculinity in a racist world.

42. Blitz the Ambassador, private interview, March 2012.

43. Hashim Haruna, private interview, March 2007.

44. Livingston, private interview, 2006.

45. These events were hosted in Accra at Globe, Keteke Club, Baby's Inn, Miracle Mirage, She Club, and Felisa, and in nearby Tema at Dzato Krom. Dzato Krom showcased new urban music and styles from the United States. Kwesi Kyei Darkwa (KKD) was also important in encouraging kids to rap by hosting hip-hop radio programs and live rap shows.

46. M.anifest, private interview, March 2007.

47. DJ Black, private interview, May 2009.

48. Anonymous, private interview, January 2005.

49. Panji Anoff, private interview, January 2005.

50. Kweku T, private interview, June 2006.

51. Panji Anoff, private interview, January 2005.

52. Mohammed Ben Abdallah, private interview, November 1999.

53. Adjetey Sowah, the 1986 world freestyle dance champion, directed the dance aspects of Kiddafest.

54. Korkor Amartefio, Artistic Director, National Theatre of Ghana, private interview, September 1999.

55. Komla Amoako, Director, National Theatre, private interview, December 1999.

56. Korkor Amartefio, Artistic Director, National Theatre of Ghana, private interview, September 1999.

57. Ibid.

58. Ibid.

59. Korkor Amartefio, private interview, December 1999.

60. Ibid.

61. Adjetey Sowah, Director of Dance Factory, National Theatre, private interview, December 1998.

62. Kwesi, private interview, November 1999.

63. Anonymous, private interview, November 1999.

64. Nana Brefo Boateng, private interview, May 1999

65. Anonymous, private interview, December 2005.

66. Anonymous, private interview, January 2000.

67. Anonymous, sermon, Assemblies of God Adenta, January 2000.

68. Adowa is a pseudonym. Private interview, December 2005.

69. Anonymous, private interview, January 2005.

70. Blakofe, private interview, May 2006.

Chapter 3

1. Rab Bakari, private interview, November 2004.

2. Mahoney P returned to Ghana from Holland around the same time as Rockstone. He recorded Twi rap but did not gain widespread popularity.

3. Rab Bakari, private interview, November 2004.

4. Ibid.

5. Sidney, private interview, July 2005.

6. Reggie Rockstone, private interview, June 2004.

7. Rab Bakari, private interview, October 2004.

8. Chapter 12, Article 162 of the 1992 Constitution, "Freedom and Independence of the Media," outlines the mandate to privatize media. Constitution of the Republic of Ghana, May 8, 1992.

9. John Mahama, Minister of Communications, private interview, February 2000.

10. Important DJs in this period included Blakofe, KKD, Azigiza Jr., BiBi Menson, Black, Sammy B, Fifi Banson, Bola Ray, and KOD.

11. At first, TV3 and Metro TV only broadcast in Accra, while GTV remained the only national broadcast station. This soon changed as they expanded the reach of their transmitters. Other new stations also went on the air in Accra and Kumasi. By 2011 over ten channels with varying degrees of broadcast reach played local programming in Accra. The establishment of South African–based music television stations Channel O in 1998, and MTV Base Africa in 2005, circulated music videos across Africa.

12. Paa Kwesi Holdbrook-Smith, private interview, January 2000.

13. Blakofe, private interview, January 2005.

14. Paa Kwesi Holdbrook-Smith, private interview, January 2000.

15. BiBi Menson, private interview, January 2004.

16. Reggie Ossei Rockstone, private interview, June 2004.

17. Rab Bakari, private interview, November 2004.

18. Anonymous, private interview, November 1998.

19. The *Ma Ka Ma Ka* EP was released with five tracks under the name Asei Mix Records: "Tsoo Boi"; "Nightlife in Accra" featuring Cy Lover, Chocolate, and Sammy B; "Agoo"; "My Sweetie, Sweetie" featuring Root I; and "My Turn to Burn" featuring Freddie Funkstone. Production by Rab Bakari, Michael Smith-Horthman, and Zap Mallet.

20. Rab Bakari, private interview, November 2004.

21. Translation by Kwesi Brown.

22. Rab Bakari, private interview, April 2004.

23. Ibid.

24. To keep their music in the public ear, in the year before the new album's re-lease they put out a remix of "Sweetie Sweetie" and a new single "Plan Ben?" (What's the plan?), which tells humorous stories in Twi about Accra night-life, over a sample of American Jean Carn's obscure 1978 R&B disco hit "Don't Let It Go to Your Head."

25. CD liner notes to *Me Na Me Kae*, by Rab Bakari, 1998.

26. Rab Bakari, private interview, November 2004.

27. Paa Kwesi Holbrook-Smith, private interview, June 2006.

28. Rab Bakari, private interview, April 2004.

29. Approximately $1,000 (U.S.).

30. Reggie Rockstone, private interview, January 2005.

31. Rab Bakari, private interview, Novmember 2004.

32. Translated by Reggie Rockstone and Jesse Weaver Shipley.

33. Reggie Rockstone, private interview, January 2005.

34. This type of Ghanaian verbal playing with the English language is reminis-cent of the way in which concert party popular comedians create long lists of introductory titles that go on for several minutes (e.g., "My name is Alhaji, Pastor, North America, Mr., Dr., Sister, Brother, President, Minister . . .") or speak in nonsensical English with long names and words. The early twentieth-century Gold Coast intellectual Kobina Sekyi's play *The Blinkards* ([1915] 1994) also satirizes the paradoxes of the West African use of English as a way to appear elite and refined (cf. Cole 2001).

35. Ama Ata Aidoo, private interview, November 2005. Writer Ama Ata Aidoo's work such as *No Sweetness Here* (1970) and *Our Sister Killjoy* (1977) speaks of the profound emotional displacement of Ghanaians caught in circuits of movement, often focusing on the effects of life abroad for Ghanaian women who return home and the ambivalent ways they are treated upon returning.

36. Reggie Rockstone, private interview, June 2004.

Chapter 4

1. Anonymous, private interview, January 2000.

2. Recall Marx's (1993) insistence that class is defined not simply by conditions of labor but through a group's self-conscious recognition that they are part of a shared cohort.

3. Ideas of place are made through ideas out of place. Appadurai (1996), follow-ing Frederik Barth (1969), points out that locality is not something that pre-exists contact with others but is produced and reproduced in specific engage-ments with outsiders and outsideness.

4. Paa Kwesi Holbrook-Smith, private interview, June 2006.

5. Nkonyaa, private interview, June 2005.

6. The shift to focusing on individual stars is true in gospel and highlife as well, though in hiplife it is more pronounced.

7. See Jackson (2005) for naming in hip-hop.

8. Sidney, private interview, January 2004.

9. Panji, private interview, January 2005.

10. Tic Tac, private interview, January 2004.

11. Translated by Judith Nketia and Jesse Weaver Shipley.

12. Lazzy, private interview, June 2004.

13. Translated by Judith Nketia and Jesse Weaver Shipley.

14. Reggie Rockstone, private interview, June 2006.

15. Regional subgenres have developed with distinctive sounds and language practices, which remain confined to those areas of the country. For example, Tamale, the capital of the Northern Region, developed a Dagbane-language rap scene. Artists such as Tuba Clan and Big Adams use electronic reggae beats with Islamic musical inflections and sometimes sample versions of the *dondo,* the talking drum from that region.

16. Buk Bak's album *Gold Coast* features melodic kpanlogo and highlife harmonies. Songs like "Gonja Barracks" recall an older highlife storytelling sensibility, describing a man who would rather go to the infamous Gonja Barracks prison than not be with his woman. "Helepu" has a Pidgin chorus: "Make you no leave me for this place ooo. I go die." It invokes highlife laments of lost love. While Buk Bak dress in hip-hop styles, their music is extremely close to 1970s highlife, with little explicit rap and mostly Ga language lyrics.

17. DJ Black, private interview, January 2009. Lord Kenya's later track "Sika Mpo Nfa Neho" ("To hell with money") also reflected on the ambivalences of money through rich lyrical metaphors that end with the proverb-like statement of the song's title. As DJ Black points out, he was seen as an early "rap champion" because of his skill in using a proverb to define a song and expand on a theme.

18. Translated by Judith Nketia.

19. Ibid.

20. Okyeame (Quoami) Kwame would go on to a successful solo career, calling himself the "rap doctor" and the "best rapper in Ghana," remaining one of the biggest hiplife stars.

21. Around this time Omanhene Pozo, formerly of Nananom, collaborated with several old highlife artists, including Awurama Badu for "Me Dofo A Daadaa Me" (My lover fooled me), C. K. Mann for "Afa," and Alhaji K. Frimpong for "Kyenkyen Bi Edi Me Ewu," the same track that Reggie and Rab used for "Keep Your Eyes on the Road." The videos for these songs intercut images of Pozo's urban hip-hop style and flair with the older artists' highlife dance movements and traditional lives. Obour's later collaboration album with highlife legend A. B. Crentsil also demonstrates these contrasts. The video for one track, "Adowa" (Asante funeral dance), shows the elder musician seated wearing a tuxedo, in front of Obour, who in a red track suit, sneakers, and backward baseball cap. Young dancers gyrate in front of a giant sign reading "The Best of the Life's: HighLife Meets HipLife."

22. Obour, private interview, December 2005.

23. Obrafour, private interview, June 2010.

24. Rab Bakari, private interview, March 2004.

25. Grey, private interview, June 2006.

26. Hammer, private interview, June 2008.
27. For one Ga listener not fluent in Twi, the album title is obscure. "It's interesting, it makes me think, but I don't really know what it means." In multilingual Accra, listeners often do not understand everything, but misunderstanding and partial interpretations drive curiosity.
28. Akramah Cofie, private interview, September 2008.
29. Lyrics translated by Kwesi Brown.
30. ghanathink.org.
31. Anonymous, private interview, June 2009.
32. Anonymous, private interview, July 2009.
33. "Samuel" is a pseudonym, private interview, June 2010.
34. Aminata Abdallah, private interview, January 2010.
35. Anonymous, private interview, March 2007.
36. Ibid.
37. "50th Anniversary of *Things Fall Apart*," Chinua Achebe, Bard College, Red Hook, NY, April 11, 2008.
38. Blakofe, private interview, May 2006.

Chapter 5

1. Hiplife parodies by young men about politicians, pastors, and figures of authority can be seen as a form of joking relationship structured around "permitted disrespect" (Radcliffe-Brown 1940, 196). In a variety of contexts, humor mediates political, material, and kinship relations that are otherwise antagonistic, dangerous, or ill-suited to direct forms of address. Joking relationships can constitute a form of intimacy or alliance or "a definite and stable system of social behavior in which conjunctive or disjunctive components . . . are maintained and combined" (ibid., 200). Singing and poetry in a variety of West African contexts intermingle praise, intimacy, humor, insults, and innuendo.
2. Esi Sutherland-Addy, private interview, December 2004.
3. The opposition boycotted the 1996 parliamentary elections, leading to an overwhelming majority for the NDC. Early Rawlings supporters saw him as betraying his revolutionary stance by acquiescing to IMF and World Bank changes that appeared to benefit the wealthy. At the same time, his opponents criticized him for maintaining the trappings of military rule for too long and preventing the progress of free-market capital.
4. Kenkey is a staple food made from mashed cassava or yam and sold on the streets wrapped in corn husks or banana leaves.
5. Eddie Blay, private interview, June 2008.
6. Ibid.
7. BiBi Menson, private interview, May 2008.
8. Exact figures are hard to determine; cassette and CD duplication and sales figures are not kept carefully. These estimates are based on discussions with numerous producers and artists.
9. Anonymous, private interview, June 2004.

10. Hammer, private interview, June 2004.

11. Motia, private interview, June 2004.

12. Hammer, private interview, June 2008.

13. Sidney claims that his great-grandfather, Osei Kwame, was the first Gold Coaster to have a song recorded on a gramophone.

14. Esi Sutherland-Addy, private interview, February 2004.

15. Sidney's manager told me that it had reported sales of 500,000 copies. I cannot confirm this figure. While it reflects the extreme popularity of the song, the figure is much higher than most other estimates for sales in Ghana.

16. Sidney, private interview, January 2004.

17. Song lyrics translated by Kwesi Brown and Jesse Weaver Shipley.

18. Some music insiders were critical of Sidney's sale of songs to political parties. Others claim that the songs had no effect on public opinion. Some even deny that "Scenti No" was actually sold to the campaign.

19. Sidney, private interview, January 2004.

20. In 2008 hiplife artist Obour put out a song called "President" just before the election, in which he described the types of responsibility he would take on if he was made president. Rather than parodying the state, the song sought to align hiplife and youth culture with good governance, though Obour was seen by some as using music to try to enter politics himself.

Chapter 6

1. "'I Cannot Be Blamed for My Own Assault'—Mzbel," Music in Ghana, www
.musicinghana.com/migsite/artist/readnews.php?artid=43&cid=107.

2. Charles Nimmo N-Mensah aka Mr. CNN, "Mzbel Attackers Must Face the Music," GhanaWeb, September 25, 2006, www.ghanaweb.com/GhanaHome Page/entertainment/artikel.php?ID=111047.

3. MzbelOnline, www.mzbelonline.com; "Mzbel," Myspace profile, www.my space.com/158160758.

4. Following Abrewa Nana and Mzbel, there have been a handful of female artists, notably Becca, Triple M, Efya, Eazzy, and Tiffany. The 2011 season of the reality TV show *Idols* focused on finding a female group, which would win a record contract. Jyoti Chandler Ohemaa, the queen mother figure, an original member of Sidney's group Nananom, switched to gospel music, later moving to Germany.

5. Esi Sutherland-Addy, private interview, January 2004.

6. For examinations of women in highlife and Concert Party, see Cole 2001; Collins 1996.

7. Throughout the twentieth century, women in Asante—and across colonial Africa—took advantage of ambiguities in changing legal and commercial orders to gain economic and sexual autonomy and challenge the constraints of patriarchal land and marriage rights (Allman and Tashjian 2000; Clark 1994). Colonial rule favored male ownership of property and political leadership, foregrounding the patriarchal aspects of African political systems (Mikell 1992). The language of culture was deployed to authenticate legal and

political claims on both sides, as women used commerce to gain access to spheres previously unavailable to them (Clark 1994).

8. Warner (2005) and Berlant (1997), following Foucault (1990), have argued that in the context of the Euro-American liberal state, a normative public sphere populated by rights-bearing citizens is produced against the backdrop of the policing of intimate spaces and sexual differences. Heteronormative publicness relies on containing deviance. In this sense, the struggle over respectable public sexuality is central to the production of the notions of a universal rights-bearing citizen.

9. Around the same time, there were a number of incidents of public policing of youths across Africa that reveal anxieties about modern fashions, hip-hop style, and female sexuality. Local and international media interest in these episodes only further emphasized their significance as flash points for incendiary discussions about public morality. For example, in an incident in mid-2007, skimpily dressed women in Lagos were arrested en mass by police. While the officers admitted that their clothing was not illegal, they claimed that women dressed in a provocative manner encouraged immorality and illegal activity. In 2007 Liberia banned students in school from wearing artificial hair extensions and weaves as well as trousers and skirts that were "sagging" to reveal undergarments. The country's "Education Minister Joseph Korto told the BBC it was a way of 'instilling moral discipline in our young people'" (Jonathan Paye-Layleh, "Liberia 'Immoral Dress' Crackdown," BBC News, August 24, 2007, http://news.bbc.co.uk/2/hi/africa/6962871.stm).

10. In 2006 the first widely acknowledged pornographic videos made in Ghana became available for purchase online and circulated among Ghanaians around the world. They show Ghanaians having sex in a hotel room that is purportedly abroad but is clearly in Ghana. While both men and women performed in the films, criticism tended to focus on the fact that Ghanaian women were, as one man told me, "willing to act as prostitutes for the whole world to see." Others said pornography was un-Ghanaian and showed a desire to get money at the expense of values: "Pornography is not for us. Some people are taking private entrepreneurship too far." See "Pornography Brewed in a Ghanaian Pot: Actors Speak Twi," http://ghanaweb.com/GhanaHome Page/NewsArchive/artikel.php?ID=118064.

11. Translation by Judith Nketia.

12. Interviews were conducted with Kelvin Asare Williams and Samuel Otoo (Ghana Boy).

13. In mid-2002 the exchange rate hovered around $1 (U.S.) to 9,000 Ghanaian cedis.

14. Translation by Judith Nketia.

15. Sidney, private interview, January 2004.

16. Sidney's management claims that the album sold 400,000 copies.

17. Paa Kwesi Holdbrook-Smith, January 2006.

18. Reggie Rockstone, private interview, January 2006.

19. Esi Sutherland-Addy, private interview, January 2004.

20. Translation by Kwesi Brown.

21. Comfort is a pseudonym, private interview, June 2005.

22. "Kwame Nkrumah University of Science and Technology, Kumasi Fact-Finding Committee's Report on the Alleged Manhandling and/or Harassment of the Hip-Life Artiste, Nana Akua Amoah (A.K.A. Mzbel)," October 17, 2005, KNUST Internal Publication.

23. "Our University Students Are Useless," Music in Ghana, www.musicinghana .com/migsite/artist/readnews.php?artid=43&cid=144; "University Students React to Alleged Remarks by Singer Mzbel," Music in Ghana, www.musicinghana .com/migsite/artist/readnews.php?artid=43&cid=149.

24. "Watch It Mzbel," Music in Ghana, www.musicinghana.com/migsite/artist /readnews.php?artid=43&cid=108.

25. "Mzbel's Stagecraft Attracts More Comments," Music in Ghana, www .musicinghana.com/migsite/artist/readnews.php?artid=43&cid=140.

26. Esther is a pseudonym, private interview, January 2007.

27. Prof. Mawere Opoku Legon, private interview, November 1999.

28. Ibid.

29. The notion that Kumasi is a bastion of traditional culture has a long history (see McCaskie 1995).

30. Nii is a pseudonym, private interview, February 2006.

31. "Mzbel's One Hour Agony," *Graphic Showbiz*, September 17, 2006. Also available online, GhanaWeb, www.ghanaweb.com/GhanaHomePage/entertainment /artikel.php?ID=110702.

32. Later in 2006 a well-known female gospel singer suffered a similar house break-in and robbery. It did not cause the same public controversy because the singer was married and was seen as a pious Christian. She claimed that she prayed when the robbers arrived. Here violence was portrayed not as shaming and moral retribution but rather as demonic. The "gospel" image reflects the fact that most female artists are religious gospel singers. Images of piety provide an acceptable female pathway to success.

33. Ghana Boy, private interview, January, 2007.

34. "Mzbel's Brother Speaks Out," GhanaWeb, September 17, 2007, www.ghana web.com/GhanaHomePage/entertainment/artikel.php?ID=110701.

35. Mimi Victor, Naijarules.com, September 17, 2006, www.naijarules.com/vb /news-current-affairs-art-culture-politics/18195-armed-robber-robbed -raped-singer-mzbel-5.html.

36. "Mzbel: Her Story, in Her Own Words," GhanaWeb, October 31, 2006, www .ghanaweb.com/GhanaHomePage/entertainment/artikel.php?ID=113099.

37. "Mzbel Attackers Must Face the Music," GhanaWeb, September 25, 2006, www .ghanaweb.com/GhanaHomePage/entertainment/artikel.php?ID=11405.

38. Comments in response to "Mzbel Attackers Must Face the Music," Ibid.

39. Osabarmia, Comment in response to "Mzbel Attackers Must Face the Music," ibid.

40. In 2007 she performed in Europe and throughout Ghana. She also came to the United States performing along with VIP and Tic Tac, August 4, 2007, for the Ghana Picnic at Orange County Fairgrounds in Middletown, New York.

41. Esther Dovi, private interview, March 2007.

42. Kwame is a pseudonym, private interview, December 2006.

43. Alhaji, Radio Univers, private interview, February 2000.

44. Papa Nii, comment in response to "Mzbel: Her Story, in Her Own Words," GhanaWeb, October 31, 2006, http://www.ghanaweb.com/GhanaHomePage /entertainment/artikel.php?ID=113099&comment=2377344#com.

45. For parallels to how witchcraft is invoked in relation to jealousy and the dangers of accumulation, see Mbembe (2005) and Geschiere (1997).

46. "Mzbel Drops Her Old Image," Pope Breezy, May 2, 2012, http://www.ghana showbiz.com/music/mzbel-drops-her-old-image/.

Chapter 7

1. M3nsa uses "3" in his name to stand in for the short "e" sound.

2. M3nsa, private interview, November 2009.

3. A Facebook posting to M3nsa's page on November 25, 2009, from Edmund Daniel recalls M3nsa's early style and fame. "D'u still have copies of the songs you did with Lifeline? I mean the tracks you featured in? With Shepherd etc? I think you were known as Shyne, right? Or that was someone else? '. . . I remember back in the days, things were going right in my way. Now I dont even see your face, dont even know just where you stay, think I'm gonna go astray. . . . LoL' . . . infact I loved the whole album. And you were my favorite cuz you sounded and felt like my Idol, Nas! If you still have copies of those sounds, make I feel them. I beg you waaaaaah!" M3nsa Ansah, Facebook, www.facebook.com/event.php?eid=348034975301&ref=mf#/M3NSA.

4. M3nsa, private interview, November 2010.

5. D-Black, private interview, August 2009.

6. MA Peters, private interview, August 2009.

7. Reggie Rockstone, private interview, August 2009.

8. Pronounced "fucking boys" as in "those fucking boys!"

9. Panji Anoff, private interview, July 2010.

10. Numerous albums by mobile Ghanaian artists have money, travel, and borders as central themes. They include Gibril's *Diplomatic Passport*, Wanlov the Kubolor's *Green Card*, and M.anifest's *Immigrant Chronicles: Coming to America*.

11. Grime comes out of East London and builds on drum'n'bass, garage, dancehall, and American hip-hop. Marked by fast minimalist beats and heavy distorted bass, its lyrics are rendered with working-class English accents deploying imagery representing East London and black British life.

12. Wet or dry as sonic aesthetic in studio mixing bears an interesting relation to "wet" and "dry" in Akan epistemology, in which speaking clearly versus improperly have moral and aesthetic implications (Yankah 1995).

13. Bosco's stage name, Kwabena Jones, is taken from Sekyi's play *The Blinkards* about Gold Coast elites in the early twentieth century putting on airs and speaking and acting with exaggerated English affect.

14. "Anaa?" is a track with a classic Afrobeat sound. In contrast "Yen Ko'o," featuring Bosco, who finished the song while M3nsa was in New Jersey, has an

ominous hard-core hip-hop sound with looming Twi rap lyrics and thunder and lightning composed in piano and guitar riffs.

15. Rab Bakari, private interview, December 2009.
16. Blitz the Ambassador, private interview, April 2012.
17. Blitz the Ambassador, "About," Facebook, www.facebook.com/BlitzAmbas sador/info. See also http://blitz.mvmt.com/.
18. Blitz the Ambassador, private interview, April 2012.
19. Rab Bakari, private interview, December 2009.
20. Sam Kessie, private interview, Novemver 2010.
21. "Ajuma" is sometimes spelled "Edwuma."
22. After the December 19 program, the promo statement initially posted was elaborated on at DJ Black's Joy FM page. Three video clips were posted: footage of M3nsa live on air, Wanlov freestyling in the studio, and the video for "Adjuma." The writeup read: "M3NSA PROMOTES HIS NEW ALBUM ON THE OPEN HOUSE PARTY 12/19/2009. Ghanaian MC, M3nsa was the guest on the Open house party last Saturday night. He promoted his new album 'NO 1 MANGO STREET' on the show. M3nsa is not a strange name in the Ghanaian music scene. He spoke about his recent album and a movie album he was working with Wanlov at the same time whilst trying to merge that with producing other artistes work and ads."
23. "M3NSA ADJUMA (WORK!! HUSTLE!)," YouTube, December 3, 2009, www.you tube.com/watch?v=geWUQxMvqyc&p=2444F74F6162141F&playnext=1& index=43.
24. About $6 (U.S.) at the time.
25. "Mango Street's No 1 Son," BBC World Service, Africa, October 19, 2010, www .bbc.co.uk/worldservice/africa/2010/10/101019_m3nsa_interview_session .shtml.
26. www.thehiphopchronicle.com/2010/09/28/m3nsa-no-one-knows/; Toksala, "Ghana Rapper M3nsa's New Video Will Make You Stop Worrying," music video review, MTV Iggy, January 31, 2011, http://blog.mtviggy.com/2011/01 /31/ghana-rapper-m3nsas-new-video-will-make-you-stop-worrying/.

Chapter 8

1. Hashim Haruna, private interview, March 2007.
2. Ronny Boateng, private interview, March 2007.
3. According to U.S. Census records, the West African–born population in the United States was 326,507 in 2000: 134,940 from Nigeria, 65,572 from Ghana, and 20,831 from Sierra Leone. New York City had the most African-born residents, with 99,126. Washington, DC, had 93,271. Real figures are likely much higher than official statistics. See Jill Wilson, "African-Born Residents of the United States," Migration Information Source, August 2003, "Foreign Born," United States Census Bureau.
4. There are many Ghanaians who would not come to events like this. Some who move to the United States attempt to break their ties to Ghana, cutting off those they know from home as well as Ghanaian networks more gener-

ally. While most legal and illegal immigrants rely on these kinship and fictive kinship networks, severing ties to home usually occurs for two reasons: pressure from kin for economic support and the intensity of rumors about Ghanaians abroad. These rumors often focus on sexual promiscuity, illegal trafficking, marriage fraud, or other morally disreputable activities. One nurse living in New Jersey commented to me that she would never go to Ghanaian concerts and in fact had cut ties to others she knew from Ghana. "I am trying to make a new life here. I do not want to get caught in rumors. You know how Ghanaians talk about each other. I just cannot stand it anymore."

5. Eli Jacobs-Fantauzzi has been a close collaborator with VIP for over ten years since meeting them as a visiting student in Ghana. Supporting himself through his videography, Eli's work under the rubric of Clenched Fist Productions focuses on global hip-hop as a radical political project and form of community organization and empowerment. After releasing a film on Cuban hip-hop he filmed a feature documentary depicting VIP's rise to fame titled *Homegrown*.

6. "Ghana's Golden Jubile Concert—NYC," YouTube, March 15, 2007, www.youtube.com/watch?v=7Oy4j_wCAfo. As of October 6, 2008, it had 33,467 viewings and thirty-three comments.

7. Each diaspora privileges specific symbols in forming relations to home and movement. For examinations of the relationship between memory, locale, and diaspora, see Engseng Ho (2006). He is concerned with the long duration and multiple sites of settlement for Hadrami diaspora around the Indian Ocean arguing that, in this case, graves are symbolically dense focal points of return, centering spatial, bodily, and temporal forms of cohesion.

Conclusion

1. I thank the anonymous reader for specific help in clarifying and condensing this concept.

2. Across the continent, fans noted Jay-Z's reluctance to get close to people. For example, Kenyans complained that he was uncomfortable shaking hands.

3. They reportedly invested $420 million in Ghana's "network infrastructure," adding Ghana as the seventeenth country under their global campaign slogan "One Network." Only two years later, however, they sold most of their African networks to the Indian company Airtel for a reported $10.7 billion.

4. D-Black, private interview, August 2009.

5. R2Bees, radio interview, Joy FM, July 2010.

6. DJ Jazzy Jeff, private interview, March 2011.

BIBLIOGRAPHY

Abu-Lughod, Lila. 2004. *Dramas of Nationhood: The Politics of Television in Egypt.* Chicago: University of Chicago Press.

Agamben, Giorgio. 1998. *Homo Sacer: Sovereign Power and Bare Life.* Stanford, CA: Stanford University Press.

Agawu, Kofi. 2003. *Representing African Music: Postcolonial Notes, Queries, Positions.* New York: Routledge.

Agha, Asif. 2005a. "Introduction: Semiosis across Encounters." *Journal of Linguistic Anthropology* 15(1).

———. 2005b. "Voicing, Footing, Enregisterment." *Journal of Linguistic Anthropology* 15(1): 38–59.

Agovi, Kofi. E. 1990. "The Origin of Literary Theatre in Colonial Ghana." *Institute of African Studies Research Review* 6(1): 1–23.

———. 1989. "The Political Relevance of Ghanaian Highlife Songs since 1957." *Research in African Literatures* 20(2): 194–201.

Aidoo, Ama Ata. 1977. *Our Sister Killjoy.* London: Longman.

———. 1970. *No Sweetness Here.* London: Longman.

Akudinobi, Jude G. 2001. "Nationalism, African Cinema, and Frames of Scrutiny." *Research in African Literatures* 32(3): 123–142.

Akyeampong, Emmanuel. 1997. "Sexuality and Prostitution among the Akan of the Gold Coast, c. 1650–1950." *Past and Present* 156(1): 144–173.

Alim, Samy, Awad Ibrahim, and Alastair Pennycook. 2008. *Global Linguistic Flows: Hip Hop Cultures, Youth Identities, and the Politics of Language.* New York: Routledge.

Allman, Jean, and John Parker. 2005. *Tongnaab: The History of a West African God.* Bloomington: Indiana University Press.

Allman, Jean Marie. 1993. *The Quills of the Porcupine: Asante Nationalism in an Emergent Ghana.* Madison: University of Wisconsin Press.

Allman, Jean Marie, and Victoria B. Tashjian. 2000. *I Will Not Eat Stone: A Women's History of Colonial Asante.* Oxford: Heinemann.

Angelou, Maya. 1991. *All God's Children Need Traveling Shoes.* New York: Vintage.

Anyidoho, Akuosua. 1994. "Tradition and Innovation in Nnwonkoro, an Akan Female Verbal Genre." *African Literatures* 25(3).

Anyidoho, Kofi. 1983. "Oral Poetics and Traditions of Verbal Art in Africa." PhD dissertation, University of Texas, Austin.

Appadurai, Arjun. 1996. *Modernity at Large: Cultural Dimensions of Globalization.* Minneapolis: University of Minnesota Press.

Apter, Andrew. 2005. *The Pan-African Nation: Oil and the Spectacle of Culture in Nigeria.* Chicago: University of Chicago Press.

———. 1999. "IBB = 419: Nigerian Democracy and the Politics of Illusion." In *Civil Society and the Political Imagination in Africa*, ed. John L. Comaroff and Jean Comaroff, pp. 267–306. Chicago: University of Chicago Press.

Armah, Ayi Kwei. [1968] 1988. *The Beautyful Ones Are Not Yet Born.* London: Heinemann.

Arvamudan, Srinivas. 2005. *Guru English: South Asian Religion in a Cosmopolitan Language.* Princeton, NJ: Princeton University Press.

Aryeetey, Ernest, Jane Harrian, and Machiko Nissanke. 2000. *Economic Reforms in Ghana: The Miracle and the Mirage.* Oxford: Africa World Press.

Asare, Charles Agyin. 1997. *It Is Miracle Time: Experiencing GOD's Supernatural Working Power, Volumes I & II.* Accra: Type Company Ltd.

Askew, Kelly M. 2002. *Performing the Nation: Swahili Music and Cultural Politics in Tanzania.* Chicago: University of Chicago Press.

Avorgbedor, Daniel. 2008. "In and Out of Song." *Research in African Literatures* 39(2): 131–137.

Baker, Houston A. 1993. *Black Studies, Rap, and the Academy.* Chicago: University of Chicago Press.

Bakhtin, M. M. 1986. *Speech Genres and Other Late Essays.* Austin: University of Texas Press.

———. 1981. *The Dialogic Imagination*, ed. Michael Holquist. Austin: University of Texas Press.

Bald, Vivek. 2004. *Mutiny: Asians Storm British Music.* Documentary film.

Bame, Kwabena N. 1985. *Come to Laugh: African Traditional Theatre in Ghana.* New York: Lilian Barber Press.

Barber, Karin. 2003. *The Generation of Plays: Yoruba Popular Life in Theater.* Bloomington: Indiana University Press.

———. 1997. "Preliminary Notes on Audiences in Africa." *Africa* 67(3).

———. 1987. "Popular Arts in Africa." *African Studies Review* 30(3): 1–78.

Barber, Karin, John Collins, and Alain Ricard. 1997. *West African Popular Theatre.* Bloomington: Indiana University Press.

Barth, Fredrik. 1969. *Ethnic Groups and Boundaries: The Social Organization of Cultural Difference.* Oslo: Universitetsforlaget.

Basu, Dipannita, Sidney Lemelle, and Robin Kelley. 2006. *The Vinyl Ain't Final: Hip-hop and the Globalisation of Black Popular Culture.* London: Pluto Press.

Bate, Bernard. 2009. *Tamil Oratory and the Dravidian Aesthetic: Democratic Practice in South India.* New York: Columbia University Press.

Baucom, Ian. 2005. *Specters of the Atlantic: Finance Capital, Slavery and the Philosophy of History.* Durham, NC: Duke University Press.

Bauman, Richard. 2002. "Disciplinarity, Reflexivity, and Power in Verbal Art as Performance: A Response." *Journal of American Folklore* 115: 455.

———. 1995. "Contextualization, Tradition, and the Dialogue of Genres: Icelandic Legends of the Kraftaskald." In *Rethinking Context: Language as an Interactive Phenomenon*, ed. Alessandro Duranti and Charles Goodwin. Cambridge: Cambridge University Press.

Bauman, Richard, and Charles Briggs. 1990. "Poetics and Performance as Critical Perspectives on Language and Social Life." *Annual Review of Anthropology* 19: 59–88.

Bayart, Jean-Francois. 1993. *The State in Africa: The Politics of the Belly*. London: Longman.

Beidelman, Thomas. 1980. "The Moral Imagination of the Kaguru: Some Thoughts on Tricksters, Translation, and Comparative Analysis." *American Ethnologist* 7(1): 27–42.

Benjamin, Walter. 1969. "The Storyteller: Reflections on the Works of Nikolai Leskov." In *Illuminations: Essays and Reflections*. New York: Shocken Books.

Berlant, Lauren. 1997. *The Queen of America Goes to Washington City: Essays on Sex and Citizenship*. Durham, NC: Duke University Press.

Berry, Jack. 1961. *Spoken Art in West Africa*. London: University of London Press.

Bhabha, Homi K. 1994. *The Location of Culture*. London: Routledge.

Bhattacharjee, Sudip, et al. 2007. "The Effect of Digital Sharing Technologies on Music Markets: A Survival Analysis of Albums on Ranking Charts." *Management Science* (53)9: 1359–1374.

Bohannan, Paul. 1955. "Some Principles of Exchange and Investment among the Tiv." *American Anthropologist* 57(1): 60–70.

Bourdieu, Pierre. 1984. *Distinction: A Social Critique of the Judgement of Taste*. Cambridge, MA: Harvard University Press.

Bourgault, Louise M. 1995. *Mass Media in Sub-Saharan Africa*. Bloomington: Indiana University Press.

Boyer, Dominic. 2005. *Spirit and System: Media, Intellectuals, and the Dialectic in Modern German Culture*. Chicago: Chicago University Press.

Boyer, Dominic, and Alexei Yurchak. 2010. "American Stiob: Or, What Late Socialist Aesthetics of Parody Reveal about Contemporary Political Culture in the West." *Cultural Anthropology* 25(2): 179–221.

Braudy, Leo. 1997. *The Frenzy of Renown: Fame and Its History*. New York: Vintage.

Brennan, Vicki. 2010. Mediating "'The Voice of the Spirit': Musical and Religious Transformations in Nigeria's Oil Boom." *American Ethnologist* 37 (2): 354–370.

Briggs, Charles, and Richard Bauman. 1992. "Genre, Intertextuality and Social Power." *Journal of Linguistic Anthropology* 2: 131–172.

Buggenhagen, Beth. 2010. "Killer Bargain: The Global Networks of Senegalese Muslims and Policing Unofficial Economies in the War on Terror." In *Hard Work, Hard Times: Global Volatilities and African Subjectivities*, ed. Anne-Maria B. Makhulu, Beth A. Buggenhagen, and Stephen Jackson. Berkeley: University of California Press.

Burrell, Jenna. 2012. *Invisible Users: Youth in the Internet Cafes of Urban Ghana*. Cambridge, MA: MIT Press.

Caldeira, Teresa P. R. 2006. "'I Came to Sabotage Your Reasoning!' Violence and Resignifications of Justice in Brazil." In *Law and Disorder in the Postcolony*, ed. Jean Comaroff and John L. Comaroff. Chicago: University of Chicago Press.

Campt, Tina. 2012. *Image Matters: Archive, Photography, and the African Diaspora in Europe*. Durham, NC: Duke University Press.

Carby, Hazel. 2007. " Lost (and Found?) in Translation." Reading at the Reconstructing Womanhood: A Future beyond Empire Symposium, November 26, Barnard College.

Cashmore, Ellis. 1997. *The Black Culture Industry*. London: Routledge.

Chalfin, Brenda. 2010. *Neoliberal Frontiers: An Ethnography of Sovereignty in West Africa*. Chicago: University of Chicago Press.

Charry, Eric, ed. 2012. *Hip Hop Africa: New African Music in a Globalizing World*. Bloomington: Indiana University Press.

———. 2000. *Mande Music: Traditional and Modern Music of the Maninka and Mandinka of Western Africa*. Chicago: University of Chicago Press.

Chernoff, John Miller. 2003. *Hustling Is Not Stealing: Stories of an African Bar Girl*. Chicago: University of Chicago Press.

———. 1981. *African Rhythm and African Sensibility: Aesthetics and Social Action in African Musical Idioms*. Chicago: University of Chicago Press.

Clark, Gracia. 1994. *Onions Are My Husband: Survival and Accumulation by West African Market Women*. Chicago: University of Chicago Press.

Clarke, Kamari. 2004. *Mapping Yoruba Transnational Networks: Power and Agency in the Making of Transnational Communities*. Durham, NC: Duke University Press.

Coe, Cati. 2005. *Dilemmas of Culture in African Schools: Youth, Nationalism, and the Transformation of Knowledge*. Chicago: University of Chicago Press.

Cogdell DjeDje, Jacqueline. 2008. *Fiddling in West Africa: Touching the Spirit in Fulbe, Hausa, and Dagbamba Cultures*. Bloomington: Indiana University Press.

Cole, Catherine M. 2001. *Ghana's Concert Party Theatre*. Bloomington: Indiana University Press.

Collins, John. 2012. "Contemporary Ghanaian Popular Music since the 1980s." In *Hip Hop Africa: New African Music in a Globalizing World*, ed. Eric Charry. Bloomington: Indiana University Press.

———. 2009a. "Ghana and the World Music Boom." In *World Music: Roots and Routes*, ed. Tuulikki Pietilä, pp. 57–75. Helsinki: Helsinki Collegium for Advanced Studies.

———. 2009b. *Fela: Kalakuta Notes*. Amsterdam: Dutch Royal Tropical Institute.

———. 2002. "African Popular Music: A Historical Review of Sub-Saharan Africa." Unpublished paper.

———. 1996. *Highlife Time*. Accra: Anansesem.

———. 1985. *Music Makers of West Africa*. Washington, DC: Three Continents Press.

Comaroff, John L., and Jean Comaroff. 2006. "Law and Disorder in the Postcolony: An Introduction." In *Law and Disorder in the Postcolony*, ed. Jean Comaroff and John L. Comaroff. Chicago: University of Chicago Press.

————. 2000. "Millennial Capitalism: First Thoughts on a Second Coming." *Public Culture* 12(2): 291–343.

Condry, Ian. 2006. *Hip-Hop Japan: Rap and the Paths of Cultural Globalization*. Durham, NC: Duke University Press.

Cooper, Carolyn. 2004. *Sound Clash: Jamaican Dancehall Culture at Large*. London: Palgrave Macmillan.

Coplan, David. [1985] 2008. *In Township Tonight! South Africa's Black City Music and Theatre*. Chicago: University of Chicago Press.

Cornyetz, Nina. 1994. "Fetishized Blackness: Hip Hop and Racial Desire in Contemporary Japan." *Social Text* 41: 112–139.

Coronil, Fernando. 1997. *The Magical State: Oil Money, Democracy, and Capitalism in Venezuela*. Chicago: University of Chicago Press.

DeGenova, Nicholas. 1995a. "Check Your Head: The Cultural Politics of Rap Music." *Transition* 67: 123–137.

————. 1995b. "Gangster Rap and Nihilism in Black America: Some Questions of Life and Death." *Social Text* 43: 89–132.

Dent, Alexander. 2009. *River of Tears: Country Music, Memory, and Modernity in Brazil*. Durham, NC: Duke University Press.

Dent, Gina, ed. 1992. *Black Popular Culture*. Seattle: Bay Press.

De Witte, Marleen. 2005. "The Spectacular and the Spirits: Charismatics and Neo-Traditionalists on Ghanaian Television." *Material Religion* 1(3): 314–335.

Diawara, Manthia. 2002. "The 1960s in Bamako: Malick Sidibé and James Brown." *Black Renaissance/Renaissance Noire* 4.

Drake, St. Clair. 1982. "Diaspora Studies and Pan-Africanism." In *Global Dimensions of the African Diaspora*, ed. Joseph Harris. Washington, DC: Howard University Press.

DuBois, W. E. B. [1939] 1990. *Black Folk: Then and Now*. White Plains, NY: Kraus-Thomson.

Durand, Alain-Philippe, ed. 2003. *Black, Blanc, Beur: Rap Music and Hip-Hop Culture in the Francophone World*. Lanham, MD: Scarecrow Press.

Duranti, Alessandro, and Charles Goodwin, eds. 1995. *Rethinking Context: Language as an Interactive Phenomenon*. Cambridge: Cambridge University Press.

Dyson, Michael E. 1993. *Reflecting Black: African-American Cultural Criticism*. Minneapolis: University of Minnesota Press.

Eagleton, Terry. 1990. *The Ideology of the Aesthetic*. Oxford: Blackwell.

Ebron, Paulla. 2002. *Performing Africa*. Princeton, NJ: Princeton University Press.

Edwards, Brent Hayes. 2003. *The Practice of Diaspora: Literature, Translation, and the Rise of Black Internationalism*. Cambridge, MA: Harvard University Press.

Eisenlohr, Patrick. 2006. *Little India: Diaspora, Time, and Ethnolinguistic Belonging in Hindu Mauritius*. Berkeley: University of California Press.

Elias, Norbert. 1978. *The Civilizing Process: The History of Manners*. New York: Urizen Books.

Engelke, Matthew. 2007. *A Problem of Presence: Beyond Scripture in an African Church*. Berkeley: University of California Press.

————. 2004. "Text and Performance in an African Church: The Book, 'Live and Direct.'" *American Ethnologist* 31(1): 76–91.

Erlmann, Veit. 1999. *Music, Modernity, and the Global Imagination: South Africa and the West*. New York: Oxford University Press.

————. 1991. *African Stars: Studies in Black South African Performance*. Chicago: University of Chicago Press.

Fanon, Frantz. [1952] 2008. *Black Skin, White Masks*. New York: Grove Press.

Feld, Steven. 2012. *Jazz Cosmopolitanism in Accra: Five Musical Years in Ghana*. Durham, NC: Duke University Press.

————. 1990. *Sound and Sentiment: Birds, Weeping, Poetics, and Song in Kaluli Expression*. Philadelphia: University of Pennsylvania Press.

Ferguson, James. 2006. *Global Shadows: Africa in the Neoliberal World Order*. Durham, NC: Duke University Press.

————. 1999. *Expectations of Modernity: Myths and Meanings of Urban Life on the Zambian Copperbelt*. Berkeley: University of California Press.

Fernandes, Sujatha. 2011. *Close to the Edge: In Search of the Global Hip Hop Generation*. London: Verso.

————. 2006. *Cuba Represent!: Cuban Arts, State Power, and the Making of New Revolutionary Cultures*. Durham, NC: Duke University Press.

Forman, Murray, and Mark Anthony Neal. 2011. *That's the Joint!: The Hip-Hop Studies Reader*. New York: Routledge.

Foucault, Michel. 1990. *The History of Sexuality Vol. 1: An Introduction*. New York: Vintage Books.

Fox, Aaron. 2004. *Real Country: Music and Language in Working Class Culture*. Durham, NC: Duke University Press.

Friedson, Steven M. 2009. *Remains of Ritual: Northern Gods in a Southern Land*. Chicago: University of Chicago Press.

Gaines, Kevin. 2006. *American Africans in Ghana: Black Expatriates in the Civil Rights Era*. Chapel Hill: University of North Carolina Press.

Gal, Susan. 2005. "Language Ideologies Compared: Metaphors of Public/Private." *Journal of Linguistic Anthropology* 15(1): 23–37.

————. 1990. "Between Speech and Silence: The Problematics of Research on Language and Gender." *Pragmatics* 3(1): 1–38.

Gaonkar, Dilip Parameshwar. 2002. "Toward New Imaginaries: An Introduction." *Public Culture* 14(1): 1–19.

Geertz, Clifford. 1985. "Blurred Genre." In *Local Knowledge*. New York: Basic Books.

Geschiere, Peter. 1997. *The Modernity of Witchcraft: Politics and the Occult in Postcolonial Africa*. Charlottesville: University of Virginia Press.

Geschiere, Peter, and Francis Nyamnjoh. 2000. "Capitalism and Autochthony: The Seesaw of Mobility and Belonging." *Public Culture* 12(2): 423–452.

Gifford, Paul. 2004. *Ghana's New Christianity: Pentecostalism in a Globalizing African Economy*. Bloomington: Indiana University Press.

Gilroy, Paul. 1993. *The Black Atlantic: Modernity and Double Consciousness*. Cambridge, MA: Harvard University Press.

Giroux, Henry A. 2008. *Against the Terror of Neoliberalism: Politics beyond the Age of Greed*. London: Paradigm.

Goffman, Erving. 1981. *Forms of Talk*. Philadelphia: University of Pennsylvania Press.

Goldberg, David Theo. 2002. *The Racial State*. Malden, MA: Blackwell.

Goodman, Jane. 2005. *Berber Culture on the World Stage: From Village to Video*. Bloomington: Indiana University Press.

Graeber, David. 2011. *Debt: The First 5,000 Years*. Brooklyn, NY: Melville House.

———. 2001. *Towards an Anthropological Theory of Value: The False Coin of Our Own Dreams*. New York: Palgrave.

Guha, Ranajit. 1997. *Dominance without Hegemony: History and Power in Colonial India*. Cambridge, MA: Harvard University Press.

Guilbault, Jocelyne. 2007. *Governing Sound: The Cultural Politics of Trinidad's Carnival Musics*. Chicago: University of Chicago Press.

Guillory, Monique, and Richard C. Green. 1998. *Soul: Black Power, Politics, and Pleasure*. New York: New York University Press.

Guyer, Jane. 2004. *Marginal Gains: Monetary Transactions in Atlantic Africa*. Chicago: University of Chicago Press.

Gyekye, Kwame. 1987. *An Essay on African Philosophical Thought: The Akan Conceptual Scheme*. Cambridge: Cambridge University Press.

Habermas, Jurgen. 1996. "Further Reflections on the Public Sphere." In *Habermas and the Public Sphere*, ed. Craig Calhoun, pp. 421–461. Cambridge, MA: MIT Press.

Hackett, Rosalind. 1999. "The Gospel of Prosperity in West Africa." In *Religion and the Transformations of Capitalism*, ed. R. H. Roberts. London: Routledge.

Hall, Stuart. 1993. "Cultural Identity and Diaspora." In *Colonial Discourse & Postcolonial Theory: A Reader*, ed. Patrick Williams and Laura Chrisman. Essex: Harvester Wheatsheaf.

Hanchard, Michael. 1999. "Afro-Modernity: Temporality, Politics, and the African Diaspora." *Public Culture* 11(1): 245–268.

Hanks, William. 1996. *Language and Communicative Practices*. Boulder, CO: Westview Press.

Hansen, Karen. 2000. *Salaula: The World of Secondhand Clothing and Zambia*. Chicago: University of Chicago Press.

Hart, Keith. 2009. "The Persuasive Power of Money." In *Economic Persuasions*, ed. Stephen Gudeman. New York: Berghahn Books.

———. 1973. "Informal Income Opportunities and Urban Employment in Ghana." *Journal of Modern African Studies* 11: 61–89.

Hartman, Saidiya. 2007. *Lose Your Mother: A Journey along the Atlantic Slave Route*. New York: Farrar, Straus and Giroux.

Harvey, David. 2005. *A Brief History of Neoliberalism*. New York: Oxford University Press.

Hasty, Jennifer. 2005. *The Press and Political Culture in Ghana*. Bloomington: Indiana University Press.

———. 2002. "Rites of Passage, Routes of Redemption: Emancipation Tourism and the Wealth of Culture." *Africa Today* 49(3): 47–76.

Haupt, Adam. 2008. *Stealing Empire: P2P, Intellectual Property and Hip-Hop Subversion*. Johannesburg: Human Sciences Research Council Press.

Heath, R. Scott. 2006. "True Heads: Historicizing the Hip-Hop 'Nation' in Context." *Callaloo* 29(3): 846–866.

Hebdige, Dick. [1979] 1996. *Subculture: The Meaning of Style*. Routledge: London.

Herskovits, Melville J. [1941] 1990. *The Myth of the Negro Post*. Boston: Beacon Press.

Herson, Ben. 2007. *Democracy in Dakar: Hip Hop and Politics in Senegal*. Feature documentary film. Nomadic Wax.

Hertzfeld, Michael. 2004. *Cultural Intimacy: Social Poetics in the Nation-State*. New York: Routledge.

Hesmondhalgh, David, and Caspar Melville. 2001. "Urban Breakbeat Culture: Repercussions of Hip-Hop in the United Kingdom." In *Global Noise: Rap and Hip-Hop outside the USA*, ed. Tony Mitchell. Middletown, CT: Wesleyan University Press.

Hess, Janet Berry. 2000. "Imagining Architecture: The Structure of Nationalism in Accra, Ghana." *Africa Today* 47(2): 35–58.

Hill, Jane H. 2005. "Intertextuality as Source and Evidence for Indirect Indexical Meanings." *Journal of Linguistic Anthropology* 15(1).

———. 1987. "Women's Speech in Modern Mexicano." In *Language, Gender and Sex in Comparative Perspective*, ed. Susan Philips, Susan Steele, and Christine Tanz, pp. 121–159. Cambridge: Cambridge University Press.

Hirschkind, Charles. 2006. *The Ethical Soundscape: Cassette Sermons and Islamic Counterpublics*. New York: Columbia University Press.

Ho, Engseng. 2006. *The Graves of Tarim: Genealogy and Mobility across the Indian Ocean*. Berkeley: University of California Press.

Hoffman, Danny. 2007. "The City as Barracks: Freetown, Monrovia, and the Organization of Violence in Postcolonial African Cities." *Cultural Anthropology* 12(3): 400–428.

Holsey, Bayo. 2008. *Routes of Remembrance: Refashioning the Slave Trade in Ghana*. Chicago: University of Chicago Press.

Irvine, Judith. 1996. "Shadow Conversations: The Indeterminacy of Participant Roles." In *Natural Histories of Discourse*, ed. Michael Silverstein and Greg Urban, pp. 131–159. Chicago: University of Chicago Press.

Jackson, John. 2005. *Real Black: Adventures in Racial Sincerity*. Chicago: University of Chicago Press.

Jefferies, Michael. 2010. *Race, Gender, and the Meaning of Hip Hop*. Chicago: University of Chicago Press.

Kapchan, Deborah. 2007. *Traveling Spirit Masters: Moroccan Gnawa Trance and Music in the Global Marketplace*. Middletown, CT: Wesleyan University Press.

———. 1996. *Gender on the Market: Moroccan Women and the Revoicing of Tradition*. Philadelphia: University of Pennsylvania Press.

Keane, Webb. 2003. "Semiotics and the Social Analysis of Material Things." *Language and Communication* 23: 409–425.

————. 1997. *Signs of Recognition: Powers and Hazards of Representation in an Indonesian Society*. Berkeley: University of California Press.

Keeler, Ward. 2009. "What's Burmese about Burmese Rap? Why Some Expressive Forms Go Global." *American Ethnologist* 36(1): 2–19.

Kelley, Robin. 2003. *Freedom Dreams: The Black Radical Imagination*. Boston: Beacon.

Kitwana, Bakari. 2002. *The Hip Hop Generation: Young Blacks and the Crisis in African American Culture*. New York: Basic Books.

Klein, Debra L. 2007. *Yoruba Bata Goes Global: Artists, Culture Brokers, and Fans*. Chicago: University of Chicago Press.

Knight, Arthur. 2002. *Disintegrating the Musical: Black Performance and American Musical Film*. Durham, NC: Duke University Press.

Kockelman, Paul. 2010. "Enemies, Parasites, and Noise: How to Take Up Residence in a System without Becoming a Term in It." *Journal of Linguistic Anthropology* 20(2): 406–421.

Larkin, Brian. 2008. *Signal and Noise: Media, Infrastructure and Urban Culture in Nigeria*. Durham, NC: Duke University Press.

Lee, Benjamin. 1997. *Talking Heads: Language, Metalanguage, and the Semiotics of Subjectivity*. Durham, NC: Duke University Press.

Lee, Benjamin, and Edward LiPuma. 2002. "Cultures of Circulation: The Imaginations of Modernity." *Public Culture* 14(1): 191–213.

LiPuma, Edward and Benjamin Lee. 2004. *Financial Derivatives and the Globalization of Risk*. Durham, NC: Duke University Press.

Lubiano, Wahneema, ed. 1997. *The House That Race Built: Black Americans, U.S. Terrain*. New York: Pantheon.

Maira, Sunaina. 2000. "Henna and Hip Hop: The Politics of Cultural Production and the Work of Cultural Studies." *Journal of Asian American Studies* 3(3): 329–369.

Mamdani, Mamhood. 1996. *Citizen and Subject: Contemporary Africa and the Legacy of Late Colonialism*. Princeton, NJ: Princeton University Press.

Marx, Karl. 1993. *Capital: A Critique of Political Economy*. 3 vols. New York: Penguin Classics.

Matory, J. Lorand. 2005. *Black Atlantic Religion: Tradition, Transnationalism, and Matriarchy in the Afro-Brazilian Candomblé*. Princeton, NJ: Princeton University Press.

Mauss, Marcel. 2000. *The Gift: The Form and Reason for Exchange in Archaic Society*. New York: W. W. Norton and Company.

Mazzarella, William. 2004. "Culture, Globalization, Mediation." *Annual Review of Anthropology* 33: 345–367.

Mbembe, Achille. 2005. "Sovereignty as a Form of Expenditure." In *Sovereign Bodies: Citizens, Migrants, and States in the Postcolonial World*, ed. Thomas Blom Hansen and Finn Stepputat. Princeton, NJ: Princeton University Press.

————. 2002. "African Modes of Self-Writing." *Public Culture* 14(1): 239–273.

————. 2001. *On the Postcolony*. Berkeley: University of California Press.

McAnany, Emile G., and Kenton T. Wilkinson, eds. 1996. *Mass Media and Free Trade: NAFTA and the Cultural Industries*. Austin: University of Texas Press.

McCaskie, T. C. 2000. *Asante Identities: History and Modernity in an African Village: 1850–1950*. London: Edinburgh University Press.

———. 1995. *State and Society in Pre-colonial Asante*. Cambridge: Cambridge University Press.

———. 1983. "Accumulation, Wealth, and Belief in Asante History, I: To the Close of the Nineteenth Century." *Africa: Journal of the International African Institute* 53(1): 23–43.

Meintjes, Louise. 2003. *Sound of Africa: Making Music Zulu in a South African Studio*. Durham, NC: Duke University Press.

Meyer, Birgit. 2006. "Religious Revelation, Secrecy and the Limits of Visual Representation." *Anthropological Theory* 6(4): 431–453.

———. 2004a. "Christianity in Africa: From African Independent to Pentecostal-Charismatic Churches." *Annual Review of Anthropology* 33: 447–474.

———. 2004b. "'Praise the Lord': Popular Cinema and Pentecostalite Style in Ghana's New Public Sphere." *American Ethnologist* 31(1): 92–110.

———. 1998a. "Commodities and the Power of Prayer: Pentecostalist Attitudes towards Consumption in Contemporary Ghana." *Development and Change* 29: 751–776.

———. 1998b. "'Make a Complete Break with the Past': Memory and Postcolonial Modernity in Ghanaian Pentecostal Discourse." *Journal of Religion in Africa* 28(3): 316–349.

———. 1998c. "The Power of Money: Politics, Occult Forces, and Pentecostalism in Ghana." *Africa Studies Review* 41: 15–37.

Mikell, Gwendolyn. 1992. *Cocoa and Chaos in Ghana*. Washington, DC: Howard University Press.

Miller, Kiri. 2012. *Playing Along: Digital Games, YouTube, and Virtual Performance*. New York: Oxford University Press.

Mintz, Sidney W. 2012. *Three Ancient Colonies: Caribbean Themes and Variations*. Cambridge, MA: Harvard University Press.

Mitchell, Tony, ed. 2001. *Global Noise: Rap and Hip-Hop outside the USA*. Middletown, CT: Wesleyan University Press.

Morris, Rosalind C. 2006. "Mute and the Unspeakable: Political Subjectivity, Violent Crime and 'the Sexual Thing' in a South African Mining Community." In *Law and Disorder in the Postcolony*, ed. Jean Comaroff and John L. Comaroff. Chicago: University of Chicago Press.

Mudimbe, V. Y. 1988. *Gnosis, Philosophy, and the Order of Knowledge*. Bloomington: Indiana University Press.

Munn, Nancy. 1986. *The Fame of Gawa: A Symbolic Study of Value Transformation in a Massim Society*. Durham, NC: Duke University Press.

Nketia, J. H. K. 1982. "Developing Contemporary Idioms Out of Traditional Music." *Studia Musicologica Academiae Scientiarum Hungarica* 24: 81–97.

———. 1976. *Cultural Development and the Arts*. Legon: Institute of African Studies, University of Ghana.

———. 1962. *African Music in Ghana*. Accra: Longmans.

Ntarangwi, Mwenda. 2009. *East African Hip Hop: Youth Culture and Globalization.* Urbana: University of Illinois Press.

Nugent, Paul. 1995. *Big Men, Small Boys and Politics in Ghana.* London: Pinter.

Obeng, Samuel Gyasi. 2000. "From Praise to Criticism: A Pragmalinguistic Discussion of Metaphors in African (Ghanaian) Political Rhetoric." In *IUWPL 2: The CVC of Sociolinguistics: Contact, Variation, and Culture*, ed. Julie Auger and Andrea Word-Allbritton. Bloomington, IN: IULC Publications.

———. 1999. "Requests in Akan Discourse." *Anthropological Linguistics* 41(2).

———. 1997. "Language and Politics: Indirectness in Political Discourse." *Discourse and Society* 8(1): 49–83.

Ong, Aihwa. 2006. *Neoliberalism as Exception: Mutations in Citizenship and Sovereignty.* Durham, NC: Duke University Press.

———. 1999. *Flexible Citizenship: The Cultural Logic of Transnationality.* Durham, NC: Duke University Press.

Osumare, Halifu. 2007. *The Africanist Aesthetic in Global Hip-Hop: Power Moves.* London: Palgrave Macmillan.

Otabil, Mensa. 2002. *Buy the Future: Learning to Negotiate for a Future Better Than Your Present.* Lanham, MD: Pneuma Life Publishing, Inc.

Palumbo-Liu, David, and Hans Ulrich Gumbrecht, eds. 1997. *Streams of Cultural Capital: Transnational Cultural Studies.* Palo Alto, CA: Stanford University Press.

Parmentier, Richard J. 1994. *Signs in Society: Studies in Semiotic Anthropology.* Bloomington: Indiana University Press.

Peirce, Charles S. 1992. *The Essential Peirce: Selected Philosophical Writings.* Bloomington: Indiana University Press.

Pellow, Deborah. 2002. *Landlords and Lodgers: Socio-Spatial Organization in an Accra Community.* Westport, CT: Praeger.

Perry, Imani. 2004. *Prophets of the Hood: Politics and Poetics in Hip Hop.* Durham, NC: Duke University Press.

Perullo, Alex. 2011. *Live from Dar es Salaam: Popular Music and Tanzania's Music Economy.* Bloomington: Indiana University Press.

———. 2005. "Hooligans and Heroes: Youth Identity and Hip-Hop in Dar es Salaam, Tanzania." *Africa Today* 51(4): 75–101.

Peterson, Marina. 2010. *Sound, Space, and the City: Civic Performance in Downtown Los Angeles.* Philadelphia: University of Pennsylvania Press.

Pierre, Jemima. 2012. *The Predicament of Blackness: Postcolonial Ghana and the Politics of Race.* Chicago: University of Chicago.

Pierre, Jemima, and Jesse Weaver Shipley. 2003. "African/Diaspora History: W. E. B. Du Bois and Pan-Africanism in Ghana." In *Ghana in Africa and the World*, ed. Toyin Falola. Trenton, NJ: Africa World Press.

Piot, Charles. 2010. *Nostalgia for the Future: West Africa after the Cold War.* Chicago: University of Chicago Press.

Plageman, Nate. 2013. *Highlife Saturday Night: Popular Music and Social Change in Urban Ghana.* Bloomington: Indiana University Press.

Pough, Gwendolyn D., Elaine Richardson, Aisha Durham, and Rachel Raimist, eds. 2007. *Home Girls Make Some Noise!: Hip Hop Feminism Anthology*. Mira Loma, CA: Parker Publishing.

Povinelli, Elizabeth A. 2006. *Empire of Love: Toward a Theory of Intimacy, Genealogy, and Carnality*. Durham, NC: Duke University Press.

———. 2002. *The Cunning of Recognition: Indigenous Alterities and the Making of Australian Multiculturalism*. Durham, NC: Duke University Press.

Radcliffe-Brown, A. R. 1940. "On Joking Relationships." *Africa: Journal of the International African Institute* (13)3: 195–210.

Ralph, Michael. 2009. "'It's Hard Out Here for a Pimp . . . with . . . a Whole Lot of Bitches Jumpin' Ship': Navigating Black Politics in the Wake of Katrina." *Public Culture* 21(2): 343–376.

Rattray, R. S. [1923] 1969. *Ashanti*. New York: Negro Universities Press.

Reed, Susan A. 2002. "Performing Respectability: The *Berava*, Middle-Class Nationalism, and the Classicization of Kandyan Dance in Sri Lanka." *Cultural Anthropology* 17(2): 246–277.

Robinson, Cedric J. [1985] 2000. *Black Marxism: The Making of the Black Radical Tradition*. Chapel Hill: University of North Carolina Press.

Roitman, Janet. 2003. "Unsanctioned Wealth; or, the Productivity of Debt in Northern Cameroon." *Public Culture* 15(2): 211–237.

Rose, Tricia. 2008. *The Hip Hop Wars: What We Talk about When We Talk about Hip Hop—And Why It Matters*. New York: Basic Civitas Books.

———. 1994. *Black Noise: Rap Music and Black Culture in Contemporary America*. Hanover, NH: University Press of New England.

Rutherford, Danilyn. 2001. "Intimacy and Alienation: Money and the Foreign in Biak." *Public Culture* 13(2): 299–324.

Saada-Ophir, Galit. 2006. "Borderland Pop: Arab Jewish Musicians and the Politics of Performance." *Cultural Anthropology* 21(2): 205–223.

Samuels, David W., Louise Meintjes, Ana Maria Ochoa, and Thomas Porcello. 2010. "Soundscapes: Toward a Sounded Anthropology." *Annual Review of Anthropology* (39) 329–345.

Schulz, Dorothea. 2002. "'Charisma and Brotherhood' Revisited: Mass-Mediated Forms of Spirituality in Urban Mali." *Journal of Religion in Africa* 33(2): 146–171.

Scotton, Carol Myers, and William Ury. 2009. "Bilingual Strategies: The Social Functions of Code-Switching." *Linguistics* 15(193): 5–20.

Sekyi, Kobina. 1994 [1915]. *The Blinkard's: A Comedy*. Oxford: Heinemann Educational Publishers.

Shannon, Jonathan. 2003. "Emotion, Performance, and Temporality in Arab Music: Reflections on Tarab." *Cultural Anthropology* 18(1): 72–98.

Sharpley-Whiting, Tracy. 2007, *Pimps Up, Ho's Down: Hip Hop's Hold on Young Black Women*. New York: New York University Press.

Shaw, Rosalind. 2007. "Displacing Violence: Making Pentecostal Memory in Postwar Sierra Leone." *Cultural Anthropology* 22(1): 66–93.

———. 2002. *Memories of the Slave Trade: Ritual and the Historical Imagination in Sierra Leone*. Chicago: University of Chicago Press.

Shepperson, George. 1960. "Notes on Negro American Influences on the Emergence of African Nationalism." *Journal of African History* 1(2): 299–312.

Shipley, Jesse Weaver. 2009a. "Aesthetic of the Entrepreneur: Afro-Cosmopolitan Rap and Moral Circulation in Accra, Ghana." *Anthropological Quarterly* 82(3): 631–668.

———. 2009b. "Comedians, Pastors, and the Miraculous Agency of Charisma in Ghana." *Cultural Anthropology* 24(3): 523–552.

———. 2004. "'The Best Tradition Goes On': Audience Consumption and the Transformation of Popular Theatre in Neoliberal Ghana." In *Producing African Futures: Ritual and Reproduction in a Neoliberal Age*, ed. Brad Weiss, pp. 106–140. Leiden: Brill.

Silverstein, Michael. 2005. "Axes of Evals Token versus Type Interdiscursivity." *Journal of Linguistic Anthropology* 15: 1.

———. 1976. "Shifters, Linguistic Categories, and Cultural Description." In *Meaning in Anthropology*, ed. Keith Basso and H. A. Selby Jr., pp. 11–55. Albuquerque: University of New Mexico Press.

Silverstein, Paul. 2004. *Algeria in France: Transpolitics, Race, and Nation*. Bloomington: Indiana University Press.

Simmel, Georg. 2004. *Philosophy of Money*. New York: Routledge.

Spitulnik, Debra. 1998. "Mediating Unity and Diversity: The Production of Language Ideologies in Zambian Broadcasting." In *Language Ideologies: Practice and Theory*, ed. Bambi B. Schieffelin, Kathryn A. Woolard, and Paul V. Kroskrity. Oxford: Oxford University Press.

———. 1996. "The Social Circulation of Media Discourse and the Mediation of Communities." *Journal of Linguistic Anthropology* 6(2): 161–187.

Stavrias, George. 2005. "Droppin' Conscious Beats and Flows: Aboriginal Hip Hop and Youth Identity." *Australian Aboriginal Studies* 2: 44–54.

Stokes, Martin. 2004. Music and the Global Order. *Annual Review of Anthropology* (33): 47–72.

Stoller, Paul. 2002. *Money Has No Smell: The Africanization of New York City*. Chicago: University of Chicago Press.

Sutherland, Efua. 1975. *The Marriage of Anansewa*. London: Longman.

Taussig, Michael. 1992. *Mimesis and Alterity: A Particular History of the Senses*. New York: Routledge.

Taylor, Charles. 2002. "Modern Social Imaginaries." *Public Culture* 14(1): 91–124.

Thomas, Deborah. 2004. *Modern Blackness: Nationalism, Globalization, and the Politics of Culture in Jamaica*. Durham, NC: Duke University Press.

Thompson, Robert Farris. 1973. "An Aesthetic of the Cool." *African Arts* 7(1): 40–43, 64–67, 89–91.

Trouillot, Michel-Rolph. 1997. *Silencing the Past: Power and the Production of History*. Boston: Beacon Press.

Tsing, Anna Lowenhaupt. 2005. *Friction: An Ethnography of Global Connection*. Princeton, NJ: Princeton University Press.

Turner, Terrence. 2007. "The Social Skin." In *Beyond the Body Proper: Reading the Anthropology of Material Life*, ed. Margaret Lock and Judith Farquhar, pp. 83–103. Durham, NC: Duke University Press.

———. 1984. "Value, Production, and Exploitation in Non-Capitalist Societies." Unpublished essay based on a paper presented at the AAA 82nd Annual Meeting.

Van de Port, Mattijs. 2006. "Visualizing the Sacred: Video Technology, 'Televisual' Style, and the Religious Imagination in Bahian Candomblé." *American Ethnologist* 33(3): 444–462.

Van der Veer, Peter, ed. 1996. *Conversion to Modernities: The Globalization of Christianity.* New York: Routledge.

Veal, Michael. 2007. *Dub: Soundscapes and Shattered Songs in Jamaican Reggae.* Middletown, CT: Wesleyan University Press.

———. 2000. *Fela: The Life and Times of an African Musical Icon.* Philadelphia: Temple University Press.

Von Eschen, Penny M. 2006. *Satchmo Blows Up the World: Jazz Ambassadors Play the Cold War.* Cambridge, MA: Harvard University Press.

Wainaina, Binyavanga. 2011. *One Day I Will Write about This Place.* Minneapolis, MN: Greywolf Press.

Walcott, Rinaldo. n.d. *Black Diaspora Faggotry: Frames, Readings, Limits.* Durham, NC: Duke University Press.

Wallach, Jeremy. 2008. *Modern Noise, Fluid Genres: Popular Music in Indonesia, 1997–2001.* Madison: University of Wisconsin Press.

Warner, Michael. 2005. *Publics and Counterpublics.* New York: Zone Books.

———. 2002. "Publics and Counterpublics." *Public Culture* 14(1): 49–90.

Waterman, Christopher Alan. 1990. *Juju: A Social History and Ethnography of an African Popular Music.* Chicago: University of Chicago Press.

Watkins, Craig S. 2005. *Hip Hop Matters: Politics, Popular Culture, and the Struggle for the Soul of a Movement.* Boston: Beacon.

Weiss, Brad. 2009. *Street Dreams and Hip Hop Barbershops: Global Fantasy in Urban Tanzania.* Bloomington: Indiana University Press.

———. 2002. "Thug Realism: Inhabiting Fantasy in Urban Tanzania." *Cultural Anthropology* 17(1): 93–124.

Werbner, Richard, ed. 1998. *Memory and the Postcolony: African Anthropology and the Critique of Power.* London: Zed Books.

White, Hylton. 2010. "Outside the Dwelling of Culture: Estrangement and Difference in Postcolonial Zululand." *Anthropological Quarterly* 83(3): 497–518.

Woolard, Kathryn A., and Babmi B. Schieffelin. 1994. "Language Ideology." *Annual Review of Anthropology* 23: 55–82.

Yankah, Kwesi. 1998. *Free Speech in Traditional Society: The Cultural Foundations of Communication in Contemporary Ghana.* Accra: Ghana University Press.

———. 1995. *Speaking for the Chief: Okyeame and the Politics of Akan Royal Oratory.* Bloomington: Indiana University Press.

———. 1989. *The Proverb in the Context of Akan Rhetoric: A Theory of Proverb Praxis.* Bern: Peter Lang.

Yurchak, Alexei. 2003a. "Russian Neoliberal: The Entrepreneurial Ethic and the Spirit of "True Careerism." *Russian Review* 62: 72–90.

———. 2003b. "Soviet Hegemony of Form: Everything Was Forever, until It Was No More." *Comparative Studies in Society and History* 45(3): 480–510.

INDEX

Commodity, 54–57, 253, 279–280, foreign 31, 51; success as, 105

Community, 110, black, 15, 26, 60; Ghanaian, 194, 230–231, 234, 238–239, 242; sonic, 247, 265. *See also* Affiliation; Interpretation; Speaking and speech

Concert Party, 32–33; and Worker's Brigade, 32

Constitution of Ghana, 6, 87

Consumption, 4, 11, 15, 17, 35, 81–82, 135–136, 141–142, 162, 172, 175, 179, 194, 196; male, 102, 170, 174, 180; personal, 20; public, 10, 72

Context, 5, 50, 128, 135, 210, 267; colonial, 49, 166; of interpretation, 106, 109–110; social, 5, 79, 81–82, 99; urban, 91, 147, 174

Control, 11–14, 101, 194; aesthetics of, 48, 127, 268, 283; linguistic and bodily, 37–41, 51–53, 55, 107, 132, 232, 154, 179, 184, 189; and power, 161–162, 169, 178; public, 136, 158

Convention People's Party (CPP), 32

Cool, 18–19, 25, 40, 61, 108, 111, 129

Copying, 18, 35, 42–43, 48–50, 103; of music, 69, 205, 224; of styles, 8, 44, 85. *See also* File sharing

Copyright, 35

Corporate, corporation, 17, 269, 273, 282–283; and sponsorship, 1–3, 5, 22, 71, 80, 147, 151

Corrupt, corruption, 16, 38, 54, 56, 55, 193; moral 17, 76, 156; musical references, 38, 138–144; political, 54–56, 127, 138, 155

Cosmopolitanism, Afro-Cosmopolitanism, 6, 9, 17, 29–30, 33, 41, 47, 265, 272. *See also* Accra; Blackness

Coz Ov Moni, 209, 223

Cubase, 112, 123

Culture, and collectivity, 13, 27; black, 30, 65, 81, 86, 233; discourse, 29–20; and meaning, 19, 106; and national-ism, 7–8, 25–27, 32–33, 46, 52–53, 70–71, 76, 126; popular, 4, 9, 14–16, 25, 30, 152

Culture broker, 81

Curfew, 56–57

Currency, celebrity as a form of, 267–270, 279, 284

D-Black, 273, 276–278, 282

Daddy Lumba, 157

Dagbane, 8, 63

Dance, 12, 21–22, 57–60, 108, 184; danceability, 21, 115; dance bands, 31, 34

Danquah, J. B., 290 n. 16

Darko, George, 58

D'Banj, 205

Debt, 48, 279–282, 284

Def Jam Records, 271

Deictics, 13

Democracy, 6, 159, 189, 193

Diaspora, 4, 7, 14–18, 25–26, 28–30, 31, 35–37, 44–45, 50, 86, 229; Ghanaians in, 41–42, 63–66, 230–232, 246, 265; and globalization, 265, and ideas of home, 86, 230–232, 245, 247, 265; return to Ghana, 6, 43, 52, 58, 83, 88–90, 129; and travel, 229. *See also* Affiliation; Soul to Soul; Style

Diawara, Manthia, 43–44

Digital, 200–201, 218–219; circulation, 5, 10, 19, 23, 25, 194; copying and file sharing, 147–148, 152, 205, 232, 240

Disco, 34, 57–60

Disjuncture, 14–18, 30, 41–43, 46, 49–50

District Six, 47,

Dizzee Rascal, 211,

DJ, DJing, 6, 9, 11, 15, 23, 58, 68–69, 73, 88–90, 112, 147–149, 187, 219–220, 238–242, 251–252, 258–261

DJ Black, 220–221

DJ Jazzy Jeff, 278

Dreadlocks, 74–75, 80, 89, 102, 208, 212. *See also* Hair

Dry, 299 n. 12

Du Bois, W. E. B., 45, 49

Ebi Te Yie, 37–41

Economic, 15, 18–21, 31–32, 78, 196, 278; success, 118, 166, 228, 255, 194, 228;

Music: industry, 22, 31, 149, 221, 283; video, 23, 103, 119, 177. *See also* Aesthetics; Africa; African American; America, American; Circulation; Copying; Digital, circulation; Electronic; File sharing; Highlife; Hip-hop; Innovation, individual; Labor; Nigeria, Nigerians; Production; Proverbs, proverbial speech; Registers

Music Music, 88

Mzbel, 163–168, 175–197, 247

Nana King, 69, 112

Nananom (hiplife group), 69, 73, 112, 152

Nana NYC, 249, 254, 266

Narration and narrative, 11, 17, 42, 66, 99, 128, 149, 155

National Commission on Culture, 57, 74

National Democratic Congress (NDC), 139, 159, 295 n. 3

National Theatre of Ghana, 8, 52, 57, 71, 72–76, 114–115, 127, 158, 224

National Theatre Movement, 32–33

Nation and nationalism, 6, 10, 16, 25–26; dispersed, 233–234; sonic, 26, 29–30, 32–33, 46, 50. *See also* Culture, and collectivity

Native Funk Lords (NFL), 69, 112, 137, 141

Native Sun, 216

Neoliberalism, 5, 76, 162, 166, 196, 283. *See also* Economic, transformation; Free market; Hip-hop

Nestlé and Nescafé, 1–4, 21

Newness, 9, 30, 49, 110, 120, 132, 269, 280

New Patriotic Party (NPP), 139, 146, 158–159, 161

New York, 15, 16, 26, 51, 57; Ghanaians living in, 26, 231, 233–234, 250, 251, 256; recording in, 212–216; sound, 86, 92

Nigeria, Nigerians, 6, 17, 47, 56, 138, 198; and Ghana relations, 138; music from, 6, 17, 34, 47, 205. *See also* Asa; Kuti, Fela; Nneka

"Nightlife in Accra" (Song Reggie Rockstone), 103

Nima, 54, 67–68, 115, 147, 238

Nkonson Konson, 117

Nkrumah, Kwame, 32–33, 38, 54, 120–126, 140, 237, 241, 243

Nneka, 225

"No One Knows Tomorrow," 219, 225

No. 1 Mango Street (Album Mensa), 198–199, 203–204, 209–213, 217, 220, 224–225

"No. 1 Mango Street" (Song Mensa), 213

North Africa, 16

Nostalgia, 39, 93, 128, 139, 140, 143, 231, 256

Notorious BIG, 291 n. 41

Nyame, E. K., 32, 126

Obour, 120, 131

Obrafour, 77, 109, 112, 121, 120–128, 149, 152, 272, 282

Ohene-Gyan, Abraham, 103, 261

Okomfour Kwadee, 117

Okyeame, 12, 112, 119

Okyeame Kofi (Quophi), 119, 220

Okyeame Kwame (Quoami), 119, 277

Omanhene Pozo, 294 n. 21

Omar, Rex, 120

Opoku, Mawere, 184

Oratory, 12–13, 15, 109, 128, 131, 168, 194

Organization of African Unity, 33

Origins, 14–15, 46, 50, 132

Osei, Teddy, 34

Osibisa, 34, 41, 202, 204

Osofo Dadze, 95

Ossei, Ricci, 59, 90–91

Our Sister Killjoy, 195

Padmore, George, 287 n. 7

Pae Mu Ka (Album Obrafour), 123

Pan-African Congress, 32

Pan-Africanism, 7, 16–18, 25, 32–33, 51, 93, 255, 263

Pan African Historical Theatre Festival (PANAFEST), 7, 83

Paris, 16

Parody, 49–50, 134–136, 143, 161–162

Rockstone, Reggie, 59–67, 80–85, 90–107, 128–130, 240–248, 260–281
Rockstone's Office, 224, 267, 273–276
Romanticization, 14, 15
R2Bees, 277, 301 n. 5
Rumor, 13, 130, 155, 195
Run-DMC, 61, 69
Rural, 1, 9, 13, 36, 68, 73, 77

Samini (or Batman), 117, 205–206, 208, 225, 231
Sampling, 4, 8, 81, 85, 97, 110
Santana, 35, 41
Sarkodie, 150
"Scenti No" (Song Sidney), 134, 151–161
Sekyi, Kobina, 299 n. 13
Selah, Scooby, 9
Self-expression, 4, 168, 176–177, 191, 210
Self-fashioning, 4, 11, 19, 29–30
Self-making, 76, 95, 109, 233
Semiotics, 11, 18–21, 25, 44, 50, 99
Senegal, 16–17
Sexuality, 10, 15, 28, 39–41, 49, 164–167, 175, 178; sovereign sexuality, 192–197
Shakur, Tupac, 291 n. 41
"Shepherd's Pie," 211
Sidibe, Malick, 44
Sidney, 85, 151–161, 170–173, 195
Sierra Leone, 31, 39, 63, 160
Signs, 5–6, 13, 44, 49–50, 81–83, 101, 109; shared, 86, 157, 245; theory of, 106
"Sika Baa," 117
"Sika Mpo Nfa Neho," 294 n. 17
"Simigwa Do" (Song Ambolley), 28, 38–41, 135
Simultaneity, 79, 132, 232
Simmons, Russell, 271
"16 Years" (Song Mzbel), 164, 176–180, 190, 191, 195
Smash TV, 88, 129
Socialism, 32–33, 53–53, 78
Socially conscious music, 15
Social network, 10, 23, 78, 111, 200–201, 212, 232. See also Facebook; Twitter

Sociolinguistics, 5
Software, music. See Production
Sonic nationalism. See Nation and nationalism
Soukous, 47
Soul, 6, 28, 34, 35, 41, 44, 47, 51
Soul to Soul, 35–37
Soul Train, 58
South Africa, 17, 47, 68, 145, 192, 203, 220, 271
Sovereignty, 11, 32, 137, 143, 196
Sowah, Adjetey, 59, 291 n. 53
Space, spatiality, 46, 230–234; spatial displacement, 66, 78
Spacefon, 82, 273
Spacetime, 19–20
Speaking and speech, 4, 12–13; community, 80, 91–92, 101, 107–110, 127, 174; culture, 127, 132–135, 151, 160, 162, 268. See also Akan; Ambiguity; Authority; Proverbs, proverbial speech
Stance, stance-taking, 5, 6, 19, 50, 132, 161
Staple Singers, 35
Stars and stardom, 4, 5, 105, 107, 147; iconography of, 112
State, 5, 7–8, 25–26, 51, 143; corruption, 16, 54, 56, 127, 138, 146; interests, 35, 138; sponsorship, 35, 56, 70–72. See also Privatization; Violence
Steneboofs, 39
Stereotype (Album Blitz the Ambassador), 216
Storytelling, 4, 8, 28, 32, 37–38. See also Akan; Ananse, Anansesem
Style, 4, 13, 14, 21, 26–27, 30, 33–34, 36, 43, 48, 51, 107; black, 29, 35, 43, 48, 65, 81, 272; diasporic, 37, 43–44, 49, 61, 68, 132; youth, 62, 65–66. See also Copying; Hair; Hip-hop
Subjectivity, 11, 24–25, 41, 50, 136, 269
Success, 111, 114–115; as commodity, 105–107; entrepreneurial, 5, 164, 179; image of, 21–22, 79, 105, 280, 283–284; individual, 11, 52, 77, 115, 164, 175, 193, 196, 269
Sutherland, Efua, 32–33

Sutherland-Addy, Esi, 152

Swagger, 6, 19, 67, 77; hip-hop 91, 112, 117, 129

Sway, 211–212, 217

"Sweetie Sweetie" (Song Reggie Rockstone), 102, 293 n. 24

Symbolic, 19, 47, 133; language, 68, 83; mediation, 81; value, 159, 172, 194

Takoradi, 30–31, 173

Talking Drums, 69–70, 112, 131, 144

Tanzania, 17, 44

Taste, 20, 21–24, 27, 30, 61; popular, 24, 27, 79, 190; youth, 76. *See also* Commercial

Taylor, Ebo, 41

Technology, 8, 11–12, 21–23, 25–26, 229, 252, 259. *See also* Digital; Electronic; Production

Television, 6, 23, 88, 159

Temporality, 46–47, 228

Tempos, 31

Texting, 248, 259, 276

Thatcher, Margaret, 66

TH4 Kwages, 9

Things Fall Apart, 130–131

Tic Tac, 73, 75, 112, 114, 169, 248, 253

Tinchy Stryder, 211

Tinny, 117

Tontoh, Mac, 34

Tradition, 13, 72, 106, 110, 112, 152, 179, 185, 192, 196; cultural, 26, 250; national, 25. *See also* Ghana

Translate, translation, 13–14; and mistranslation, 30

Transnational, 7, 10, 16–18, 24, 26, 50, 195, 210, 264; affiliations, 186; markets, 268; media, 133;

Transportability, 14, 16, 205

Travel, 10, 19–20, 25–26, 33, 49, 98, 129–130, 210–211, 229. *See also* Diaspora

"Tsoo Boi" (Song Reggie Rockstone), 92

Tuba Clan, 294 n. 15

Tunisia, 16

Turner, Ike and Tina, 35–36

Turner, Terrence, 19–21

TV Africa, 151

TV3, 88, 151, 285 n. 1, 292 n. 11

Twi, 8; rap in, 6, 8, 65, 69–70, 72, 90–92, 94, 48, 103, 117, 239, 242, 250, 260. *See also* Code-switching; Language and linguistic

Twitter, 218, 276

Uhurus, 31

UNESCO, 159–160

Universal Music Group, 215, 218, 271

Urban, urbanity, 91; audiences, 34, 38, 150; communities, 15, 66; dwellers, 50, 107, 231; fashion, 257; life, 30, 60, 77, 155, 158, 160, 176; rural relations, 9, 73; youth, 26, 59, 71, 81, 91, 107, 149, 160. *See also* Context

Value and value transformation, 4–5, 82, 106, 194, 227–228, 268–270, 280; theory of, 18–21. *See also* Aspiration; Celebrity; Economic; Labor; Material and materiality; Morality, moral; Production; Symbolic

Vibe FM, 80, 112, 144

Violence, 15, 45, 163–168, 180–183, 185–188, 193; state, 262–263. *See also* Racial violence

VIP (Vision in Progress), 67, 73, 115, 116, 128, 131, 203, 231, 238, 242, 248, 253–255, 256, 282, 301 n. 5

"Vote for Me" (Song Native Funk Lords), 134, 137–144

Wade, Abdoulaye, 16

Wahad, Dhoruba Bin, 91, 236–237, 248–249, 262–264

Wanlov the Kubolor, 202, 208–210, 223–226, 239, 243

Warner, Michael, 86

Weiss, Brad, 44

Wet, 299 n. 12

Whites and whiteness, 15, 30, 31, 48–49, 66

Wolof, 16

Work. *See* Labor

World Bank, 56, 138, 269